K

AGEING AND LATER LIFE

DATE DUE

Also published by
SAGE Publications
in association with
The Open University

Death, Dying and Bereavement
edited by Donna Dickenson and Malcolm Johnson

Health, Welfare and Practice: Reflecting on Roles and Relationships
edited by Jan Walmsley, Jill Reynolds, Pam Shakespeare and Ray Woolfe

Disabling Barriers – Enabling Environments
edited by John Swain, Vic Finkelstein, Sally French and Mike Oliver

All four books are Course Readers for the Open University Diploma in Health and Social Welfare.

Details of the Diploma and the related courses are available from The Information Officer, Department of Health and Social Welfare, The Open University, Walton Hall, Milton Keynes MK7 6AA, UK.

AGEING AND LATER LIFE

edited by

Julia Johnson and
Robert Slater

The Open University

in association with
The Open University

SAGE Publications
London • Thousand Oaks • New Delhi

First published 1993

Sage Publications Ltd
6 Bonhill Street
London EC2A 4PU

Sage Publications Inc
2455 Teller Road
Thousand Oaks, California 91320

Sage Publications India Pvt Ltd
32, M-Block Market
Greater Kailash – I
New Delhi 110 048

British Library Cataloguing in Publication data

Ageing and Later Life
 I. Johnson, Julia   II. Slater, Robert
 305.26

 ISBN 0-8039-8965-2
 ISBN 0-8039-8966-0 (pbk)

Library of Congress catalog card number 93-086213

Typeset by Mayhew Typesetting, Rhayader, Powys
Printed in Great Britain by The Cromwell Press Ltd,
Broughton Gifford, Melksham, Wiltshire

Contents

CONCEPTS AND VALUES

POLICY AND POLITICS

Acknowledgements

The editors and publishers wish to thank the following for permission to use copyright material.

Age Concern for material from M. Herwood, 'No sense of urgency: age discrimination in health care' in E. McEwen, ed., *Age: The Unrecognised Discrimination* (1990) pp. 43–57; 'Mr and Mrs Cosgrove' in Jeremy Seabrook, *The Way We Are: Old People Talk About Themselves, Conversations With Jeremy Seabrook* (1980) pp. 38–43; and M. Abrams, 'Born 1898: a brief group biography' in *Beyond Three-score Years and Ten: A First Report Survey of the Elderly* (1978) pp. 6–7;

Ashgate Publishing Ltd for Robin Means, 'The development of social services for elderly people: historical perspectives' in C. Phillipson and A. Walker, eds, *Ageinq and Social Policy* (1986) Gower;

The Beth Johnson Foundation for Chris Phillipson, 'Approaches to advocacy' in M. Bernard and F. Glendenning, eds, *Advocacy, Consumerism and the Older Person* (1990) Beth Johnson Foundation and The University of Keele, pp. 30–5;

Blackwell Publishers for Georges Minois, 'History of old age in western culture and society' in *History of Old Age: From Antiquity to the Renaissance* (1989) Polity Press, pp. 303–7;

BBC Enterprises Ltd and Peters Fraser and Dunlop Group Ltd on behalf of the author, for Alan Bennett, 'A cream cracker under the settee' in *Talking Heads* (1988) Forelake Ltd and *Single Spies and Talking Heads*, Simon & Schuster Inc. Copyright © 1988 Forelake Ltd;

Cambridge University Press for figures from David Thomson, *Ageing and Society*, 4 (1984) p. 453, and T. Kitwood, *Ageing and Society*, 10 (1990) p. 187; and A. Blaikie, 'The emerging political power of the elderly in Britain 1908–48', *Ageing and Society* 10 (1990) 1, pp. 17–40;

Centre for Policy on Ageing for Alison Norman, 'Losing your home' in *Rights and Risk* (1980), pp. 14–28 and Alison Norman, 'Risk' in *Aspects of Ageism* (1987);

Community Care for Evan Marsh, 'Home from Home', *Community Care*, 1.12.88, pp. 18–19, and Phyllida Parsloe and Olive Stevenson, 'A powerhouse for change: empowering users', *Community Care*, 18.2.93, pp. 24–5;

Consumers' Association, London for 'Elderly people: their medicines and their doctors', *Drug and Therapeutics Bulletin*, 1.10.90;

The Gerontological Society of America for J.S. Grigsby, 'Paths for future population ageing', *The Gerontologist* 31 (1991) 2, pp. 195–203;

Victor Gollancz for material from Barbara Strachey and Jayne Samuels, *Mary Berenson: A Self Portrait from her Letters and Diaries* (1983);

HarperCollins Publishers for material from Michael Young and Tom Schuller *Life After Work* (1991) pp. 1–26;

The Controller of Her Majesty's Stationery Office for Roy Parker, 'Ideology and the private sector of welfare' in I. Sinclair, R. Parker, D. Leat and J. Williams, eds, *The Kaleidoscope of Care* (1990) pp. 349–61;

Hodder & Stoughton Ltd for material from O. Stevenson, *Age and Vulnerability: a guide to better care* (1989) pp. 15–29, Edward Arnold; and John Young and James George, 'History of migration to the United Kingdom' in A. Squires, ed., *Multicultural Health Care and Rehabilitation of Older People* (1991) pp. 17–27, Edward Arnold with Age Concern;

Hughes Massie Ltd for Agatha Christie, 'Epilogue' to *An Autobiography* (1977). Copyright © 1977 Agatha Christie Ltd.;

Indiana University Press for material from K. Woodward, *Aging and its Discontents: Freud and Other Fictions* (1990) pp. 1–2, 195–6;

J.B. Lippincott Company for material from Russell A. Ward, *The Aging Experience: An Introduction to Social Gerontology* (1979) pp. 371–7;

Little, Brown and Company for an extract from Edward M. Brecher and the Editors of Consumer Report Books, *Love, Sex and Aging: A Consumer's Union Report* (1984) pp. 403–8. Copyright © 1984 by Consumer's Union of the United States;

Longman Group UK for Robin Means, 'Community care, housing and older people: continuity or change', *Housing Studies*, 6, 4, pp. 273–84;

Macmillan London Ltd for material from Elaine Murphy, 'Depression in later life' in *Dementia and Mental Illness in Older People* (1993) pp. 147–65;

Manchester University Press for P. Johnson, C. Conrad and D. Thompson 'Introduction' to *Workers Versus Pensioners* (1989). Copyright © 1989 Centre for Economic Policy Research;

Nursing Times for Peter Blackburn, 'Freedom to Wander' (1988) *Nursing Times*, 7.12.88, 84, 49; Helen Passant, 'A holistic approach in the ward' (1990) *Nursing Times*, 24.1.90, 86, 3; and Grainne Sheridan, 'Baffle locks: in whose best interest?' (1989) *Nursing Times*, 31.5.89, 85, 22;

Office for Official Publications of the European Communities for material from Alan Walker, Jens Alber, Anne-Marie Guillemard et al., 'Older people in Europe: social and economic policies: The 1993 Report of the European Observatory' (1993);

Oral History Society and the author for Joanna Bornat, 'Oral history as a social movement' (1989) *Oral History*, Autumn 1989, pp. 16–24;

Oxford University Press for material from Paul Thompson, Catherine Itzin and Michele Abendstern, *I Don't Feel Old: Understanding the Experience of Later Life* (1990) pp. 19–43. Copyright © 1990 Oxford University Press; and Liam Donaldson and Marie Johnson, 'Elderly Asians' in B.R. McEvoy and L.J. Donaldson, eds, *Health Care for Asians* (1990) pp. 237–49. Copyright © 1990 by Oxford University Press;

Piatkus Books for Maxine Myers, 'Coming out of the age closet' in *Growing Old Disgracefully* (1993) pp. 62-6, The Hen Co-op. Copyright © 1993 The Hen Co-op;

Random Century Group and Tessa Sayle Agency on behalf of the author for material from Margaret Forster, *Have the Men Had Enough?* (1990);

Routledge for material from M. Bury and A. Holme, *Life After Ninety* (1991) pp. 82-96;

Sage Publications Ltd for material from S. Arber and J. Ginn, *Gender and Later Life* (1991) pp. 40-9; and Beverley Hughes, 'Quality of Life' in S.M. Peace ed., *Researching Social Gerontology: Concepts, Methods and Issues* pp. 46-58;

Bertrand Schneider for Alexander King and Bertrand Schneider, 'Can we survive the world revolution?' in *The First Global Revolution*, Simon & Schuster;

Sheil Land Associates Ltd on behalf of the author, for J. Shapiro, 'Osteoporosis' in *Ourselves Growing Older* (1989) pp. 342-66, Simon & Schuster/Touchstone Books 1987, Fontana Paperbacks 1989. Copyright © 1987 Jean Shapiro;

Spinsters Ink for material from Barbara Macdonald, 'Look me in the eye' in Barbara Macdonald with Cynthia Rich *Look Me in the Eye: Old Women, Aging and Ageism* (1983) pp. 25-33, The Women's Press. Copyright © Spinsters Ink;

Springer Publishing Company for David Moberg, 'Religion and Aging' in Ferraro, ed., *Gerontology: Perspectives and Issues* (1990), Chap. 10;

The Women's Press Ltd for material from Janet Ford and Ruth Sinclair, 'Mrs Hatter' in *Sixty Years On: Women Talk About Old Age* (1987) pp. 31-6; and Jenny Morris, '"Us" and "them"? Feminist research, community care and disability' based on material from *Pride Against Prejudice* (1991) The Women's Press;

Every effort has been made to trace all the copyright holders, but if any have been inadvertently overlooked the publishers will be pleased to make the necessary arrangement at the first opportunity.

Introduction

Julia Johnson and Robert Slater

We are constantly being reminded that we are part of an ageing society. The publication of the 1991 Census results, for example, triggered the alarmist headline in the quality press: 'We're already feeling our age, but new census results reveal an unpredicted explosion in Britain's elderly population.' In 1993, the government now expects there to be some 6.1 million people aged 75 and over in Britain in 2031 – 18 per cent more than the official forecast made two years earlier, and many more than the 3.6 million people aged 75 and over in 1991.

It is for the very reason that the idea of an ageing society tends to be presented as a matter of statistics, divorced from the experience of ageing and later life, that we chose to start this reader with a collection of *Personal Accounts*. It is important to remember not only that it is individuals who comprise statistics, but also that all of us are ageing. It is *we* and not just the 'elderly population' who comprise the ageing society. However, it is critical that a book called *Ageing and Later Life* should include first-hand accounts from older people, because those who are younger have not had the same experience of age. The contributors to the other eight sections of this book, who incidentally are of a wide range of ages themselves, call upon a variety of expertise and experience. But, as you read what they have to say, you might bear in mind the accounts in this first section.

Although the term 'elderly' occurs in this selection of readings, we prefer the term 'older' because, being relative, it avoids categorisation and the attendant stereotyping. We do not consider this to be a case of pedantic semantics.

But others do. Another newspaper headline declared 'Older but no wiser, the borough where the elderly don't exist.' What followed were criticisms of Islington Council for suggesting that the phrase 'the elderly' be replaced by 'older people'. One 71-year-old letter-writer to *The Independent* similarly considered this creeping 'political correctness' deplorable and urged the cultivation of a metaphorical thick skin. Certainly some older people prefer to identify with a group called 'Senior Citizens' or 'The Retired'. But it is our belief that these homogenising and stereotyping labels promote ageist policies which detract from the diversity and individuality revealed in the personal accounts of our first section. A 70-year-old writing to *The Observer* asked why should he be called a 'wrinklie'; he and his friends didn't call their teenage friends 'spotties'.

In our efforts to select material that covers the enormous range of social gerontology, we have grouped our chapters under a number of sectional headings. Following personal accounts, we included several readings relating to *Images and Identity*. Just how much is our self-image and behaviour in later life influenced by labelling and stereotypes? How are images created and how do we react? We include examples from fiction and photography for you to consider. The relationship between image and identity is further explored in the chapters on disability, gender and ethnicity. Echoing the personal accounts of the first section, these chapters indicate how other basic social dimensions that divide us continue to sustain inequalities and diversity in later life - age is not the great leveller that some would have us believe.

This process of disaggregating 'the elderly population' is continued in the third section, on *Ill-health and Well-being*, where different aspects of health are examined. This section raises questions about the potential clash between cultural and professional responses, issues about taking control of our own bodies, and about what is perceived to be 'normal' and 'natural'. In the range of topics covered, which include dementia, depression, sexual activity and hormone replacement therapy (HRT), we can see how the interplay between intrinsic and extrinsic factors, as well as matters of meaning and interpretation, affect our thinking about ageing and health.

The final chapter of this section, on age discrimination in health care, is particularly topical in the 1990s when the subject of health service rationing is getting so much attention, and older people are portrayed as a burden to society. What is alarming is not just the health care that may be denied to older people, but also the belief - often held by older people themselves - that they should make way for others.

Our fourth section, *Intervention and Therapy*, focuses on the benefits and risks that arise in care settings. It begins with two accounts of how change for the better in service provision can be brought about at no extra financial cost. What is needed, however, is vision and determination from the person in charge. With this, group living in a residential home built to a traditional design can be successful. So too can alternative ways be made available of relieving pain on a continuing care ward in an ordinary NHS hospital. The risks of conventional medical treatment, and other forms of intervention and therapy, are considered in the following chapters. The extract from the *Drug and Therapeutics Bulletin*, summarising the findings of a national survey of older people and their medicines, indicates that older people continue to be prime marketing targets of an aggressive drugs industry and to be at risk from poor prescribing practices. Medication can be the basis of the abuse and restraint of older people and these two issues are explored more generally in the last three chapters of this section. What constitutes good practice when it is felt that the freedom of someone with diminished responsibility needs to be circumscribed?

In the light of these possible threats from intervention or therapy, empowering service-users seems a self-evidently 'good thing'. This theme begins our next section on *Power and Control*. The term 'empowerment' has now acquired academic respectability, as well as being much in evidence in government rhetoric: 'Where is the user's voice? Service must be designed around the user's agenda!' We must beware that lip service is not mistaken for reality, that the gloss is not mistaken for the substance. So, to end this section, we move from the empowerment of service-users to the power of 'pensioners'. Will older people ever acquire the real power that is necessary to maintain control over the course and quality of their lives?

Concepts and Values, the subject of the sixth section, are critical to understanding attitudes and expectations and to engineering change. Ageism is a matter of growing concern and one essential feature of it is the contrast between 'us' and 'them'. It is possible to see it clearly in the rhetoric over empowerment: 'Our objective is to empower older people to make choices.' This is fine except who is this 'we' claiming to have the power to empower? Two other concepts that have leapt on to the stage are quality of life and life satisfaction. Again, however, there are ambiguities in these terms which arise from conflicting values. We can all approve the objective of raising the quality of life only if we can all agree upon what constitutes a rise. Without questioning, the debate over euthanasia for the terminally ill could easily influence plans to provide older people with a 'high-quality' package of care.

Policy and Politics are the focus of the seventh section, and we should not forget that concepts and values both create and flow from policy, which in turn arises from the political process. These chapters well illustrate that, while an ageing society and some of its inherent long-term challenges are acknowledged politically, appropriate integrated policies are marked by their absence. As historical studies tell us, division is easier to achieve than solidarity. In the absence of consensus and long-term strategies, the conflicting interests of different generations, as well as those relating to other divisions in society, will continue to dominate. These chapters document some of the many rapid changes currently affecting the lives of older people: the privatisation of welfare; the development of markets; the neglect of housing in the launching of the NHS and Community Care Act (1990); and changing patterns of retirement. It is possible that, with increased international migration, the future well-being of an ageing society rests in the development of cross-national strategies and policies.

The final two sections focus upon *Pasts* and *Futures*. Placing individuals in a personal and historical context should help sensitise us to the pressures that moulded older generations and to those which now mould us. The study of the past, however, is a complex enterprise. There is a diversity of biographies and reminiscences which ensures that the individual perspective will be idiosyncratic. Institutional histories, regarding the services or the professions, are bounded up with the politics of the time as well as with the enterprise of the individual. Nevertheless, all societies – ageing or otherwise – should endeavour to judge the past and to learn from it in order better to understand the present. Knowledge of what might have been can engender an increased level of awareness of possibilities to come – futures which, as some of the chapters in our last section suggest, we should play a part in constructing. After all the future is *our* future and, in an ageing society, more of us will be able to take advantage of past successes, such as improvements in hygiene and living standards. Such successes have given us the opportunity to make the best of the years to come.

This reader was compiled to accompany a new Open University course *An Ageing Society (K256)*. It is anticipated that many of the students on this course will be working in the health and social services. The course, like this reader, is multidisciplinary and all of it is relevant to practice. However, our hope is that students of all ages and from all kinds of life situations will be attracted to the course. In particular we hope that some of the older people with whom health and social services professionals are working will also become students. For these reasons, this reader is not narrowly focused on practice of policy issues, but endeavours to offer a wide overview of ageing and later life in an ageing society.

We owe a great deal of thanks for the hard work put in by the many contributors to this reader. But we would also like to thank many other people who have helped us to get this book into print: our colleagues on the Open University K256 course team – Brian Gearing and Sheila Peace who have given invaluable editorial assistance and Caroline Malone and Antonet Roberts for their practical support; Eric Midwinter, Alan Walker, Christine Kalus, Christina Victor, Joanna Bornat, Moyra Sidell, Jim Leeming, Ioan Davies, Laura Sutton, Robert Baldwin and Helen Evers who have worked on, or suggested, inclusions for this reader; and Bill Bytheway for his many suggestions and for his help with some of the editing.

PERSONAL ACCOUNTS

1

Look me in the eye

Barbara Macdonald

Cynthia and I decided to go on the March to Take Back the Night. It wasn't a decision we came to easily. [. . .]

I always try to win an argument by throwing in a lot of words and flailing my arms around, but Cynthia didn't raise her fork or her voice. 'Barbara, everything women do invites violence. We can't let others go out and not stand with them, and we need numbers, especially because it's going to rain tonight. Besides, you need the exercise.' [. . .]

Women were dressed in somber colors, parkas, capes and slickers because of the rain. Kenmore Square was dark except for a few lights from the closed shops reflected on Commonwealth Avenue's dark wet pavement. We were lined up along the edge of the center green so as not to block traffic while we waited for the march to begin.

Monitors carrying flashlights, dressed in bright yellow slickers and hoods, moved like monks down dark corridors, back and forth along the lines, giving instructions, advising us about how long the wait would be, reminding us to watch out for the curb when we stepped into the street as we would be marching in close ranks and unable to see the curb ahead. [. . .]

I don't know exactly when I sensed that something was wrong and noticed that Cynthia was no longer beside me but a few feet away where the monitor was talking to her. I joined them. At first the conversation was not clear to me and I glanced at Cynthia's face for some clue. There was none. The monitor was at first evasive and then chose her words with care, 'If you think you can't keep up, you should go to the head of the march.' Gradually, I took in, like a series of blows, what the situation was, that the monitor had thought that, because my hair is grey, because I am 65 and because I look 65, I might be unable to keep up; that her concern was that I might, if slower, leave a gap between the ranks in which men might try to

From B. Macdonald and C. Rich, *Look Me in the Eye: Old Women, Aging and Ageism.* London: Women's Press, 1983, pp. 25–33 (abridged).

enter; and that she could not say this to me. I stepped directly in front of the monitor for eye to eye contact to force her to talk to me instead of about me, saying only to Cynthia, 'She means me, Cynthia.'

I faced the monitor with rage. 'You have got to be kidding; I don't believe this.' My fists were clenched at the injustice as I felt the all too familiar wave of helplessness and fury engulf me. Then, in the glow of the flashlight, I saw the monitor's face and heard her words of discomfort and confusion. She said that she was sorry, that she had not known what to do, whether to say anything to me or not, and finally she had asked others if she should. She wanted to apologize. I said it was all right but it wasn't all right. Sometimes I wonder if it will ever be all right.

She went back to her monitoring and I tried to go back to where I had been in my head before the encounter. Back to the exhilaration, back when I was feeling and remembering Cynthia's words, 'if the march doesn't accomplish anything else, it is good for the women doing it'. But there was no way back. I took my place beside Cynthia but I knew that this march could not be good for me. The monitor came back to me a second time; she wanted to apologize again, she explained that she had not known what to do. I assured her I understood that she had not known what to do. For at that moment, I did not know, myself, what I thought she should have done.

We continued to wait in the darkness but nothing was the same. I felt the old caution I used to feel entering a bar not knowing whether or not it was a men's only bar – the dread of being told I did not belong there. With the same furtiveness, I now glanced at the women around me, at the six women in the rank ahead of me. We had been laughing together earlier at the man who wanted to convince us that capitalism was our oppressor; at least, I had thought we were laughing together – now I wondered. I looked at the women in the row behind me. I wondered how I looked to them. My short stature, my grey hair, my wrinkled face – I wondered how 65 years looked to them. And finally I looked at the four other women who were to walk beside me. I wondered how they felt about being with me. I wondered if I should take the arm of the woman next to me and tried to remember the instructions, but all I could recall was my shock and shame, hearing the monitor's words, 'If you can't keep up, go to the head of the march.' Hearing once more that I was a problem and did not fit. All my life in a man's world, I was a problem because I was a woman; now I'm a problem in a woman's world because I'm a 65-year-old woman. Hearing once more that I was not in the right place and thinking, 'If not here, where?' [. . .]

I was left with the experience – with the rage that had no place to go. I could see no way to put the anger on the monitor and I fought not to put it on my aging body. I recalled the monitor's face above her flashlight, sincere in her discomfort and apology – that she 'had not known what to do'. I tried to look at it from where she was. What could she do? The ranks were expected to stay close together in order that men could not enter. There might be a lot of women who could not keep up. And how could she know whether they could or not without asking? And why should I find her assumption that I might not be able to keep up so painful?

Repeatedly, I told myself that there would be nothing wrong with being physically weak. Lots of people are. If it does not happen to be true of me now, it will be true of me soon. If I have pride in my strength now, it is false pride and if I feel shame in my lack of strength later, I will have let someone else in my head for the rest of my life.

I would go over it all again in my mind. The monitors were looking for women who would march slower, I told myself, and I looked 65 and they picked me. But why me? Out of five thousand women there must have been thirty about to come down with the flu, fifty suffering from a hang-over, and at least a hundred who were going to get a blister on their heel before the march was over. So why me? If you are a woman about to come down with the flu or your head is bursting with a hang-over you will either decide not to march or have sense enough to quit. Why can't it also be assumed that if a 65-year-old woman doesn't feel up to a march, she won't choose to march? I still come to only one conclusion: the monitor didn't pick me out because I looked weak; she picked me out because she believes that a 65-year-old woman lacks judgment about what she can do. She thought I did not perceive the situation and that I did not know what I was doing.

We had chanted:

Our bodies, our lives
Our right to decide.

Did she think I had no right to decide?

Sixty-five is older – that's true. Sixty-five may be slower – that's also true. But who should know more about what 65 can do than the woman who is living it? All our lives, we look over a situation and decide whether or not to participate according to our ability. From 6 to 96, we measure our strength and our agility for the situation at hand. Why did the monitor assume that I had suddenly lost that ability at 65?

One may reply to this that it is well known that very old people lack judgment. I'm not willing to accept even that general statement. Lots of people lack judgment – drunk people, psychotic people, plain happy excited people. But old and lacking judgment don't go together – old and cautious sometimes do. When I was young, it seemed like everybody over 30 thought, 'The young lack judgment.' Now I'm 65, and the women in their thirties think I lack judgment, and I am not about to go through that round for a second time without examining very carefully this movement that is rejecting me. [. . .]

2

Coming out of the age closet

Maxine Myers

I am 63 years old and for the first time in my life I feel that my age fits me. Or I fit my age. It hasn't always been so.

All during my childhood, I looked several years older than my actual age, and I was expected to act that way. I was given the responsibilities and freedoms of a much older child. Early on, I developed a fierce independence that belied my years.

My parents, upon advice from my schoolteachers, agreed to have me moved ahead two grades with the consequence that throughout my academic years my classmates were always older than I. I usually lied to strangers about my age by adding on a few years to achieve congruence with my physical appearance, grade level and friends.

Having lied, or at least having omitted the truth about my age, I would then have a devilish time explaining to ticket sellers and tram conductors why I was still asking for youth fares when my friends weren't. I took to carrying my birth certificate to use on such occasions as it was to my advantage to prove that I was young, and conveniently misplacing it when I wanted the status of my peers.

My body began to mature very early. I started menstruating at the age of 9, and by the time I was 12, I was tall and full-breasted. I seemed to leap from childhood to adulthood with little or no transition. I finished school at 14, but since I was a girl, higher education wasn't considered necessary (my parents couldn't have afforded it anyway). I was too young to marry, so three months before my fifteenth birthday, I entered the job market.

I had to lie again about my age when I filled out job applications. It was wartime when any civilian who could spell her name and count to 10 got hired. Since I had finished all my compulsory schooling, it was easy to convince the interviewer that I was 16 years old (the legal working age). So just before my fifteenth birthday, I began as a mail clerk at a bank, earning the grand sum of 80 dollars per month.

Given my newly-found 'wealth' I began to acquire stylish clothing, wear make-up, and adopt other fashionable trappings of the

From The Hen Co-op, *Growing Old Disgracefully*. London: Piatkus, 1993, pp. 62–6.

sophisticated working woman, all of which added to the illusion of maturity. I had my own charge accounts, none of which would have been approved had they thought I was under 18 and still living with my parents.

I was never popular with schoolboys, but now men were beginning to notice me. I took weekend trips with girlfriends, and flirted shamelessly with uniformed servicemen. My suitors all thought I was much older, and I did nothing to disabuse them of the notion.

Later, during the 1950s, my age seemed fairly appropriate to my activities as wife and mother, but when I divorced in 1969, just before my fortieth birthday, age suddenly seemed salient again. Because I didn't become aware of alternatives until much later, I assumed that the only way to restart my life would be to find a new husband; however, a 40-year-old woman with three children does not have great marketability in the romance department.

It was about that time that the student movements were proclaiming anyone over 30 as the enemy, and all public attention was being directed toward youth. At 42, I was in the process of taking some college courses for the first time, and I was thrown into a system designed for and populated by 18–21 year olds. Now, rather than being older than me, my schoolmates were half my age. Once more I was out of step.

I'd like to say that age was unimportant, and to some extent that would be true. As students we were all subjected to the same exams and assignments. I became acquainted with some wonderful young people with whom I talked, lunched, studied. Then they would go off to their parties and dates and I would go home to the responsibilities of a house, three children and two dogs. Even my teachers were younger than I.

The incongruity between my chronological age and my student status was disconcerting. To reduce the dissonance, I began to deny that I was like other women in their forties. I didn't want to be my age. I took much younger men as lovers, went to rock concerts, wore flowers in my hair, sewed long dresses from Indian bedspreads, hippie fashion, and stayed barefoot much of the year. I took great delight in hearing people say that I didn't 'look my age'.

What ageist nonsense! I was naive, unaware of the politics of age, untouched (I thought) by ageism. I was finishing my basic courses with high marks, and with a counsellor's encouragement, I had applied to and been accepted at a major university to complete a bachelor's degree. At the same time I wanted to apply for a State Scholarship to help with tuition. Stated clearly on the application form was the following: 'Available to students under 25 years of age.' CLICK!

Now, I'm hardly a person one could ordinarily call confrontational, but seeing blatant injustice makes me break through my passivity and pushes me to action. I didn't know how to use the words 'age discrimination' but I perceived the wrongness of denying aid to someone strictly on the basis of age. My first thought was to hire an attorney, but I hadn't the money, so I rang the local chapter of the American Civil Liberties Union (ACLU), an organization that works at no charge to defend civil and constitutional rights. I left my message, explaining the problem.

Several days later I received a call from an ACLU attorney, who said that they had agreed to take on my case. In their opinion, there was not only ageism but sexism as well, since most adult returners were women who had left education to care for families. They were prepared to go to court and so was I, but the State Legislature got wind of it and quickly decided to amend the application to exclude reference to age. And yes, I received my scholarship, as well as later fellowships for graduate work.

By the time I had earned my doctorate, I was 54 years old. I found a great job, my sons and daughter were grown, and I was in a long-term relationship. I had learned much from the Women's Movement about sexism, racism, ageism, anti-Semitism and other forms of oppression. I had also begun to examine and work on my own internalized oppression, which had kept me feeling that being old was not OK. I began to reject the Jewish Mother stereotype as being sexist and anti-Semitic, and started to celebrate the strengths and courageousness of my traditions. I challenged the negative labels put on mothers-in-law, stepmothers and old women in general.

I no longer lie about my age. I have come out of the age closet. I say how old I am and it feels just right. I like calling myself an old woman – it makes me feel strong and wise and important.

Other people sometimes seem embarrassed when I say I'm old. They're quick to reassure me that I'm not *really* old, as if it were some horrible disfigurement, or a disease they're worried about catching, like being (heaven forbid) single, which I am again by choice. My life is far from perfect and I have much to learn, but I feel more authentic than ever before. I'm growing old disgracefully and enjoying each step along the way.

I am 63 years old.

3

The ageing of Mary Berenson

Bill Bytheway

Gubrium and Wallace (1990) have argued the case for research into the ways in which people ordinarily talk about ageing. Many theories and ideas are articulated in everyday talk and writing. It is often what is heard and read that determines how people think and interpret their experience of age.

Mary Berenson was closely involved in the world of art in the first half of this century. She constantly wrote letters to her family and friends. I have undertaken a detailed analysis of what is written about age in Strachey and Samuels (1983 – abbreviated below to S&S), a published collection of her diaries and letters (Bytheway, 1993).

The extracts

Mary Smith was born in 1864 in Philadelphia. In 1885, aged 21, she married Frank Costello, aged 30, and moved to live in London. Two daughters were born in 1887 and 1889. Aged 26, she wrote in her diary:

> [1889] I feel quite sure that there could not be a more unselfish self-sacrificing husband. I am far more selfish in every way. Yet whose life is it we lead? *Frank's of course.* . . . Up to the end of our third year, I still hoped to have a chance to study a little and fill up, if only a little, the dreadful gap in my desultory education. [. . .] *He* has had his splendid education – he cannot conceive what it is to be without it – and *constantly feeling the lack.* . . . As a matter of fact what it comes to is this. What capacities for development etc. I have which do not coincide with the plan he has formed for himself of his own life – may lie dormant – may die for lack of nourishment. [. . .] To say I married too young a man who had already passed beyond the requirements of my age, that we lived a life of *his* age and education since [. . .], that my occupations leave me no chance for the things I would naturally have chosen – all this does not help matters a bit. (S&S: 40–1)

She met Bernard Berenson a few months later in 1890. He was one year younger than Mary. By December 1891 they had settled next door to each other in Florence and there 'they worked and loved' (S&S: 46). When 28, she wrote in her diary:

[1892] When we grow old, we won't look back upon our famous books, on the flattery we have had, but to our early loves [. . .]. I shall never forget the charm of these days. (S&S: 49)

Three years later, separated from her children, she sent her younger daughter a birthday letter:

[1895] To think that nobody on earth can stop thee, or keep thee little - thee *will* go on getting older and older, and more and more grown up! (S&S: 62–3)

Frank died suddenly at the end of 1899. During 1900, Bernard and Mary married and moved to a villa, 'I Tatti', near Florence, which was their home for the rest of their lives. Now aged 40, she wrote to her mother about a new diet:

[1904] There is no doubt I needed this discipline, for I begin to *feel fat*, to be too heavy to enjoy walking, to feel buried somehow in flesh. It's no longer the vanity of looks that spurs me on, for I gave that up on my fortieth birthday. (S&S: 118)

In January 1907, she wrote to her daughters about Bernard. He had told her he was at a great crisis:

[1907] I said 'The truth is that THIS time you have really and truly come to the end of your mental energy. *All is over*. You will never write or think again. Your brain is already attacked with fatty degeneration and you are doomed to pass a dull, idle unthinking existence. Of course these symptoms, in the past, have come about as regularly as the trees shed their leaves, about once a year, but THIS time it is of course utterly different; this time it really is all over!' He could not deny that I had hit off his mysterious complaint pretty well. I have noticed that he always feels like that a few months before he sets to work on something new. [. . .] Are we all as unconscious as that, taking our habitual peculiarities with such gravity? (S&S: 137–8)

Aged 54, she wrote to her family about her health following a journey from England:

[1918a] You can't think how seriously ill I've been - or perhaps you can, from the cessation of my in normal circumstances incessant letters! It was of course crazy of me to take that journey with the kind of cough I had, and I realize now that at my age there's no chance of not paying for our imprudence! (S&S: 220–1)

Relations between Bernard and Mary were never harmonious and each had a series of affairs. She had growing anxieties about Bernard's wartime affairs in Paris:

[1918b] Dearest Bernard. I can't, I just can't bear it if you go off to spend July with Mme. La Caze. I have fought and fought all day, and tried to feel old and take on the passive spectator attitude of old age, but I can't do it, Bernard! (S&S: 225)

Nicky Mariano became a lifelong friend of them both and all three frequently travelled together (S&S: 240-1). During a visit to Egypt, Mary wrote to one of Bernard's friends:

[1922] He works like a demon to prove that he can grasp & retain it with the same ease & tenacity that he had for Italian art 30 – ahime! 35 – years ago. But Anno Domini is too much for him. Dear Nicky remembers it all much better, no detail escapes her & she has become an animated History of Egyptian Art. Whereas B.B. & I muddle up places & things & names with the inevitability that belongs to what we always have called 'Middle Age'. The only difference is that I feel no responsibility at all towards 4000 B.C. & forget as easily as I enjoy & without vain regrets; whereas B.B. is striving to show he is still young enough to learn new tricks. (McComb, 1965: 92)

Back at 'I Tatti' and aged 59, Mary wrote the following diary entry regarding Nicky:

[1923] I am so old that all I can do is to take care of my own health. . . . It is a very difficult situation for me, this continual contrast between my age and infirmities of body *and* character with a young woman who is such an angel. (S&S: 248)

Mary felt that she was entitled to some portion of Bernard's earnings, but he disapproved of her often devious efforts to 'shower it on her children and grandchildren' (S&S: 250). In January 1924 and approaching 60, she wrote to her sister:

[1924] The bottom truth is that B.B. and I grow more and more uncongenial every year. [. . .] I'm not living the life I should enjoy, not the life I can approve of, but there is no way out while I remain with him [. . .]. When I'm well I can get along somehow. But Bernard always falls into a rage with me for small illnesses, and the fact of being below par makes me take it hard. (S&S: 251)

Three years later, aged 63, she visited Berne, where she re-read her old letters to Bernard:

[1927a] Apparently, it was because thee found me *real* in a world of shadows that thee cared so much. Well, well! Life took its course. But thank the gods it left us still together, still loving, still pursuing many of the same ends. (S&S: 264)

On a different topic, she wrote two days later to her mother:

[1927b] I decided [. . .] to take advantage of the famous Dr Kocher and his Cure. I couldn't scrape up any symptoms, except perhaps a bit of old-age laziness, and he rather laughed at me. However, he said that fat old ladies did tend to lose their grip, and that he could help them by his system of feeding the glands by means of injections of (as I understand) gland extract. So I am trying it. (S&S: 264)

The following year, now 64, she wrote to her family:

[1928] It is a bore to have lost faith in Drs Freeman and Kocher! But I mean to have a few more trials before I settle down to the life of an old invalid. (S&S: 272)

She began writing a book about a tour of Syria and Palestine. She wrote to Bernard's mother:

> [1929] In a sense I have never enjoyed myself so much as I have done in writing this book! It is wonderful what pleasures life stores up for one's old age. (S&S: 275)

Two years later, now 67, her health deteriorated sharply. In November she wrote to her sister:

> [1931] I dare say I shall get over this attack. The analysis is always showing improvement. But *is* it worthwhile to make such a fight for a few more years of an old woman's existence? (S&S: 285–6)

The following October, she wrote to Bernard's sister:

> [1932] The doctors, with their examinations and endless 'remedies', seemed to make me worse, so at last I threw away their horrid brews and betook myself to the Milk Diet that cured me last spring. (S&S: 290)

Her health never recovered. Eleven years later, in the middle of the War, Bernard went into hiding. Mary, now 79, described to him how her memory 'grows and grows':

> [1943] I look back to 55 years ago when it was all so difficult that it seemed *impossible* that I should ever be able to write so freely, and when a stretch of years as great was unimaginable. (S&S: 305)

In May the following year, she wrote to Bernard again:

> [1944] I have a very good memory and thousands of things come back to my mind in their settings, and it is in a way so impersonal now – as if I were really dead and reading my own autobiography. (S&S: 307)

Bernard returned to 'I Tatti' in the autumn of 1944. Mary died the following spring at the age of 80 years.

Analysis

Many of Mary's comments on the processes and patterns of change reflected her 'models of ageing'. A 'model' is not so much an explanation of ageing as a way of typifying the experience of ageing. The 1907 extract is a good example. What Mary put to Bernard is a 'model' of ageing: you are suffering from fatty degeneration in the brain and are doomed to an idle existence. She had come to recognise how periodically he held this distinctly negative model of his ageing.

In the analysis of this material I have identified eight models but this is not a complete or definitive list.

The first, the DEVELOPMENTAL model, is the basis of being *more and more grown up* (1895). It is clearly evident in the first extract (1889): ageing as *development – filling gaps* through *nourishment*. The model includes *growth* (1892), and explains the learning of *new tricks* (1922).

Although this model dominates her thoughts about early life note how, in her final years, her memory *grows and grows* (1943).

A second model is that of the STATUS QUO. It lies behind words such as *constantly* (1889), *never forget* (1892), *always* (1922) and *same* (1922). The idea of an unageing self detached from an ageing body is apparent in phrases such as *a life being led* (1889), *buried somehow in flesh* (1904), *one's old age* (1929) and *an old woman's existence* (1931). The search for the 'real' age-free Mary is apparent in her review of her old love-letters (1927a), and is most dramatically expressed in the last: 'as if I were really dead and reading by own autobiography' (1944).

Similar to this is the third model: ageing as ROUTINE. Ageing is the experience of events happening routinely: *regular symptoms* (1907), *habitual peculiarities* (1907), *incessant letters* (1918a), and attacks to be got over (1931).

Fourth, there is the STAGES model. As one stage succeeds another, you accept that things will be *utterly different* (1907), that significant changes *tend* to happen when a stage is reached (1927b). *Middle age* is an inevitable muddling of places and names (1922), and you anticipate *old age* (1918b), the pleasures that life *stores up* for it (1929), and then *settling down* to become an invalid (1928). The discontinuities between stages is enhanced by the contrasts between the generations (mothers, sisters, daughters and Nicky).

Fifth, there is negative change, the DECLINE model. This underlies not only the 1907 model of Bernard's ageing, but also her comments about *giving up* (1904), and *loss* (1927b). 'B.B. and I grow more and more uncongenial every year' (1924). The phrase 'more and more' is used to represent both growth and decline.

Sixth, we have the model of EXTREMES. It is represented by extremes of (1) experience: 'You can't think how seriously ill I've been' (1918a), 'never enjoyed myself so much' (1929), 'You will never write or think again' (1907); and (2) age: *so old* (1923), a *stretch of years as great* (1943). This model is implicit when extremes are perceived not yet to have occurred: *still* young enough (1922), *still* together (1927a).

Seventh, there is age the ADVERSARY. Consider her comments on Bernard's crises: his brain was *attacked* and he was *doomed* (1907), and Anno Domini was too much for him (1922).

The short sentence 'Life took its course' (1927a) raises the crucial question of whether Mary ever felt she could resist the changes that were happening in her life. She only seemed to be positively self-determining when she became ill. Then she decided to *take care* of her own health (1923), to *take advantage* of the famous doctor (1927b), and to *fight* for a few more years (1931). She *threw away* the doctors' medicines (1932).

Finally, there is the CONTINGENCY model. The first extract is full of thoughts about the course her life might have taken but for her obligations to Frank: 'my occupations leave me no chance for the things I would naturally have chosen' (1889). Later she recognises that so long as she is *prudent* then she can hope to avoid ill-health (1918a). Her ageing experience becomes increasingly contingent upon circumstances: 'there is no way out while I remain with him. . . . [. . .] When I'm well I can get along somehow' (1924).

Conclusion

This analysis demonstrates how the experience of ageing is full of the changing images of life, past, present and future, and how this is reflected in the changing views of people as they age. Throughout her letters, Mary Berenson uses words and phrases in still familiar ways.

Other models could be identified and discussed – relating to control, generation and denial, for example. Of the eight considered, four – the Developmental, Stages, Decline and Adversary models – are familiar to gerontologists. Gubrium and Wallace (1990) also found 'striking parallels' between ordinary and academic theories. What we need to consider is what we should make of the other less familiar four: the Status Quo, Routine, Extremes and Contingency models.

References

Bytheway, B. (1993) 'Ageing and biography: the letters of Bernard and Mary Berenson', *Sociology*, 27(1): 153–165.

Gubrium, J. and Wallace, B. (1990) 'Who theorises age?', *Ageing and Society*, 10(2): 131–50.

McComb, A.K. (1965) *The Selected Letters of Bernard Berenson*. London: Hutchinson.

Strachey, B. and Samuels, J. (1983) *Mary Berenson: a Self-Portrait from her Letters & Diaries*. London: Victor Gollancz.

4

Home from home?

Evan Marsh

My day starts at about seven when one of the night staff brings my breakfast. Cereal, a slice of rather flabby toast, and tea. That eaten, I get up, dress partly and shave, during which time the tray is taken away. Shaved and washed, I finish dressing, tidy up and turn on BBC 1 without the sound.

(I watch quite often like this, especially in the evenings when I am feeling tired. It occupies my mind – and anyway much of it is not worth listening to.)

My room is long and narrow – 18 feet by 8 feet – with the door at the end of one long wall. There are two windows, facing North and East.

Starting at the door, I have the little table I am using now – just big enough to hold the typewriter.

Next comes a chest of drawers, an electric fire, and then the very comfortable four-foot wide bed. The bedside table is like the one I am using now, and then the handbasin, with mirror over and good hot and cold water. Next is a small easy chair with wooden arms and, at the end of the room, a wardrobe.

The room is one of three, sharing a shower and separate lavatory, on the first floor of a specially built addition to a large Victorian villa. Into that room I have introduced my large easy chair, my television set, bedside light and photographs of my late parents and brother. And here I spend 23 hours out of 24. After 82 years as a bachelor, solitude is no problem.

The large lounge of the house is exactly like the ones shown on television whenever a home like this hits the news. Easy chairs, cheek by jowl, facing inwards all round the walls and a television set at one end. I spent my first half-hour there, and have not been back since.

The daily procedure continues as someone comes and makes my bed. Someone comes and cleans my basin. Someone comes and vacuums the carpet – and on Saturday the furniture is dusted. That is

From *Community Care*, 1 December 1988: 18–19.

the only way I can put it because of the odd staff, none of whom lives on the premises.

No qualifications

The manageress is a woman of about fortyish, without any technical qualifications and who has another outside interest. She is here from about nine to five but not on Saturdays and Sundays. We all dislike her intensely.

There is the very nice young housekeeper, who lives about a dozen miles away – also away at the weekend – and there is the 19-year-old youth who is the chef, replaced at weekends by a lady. So on Saturdays and Sundays the place is run by part-time amateurs.

They too, during the week, do all the cleaning, waiting and washing. There seem to be about 20 of them. In the six months I have been here, there has been a new girl nearly every week, and several of the old hands work more than once a week. I understand that by local standards the pay is good. This constant change is irritating as we have to keep telling newcomers how we like things.

My neighbour Alice visits me in my room each day and being the kindest person in the house, has taken it on herself to distribute the daily papers. Only seven of the 22 residents take a daily paper. Two or three more also watch the news on television. The rest are apparently content to be vegetables.

Their example has made me realise that it may be a struggle to avoid joining them. To this end, I have asked my kind sister-in-law to send me three monthly magazines. I read *The Times* almost from cover to cover. I do the crossword puzzle – a mind honer. And I read novels.

After breakfast James, the young chef, arrives in my room with coffee and biscuits. Later still, mail, if any, is brought up.

Then, in time for the 12.30 lunch, I descend to the dining-room. This is actually two adjoining rooms – mine holds 11 at three tables.

On my right sits James, who had a stroke four years ago. He walks with some difficulty, with a stick to help him, and has difficulty lowering himself on to his chair. All his cutting of meat and eating has to be done with his right hand. We always greet each other when we meet, but after that I never know whether he will be talkative or silent – generally the former at lunch and the latter at tea, and all conversation must be simple and factual.

On my left is the very nice Dora, from Lancashire. She is almost stone deaf, but often picks up the quiet word. She is quite unaware of the fact that when she eats she makes rather endearing little grunting sounds.

Opposite me is Bessie – a little mouse of a woman who is just not there at all. She never speaks. The other table for four holds the already-mentioned Alice, plus Annie and Gwen. Annie is alleged to be very rich and mean. I am told that she sleeps for most of the day. I have only spoken to her once. Gwen is from my village. I have known her for more than 40 years. She is here because she has fits of forgetfulness and was not safe living alone in the village.

The third table has another lady from my village, very deaf indeed. She always answers questions, whether fully heard or not – sometimes with very comic results. The last lady is Mrs Howard – the grande dame of the establishment. She is always referred to as Mrs – the rest of us are known by our Christian names.

The round wooden tables have place mats and we each have a knife, fork and spoon. A pudding fork can be obtained on Fridays to deal with prunes. No side plate. No napkin (I use a handkerchief). We are each provided with a glass of lemonade.

When we assemble there is a certain amount of chat and greeting, but when the food arrives we concentrate on that. Very plentiful – heaped plates – but very monotonous. At the moment carrots and cabbage nine days out of ten. Like several others, on many days I cannot finish my helping.

The pudding, fruit or suet, is always covered with custard.

The whole thing takes no more than 20 minutes – we have done it in less – so that I am easily back in my room for the *One O'clock News*. That over, I have more than three hours to fill. I read, play Patience, may watch television, and if need be I finish the crossword.

One sunny afternoon recently I went for a short walk with three other residents and one of the attendants. We walked past a lot of bungalows and came back past more bungalows, with two stops for rest on the way. But did it do any of us any good?

For more than four years I have had to use a stick when walking and now I would feel naked without it. My shaky legs are due, so my doctor tells me, to half a century of drinking pints in public bars – public, not saloon, I emphasise. No regrets – no regrets at all. What fun I have had in those bars, and what fine men I have met, including all my best friends.

French dressing

Tea is at 4.45. An egg dish, fish fingers or a meat sandwich. I reject all three – either they do not like me, or I them. So every day I have a salad of lettuce, cucumber, tomato and apple or orange. I remember what a French chef once told me and add a little sugar to the dressing.

Back upstairs again at about five, I settle down to an evening of television, sometimes with sound, sometimes without. At seven I get my bed ready for the night, for by this time I am beginning to feel very tired. Sometimes between seven and eight my supper appears – a meat soup with two slices of bread and butter.

Then, at 8.45, comes the happy moment when I have my first large whisky. I watch the *Nine O'clock News* headlines and then go to bed with my second, even larger whisky.

About 20 minutes of reading, then lights out, my prayers to God and, mercifully, sleep.

And so, along with all the others, I wait for death, not sure whether I will die of old age or boredom.

But not quite – for I have a friend. For more than four years he has been to see me at least once a week – at many times more frequently. When I had a stroke he came at once in answer to my telephone call, and then came every evening for 10 days. I have now given him my few good possessions – he knows he will get no more for I live on an annuity and my old age pension.

He is a fisherman – a very hard-working and successful fisherman – and at 30, is 52 years younger than me. He is that rare thing these days, *good* – as my dictionary tells me, 'promoting health, wealth and happiness'. I thank God for him every night. After he says goodnight and leaves, I feel a glow of happiness as I fall asleep.

But then I wake up to another 14 hours of boredom – and possibly something worse. The way we are all unnaturally boxed in together, with nothing to do all day, it is not surprising that we have all become a bit peculiar, including probably myself. I may already be a bit crackers.

Bored, uncertain, unhappy. Is this how we have to end our lives?

5

Mrs Hatter

Janet Ford and Ruth Sinclair

I came here about four years ago but I wish I hadn't done so. Before that I lived with my son and his wife for about three years. I went there when my husband died. I'd been away in hospital for an operation on my eyes – I've had three operations for cataracts – and I was not long home when he died. I couldn't see too well but I managed to get help. It was an awful shock, he died of heart failure. After that my son said that on account of my eyes and the shock, that I couldn't stay in the bungalow on my own, so I went to live with him. We were comfortable enough, but, you know, you feel a bit in the way when they're young. I wasn't a lot of trouble. I never interfered with them, and they used to go out when they wanted and I never got lonely. I was all right, only it felt wrong sometimes, like I was a bit in the way. I used to go to Faringdon House on a Wednesday and I'd been to one or two other places for a fortnight while they'd been on their holidays. One time I'd been here. In the end they said I'd be better looked after, so when it was decided I'd move for good I said I'd come here, but I wish I hadn't done. I think it would have been better if I'd have gone to Faringdon House. Do you know it? There are one or two nice little places, better than here. Not so big and more friendly. Now if anyone asks me I always say that if you can keep your own home it's best to do so as long as possible because however nice a place is it's not like home is it? When you're at home you can do as you like, although when you get as you can't manage you've got to go somewhere like this. [She laughed.] You've no choice about being old. It's just one of those things you have to take. I don't think anyone wants to be old if they can't do for themselves, and there is such a lot like that now, they're really living too long.

I've not got many friends left, a lot of them have passed away but I have a cousin in Huddersfield. She's in a home. She's the last of the family apart from me. She'll be 84 this September. I write to her but I can't write a lot now because of my eyes. You do miss

From J. Ford and R. Sinclair (eds), *Sixty Years On: Women Talk About Old Age*. London: Women's Press, 1987, pp. 31–6.

your friends really and so you have to think of the past. You sit
and think about what happened because you haven't much future,
have you?

Did you see in the paper where a woman was 105? She looked well,
didn't she? I shouldn't want to live as long as that, though. I don't
think anyone really wants to. As it is you spend most of your time
thinking about the past, that's if you haven't dozed off! There is not
much future to think about. I can't go on holidays now. We had some
good ones in the past, but I never went abroad. My husband would
not fly, he didn't like it at all so we never went.

Can you tell me how you spend your day?

What? . . . Oh yes, spend the day? Well, I get up by half past six,
between six and half past, and of course it takes a bit longer getting
dressed now, washing yourself and doing, than it used to. Then we
have a cup of tea about seven, and they come and give you a
tablet. It's a water tablet [she whispered, and grinned at me and
laughed]. I don't need it but you have to take it from them so then
I put mine down the sink. Breakfast is at half past eight. I usually
go down there about eight o'clock with Mrs Mullard. She's not well
now and she's become really depressed. We get a cup of tea around
quarter past ten but I've already told them I won't bother this
morning because I don't want them coming in. After breakfast you
just have to sit and shut your eyes [she laughed]. I used to be able
to crochet and do, and after dinner I come in here and either have
a rest or rub through my hankies and do any bits of mending I've
got. I do as much as I can. The others, them that can't, they have
to do it for them. Later in the afternoon you just go and sit and
perhaps talk, but Mrs Mullard doesn't talk much now. I do an
awful lot of just sitting! They bring more tea and you can have a
biscuit but then at half past five it's supper. That's what they call it
but it's really tea. Later they bring you a milk drink, you can have
what you want. But I tell you what: least said, best said about lots
of things here. I watch television at night. Not up here, this one is
no good and I go down to one of the rooms that has a colour one.
There's only three of us so it's nice and quiet. I shouldn't want it
on all day. I like a good film but not all that pop stuff and I'm not
keen on Shakespeare. [There was a knock at the door and an
attendant came in without waiting for a reply. He did not seem to
have come in for any particular reason and looked around and went
out again.] You see, that's the trouble with this place [she
whispered]. Often they don't even knock. I told them not to come
in today.

Are there people here who give you some company?

No. There's nobody much that you can really have a conversation with. They're all getting past it, same as some of them that's out there [Mrs Hatter pointed out of her window to the courtyard where several elderly people were sitting on benches]. They make them go outside whether they want to or not. I don't want to live to be crippled up. A lot of them here are turned 90 and there's all sorts, in wheelchairs as well, so I've something to be thankful for. I look forward to our visitor who comes on a Wednesday, she's very nice, and then of course I have my family and I go out occasionally. My niece fetches me sometimes for the day on a Sunday and it's a nice change, and nice food; a bit different from this place. A change all round and I love sitting in her garden.

I'm not really lonely here, but it is a big place. One real trouble is if you are down at the table it echoes and if anybody says anything, everybody can hear it. It's a big drawback I think, as you don't want everyone to hear what you've got to say. Say the matron or anyone comes and says something to you . . . well, everyone is looking and listening. Their eyes and ears are always on. That's the trouble in these big places. I really want somewhere private. The people here are always arguing, you know, and grumbling on one with another. I mean you don't find that in every place. Here, there are not enough staff to look after them all. As I am, I'm all right, but you never know how you're going to be. They're often busy and if you say you don't feel well often they won't take much notice. They won't call the doctor when you ask, they just give you an aspirin. Mind you, I never say anything because it could be worse.

I'll tell you what happened with my pension book. They have it here, they take it when you come in to help keep you and they give you so much back as spending money. I think they decide how much you get. In fact I do not know how much the pension is now. I've told them that they are to let me know when it's due again. It's nice to know. I know it belongs to me, but they have it. You never see the book. They never say anything to you about it. The spending money's not bad and if you don't want it they'll bank it for you. I've so many grandchildren that as the birthdays come round I spend it. Odd times I go shopping too if I need a dress. Then my niece takes me so I need the money. I've told them they've got to let me know what I get.

Sometimes I cannot believe I'm 88 next month. I left school when I was 12 because my mother needed the help to look after my Grandma. Then at 13 I was apprenticed to millinery. You had to work 18 months for nothing, and then I went to another shop and got two-and-six a week. When I got married in 1920 we came to Loughborough. We went to London for a while but things weren't too rosy, so we came back by the Second World War. . . . Listen that's the bell. I shall have to go dear, we get dinner now and I take a while to get down. I'm thankful I can do it on my own. I've got a walker that is a help sometimes, especially getting up from old chairs and things. I never thought I'd get like this and this old, who'd have thought it?

6

Mr and Mrs Cosgrove

Jeremy Seabrook

In any case, I wouldn't exaggerate. We weren't exactly the happiest marriage. We used to fight. She had her sulks. Once or twice she was going to pack her bags and leave, but we neither of us had any place to go. She was a good wife, and I hope I was a good husband. You don't expect your whole life to be a honeymoon. She had these terrible moods. I never actually went with another woman, but it wasn't for want of thinking about it at times. I used to hang about after some of the girls at work, harmless enough really; nothing ever came of it. . . . You get so used to one another really, somebody snoring the other side of the bed, but that's what it's all about isn't it? . . .

She didn't have a happy young life. Her mother finished up in an asylum, the old man drank. She used to be scared she would finish up like that. Funny, she was much too sharp to go off her head. The thing you dread never really happens. It comes, but it always comes some other way. . . . But she was my old girl, and I was her chap, and that's all there was to it really. I don't want no medals for looking after her. It was lonely, because I knew I was the one going to be left. I couldn't have done anything else could I – what would I have done, run away? If I was going to do that, I'd 've done it in life, not death. I think I'm not afraid of death now, because I lived with it every day. It's now I suffer, believe me. I can feel the gap where she was; I wake up in the night, and I swear I can still hear her breathing and I have to turn round to make sure she's not there. I look at the clock in the afternoon and think 'Oh, time to get Doris a cup of tea', or 'She'll be wanting her tablets about now.' I used to give her those tablets – strong painkillers they were – in the early evening; you know, you had to give them to prevent the pain from coming on. You get an instinct for it; I got so I used to be all alert, listening for the pain, if you understand what I mean.

But I've nothing to be ashamed of in the way I looked after her. She never suffered like she would have if she'd been left to the professional indifference of hospital. Believe me, I used to say to

From *The Way We Are: Old People Talk about Themselves. Conversations with Jeremy Seabrook*. Mitcham: Age Concern, England, 1980, pp. 38–43.

myself every day of that last year with her, 'the last winter, the last spring'; and we watched the bulbs come out and the spring flowers, and the sun coming in the window and getting higher day by day, and she thought she was getting a bit better; and that summer, I don't care what anybody says, she did get a lot better, she even went out for a few walks. One Sunday night the neighbours took us out in the car for a drink down by the river. She did definitely gain a few months she would never have had in hospital. I gave her that, and I'm proud of it. There's only me knows what it was like, the way the illness developed, the way she felt about it. I was having to prepare myself to lose her, and she was having to prepare herself to die. It was the hardest year's work either of us ever did in our lives, poor old girl. She didn't know at first, and she wouldn't accept it. She swore it was an ulcer, and then felt she was getting over it. Then she had to come to terms, had to admit it was something worse; and to do that, she had to make out life wasn't worth living; and some days she talked about herself as it she was already dead. Then she lived from day to day, and picked up for those few months in the summer. Then she got very sulky and sorry for herself, and she cried a lot. Then she tried to hope again, and then she did accept it, and in the end, she just let herself go and did what I told her . . ..

It's a funny thing. I knew when she was going to die. I knew it would be after the second winter, before the spring got here. And it was. In February. I got such a feel for the rhythm of her, the throb of the body, believe me, I could almost feel that cancer. I suffered with her. I seriously believe that I carried some of the pain for her, and that's why she lived on like she did. I don't know how it happened, but it did. I wasn't surprised when she died. I did what had to be done, and I never cried until she was gone. I never thought of God or anything else all the time I was looking after her. My whole life was taken up with thinking about her needs, what she wanted to make her feel comfortable. Once or twice she said 'I wonder what happens to you when you die?' and I said 'Well, it can't be all that bad, nobody's ever come back to complain.'

I don't know what went on in her mind, how she came to terms with it. Perhaps I didn't help her there as much as I should've done; but I was concerned with my own preparation for what I'd do when she'd gone. In that sense you could say I was selfish, yes. But you have to be, don't you? I wasn't going to die with her, and I had to think out a life for myself afterwards. That was the hardest bit of it. When she'd gone, that was when I started to wonder, well, where has she gone? I could see her, she got so thin at the end, just like a little girl; she wasn't the girl I'd married and lived with any more, just a shell. When she was dead, she was still real to me. I used to wake up in the night and I thought I heard her. I went over all the things we'd done together, our whole life, and I thought, surely that can't just all go away, be put out like you put out the light. I thought, well, as long as she lingers on in my thoughts, perhaps we all linger on in the world, in the universe, vibrations, echoes, all the people you've known, whoever you've loved, they all carry a bit of you; that can't all be lost, can it? Otherwise, it's got no meaning. What would be the point of it? I went to a spiritualist, privately, a medium. He didn't know who I was. I didn't give my own name. I went into his – what do you call it – consulting room, and he said he had a feeling of pain in the stomach (that was where she had the cancer); and the details he gave me, well, he convinced me. He told me how she was smiling at me and expressing her gratitude for the care I'd shown her. That convinced me, it had all been worth while, it wasn't all futile.

After that, I felt such a sense of peace. I feel she's there. We can still be close. I feel she may be here, in the room, in the house, standing at the sink peeling the potatoes like she did all those years; it isn't me going off me head, it's real. I don't fully understand it, but I know that if I talk to her, it isn't the first sign of madness. I can feel it hasn't all been in vain. I'm lonely, yes, but it's not that terrible loneliness you see some old people suffering from when they've been bereaved. There's an old boy in this street, he neglected himself when his wife died, he wouldn't eat, wouldn't bother. You could see him going downhill day by day, shuffling around with a vacant look on his face. That isn't going to happen to me. I go out now. I meet people, up the Centre, there's a lunch club. I go shopping, I cook myself a bit of tea. I'm not going to give in. As a matter of fact, I've made more friends in the last year than all the time we were married. I can accept what will happen to me when my time comes. I know I shan't have anyone to do for me what I did for her. But I'd rather it was that way than the other way round. I know she'll be there at my side. She won't be able to give me painkillers or give me medicine, or read to me bits out of the paper or talk to me through the pain, but her presence'll be with me, and that's good enough for me. Don't let anyone tell you there isn't a purpose or a meaning. We might not know what it is, but it's there; and people do live on after death.

7

Epilogue to *An Autobiography*

Agatha Christie

The longing to write my autobiography assailed me suddenly at my 'house' at Nimrud, Beit Agatha.

I have looked back to what I wrote then and I am satisfied. I have done what I wanted to do. I have been on a journey. Not so much a journey *back* through the past, as a journey *forward* – starting again at the beginning of it all – going back to the Me who was to embark on that journey forward through time. I have not been bounded by time or space. I have been able to linger where I wanted, jump backwards and forwards as I wished.

I have remembered, I suppose, what I wanted to remember; many ridiculous things for no reason that makes sense. That is the way we human creatures are made.

And now that I have reached the age of 75, it seems the right moment to stop. Because, as far as life is concerned, that is all there is to say.

I live now on borrowed time, waiting in the ante-room for the summons that will inevitably come. And then – I go on to the next thing, whatever it is. One doesn't luckily have to bother about that.

I am ready now to accept death. I have been singularly fortunate. I have with me my husband, my daughter, my grandson, my kind son-in-law – the people who make up my world. I have not yet quite reached the time when I am a complete nuisance to them all.

I have always admired the Esquimaux. One fine day a delicious meal is cooked for dear old mother, and then she goes walking away over the ice – *and doesn't come back* . . .

One should be proud of leaving life like that – with dignity and resolution.

It is, of course, all very well to write these grand words. What will *really* happen is that I shall probably live to be 93, drive everyone mad by being unable to hear what they say to me, complain bitterly of the latest scientific hearing aids, ask innumerable questions, immediately forget the answers and ask the same questions again. I shall quarrel

From *An Autobiography*. London: Fontana, 1978, pp. 548–51.

violently with some patient nurse-attendant and accuse her of poisoning me, or walk out of the latest establishment for genteel old ladies, causing endless trouble to my suffering family. And when I finally succumb to bronchitis, a murmur will go around of 'One can't help feeling that it really is a merciful relief . . .'

And it *will* be a merciful relief (to them) and much the best thing to happen.

Until then, while I'm still comfortably waiting in Death's ante-chamber, I am enjoying myself. Though with every year that passes, *something* has to be crossed off the list of pleasures.

Long walks are off, and, alas, bathing in the sea; fillet steaks and apples and raw blackberries (teeth difficulties) and reading fine print. But there is a great deal left. Operas and concerts, and reading, and the enormous pleasure of dropping into bed and going to sleep, and dreams of every variety, and quite often young people coming to see you and being surprisingly nice to you. Almost best of all, sitting in the sun – gently drowsy . . . And there you are again – remembering. '*I remember, I remember, the house where I was born . . .*'

I go back to that always in my mind. Ashfield.

O ma chère maison, mon nid, mon gîte
Le passé l'habite . . . O! ma chère maison . . .

How much that means. When I dream, I hardly ever dream of Greenway or Winterbrook. It is always Ashfield, the old familiar setting where one's life first functioned, even though the people in the dream are the people of today. How well I know every detail there: the frayed red curtain leading to the kitchen, the sunflower brass fender in the hall grate, the Turkey carpet on the stairs, the big, shabby schoolroom with its dark blue and gold embossed wallpaper.

I went to see – not Ashfield, but where Ashfield had been, a year or two ago. I knew I would have to go sooner or later. Even if it caused me pain, I had to go.

Three years ago now someone wrote to me, asking if I knew that the house was to be pulled down, and a new estate developed on the site. They wondered if I couldn't do something to save it – such a lovely house – as they had heard I had lived there once.

I went to see my lawyer. I asked if it would be possible for me to buy the house and make a gift of it to an old people's home, perhaps? But that was not possible. Four or five big villas and gardens had been sold *en bloc* – all to be demolished, and the new 'estate' put up. So there could be no respite for dear Ashfield.

It was a year and a half before I summoned up the resolution to drive up Barton Road . . .

There was nothing that could even stir a memory. They were the meanest, shoddiest little houses I had ever seen. None of the great trees remained. The ash-trees in the wood had gone, the remains of the big beech-tree, the Wellingtonia, the pines, the elms that bordered the kitchen garden, the dark ilex – I could not even determine in my mind where the house had stood. And then I saw the only clue – the defiant remains of what had once been a monkey puzzle, struggling to exist in a cluttered back yard. There was no scrap of garden anywhere. All was asphalt. No blade of grass showed green.

I said 'Brave monkey puzzle' to it, and turned away.

But I minded less after I had seen what had happened. Ashfield had existed once but its day was over. And because whatever *has* existed still *does* exist in eternity, Ashfield is still Ashfield. To think of it causes me no more pain.

Perhaps some child sucking a plastic toy and banging on a dustbin lid, may one day stare at another child, with pale yellow sausage curls and a solemn face. The solemn child will be standing in a green grass fairy ring by a monkey puzzle holding a hoop. She will stare at the plastic space ship that the first child is sucking, and the first child will stare at the hoop. She doesn't know what a hoop is. And she won't know that she's seen a ghost . . .

Goodbye, dear Ashfield.

So many other things to remember: walking up through a carpet of flowers to the Yezidi shrine at Sheikh Adi . . . the beauty of the great tiled mosques of Isfahan – a fairy-story city . . . a red sunset outside the house at Nimrud . . . getting out of the train at the Cilician Gates in the hush of evening . . . the trees of the New Forest in autumn . . . swimming in the sea in Torbay with Rosalind . . . Mathew playing in the Eton and Harrow match . . . Max arriving home from the war and eating kippers with me . . . So many things – some silly, some funny, some beautiful. Two summits of ambition fulfilled: dining with the Queen of England (how pleased Nursie would have been. 'Pussy cat, pussy cat, where have you been?'); and the proud ownership of a bottle-nosed Morris – a car of my own! Most poignant of experiences: Goldie the canary hopping down from the curtain pole after a day of hopeless despair.

A child says 'Thank God for my good dinner'.

What can I say at 75? 'Thank God for my good life, and for all the love that has been given to me.'

Wallingford. October 11th 1965

8

Old age in crime fiction

Mike Hepworth

Crime is one of the most widely read types of popular fiction. In his guide to crime literature Julian Symons writes: 'Crime literature is almost certainly more widely read than any other class of fiction in the United States, the United Kingdom, and in many other countries' (1974: 11). Public library holdings and paperback sales, he notes, abound and the readership cuts across any definition of class or income group.

In these popular novels older people appear in a number of roles: often as victims; occasionally as incidental characters; and perhaps most notably as crime investigators (often of the unofficial variety). In this chapter I suggest that crime stories are an important source of information about images of old age. Whilst there is an increasing academic interest in images of old age in 'serious' or 'high' fiction (e.g. Woodward, 1991) and there is now a discipline called 'literary gerontology', relatively little attention has been paid to representations of old age in crime fiction. The examples in this chapter have been selected from crime fiction in Britain, in order to highlight four noteworthy images of old age: physical and mental frailty; otherness; the mask of ageing; and positive ageing.

First, however, four general points about modern images as forms of knowledge should be made:

1 Images are 'mass-produced'. They are constructed and marketed to cater for the tastes, experiences and desires of the public.
2 As socially constructed mass-productions, images help us to make sense of reality and the way in which we relate to each other.
3 It is not the truth or falsity of an image which is of primary importance. What matters is how we 'make sense' of it and how this influences our beliefs, attitudes and actions.
4 Images do not exist in isolation but connect up with and invoke other images.

As a form of general public entertainment, crime fiction communicates images of ageing and old age which serve two purposes. First, it reproduces and reinforces traditional stereotypes of old age as, for example, a stage of physical and mental frailty; and secondly, it also provides us with alternative 'positive' images of old age.

Physical and mental frailty

The story in Robert Barnard's *At Death's Door* begins with the feeble mutterings of a senile old man, a writer who has been a formidable celebrity and hell-raiser:

> Upstairs in the large front bedroom that looked out to the sea the old man's voice droned feebly on, coming and going like waves against the shore. . . . The voice faded away into silence. The dim eyes in the wrinkled, sunken face stared ahead. Minutes passed. A quarter of an hour. A dribble of saliva came from the corner of the old man's mouth and coursed down his chin. Eventually the forehead wrinkled, as if pale shadows of thought were going around in his mind. At last there was some movement under the bedclothes and slowly a hand emerged from under the sheets – a hand so little fleshed as to resemble a talon. (Barnard, 1990: 5)

This is, of course, an image of old age as chronic illness and dependency. An image of physical and mental frailty which when extended to a much wider section of the population of older people transforms them into the potential victims of predatory criminals. In Celia Dale's *Sheep's Clothing* (1990), Grace Bradby and her partner Janice prey on older women living alone who have a few valuables left in their houses. They get access to these homes by posing as officials of the DHSS under the pretence that their owners are not receiving their full entitlement to benefit.

The beauty of the scheme for Grace is:

> Like as not, the old dears didn't even know they'd been robbed for quite a time after her visit, and then they probably thought they'd mislaid whatever it was, forgotten where they'd put it. And even when (and if) they did realise what had been done, they were too confused and ashamed to tell anyone. For if an old lady comes into a police station, agitated and probably deaf, and says she can't find her hubby's watch and chain that she's sure she always kept in a shoe-box at the back of the wardrobe but hadn't actually set eyes on since she couldn't remember when, what sort of tale is that? (Dale, 1990: 27)

Otherness

There is a close association between fictional images of the physical and mental vulnerability of older people and the distance which is established between them and younger characters in a story. Through this device older people are easily transformed into 'them'. In addition to descriptions of physical appearance, descriptions of the homes and property of older people can be very effective stereotypes of 'otherness', as is revealed in the following picture of the home of a murder victim aged 87:

> The house was oppressive. Not just because of the all-pervading presence of death, but because it was absolutely cluttered with the past. The walls seemed unusually honeycombed with little alcoves, nooks and crannies where painted Easter eggs and silver teaspoons from Rhyl or Morecambe nestled alongside old snuff boxes, delicate china figurines, a ship in a bottle, yellowed birthday cards and miniatures. The mantelpiece was littered with sepia photographs: family groups, stiff and formal before the camera, four women in nurses' uniform standing in front of an old-fashioned army ambulance; and the remaining wall space seemed taken up by framed samplers, and water-colours of wildflowers, birds and butterflies. Jenny shuddered. Her own house, though structurally old, was sparse and modern inside. It would drive her crazy to live in a mausoleum like this. (Robinson, 1988: 39–40)

The image of older people as an 'other' or different species can be traced in western society to the tendency to divide the life course into different 'stages' (infancy, childhood, adolescence, adulthood and old age) and thus to separate and compartmentalise them. This act of separation has resulted in the creation of age-related barriers between individuals which are experienced as a sense of difference or 'otherness'.

Some authors, however, make it possible for us to see through these barriers to the common humanity beneath. One example is Anthony Gilbert's crime story *The Spinster's Secret* (1987). The central theme is the difficulties facing Miss Janet Martin who attempts to persuade those around her (i.e. younger people in authority) that she has strong grounds for suspecting that a murder has been committed. Her problem is that she has the outward appearance of a 'typical' spinster who has devoted her best years to looking after her invalid mother. When the story opens, she is aged 74, in delicate health, and passes the time in the shops and watching passers-by from her window.

We see, through Miss Martin's eyes, her attempts to persuade others that a man has been murdered and are given access to an insider's experience of the struggle against a confining ageist stereotype. All efforts to communicate her suspicions merely confirm the perceptions of those around her that she is becoming confused.

> 'I must say', acknowledged Doreen brutally, 'she does sound as if she was suffering from brain-softening. Oh, dear! Why can't these old people die off when they're no longer any use to themselves or any one else?' (Gilbert, 1987: 116)

In contrast, of course, the reader is aware that there is much more to Miss Martin than meets the eye. He or she is admitted to the ironic knowledge that Miss Martin is a perceptive and tenacious old person: at once a testimony to the strengths of older people and to the struggle against the repressive power of the conventional stigma of old age. It is a process of sensitisation to both the objective and subjective dimensions of Miss Martin's 'otherness'.

The mask of ageing

In addition to testifying to the barrier of 'otherness' between members of different age groups, Miss Martin is an interesting example of the image of old age as a mask. If we turn for a moment from crime fiction to the 'straight' novel we can find a concise definition of the mask of ageing in Stanley Middleton's novel *Vacant Places*:

'Ageing is a peculiar process. One does not feel old. Not inside the person. Painful joints, fatigue, failing powers are more and more noticeable, but the real self is young still, indefatigable, blest, illimited. I don't expect you to understand that; you think a moment's perusal of my face in a looking glass should disabuse my mind of such mistaken ideas. It is not so.' (Middleton, 1989: 186)

The dual perspective of the mask – the tension between the inner subjective experience of ageing and changes in our outward appearance – creates a space for the older character to manipulate the mask of ageing; a strategy which can offer certain advantages to older people, as Agatha Christie classically demonstrated when she created Miss Marple.

Miss Marple, the epitome of genteel English spinsterhood, lives in the picturesque village of St Mary Mead. She is white-haired, gently appealing and, by the time of her appearance in the novel *Nemesis*, infirm:

She glanced out of the window towards the garden, withdrew her gaze and tried to put the garden out of her mind. Her garden had been the source of great pleasure and also a great deal of hard work to Miss Marple, for many, many years. And now, owing to the fussiness of doctors, working in the garden was forbidden to her. She'd once tried to fight this ban, but had come to the conclusion that she had, after all, better do as she was told. She had arranged her chair at such an angle as not to be easy to look out in the garden unless she definitely and clearly wished to see something in particular. She sighed, picked up her knitting bag and took out a small child's woolly jacket in process of coming to a conclusion. (Christie, 1971: 9)

But surface appearances are deceiving: behind the mask of ageing is the formidable criminal investigator who rescues the police from their confusion by finding the solution to tortuous murder mysteries. In this role she is wearing what Patricia Craig and Mary Cadogan (1981: 164) describe as a 'grandmotherly disguise'. Her confusion 'is on the surface only, to amuse the reader who knows what is coming' (1981: 166).

Positive ageing

The final image I want to touch upon is that of 'positive ageing'. Although in certain respects similar to the mask of ageing, positive ageing refers specifically to older characters in crime stories who, unlike Miss Marple, 'do not look their age' and whose appearance attracts a mixed reaction of surprise, approval, jealousy and awe.

In, for example, Robert Barnard's *Posthumous Papers*, we meet the retired Professor Gerald Seymour-Strachey:

> Greg pushed the door and found himself in what must have been the largest room in the cottage. Every inch of available wall space was taken up with bookshelves, and every inch of shelf-space was taken up with books – books, mostly, with tattered jackets or sun-faded bindings and dating, Greg guessed, from the 'twenties, 'thirties and 'forties – presentation copies, review copies and remaindered copies amongst them. The room itself, however, was perfectly neat, and provided an excellent foil for Gerald Seymour-Strachey, who was no drivelling dotard, but a smart, upright, handsome old man, his clothes admirably cut and suitable for the occasion, his profile cunningly arranged to impress, his mane of white hair, thick and shiny, suggesting intellect and a sense of the aesthetically satisfying. He was the Patriarch, the Fountain of Wisdom, the man to whom pilgrimages are made. Here I am, he seemed to say, in the fullness of my years. Come and sit at my feet and drink the wisdom learned of experience. (Barnard, 1992: 103)

In similar style, the physical appearance of Simon Brett's Mrs Melita Pargeter is a clear signal of a positive approach to later life by someone who has no illusions about her age but is determined to extract the maximum enjoyment out of her remaining years. She is described as:

> An ample white-haired woman [who] must have been in her sixties, but was carefully and expensively preserved. Bright silk print dress, fur coat draped over shoulders, gleams of substantial jewellery, surprisingly high heels accentuating fine legs. There was about her a quality which, while not extreme enough to be dubbed 'flashy' or 'vulgar', would still have disqualified her from being called 'self-effacing'. (Brett, 1990: 11)

Mrs Pargeter

> had encountered so much distressing defeatism amongst the old too [. . .] many of whom seemed to regard their remaining years as a spiralling down process. This was not Mrs Pargeter's approach to any part of her life. Though she could not possibly know how many more years she would be allotted, she was determined to enjoy every one of them to the full. (Brett, 1990: 15)

Conclusion

I have argued that crime fiction is an important source of images of old age. These images have a good deal to tell us about our attitudes towards older people. But, the field is enormous and the four themes I have selected here should be read as an invitation to a personal exploration and critical evaluation of this literature. In doing this, three questions might be addressed. First, how do images of ageing reflect the value placed upon older people? Secondly, do these images have any influence on the self-images of older people? Finally, what, if any, are the alternatives to the images in current circulation?

References

Barnard, R. (1990) *At Death's Door*. London: Corgi.
Barnard, R. (1992) *Posthumous Papers*. London: Corgi.
Brett, S. (1990) *Mrs Presumed Dead*. London: Pan.
Christie, A. (1971) *Nemesis*. London: Fontana.
Craig, P. and Cadogan, M. (1981) *The Lady Investigates: Women Detectives and Spies in Fiction*. London: Gollancz.
Dale, C. (1990) *Sheep's Clothing*. Harmondsworth: Penguin.
Gilbert, A. (1987) *The Spinster's Secret*. London: Pandora. (Originally published 1946).
Middleton, S. (1989) *Vacant Places*. London: Arena.
Robinson, P. (1988) *Gallows View*. Harmondsworth: Penguin.
Symons, J. (1974) *Bloody Murder: From the Detective Story to the Crime Novel: a History*. Harmondsworth: Penguin.
Woodward, K. (1991) *Aging and its Discontents: Freud and Other Fictions*. Bloomington and Indianapolis: Indiana University Press.

Further reading

Featherstone, M. and Hepworth, M. (1993) 'Images of ageing', in J. Bond, P. Coleman and S. Peace (eds), *Ageing in Society: an Introduction to Social Gerontology* (2nd edn.). London: Sage, pp. 304–32.
Hepworth, M. (1991) 'Positive ageing and the mask of age', *Journal of Educational Gerontology*, 6(2): 93–101.
Light, A. (1991) 'Agatha Christie and conservative modernity', in *Forever England: Femininity, Literature and Conservatism between the Wars*. London: Routledge, pp. 61–112.
Shaw, M. and Vanacker, S. (1991) *Reflecting on Miss Marple*. London: Routledge.

9

A cream cracker under the settee

Alan Bennett

Doris is in her seventies and the play is set in the living-room and hallway of her semi-detached house. She is sitting slightly awkwardly on a low chair and rubbing her leg. Morning.

It's such a silly thing to have done.

Pause.

I should never have tried to dust. Zulema says to me every time she comes, 'Doris. Do not attempt to dust. The dusting is my department. That's what the council pay me for. You are now a lady of leisure. Your dusting days are over.' Which would be all right provided she did dust. But Zulema doesn't dust. She half-dusts. I know when a place isn't clean.

When she's going she says, 'Doris. I don't want to hear that you've been touching the Ewbank. The Ewbank is out of bounds.' I said, 'I could just run round with it now and again.' She said, 'You can't run anywhere. You're on trial here.' I said, 'What for?' She said, 'For being on your own. For not behaving sensibly. For not acting like a woman of seventy-five who has a pacemaker and dizzy spells and doesn't have the sense she was born with.' I said, 'Yes, Zulema.'

She says, 'What you don't understand, Doris, is that I am the only person that stands between you and Stafford House. I have to report on you. The Welfare say to me every time, "Well, Zulema, how is she coping? Wouldn't she be better off in Stafford House?"' I said, 'They don't put people in Stafford House just for running round with the Ewbank.' 'No,' she says. 'They bend over backwards to keep you in your own home. But, Doris, you've got to meet them half-way. You're seventy-five. Pull your horns in. You don't have to swill the flags. You don't have to clean the bath. Let the dirt wait. It won't kill you. I'm here every week.'

From *Talking Heads*. London: BBC Books, 1988, pp. 81–91.

I was glad when she'd gone, dictating. I sat for a bit looking up at me and Wilfred on the wedding photo. And I thought, 'Well, Zulema, I bet you haven't dusted the top of that.' I used to be able to reach only I can't now. So I got the buffet and climbed up. And she hadn't. Thick with dust. Home help. Home hindrance. You're better off doing it yourself. And I was just wiping it over when, oh hell, the flaming buffet went over.

Pause.

You feel such a fool. I can just hear Zulema. 'Well, Doris, I did tell you.' Only I think I'm all right. My leg's a bit numb but I've managed to get back on the chair. I'm just going to sit and come round a bit. Shakes you up, a fall.

Pause.

Shan't let on I was dusting.

She shoves the duster down the side of the chair.

Dusting is forbidden.

She looks down at the wedding photo on the floor.

Cracked the photo. We're cracked, Wilfred.

Pause.

The gate's open again. I thought it had blown shut, only now it's blown open. Bang bang bang all morning, it'll be bang bang bang all afternoon.
     Dogs coming in, all sorts. You see Zulema should have closed that, only she didn't.

Pause.

The sneck's loose, that's the root cause of it. It's wanted doing for years. I kept saying to Wilfred, 'When are you going to get round to that gate?' But oh no. It was always the same refrain. 'Don't worry, Mother. I've got it on my list.' I never saw no list. He had no list. I was the one with the list. He'd no system at all, Wilfred. 'When I get a minute, Doris.' Well, he's got a minute now, bless him.

Pause.

Feels funny this leg. Not there.

Pause.

Some leaves coming down now. I could do with trees if they didn't
have leaves, going up and down the path. Zulema won't touch them.
Says if I want leaves swept I've to contact the Parks Department.

I wouldn't care if they were my leaves. They're not my leaves.
They're next-door's leaves. We don't have any leaves. I know that for
a fact. We've only got the one little bush and it's an evergreen, so I'm
certain they're not my leaves. Only other folks won't know that. They
see the bush and they see the path and they think, 'Them's her
leaves.' Well, they're not.

I ought to put a note on the gate. 'Not my leaves.' Not my leg either,
the way if feels. Gone to sleep.

Pause.

I didn't even want the bush, to be quite honest. We debated it for
long enough. I said, 'Dad. Is it a bush that will make a mess?' He
said, 'Doris. Rest assured. This type of bush is very easy to follow,'
and fetches out the catalogue. '"This labour-saving variety is much
favoured by retired people." Anyway,' he says, 'the garden is my
department.' Garden! It's only the size of a tablecloth. I said, 'Given
a choice, Wilfred, I'd have preferred concrete.' He said, 'Doris.
Concrete has no character.' I said, 'Never mind character, Wilfred,
where does hygiene come on the agenda?' With concrete you can
feel easy in your mind. But no. He had to have his little garden
even if it was only a bush. Well, he's got his little garden now.
Only I bet that's covered in leaves. Graves, gardens, everything's to
follow.

I'll make a move in a minute. See if I can't put the kettle on. Come
on leg. Wake up.

Go to black.

*Come up on Doris sitting on the floor with her back to the wall. The edge
of a tiled fireplace also in shot.*

Fancy, there's a cream cracker under the settee. How long has that
been there? I can't think when I last had cream crackers. She's not
half done this place, Zulema.

I'm going to save that cream cracker and show it her next time she
starts going on about Stafford House. I'll say, 'Don't Stafford House
me, lady. This cream cracker was under the settee. I've only got to
send this cream cracker to the Director of Social Services and you'll be

on the carpet. Same as the cream cracker. I'll be in Stafford House, Zulema, but you'll be in the Unemployment Exchange.'

I'm en route for the window only I'm not making much headway. I'll bang on it. Alert somebody. Don't know who. Don't know anybody round here now. Folks opposite, I don't know them. Used to be the Marsdens. Mr and Mrs Marsden and Yvonne, the funny daughter. There for years. Here before we were, the Marsdens. Then he died, and she died, and Yvonne went away somewhere. A home, I expect.

Smartish woman after them. Worked at Wheatley and Whiteley, had a three-quarter-length coat. Used to fetch the envelopes round for the blind. Then she went and folks started to come and go. You lose track. I don't think they're married, half of them. You see all sorts. They come in the garden and behave like animals. I find the evidence in a morning.

She picks up the photograph that has fallen from the wall.

Now, Wilfred.

Pause.

I can nip this leg and nothing.

Pause.

Ought to have had a dog. Then it could have been barking of someone. Wilfred was always hankering after a dog. I wasn't keen. Hairs all up and down, then having to take it outside every five minutes. Wilfred said he would be prepared to undertake that responsibility. The dog would be his province. I said, 'Yes, and whose province would all the little hairs be?' I gave in in the finish, only I said it had to be on the small side. I didn't want one of them great lolloping, lamp post-smelling articles. And we never got one either. It was the growing mushrooms in the cellar saga all over again. He never got round to it. A kiddy'd've solved all that. Getting mad ideas. Like the fretwork, making toys and forts and whatnot. No end of money he was going to make. Then there was his phantom allotment. Oh, he was going to be coming home with leeks and spring cabbage and I don't know what. 'We can be self-sufficient in the vegetable department, Doris.' Never materialised. I was glad. It'd've meant muck somehow.

Hello. Somebody coming. Salvation.

She cranes up towards the window.

Young lad. Hello. Hello.

She begins to wave.

The cheeky monkey. He's spending a penny. Hey.

She shouts.

Hey. Get out. Go on. Clear off. You little demon. Would you credit it? Inside our gate. Broad daylight. The place'll stink.

A pause as she realises what she has done.

He wouldn't have known what to do anyway. Only a kiddy. The policeman comes past now and again. If I can catch him. Maybe the door's a better bet. If I can get there I can open it and wait while somebody comes past.

She starts to heave herself up.

This must be what they give them them frame things for.

Go to black.

Come up on Doris sitting on the floor in the hall, her back against the front door, the letter-box above her head.

This is where we had the pram. You couldn't get past for it. Proper prams then, springs and hoods. Big wheels. More like cars than prams. Not these fold-up jobs. You were proud of your pram. Wilfred spotted it in the *Evening Post*. I said, 'Don't let's jump the gun, Wilfred.' He said, 'At that price, Doris? This is the chance of a lifetime.'

Pause.

Comes under this door like a knife. I can't reach the lock. That's part of the Zulema regime. 'Lock it and put it on the chain, Doris. You never know who comes. It may not be a bona fide caller.' It never is a bona fide caller. I never get a bona fide caller.

Couple came round last week. Braying on the door. They weren't bona fide callers, they had a Bible. I didn't go. Only they opened the letter-box and started shouting about Jesus. 'Good news,' they kept shouting. 'Good news.' They left the gate open, never mind good news. They ought to get their priorities right. They want learning that on their instruction course. Shouting about Jesus and leaving gates open. It's hypocrisy is that. It is in my book anyway. 'Love God and close all gates.'

She closes her eyes. We hear some swift steps up the path and the letter-box opens as a leaflet comes through. Swift steps away again as she opens her eyes.

Hello, Hello.

She bangs on the door behind her.

Help. Help. Oh stink.

She tries to reach the leaflet.

What is it? Minicabs? 'Your roof repaired'?

She gets the leaflet.

'Grand carpet sale.' Carpet sales in chapels now. Else sikhs.

She looks at the place where the pram was.

I wanted him called John. The midwife said he wasn't fit to be called anything and had we any newspaper? Wilfred said, 'Oh yes. She saves newspaper. She saves shoeboxes as well.' I must have fallen asleep because when I woke up she'd gone. I wanted to see to him. Wrapping him in newspaper as if he was dirty. He wasn't dirty, little thing. I don't think Wilfred minded. A kiddy. It was the same as the allotment and the fretwork. Just a craze. He said, 'We're better off, Doris. Just the two of us.' It was then he started talking about getting a dog.

If it had lived I might have had grandchildren now. Wouldn't have been in this fix. Daughters are best. They don't migrate.

Pause.

I'm going to have to migrate or I'll catch my death.

She nips her other leg.

This one's going numb now.

She picks up the photo.

Come on, Dad. Come on, numby leg.

Go to black.

Come up on Doris sitting with her back against the settee under which she spotted the cream cracker. It is getting dark.

I've had this frock for years. A lame woman ran it up for me that lived down Tong Road. She made me a little jersey costume I used to wear with my tan court shoes. I think I've still got it somewhere. Upstairs. Put away. I've got umpteen pillowcases, some we got given when we were first married. Never used. And the blanket I knitted for the cot. All its little coats and hats.

She puts her hand down.

Here's this cream cracker.

She rubs it.

Naught wrong with it.

She eats it.

Making a lot of crumbs. Have to have a surreptitious go with the Ewbank. 'Doris. The Ewbank is out of bounds.' Out of bounds to her too, by the looks of it. A cream cracker under the settee. She wants reporting. Can't report her now. I've destroyed the evidence.

Pause.

I could put another one under, they'd never know. Except they might say it was me. 'Squatting biscuits under the settee, Doris. You're not fit to be on your own. You'd be better off in Stafford House.'

Pause.

We were always on our own, me and Wilfred. We weren't gregarious. We just weren't the gregarious type. He thought he was, but he wasn't.
   Mix. I don't want to mix. Comes to the finish and they suddenly think you want to mix. I don't want to be stuck with a lot of old lasses. And they all smell of pee. And daft half of them, banging tambourines. You go daft there, there's nowhere else for you to go but daft. Wearing somebody else's frock. They even mix up your teeth. I am H.A.P.P.Y. I am not H.A.P.P.Y. I am un-H.A.P.P.Y. Or I would be.
   And Zulema says, 'You don't understand, Doris. You're not up to date. They have lockers, now. Flowerbeds. They have their hair done. They go on trips to Wharfedale.' I said, 'Yes. Smelling of pee.' She

said, 'You're prejudiced, you.' I said, 'I am, where hygiene's concerned.'

When people were clean and the streets were clean and it was all clean and you could walk down the street and folks smiled and passed the time of day, I'd leave the door on the latch and go on to the end for some toffee, and when I came back Dad was home and the cloth was on and the plates out and we'd have our tea. Then we'd side the pots and I'd wash up while he read the paper and we'd eat the toffees and listen to the wireless all them years ago when we were first married and I was having the baby.

Doris and Wilfred. They don't get called Doris now. They don't get called Wilfred. Museum, names like that. That's what they're all called in Stafford House. Alice and Doris. Mabel and Gladys. Antiques. Keep them under lock and key. 'What's your name? Doris? Right. Pack your case. You belong in Stafford House.'

A home. Not me. No fear.

She closes her eyes. A pause.

POLICEMAN'S VOICE. Hello. Hello.

Doris opens her eyes but doesn't speak.

Are you all right?

Pause.

DORIS. No. I'm all right.
POLICEMAN. Are you sure?
DORIS. Yes.
POLICEMAN. Your light was off.
DORIS. I was having a nap.
POLICEMAN. Sorry. Take care.

He goes.

DORIS. Thank you.

She calls again.

Thank you.

Long Pause.

You've done it now, Doris. Done it now, Wilfred.

Pause.

I wish I was ready for bed. All washed and in a clean nightie and the bottle in, all sweet and crisp and clean like when I was little on Baking Night, sat in front of the fire with my long hair still.

Her eyes close and she sings a little to herself. The song, which she only half remembers, is My Alice Blue Gown.

Pause.

Never mind. It's done with now, anyway.

Light fades.

10

Have the men had enough?

Margaret Forster

Bridget has dressed with care. This is not so much unusual as odd: why dress carefully for King's Wood? She's wearing very bright colours as though determined to be seen from a long way off – shocking pink sweater, purple skirt, pink tights, scarf patterned in mauve and pink and blue, and on top a white flying jacket. She's even put on make-up which she hardly ever does – the old eyes are weighed down with eyeliner and the lashes with mascara. As we get into her car her perfume is strongly evident. I ask her what it is. She says Chanel No. 5, Karl bought it for her on the plane, she would never have bought it herself, waste of good money. She is smoking, of course, gets through two cigarettes before we are half way to King's Wood. I have to direct her though she swears she has been before and knows the way. She has no sense of direction at all, always turns left if I say right. When we turn into the gates she says she's dreading this. She says she knows what it will be like and she's dreading it. She says once she's in there, it won't be so bad, but the first sight of Grandma is going to make her crack up.

I tell Bridget we have to ring the bell and point to it. She puts her finger down hard on it and says, 'Bloody bell.' The man takes his time coming and peers suspiciously round the door when he does open it – visitors to King's Wood aren't usually so demanding – Bridget smiles over-brightly and says good afternoon in what I know is her best sarcastic manner. She sweeps in, her eyes raking the chairs where the old ladies are sitting. She tightens her lips, looks furious, says, 'For Christ's sake where have they dumped her?' I touch her arm, nod over to the far corner. Bridget says, 'In the name of God, what have they done to her.' She marches across the room, me scuttling behind, embarrassed by her air of authority. Grandma is half in and half out of an easy chair, her right shoulder falling over the side and her head lolling. One leg is up on a stool, the other awkwardly splayed out under it. Bridget says, 'Mother! Mother! For heaven's sake,' and hauls her upright and into the chair properly and snaps at me to get a

---

From *Have the Men had Enough?* Harmondsworth: Penguin, 1990, pp. 219–24.

cushion. I haven't the faintest idea where to get a cushion from. I go to the Sister's office. I knock. There are four of them there drinking tea. One of them comes to the door reluctantly, but then I remind myself I'm interrupting a precious tea break. I say my aunt was wondering if there was a cushion around to make my Grandma more comfortable. I hate the sound of my apologetic voice, my Mother's voice and tone. I should be like Bridget. The nurse looks puzzled but in the background Sister says, 'Give her a pillow – won't do any good but give her a pillow.' I'm taken to the dormitory. My heart thuds, with fear, what else, as we pass six corpses in chairs. I dare not look at them. Is there no mortuary? But then a creaky-cry sound comes from one, the nurse says, 'Don't start, Ruby,' as we go on. She goes to what must be Grandma's bed and hands me the pillow.

Bridget snatches it impatiently. She pummels it and puts it behind Grandma's back and arranges Grandma against it and puts both her feet on the stool, neatly together. 'Leaving her like that,' Bridget says. Then she sits on another stool beside Grandma and talks to her, entirely uninhibited by the surrounding old women. Grandma won't open her eyes. Bridget pats her hands, which she is holding, both of them, in her own. She keeps saying, 'Mother, heh, Mother it's me.' Grandma makes no response. Bridget swears under her breath and then begins to rage about Grandma's clothes. 'What have they put on her? Where're her clothes? My God, what rubbish is this, where are her own slippers?' Grandma opens her eyes. They're bleary. Bridget peers at her, says, 'Heh, Mother,' again. Grandma stares. She struggles to speak but all that comes out is an unintelligible murmur. 'What Mum? What?' Bridget shouts, 'What was that?' Grandma tries again. To me, it sounds as if she is saying, 'low bridges' but Bridget is triumphant, says, 'There you are, she's saying hello Bridget, and hello to you Mum. What have they been doing to you eh? Eh? Mum? How are you keeping? Come on, tell me, tell me?' Grandma mumbles. I only catch, 'legs'. Bridget interprets. Grandma is saying her legs are sore. Bridget examines them. (Grandma has stockings on but they're rolled down to the ankle.) She says, 'Bloody hell, she's bruised, she's *bruised*.' She stands up, flushed. She tells me to stay where I am, she's going to see Sister Grice. But at that moment Sister appears, a bag of jelly sweets in her hand.

It is a very awkward tableau. Grandma is in a corner chair with another occupant on either side and we are in front of her. I am by now on the vacant stool so Bridget and Sister seem to tower over me. Sister offers Grandma a sweet. Grandma doesn't respond (though only a month ago she'd have snatched the whole bag). Sister selects a red jelly – 'see, they're soft' – and shoves it into Grandma's mouth, expertly getting it through her closed lips. Grandma chokes slightly, but then starts sucking. 'There you are,' Sister says, 'she's happy.' And then it's like a tennis match. Bridget serves first.

My Mother doesn't seem happy to me.

Oh, goodness, she's fine, she's a bit in the dumps today, but they all have
their days you know.

I'm a nurse myself, a Sister.

You're the daughter, then?

That's right.

The one that's been on holiday a month? Very nice, where did you go?

Germany. But what I wanted to ask you about were these bruises.

What bruises?

There, and there.

Oh, they're nothing, they bruise easily at this age, I expect she knocked her
leg on a chair.

But my sister-in-law says she doesn't walk on her own any more.

That's true, but we walk her, we keep her going, don't we Mrs McKay,
don't we, darling?

And I was wondering where her clothes are?

Being name-taped, they'll be back soon.

I'd like her to be in her own clothes.

But they're awkward, they're not as comfortable as these, not as easy, look
you see, Velcro, easier for the old things.

How is she sleeping?

Fine. She was restless at first, but she's settled now.

How is she eating?

Not much, but she's plenty of fat on her yet, you don't need to worry, she
won't starve.

Well, she won't be here much longer.

Won't she?

No. I'll be taking her home next week.

Will you now, well you'll have a struggle, she can't do anything for herself
now, you know. It's a full time job.

I know, I'll do it. Just as soon as I'm properly better.

I thought you'd been on holiday?

I have but then I was ill, with flu.

Oh, bad luck. You won't have to be ill when you have your mother home.

No.

You'd be sunk then, but you've got your sister-in-law of course, you're a
lovely family. I wish you luck, you'll need it. Another jelly, Mrs McKay?

All this time Bridget has been glaring and Sister meeting her glare
and deflecting it and ignoring it and needling Bridget. It is game, set
and match to Sister. She implies, without saying a single word, that
Bridget is deluding herself, that she really knows she will never take
Grandma home. And *she* isn't in the least worried at what Bridget
implies, that Grandma is somehow being ill-treated or at least not
supervised carefully enough. Bridget, I'm sure, expected Sister to be
on the defensive but she isn't, not a bit. She doesn't give a damn what
Bridget thinks. She wanders off, doling out sweets, going from one
slobbery old mouth to another without once even wiping the finger she
inserts into them. The television blares. Doreen and May patrol, Leah
squawks. Bridget stands fuming. She makes a decision. She pursues
Sister. I hear her ask if there is a wheelchair. Sister nods, points.
Bridget gets the wheelchair and we try to get Grandma into it. We fail.

Sister saunters over. She puts an arm lock on Grandma and has her into the wheelchair in no time. She tells Bridget there's a knack, that nursing the senile demented is a specialised skill. And she smirks. She knows Bridget doesn't possess it. We wheel Grandma away, but where to? I don't know, Bridget doesn't know. Sister comes to the rescue. She says we can use the office, she won't be in there for half an hour. Bridget is obliged to thank her but not in the effusive way Mum would have done. The office is quite pleasant. There are posters, plants and a few old, but quite attractive, chintz-covered chairs. It's obviously Sister's sanctum and we are privileged. I venture to point this out and Bridget snaps at me. She says it's a disgrace not to have some kind of day room. I say that is hardly Sister's fault, probably not King's Wood's either. Bridget says, 'Oh shut up, you sound like your mother.' I am startled to see tears in her eyes. Just as I'm wondering how to cope with this, Grandma speaks. She says, quite distinctly, 'Is there any tea left in that pot?' We both stare. There is a brown tea pot on Sister's desk and Grandma is looking straight at it. Bridget bounds up, feels the pot, looks around for a mug, finds one, fills it, finds milk and sugar and lovingly takes it to Grandma who slurps thirstily. Bridget strokes her hair as she does so, crooning over her. When the mug has been drained, Grandma looks at Bridget as though seeing her for the first time. She says, 'You took your time, you hussy,' and shakes her fist at Bridget in the pretend-fierce way she used to. She smiles. Bridget smiles. They are beam-to-beam, their faces very close together as Bridget bends down over the wheelchair. I feel an intruder. I should go away. This is private. They don't even notice me slip out or if Bridget does she makes no sign. And when I'm out, although still in the ward, I feel so relieved, like being really out, in the fresh air.

11

The photographic image

Kathleen Woodward

I want to begin [. . .] with an anecdote about a photograph, not a literary text. In 1989 the theme of the annual meeting of the American Studies Association of France was the body in American culture. In conjunction with the conference, a gallery in Strasbourg organized an exhibit of photographs on the subject of the body. One photograph in particular solicited strong reactions. It was a portrait of a thin old man (actually he could have been in his early sixties) sitting on the side of his bed, his knees wide apart, his body naked except for the shuffling slippers on his feet. The black-and-white photograph told us that his old age – or his premature old age – was compounded by poverty and alcoholism. His body, positioned in the center of the photograph, was framed by his near-squalid room which was lined with a long overhead shelf full of liquor bottles, rather neatly arranged. Like his knees, his arms were spread apart on the bed. They supported the negligible weight of his upper body and his alcoholic stomach, which was as slack as his penis. His entire body seemed to be hanging down, depressed. He looked straight ahead at the photographer, and at us, expressing no particular affect, perhaps only listlessness.

We were all academics – with positions, families, futures, presumably accomplished pasts. I was finishing up this book on aging and hovered around the photograph, listening to reactions and talking with people. Many expressed disgust and outrage. They interrogated the absent photographer, Gundula Schultz, an East German. Why, several demanded to know, had the photographer *exploited* this man? (In her 'defense', the story was circulated that she had lived with him for several weeks before taking this picture, a story which was met with predictably tasteless jokes.) I wondered aloud if this anger at the unknown photographer and this moral judgment of her intentions did not represent a displacement of their own fears. Most of them quickly turned their eyes away from the portrait, although the photograph remained in their minds' eyes, generating conversation. If they were angry at the photographer, they also seemed angry at this old man

From *Aging and its Discontents: Freud and Other Fictions*. Bloomington and Indianapolis: Indiana University Press, 1990, pp. 1–2, 195–6 (abridged).

whose body expressed no particular pride. For rather than soliciting our sympathetic gaze, this portrait avoided the consoling patina of pathos. It had something neutral about it. Although the man was clearly placed in the context of his environment, paradoxically his surroundings seemed to disappear. We were left with his naked body, all the more naked for the slippers. To this nakedness people responded neither with curiosity nor with voyeurism, nor with the generalized affection with which the body of a child is greeted. In turning away from this particular portrait, it was as if people were turning away from old age itself.

I talked about the photograph with a professor from Tours, a tall, finely featured man with a deeply lined face. His sensitivity and intelligence were striking. He was thoughtful, not abruptly dismissive, either of the photograph or of my reflections. But no, he did not want to look at this picture. No, he did not want to contemplate the body of old age. He would, he said, live that time when it came to him. As he spoke I thought of Virginia Woolf's pensive seventy-some-year-old Eleanor in *The Years* who murmurs, 'old age they say is like this; but it isn't. It's different' (1937: 383). I thought, no doubt when old age came to this man, it would not be like that. But this professor, who refused to tell me his age (I would guess he was in his early fifties, but I am not very good at guessing ages), was a scholar of John Hawkes, not Virginia Woolf. I thought of the disturbing phantasy world of *The Passion Artist* which is charged with virulent representations of the aging female body. I seriously doubted that this middle-aged man from Tours would be persuaded by Woolf's gentler, yet scarcely benign world. For him the photograph of the old man, which so eloquently but matter-of-factly spoke of the circumscribed everyday life of this particular person, represented old age *in general*. We may conclude that his response to the photograph reflected his expectations about old age, the fears of a middle-aged man. [. . .]

Consider a remarkable photo essay which appeared in *The New York Times Magazine* on August 27, 1989. Entitled 'Victories of the Spirit', this piece by Mary Ellen Mark features photographs of people who participated in the second national senior olympics held in St Louis in the summer of 1989. These photographs linger in my mind's eye as counter-texts to the photographs by Gundula Schultz with which I opened [this book]. Instead of a penurious and listless old man sitting alone in his dingy room, a man who goes nameless, and whose age is undefined, we see George M. Richards, age 82, wearing running shorts and crouched at the starting line for the 100-yard dash. His body is wiry, his pose exceptionally relaxed. In another full-page photograph (not just the fact of these photographs but also their *size* is unusual), we see Catherine Cress, 79, stretching out her body in preparation for a swimming meet. She is wearing a black tank suit. The photograph is not what we would call 'flattering'. Our attention is drawn to the lumpy flesh on her thighs. But, importantly, the overall effect is not one of embarrassment, either on her part or on the part of the spectator. Her body seems just right, it is what it is, it is fit. The presence of it in public constructs a different, accepting space for the body – in all its differences – in old age.

Reference

Woolf, V. (1937) *The Years*. New York: Harcourt.

12

Ageing with a disability

Gerry Zarb

This chapter considers the experiences of disabled people who are also ageing. To be clear, this refers not to people experiencing disability as a consequence of the ageing process, but to those who become disabled in child- or adulthood and are ageing with their disabilities.

While there are no comprehensive figures, two national surveys in the late 1960s and 1980s indicate that there are now just under 100,000 people aged 50 plus who have been disabled for 20 or more years (Harris, 1971; Martin et al., 1988). It is estimated that this figure will reach 200,000 or more within the next 10 to 20 years (Zarb, 1992).

It was against this background that our three studies on the personal and social consequences of long-term disability, and on ageing with a disability[1], were initiated. The first two looked at the experiences of one particular sub-group – people who had been disabled as a consequence of spinal injury (Creek et al., 1987; Zarb et al., 1990). In the third study (Zarb and Oliver, 1993) the research was extended to cover the ageing experience amongst people with a wide variety of disabilities or disabling illnesses. A total of 300 men and women have participated in the study by providing written or oral accounts of their own experiences. One hundred and twenty five were followed up with in-depth personal interviews. Of these just over a third have been disabled since birth or early childhood. Thus at the time of the studies some had been disabled for 80 years and some for 20 years.

Physical changes over time

Despite the broad range of disabilities covered, there is considerable similarity in the kinds of physical changes reported by people in our studies. Two general themes in particular have been highlighted. First, many people's experiences are consistent with the notion of 'premature' physical ageing connected with a process of 'general deterioration' which typically becomes noticeable around 20 to 30 years from onset of disability. Further, this trend mostly appears to operate independently of chronological age.

Second, many of the physical problems/changes experienced are perceived as being long-term effects of people's original disabilities.

The most common of these is the high incidence of arthritic and rheumatic problems reported by nearly all of the groups included in the studies. For some groups, there are also common secondary impairments caused either by the original disability or by the long-term effects of medical or rehabilitation interventions: for example, blindness and neurological problems associated with long-term insulin dependence (diabetes); chronic pain resulting from building up immunity to certain drugs like morphine; chronic respiratory problems caused by spinal deformity (scoliosis); and a variety of physiological problems coming under the heading of 'post-polio syndrome'.

Satisfaction with quality of life

Amongst those who become disabled when they are young adults or middle-aged, the first 10 to 15 years are usually marked by a steady increase in quality-of-life satisfaction levels. However, this is often followed by a marked decline in satisfaction after 20 to 30 years when the effects of ageing typically become significant. The situation for people who became disabled during childhood and for those disabled from birth appears to be slightly different. For them there is the same pattern of increasing satisfaction preceding a downturn in later years, but the start of increasing satisfaction is often delayed until early adulthood (Zarb, 1991a). The biographical data suggest that negative early experiences in institutions play a major part in this. As people accommodate themselves to change experienced with ageing, satisfaction tends to rise again after 30 years from onset and amongst the 60 plus age group, but this is certainly not universal.

Although the aggregate trends are useful as a guide to understanding changes associated with ageing, it is important to consider why satisfaction increases for some individuals and decreases for others. Numerous factors influence levels of satisfaction with quality of life. Several people described the ageing process as representing the onset of a 'second disability'. Often, this realisation would be quite sudden, being triggered by a particular problem. Others who had experienced this kind of relatively sudden downturn in satisfaction pointed out that this might only be temporary. Although awareness of ageing may have been triggered by a disruptive life event, they were able to accommodate themselves to the practical and emotional changes in their lives over time.

Anxiety tends to increase as people perceive their independence to be threatened either by further physical decline or, more often, by the lack of appropriate support (Zarb, 1991b). Further, this anxiety appears to be heightened amongst older disabled women. The factors taken into account when asking people about their overall support included personal and domestic assistance, as well as material support in terms of housing and financial resources. It is likely, therefore, that structural gender inequalities in the distribution of such resources are reflected in older women being more anxious about the future.

Several people emphasised that their physical and emotional well-being were inextricably linked, and always had been throughout the disability career. Consequently, one of the most common effects of physical decline had been to reduce people's general levels of motivation. This can become a vicious circle; the drain on their emotional reserves meant that they felt less able to cope physically, which, in turn, contributed to a further drain on both their emotional and physical resources. On the other hand, some people reporting similar physical changes did not view these in exclusively negative terms as they considered them to be unavoidable.

Many people felt they were ageing faster than their able-bodied contemporaries. For some, this knowledge had given rise to the feeling that 'time is running out' and had influenced their plans for the future (eg. planning to retire early). Some anticipated not only that they would age quicker but also that they would die younger than their contemporaries. At the time when many of the people in these studies became disabled, life expectancy for people with various disabilities was low. Several people related how they had been told, or they had simply assumed, that they would not survive adolescence, or would only live for maybe 20 or 30 years. This means they had had a more or less heightened awareness of their own mortality throughout their disability career. However, most people's attitude towards this was quite accepting; often, the anticipation of dying seemed to be less traumatic than dealing with the effects of the ageing process itself.

Ageing and independence

Many older disabled people expressed significant concerns about independence, which they saw as being threatened by physical and/or personal changes they had experienced with ageing. In some cases, this only extended to personal or physical independence but, for many, ageing represented a threat to their independence in the much wider sense of losing control over how they wished to live out their lives. Several people were concerned about the possibility of having to make major changes in life-style, such as seeking more personal assistance or changing their living arrangements. Anxiety about the possibility of institutional care was a strong influence on these perceptions, particularly for women.

A few people stated that they would prefer the option of suicide or euthanasia rather than rely on support services or institutional care. Others had a more philosophical view – feeling that having extra help was probably the best way of maintaining their independence, or at least avoiding any further loss of independence. At the same time, they still intended to resist such changes for as long as possible.

A small number of people, on the other hand, had either never placed much emphasis on independence in their lives, or had never felt they had that much independence in the first place. Consequently, their anxieties about ageing were not necessarily so acute.

The important common denominator underlying these perceptions is whether or not changes associated with ageing are compatible with how an individual wishes to live his or her life. It is also essential to consider these perceptions in the context of attitudes towards independence, autonomy and responsibility developed throughout the disability career. Many people described how their independence had increased over the course of the disability career, although this had often taken many years. Further, many also talked about the efforts involved in maintaining their independence and how this had become harder as they grew older. Consequently, it is easy to see how the possibility of having to give up some of their independence was a source of great anxiety. The fact that some felt that loss of independence would be totally unacceptable and that death would literally be a preferable option shows just how important this can be.

Gender and race dimensions of ageing with a disability

Although the issues discussed in this chapter are of universal concern, it would be mistaken to imply that the subjective experience of ageing is the same for men and women, or for people of different races and cultures.

First, both old age and disability are dimensions of experience which are fundamentally linked to gender (Arber and Ginn, 1991; Morris, 1991). Gender is also particularly important in determining whether or not individuals are supported or prevented in their attempts to live independently.

Because women are generally expected to take a more dependent role in society than men, disabled women face a particularly acute struggle to overcome the obstacles to controlling their own lives, or even defining their own identities (Lonsdale, 1990; Morris, 1989, 1992). As suggested earlier, existing structural inequalities will also have an important influence on women's experience of ageing with disability. It is not surprising, then, that many disabled women place an even stronger emphasis on maintaining their independence in later life than men.

Second, practically nothing is known about the race dimension to ageing with a disability. However, what evidence there is highlights the way in which minority ethnic community elders are disadvantaged (in income, housing, health and access to services) relative to older whites. There is also considerable evidence of unmet need for support amongst black disabled people of all ages (Ahmad, 1988; Begum, 1992; GLAD, 1987). Our own research indicates that many older black disabled people live in extreme isolation, even within their own communities. In this situation, the issue of independence tends to be secondary to concerns about basic survival.

Some wider implications for social and cultural formation

The ways in which disability and old age are defined (as social, ideological and cultural categories) are a key element in the production of ideologies which serve to subordinate older disabled people. Welfare is probably the single most important arena in which these definitions become institutionalised; not surprisingly, then, it is also where many of the key contemporary political and ideological struggles around ageing and disability are actively being fought out.

Older disabled people are particularly likely to be directly affected by this. The struggle to maintain independence throughout their lives often makes the potential threat to independence associated with ageing even more acute for older disabled people than for other groups in the ageing population (most of whom will not have to consider these issues until much later on). A wider implication of this may be to create the potential for the development of a critical 'political' consciousness which challenges the ideology of dependency which has underpinned the restructuring of welfare.

Given the historical failure to address the needs or, often, to even recognise the existence of older disabled people, it is plausible to suggest that they will have a heightened consciousness of the problems facing older people in general. Further, the solutions disabled people are attempting to develop for themselves (e.g. Centres for Independent Living, Self-operated Care schemes and so on) may provide important pointers to the future empowerment of older people as a whole. The disability movement itself is becoming increasingly vociferous in pursuing its political agenda and there is a slow but increasing trend towards active forms of political protest and civil disobedience (e.g. struggles around access and public transport and the picketing of 'Telethons').

Clearly, it would be misleading to suggest these comments can be applied to the majority of older disabled people. At the same time, many people's perceptions of their position in society may still have varying degrees of congruence with those who are actively involved in disability politics. The often fierce resistance to compromising their hard-won independence is a case in point.

Conclusion

While older disabled people may well recognise the common experience of being 'older people', the biographical data from our studies indicate that this is nowhere near as important to them as is their collective identification built around the prior experience of disability. Whether or not the future will see a greater convergence between the needs and goals of disparate groups in the ageing population remains to be seen. It would, therefore, be mistaken to assume that the experience of ageing with a disability can be adequately encompassed by social gerontology's existing understanding of ageing. Clearly, issues around ageing with a disability urgently require a place on the research and policy agenda.

Note

1. The term 'ageing with a disability' has been used herewith in preference to 'ageing with an impairment'. Although the latter would be more accurate in terms of a social model of disability, the former has been retained to reflect the terminology used by the majority of people whose experiences are described in this chapter.

References

Ahmad, A. (1988) *Social Services for Black People*. London: NISW.

Arber, S. and Ginn, J. (1991) *Gender and Later Life: a Sociological Analysis of Resources and Constraints*. London: Sage.

Begum, N. (1992) *Something to be Proud of: the Lives of Asian Disabled People and Carers in Waltham Forest*. London: Waltham Forest Race Relations Unit.

Creek, G., Moore, M., Oliver, M., Salisbury, V., Silver, J. and Zarb, G. (1987) *Personal and Social Consequences of Spinal Cord Injury: a Retrospective Study*. London: Thames Polytechnic.

GLAD (1987) *Disability and Ethnic Minority Communities: a Study in Three London Boroughs*. London: Greater London Association of Disabled People.

Harris, A. (1971) *Handicapped and Impaired in Great Britain*. London: HMSO.

Lonsdale, S. (1990) *Women and Disability*. London: Macmillan.

Martin, J., Meltzer, H. and Elliot, D. (1988) *OPCS Surveys of Disability in Great Britain: Report 1 – The Prevalence of Disability among Adults*. London: HMSO.

Morris, J. (ed.) (1989) *Able Lives: Women's Experience of Paralysis*. London: Women's Press.

Morris, J. (1991) *Pride against Prejudice: Transforming Attitudes to Disability*. London: Women's Press.

Morris, J. (1992) 'Personal and political: a feminist perspective on researching physical disability', *Disability, Handicap and Society*, 7(2): 157–66.

Zarb, G. (1991a) 'Forgotten but not gone: the experience of ageing with disability'. Paper presented to the British Society of Gerontology Annual Conference, UMIST, Manchester, 20-2 September.

Zarb, G. (1991b) 'Creating a supportive environment: meeting the needs of people who are ageing with a disability', in M. Oliver (ed.), *Social Work: Disabled People and Disabling Environments*. London: Jessica Kingsley Press, pp. 177–203.

Zarb, G. (1992) 'Changes in health care: a British perspective', in G. Whiteneck and R. Menter (eds), *Ageing with Spinal Cord Injury*. New York: Demos Publications, pp. 313–26.

Zarb, G., Oliver, M. and Silver, J. (1990) *Ageing with Spinal Cord Injury: the Right to a Supportive Environment?* London: Thames Polytechnic/Spinal Injuries Association.

Zarb, G. and Oliver, M. (1993) *Ageing with a Disability: What Do They Expect after All These Years?* London: University of Greenwich.

13

Ageing and cultural stereotypes
of older women

Jay Ginn and Sara Arber

Contemporary attitudes to older women

Images of elderly women as evil goddesses, monsters and witches
appear far-fetched in contemporary industrial societies. The myths,
fairy tales and religious beliefs of ancient and feudal societies may
seem an entertaining curiosity, and enable us to feel that a dark past of
illusion and cruelty has given way, through scientific progress, to an
era of humane enlightenment.

Yet dismissive, patronising, contemptuous and hostile attitudes to
elderly women persist, and the witch image lives on in the stereotype
of the jealous, scheming mother-in-law. Elderly women are more
commonly characterised as slow, stupid, unhealthy, unattractive and
dependent. They are ridiculed in jokes which rely on these assumed
deficiencies, and referred to by derogatory colloquialisms such as 'old
bag' (Harrison, 1983). [. . .] Children's literature abounds with elderly
women as hate objects, but their cultural subordination is also
reinforced through other forms of media (partly through their
invisibility). Research and writing on older women usually implicitly
accepts and reinforces negative ideas about elderly women (Harrison,
1983). [. . .]

Women as they age have to contend with both sexism and ageism.
These prejudices in combination create a double standard of ageing, in
which growing older has a different significance for women and men.
This affects women of all ages, but is especially acute for elderly
women.

The double standard of ageing

Itzin (1990a) sees the double standard of ageing as arising from the sets
of conventional expectations as to age-appropriate attitudes and roles

From S. Arber and J. Ginn, *Gender and Later Life*. London: Sage, 1991, pp. 40–9
(abridged).

for each sex which apply in patriarchal society. These are conceptualised by Itzin as a male and a female 'chronology', socially defined and sanctioned so that transgression of the prescribed roles or of their timing is penalised by disapproval and lost opportunities. Male chronology hinges on employment, but a woman's age status is defined in terms of events in the reproductive cycle. She is therefore 'valued according to sexual attractiveness, availability, and usefulness to men' (Itzin, 1990a: 118). The social devaluation of older women occurs regardless of occupation or background, or of the fact that after childrearing they have potentially 25 years of productive working life ahead.

Because women's value is sexualised, positively in the first half of life, negatively in the second, it depends on a youthful appearance [. . .] whereas signs of ageing in men are not considered so important. [. . .] Aware that loss of a youthful appearance brings social devaluation, women are vulnerable to immense pressure to ward off the signs of ageing with an armoury of cosmetic aids and, especially in the US, surgery. Daly draws a parallel between western cosmetic surgery and the genital mutilation carried out in some African societies: both practices, although ostensibly carried out for aesthetic reasons, demonstrate the pressure on women to comply with male standards of desirability and eligibility for marriage, and the extent of male domination (Daly, 1979). For older black women, the ideal of beauty purveyed by white male culture was doubly inaccessible and alienating, until growing black consciousness subverted derogatory terminology and proclaimed 'black is beautiful'.

The double standard of ageing is not merely a matter of aesthetics: it is 'the cutting edge of a whole set of oppressive structures (often masked as gallantries) that keep women in their place' (Sontag, 1972: 38). Itzin concurs; men's preference for wives younger than themselves at *all* ages shows that the devaluation of women as they age has less to do with appearance than with the sexual division of labour and of power (Itzin, 1990a).

Material effects of the double standard

Those with the greatest power and resources in society have a disproportionate influence on widely shared beliefs. But there is a two-way interplay between material conditions and ideas, and it is the way beliefs and perceptions affect the material circumstances of older women that we consider in this section. Discriminatory prejudices – whether sexism, racism or ageism – are derived from the relations of power in society, and serve both to justify and perpetuate structured inequality in access to material resources.

In addition to the psychic penalties for women of the double standard of ageing, the material disadvantages are substantial. As a woman ages she is treated as of diminishing value by men, both as a wife and as a potential employee. The increase in the divorce rate over the last 30 years has swollen the number of women aged between 45 and 64 who must make the transition from partial or complete financial dependency in marriage to self-support. The combination of their 'redundancy' as wives and homemakers with the age/sex discrimination they encounter when trying to obtain employment has left many middle-aged women in social and economic limbo.

Since the level of personal income in retirement depends on lifetime earnings, mediated through state and occupational pension schemes, obstacles to employment and promotion after age 45 increase the likelihood of poverty in later life. This is especially so for women who have already lost earnings through caring for children [. . .].

The effect of age discrimination in employment is different for women and men. Men in their fifties are increasingly likely to leave the labour market because of redundancy, early retirement (Laczko et al., 1988) and permanent disability (Piachaud, 1986). But for women returning to employment in mid-life, the problem is to obtain employment as well as to keep it. Ageism is compounded by sexism and job segregation which restricts them to traditionally 'feminine' work in which youthful attractiveness is often required. Employers seek a combination of attributes which reflect their own prejudices; male employers 'prefer the women around them to be young, part of their own aging hang-ups' (Sommers, 1975: 270). For example, attractiveness (and therefore youth) is preferred for jobs such as receptionist, barmaid, TV presenter, air hostess or nurse. A requirement of 'recent experience' is often the ostensible obstacle to older women's re-entry into employment, but as Sommers points out, 'discounting responsible unpaid work may not seem like sex discrimination, but it just happens to eliminate older women' (Sommers, 1974: 7).

Age discrimination in employment is lawful in Britain, unless it can be proved that an age bar constitutes indirect sex discrimination under the Sex Discrimination Act (1975). Enforcing compliance with this Act is hampered by the requirement that cases must be considered individually, and cannot be taken as 'class actions'. A recent survey of large employers found that overt age discrimination, through specifying an upper age limit in advertisements, was common (Metcalf and Thompson, 1989). Informal age discrimination undoubtedly also operates in the labour market (Employment Committee, 1989) although, like any other discrimination, it is hard to prove. Even in the US, where age discrimination is illegal from age 40 to age 70, the Age Discrimination in Employment Act (ADEA 1967, amended 1978) is of limited value for women because it does not cover sex. That is, it does not specify that employers must be willing to hire older people of *both* sexes. Similarly, the 1964 Civil Rights Act (Title VII) outlaws sex discrimination but does not cover age. By ensuring that both older men and young women are hired, 'many employers can actively (although not openly) pursue a policy of discrimination against older women, yet escape the sting of the law' (Older Women's League, 1982: 12).

Thus older women lack effective legal protection in relation to employment, and suffer from 'sex and age discrimination . . . a poisonous combination' (Sommers, 1974: 7). Older black women are in triple jeopardy, suffering racism as well as sexism and ageism.

In sum, the double standard of ageing has effects on income and material circumstances which continue into later life, as well as causing anxiety for women as the visible signs of ageing increase inexorably. It would be surprising if cultural denigration or invisibility had no effect on women's own perception of their ageing selves. But the question of how far women have accepted stereotypical views of elderly women (their present or future selves), or have maintained a positive self-perception, is important. Elderly women have had a lifetime in which to internalise prejudicial attitudes to old age, before becoming the victim of them. How do they deal with this?

Stereotype and self-image: compliance and resistance

One common way of coping, Rich suggests, is to accept the stereotype in respect of other elderly women but to deny one's own old age; becoming old is then a misfortune that befalls other people (Macdonald and Rich, 1984). A false sense of self is constructed and maintained, which rests precariously on the avoidance of any sign of ageing, such as forgetfulness or fussiness. Evidence of bodily changes confronts such an elderly woman as surprising and inappropriate. Rich argues that denial alienates an elderly woman from her true identity, and from others like herself.

Itzin examines the special association 'old age' has acquired in the process of stereotyping. Among elderly people, use of the word 'old' does not refer to any particular calendar age, but to a state of decrepitude and feebleness. As one elderly person put it, 'If you're alert and you're physically well, there's no such thing as getting old' (Itzin, 1990b: 112). People do internalise an idea of what they 'should' be like at certain ages, and are then surprised to find how poorly it fits their own experience and the way they feel. What elderly people are denying is not their age, but a derogatory stereotype of incapacity and encroaching senility in which they do not recognise themselves or most of their peers. In a society which penalises old age severely, a woman's efforts to avoid the appearance of ageing may be a rational response to the prevailing prejudice, a means of escaping the consequences of age discrimination.

There are few studies on elderly people's self-image, but those there are suggest that most elderly people are painfully aware of the crude negative stereotypes, and to varying degrees resist them. Kaiser and Chandler's (1988) study of 55 elderly women and men in retirement homes in California investigated their reactions to the negative stereotypes of old age as portrayed in magazine pictures. Negative portrayals were not passively accepted by this group as accurate representations of the realities of ageing; instead, they were either taken as possibly applying to other people in less advantaged circumstances, or rejected with some resentment. The picture that emerges is of elderly people actively reinterpreting or resisting stereotypical portrayals, and wishing to see a wider range of images of elderly people in the media.

Among elderly women, Harrison (1983) contends that self-perceptions and ways of dealing with the negative stereotype of old age vary with class and background; their acceptance of the negative stereotype was greater where attitudes of men in their family had reflected sexist assumptions about women's role and capabilities, and was less among women with higher socio-economic status, higher educational level and greater commitment to employment during their earlier life. Through interviews with a small 'fortuitous' sample of elderly Australian women, she explored how their self-perceptions relate to the social, mental and physical aspects of the stereotypical view of elderly women. The social aspect of the stereotype defines elderly women as obsolete, lacking commitment, and lonely because they no longer perform the traditional female role of wife and mother raising a family. Women whose earlier lives were found to conform most closely to the homemaking model most fully internalised the perception of themselves as useless in old age. Such elderly women often described their lives an unimportant although they were full of activity and interest. Others, whose lives were less home-centred, diversified into voluntary and political activities in later life, and maintained a positive self-identity (Harrison, 1983).

A second important and potentially very damaging aspect of the stereotype of elderly women is that of assumed mental decline, including inability to make decisions, dependency on others for guidance, and lack of awareness of current affairs. But, as with social aspects, a number of women had not adopted these negative views of themselves; they saw themselves as participants in society, showing a lively understanding of topical issues.

Further, there are also physical aspects to the stereotype. The menopause is widely seen as marking the end of womanhood, viewed as a necessarily negative and distressing experience. Some of the women interviewed did describe it in these terms, yet the majority experienced little difficulty. Harrison points out Bruck's finding that in societies where 'women gain social status after the menopause, physiological and psychological symptoms are virtually non-existent' (Harrison, 1983: 223). De Beauvoir has also observed that the menopause is often experienced as a relief by working women who 'have not staked everything on their femininity' (de Beauvoir, 1968: 435). Other aspects of the physical stereotyping include frailty and passivity, but only some elderly women shared this view of themselves.

Itzin's (1990a) research with a group of North London women confirms the importance of employment in a desired occupation to the maintenance of a positive identity, and lends support to the view that low self-esteem in later life is related to the completeness of socialisation into femininity. Compliance with the prescribed 'female chronology', based on marriage and motherhood, leaves women role-less and socially devalued when their children leave home, often before age 50, and is inimical to the development of a firm sense of identity in later life. 'I was never me,' said one woman, who felt she had been defined solely in relation to her family roles (Itzin 1990a: 141). However, Itzin notes that some women had spontaneously resisted the social construction of their identity around the female chronology. The influence of feminism had also encouraged the use of various strategies, including employment, which enabled them to recover some independence and establish a positive self-image which continued into later life (Itzin, 1990a).

The conflict between feminine socialisation and a positive self-perception is also highlighted in a study of 50 lone women aged over 75 (Evers, 1984). Two types of women were distinguished. 'Passive responders', who had centred their lives on home and family, were less likely to feel in control of their lives and tended to be dependent. 'Active initiators', who had pursued many outside interests and activities, including employment in a satisfying job, were more likely to feel able to cope on their own, and to have a strong sense of independence (Evers, 1984: 307).

These studies all point to the same conclusions: that the less completely a woman has conformed to the conventional ideal of domestic femininity, the more likely she is to age with pride and independence, maintaining a positive self-image in later life; and that in spite of the pervasiveness of the female chronology (as Itzin defines it), resistance, change and a rebuilding of life-goals and identity is possible at any age.

Patriarchy, western societies and older women

If older women conformed to a stereotype as being in decline, increasingly weak, incompetent and dependent, the hostility manifested towards them in prejudicial attitudes and behaviours might seem inexplicable. But the circumstances in which they have been most maligned suggests that part of the reason why older women, more than young women or older men, have suffered hostility is that they may be perceived as capable of challenging patriarchy. Walker speculates that

> The real threat posed by older women in a patriarchal society may be the 'evil eye' of sharp judgement honed by disillusioning experience, which pierces male myths and scrutinises male motives in the hard, unflattering light of critical appraisal. It may be that the witch's evil eye was only an eye from which the scales had fallen. (Walker, 1985: 122)

No longer restricted and hampered by a reproductive role, possessing the experience of age, older women may be seen as potential contenders for a dominant position, if not kept in their place by means of social control. Persistent denigration of older women may be the defensive reaction of patriarchy, persecution an index of their potential strength.

In patriarchal societies where tradition remains strong and the accumulation of knowledge by elders is valued, older women often take on high-status roles in the extended family and in public and religious life. For example, among the patrilineal Canadian Plains Indians the Piegan sub-tribe recognises many older women as 'manly-hearted' (Leavitt, 1975). These women are independent, sexually autonomous, own their livestock, participate actively in meetings and are sought after by younger men. The 'manly-hearted' are often skilled in medicine, and acquire prestige rather than stigma as they age. Similarly in Western Australian Aboriginal culture a woman's political and religious role grows with age, especially in the mediation of tribal disputes, while in Japan and in China before the revolution, older women enjoyed considerable power and authority. In matriarchal societies, older women's status is even more favourable. Before the advent of western colonisers, older women in West Africa customarily played important roles, heading lineages and holding chieftainships and village headships (Leavitt, 1975).

In western societies the advantages of ageing which women could look forward to in traditional societies have been lost. Older people are devalued because they are seen as having reduced capacity for production in the formal economy (reflecting the priorities of industrialism), and women are devalued when deemed past fulfilling sexual, reproductive and domestic servicing roles (reflecting the priorities of men). Thus older women are doubly devalued and accorded low social status. The harsh treatment of older women is evidence of a 'powerful public need to provide a justification for social inequality by blaming those who have the rawest deal for their own fate' (Itzin 1990b: 4). The cultural images of elderly women as evil, the cruel jokes at their expense, the patronising and dismissive attitudes, all play a part in legitimising and reinforcing their social and material disadvantage.

References

Daly, M. (1979) *Gyn/Ecology*. London: Women's Press.

de Beauvoir, S. (1968) *The Second Sex*. New York: The Modern Library.

Employment Committee (1989) *Employment Patterns of the Over-50s*. Employment Committee, Fourth Special Report. London: HMSO.

Evers, H. (1984) 'Old women's self-perceptions of dependency and some implications for service provision', *Journal of Epidemiology and Community Health*, 38: 306–9.

Harrison, J. (1983) 'Women and ageing: experience and implications', *Ageing and Society*, 3 (2): 209–35.

Itzin, C. (1990a) 'Age and sexual divisions: a study of opportunity and identity in women'. PhD thesis, University of Kent.

Itzin, C. (1990b) 'As old as you feel', in P. Thompson, C. Itzin and M. Abendstern, *I Don't Feel Old: Understanding the Experience of Later Life*. Oxford: Oxford University Press, pp. 107–36.

Kaiser, S. and Chandler, J. (1988) 'Audience responses to appearance codes: old-age imagery in the media', *The Gerontologist*, 28 (5): 692–9.

Laczko, F., Dale, A., Arber, S. and Gilbert, G.N. (1988) 'Early retirement in a period of high unemployment', *Journal of Social Policy*, 17 (3): 313–33.

Leavitt, R. (1975) 'The older woman: her status and role' in E. Lasky (ed.), *Humanness: an Exploration into the Mythologies about Women and Men*. New York: MSS Information Corporation.

Macdonald, B. and Rich, C. (1984) *Look Me in the Eye: Old Women, Aging and Ageism*. San Francisco, CA: Spinsters, Ink.

Metcalf, H. and Thompson, M. (1989) *Older Workers, Employers' Attitudes and Practices*. Brighton: Institute of Manpower Studies.

Older Women's League (1982) *Gray Paper No. 8: Not Even for Dogcatcher*. Washington, DC: Older Women's League.

Piachaud, D. (1986) 'Disability, retirement and unemployment of older men', *Journal of Social Policy*, 15 (2): 145–62.

Sommers, T. (1974) 'The compounding impact of age and sex', *Civil Rights Digest*, 7 (1): 2–9.

Sommers, T. (1975) 'Social security: a woman's viewpoint', *Industrial Gerontologist*, 2 (4): 266–79.

Sontag, S. (1972) 'The double standard of aging', *Saturday Review of the Society*, 23 September.

Walker, B. (1985) *The Crone: Woman of Age, Wisdom and Power*. New York: Harper & Row.

14

Ageing and ethnicity

Ken Blakemore

The value of ethnic perspectives on ageing is to highlight a set of influences which, in comparison to other sources of conflict and identity such as class or gender, have previously been rather underplayed.[1] There are often major differences in the 'ageing experience' between ethnic groups: for example, in relation to the way we feel about ageing (self-identity, morale, life satisfaction, etc.) or the social context (family and community structures, norms affecting support, etc.).

Questions remain, however, about *how far* ethnicity makes a difference, why ethnic identities are maintained or rediscovered in later life, and how ethnic communities themselves change (Driedger and Chappell, 1987; Gelfand and Kutzik, 1979; Markides and Mindel, 1987). But, first, problems of defining ethnicity need to be considered, together with the related dimension of race.

Defining ethnicity and race

Though ethnicity has so far been mentioned without reference to race, they are clearly overlapping concepts and one cannot be fully understood without the other (Rex, 1986; Stone, 1985). This is particularly important in considering the experience of ageing among Britain's black and Asian minority communities (see Blakemore and Boneham, 1993). British Sikhs, for example, are at once an 'ethnic' and a 'racial' minority. However, it should be stressed that all groups, whether forming the majority or distinct minorities, possess both a racial and an ethnic identity: there are no 'non-ethnic' peoples.

Race

Racial distinctions are based on stereotyped beliefs about the innate characteristics of a group. Racist beliefs are reflections of a distorted picture of the biological make-up of 'white' and 'black' people. Thus differences which are actually superficial in the biological sense (for example, skin colour) are believed to signify much deeper differences and the superiority of one race over another. But distinctions of race are matters of social convention rather than being objective or firm categories. There will always be questions about who belongs to which group, and about the status of different groups. Race distinctions are socially constructed, as we are often reminded (Rex, 1986: 19).

This is well illustrated by the identity of British Asians. Should people of Asian descent be called 'black'? Some argue that, because 'blackness' refers to disadvantaged status in a minority group oppressed by racial discrimination (that is, discrimination based on perceptions of skin colour), Asians should be seen as members of the black community. Others, including a considerable number of Asians themselves, reject 'blackness' and suggest their position is better understood by use of the umbrella term 'Asian'.

Hard-and-fast definitions of 'blackness' and of racial categories are also challenged by the growing proportion of mixed race or mixed descent people in Britain (Nanton, 1992). This is mainly a feature of life among younger black (Caribbean-descent) people, about a quarter of whom now have white partners. But it is important to remember that there are also older 'black' people who have grown up in one of the long-established port communities such as Liverpool or Cardiff, and who may have had a 'white' parent, a 'black' parent and relatives with many different nationalities.

Some would argue that mixed parentage usually equates with being black, whatever actual shade of skin a person has. It is suggested that people of mixed race tend to be treated as 'black' and to be as disadvantaged as other blacks in relatively powerless minority groups. This is certainly borne out by the experience of older 'black' and mixed-race people in the settled port communities. They were either born in Britain or have been in the country for many years, but live in communities which are as disadvantaged as those of more recent black migrants.

Thus racial divisions and discrimination will continue to have sharp significance for the foreseeable future and we cannot, on the basis of past experience, hope that race will be of diminishing importance for future cohorts of older people. However, the point is that racial categories are neither fixed nor mutually exclusive.

Ethnicity

The term 'ethnicity' or 'ethnic group' is often used as a synonym for 'race' or 'racial group'. This is especially the case among medical researchers (for example, Beevers, 1981), who almost always seem to view the term 'ethnic' as a 'polite' word for 'racial'. However, race and ethnicity are not interchangeable words and there is a case for making some firm distinctions. First, 'Asians' and 'Afro-Caribbeans' and 'whites' are not single ethnic groups, and to define them as such does not do justice to the range and variety of cultural, religious and linguistic groupings among them. Second, the term 'ethnic' should not substitute for 'race' because racial distinctions primarily suggest forms of prejudice and discrimination arising from judgements about the physical characteristics of others, whereas ethnic categories rest chiefly on judgements about others' cultures, religions and ways of life.

Matters are complicated by the fact that we simultaneously derive identity, or are attributed identity, according to both racial and ethnic distinctions. But what is ethnicity? There is broad agreement that *some* if not all the following criteria are important in trying to decide how ethnically distinct a community or society is.

1 Is there a distinctive culture? 'Culture' is itself an umbrella term covering many aspects of a way of life: a community's social institutions (patterns of marriage and family, inheritance, rituals and customs), its values, ideas and traditions, and its social norms and attitudes (reflected in rules about diet, dress, and manners).

2 Is there a sense of 'peoplehood' and of personal identity being bound up with a shared destiny and a common past? Jewish identity well illustrates this notion of peoplehood, though similar feelings are expressed by many other ethnic groups, especially if identity is closely associated with a 'homeland' or land of origin. An overseas community or diaspora may continue to identify with the homeland for many generations, so that even those who have never visited the homeland regard it as a cornerstone of their identity. In old age, it is possible for ethnicity, in this sense of identifying with one's 'roots', to be strengthened. The 'East African' Sikhs, now settled in Britain, are a good illustration (Bhachu, 1985).

3 Is there a language to distinguish a minority ethnic group from the majority (for example, speaking Polish in Britain)? Or equally, is there a distinctive use of a common language (Irish or Welsh people's use of English)?

4 Is there an attachment to a particular religion (for example, Greeks and Cypriots and the Greek Orthodox Church in Britain, or Sikhs and Sikhism)? Or is identity marked by a particular approach to a world religion (for example, 'Irish' Catholicism)?

It is worth underlining the point that not all the above criteria need be present to establish that a group or community possesses a degree of ethnic distinctiveness. As with race, ethnic identity is a matter of social convention and perception. As Wallman points out, 'ethnicity refers generally to the perception of group difference' so that 'the *sense* of differences which can occur where members of a particular cultural . . . group interact with non-members' (1979: ix) is all-important.

Equally importantly, perceptions change. Saifullah Khan reminds us that 'ethnic identity is not fixed, constant or single stranded; it is flexible and shifting on different levels according to situation and context' (1982: 209). It is quite likely, therefore, that the strength of one's identification with the ethnic community and culture will wax and wane throughout the life course. A member of a minority community, for example, may seek to downplay his or her ethnic distinctiveness during a mid-life period of 'integration' at work. Drawing on the evidence of Australian minorities, Rowland (1991: 9) suggests the influence of ethnicity varies, waxing and waning at different points in the life course.

Self-identification is therefore an essential element of ethnic identity. Some people have mixed ethnic parentage or ancestry, just as they may have mixed racial identity. Such cases illustrate the general point that deciding who one is, which language to speak, etc., may be a matter of choice, or even problematic for some. But ethnicity need not be seen solely as a constraint (for example, conformity to certain religious prohibitions, or to customs such as arranged marriage), but may be viewed also as a resource or a set of strategies for living (including how to adjust to old age).

However, though ethnicity may offer protection and identity to a minority community, it is also another way for outsiders to make judgements about the distinctive group. These may be positive stereotypes (for example, the 'caring, extended families of older Asian people') or negative. But ethnic discrimination and stereotyping can be every bit as violent and barbarous as racial conflict. Similarly, the history of Irish migrants in Britain shows that a white minority may be a victim of cultural stereotyping by a white majority, though racialism as defined above is not involved (Jackson, 1963). However, British Asian and Afro-Caribbean people may be discriminated against on the basis of race *and* ethnicity. For example, a Pakistani family might be viewed negatively by white neighbours in the racial sense (perceptions of physical differences which elicit distorted views of the innate characteristics of all black people) and in the ethnic sense (the way the family's food, religion, ways of doing things are perceived).

Too much emphasis on differences of ethnicity can act as a divide-and-rule tactic to obscure the significance of race and racism. But attention to racism and discrimination does not mean that ethnicity should be left out of the picture. As Fenton puts it in relation to black and Asian older people, 'In some contexts full attention to differences within broader groupings is necessary; island or country of origin loyalties or religious differences are real and important and other people's ignorance of them can be insulting' (1986: viii).

Recognition of ethnic differences is therefore vital to a thorough understanding of older people and of ageing. The point of the three images or models of *minority* ageing, which follow, is not to show that ethnicity is only an important aspect of ageing for Asian or Afro-Caribbean older people in Britain, or that they are a special case in this respect. In expressing ethnic preferences or distinct lifestyles, the minorities are not exhibiting peculiar traits: there are also distinctly different cultural identities and lifestyles among whites, associated with ethnic groupings, social class differences, etc. What the minorities *do* illustrate particularly well, however, is the inequality of power in the relationship between a dominant ethnic and racial majority and subordinate minority groups (with consequences for who defines what are 'acceptable' forms of social and health services for older people). One of the main questions to ask about the ageing process is how far minority groups will be able to challenge or replace the 'acceptable' patterns, and how far they will be able to maintain alternative ways of growing old.

Three images of ageing

The experiences of those who migrate from one culture to another are significant, not only for understanding minority communities, but also for a general understanding of ageing and adjustment. Migrants experience – in sharper forms, perhaps – the transitions and challenges of ageing experienced by everyone: not only the practical questions such as 'where should I live?' or 'who will look after me if I am ill?' but also the existential questions: 'where do I belong?', or 'what would my life have been like if I had not come here?', or 'who am I?'

In order to try to understand the interaction between, on one hand, these kinds of personal change and transition and, on the other, older people's racial and ethnic identity, we have developed three images of ageing (Blakemore and Boneham, 1993): the *'self-reliant pioneer'* the *'gradually adjusting migrant'* and the *'passive victim'*.

These images contain elements of truth, but do not describe particular individuals or groups. There could be aspects of each in any one person's life course, with some predominating at one point and different ones at other points. Yet other images might be needed to explore other examples of change and ageing.

The term 'image' is therefore intended to suggest contested definition and debate. Each image represents common *views* of ageing among commentators in social gerontology and in the 'practical' world of health and social services; as such, the following images tell us more about the commentators and practitioners of the majority community than the people in minority communities.

Notions of *'self-reliant pioneers'* suggest that older people in minority ethnic groups will be more influenced by their roles and position in their own communities than by majority norms and expectations. It is assumed that in such communities strong links are maintained with the 'homeland' or old country by way of arranged marriages, exchanges of gifts and remittance of money. And though extended families may have to adapt to new circumstances, it is likely that the position of older people in them will be replicated as far as possible; it is also assumed, in this 'persistence of tradition' model, that the non-migrant second and third generations will largely carry on living as an immigrant minority, for example as did the Italian-Americans described by Johnson (1985).

It also follows from the 'self-reliant' element of the image either that 'rugged individuals' will care for themselves in old age or that their needs will largely be met within their communities – a concept of 'cohort self-sufficiency' (Rowland, 1991: 56) – though in reality ethnic self-reliance could be enforced by poor access to, or non-provision of, suitable services.

The *'gradually adjusting migrant'* image, on the other hand, suggests integration. While 'self-reliant pioneers' find culture-specific solutions to their problems, 'gradually adjusting migrants' will adapt to, and come to expect, an old age role which has much in common with the culture of the majority: they will learn to speak English, if they do not already know it, adopt the dress, manners and customs of the majority, and use the social and health services common to all.

While again there are elements of truth in this image – some migrants to Britain have experienced integration – it is flawed by a rather paternalistic definition of integration. It could be assumed that migrants do tend to adapt or integrate in a non-problematic way, but the barriers to equality and integration erected by the majority themselves might be conveniently forgotten. 'Failure' to adapt by the time one has become old could be seen as wholly or mainly the responsibility of the migrants. This image would be particularly irrelevant to refugees and exiles with a stake in their old countries, or to 'dependent' relatives who arrive in a 'new' country in old age, though it may more accurately depict the life of someone who has consciously and successfully adopted majority identity.

The third image, of older people in minority ethnic, especially black, communities as *'passive victims'*, challenges the complacency of those holding 'self-reliance' and 'adjustment' views. Here, the overriding significance of discrimination and disadvantage is stressed. Given the evidence of health, environmental and income inequalities between older black and white people (Blakemore, 1985), victimisation is a suitable image to describe the disadvantaged position of many in minority communities.

However, if adopted uncritically and without any recognition of the wide range of differences in income, housing, level of family support, health and other socio-economic circumstances of older people, the 'passive victim' view can just as easily lead to stereotyping as the first two images. There is a danger of over-emphasising the impact of one or two aspects of inequality, such as race and gender, when many other factors – income, housing, etc. – are relevant. Secondly, the notion of a *passive* victim devalues the resourcefulness many older people have shown in confronting discrimination and disadvantage.

Conclusion

Ethnicity and race represent a potent set of influences on ageing, but it is necessary to bring a sense of perspective to the subject. Ethnic and racial groups do not exist in isolation from each other, and the meaning of 'black' and 'white', or 'Sikh' and 'Cypriot', for example, depend very much on how groups perceive themselves, and other groups. Moreover, these definitions or perceptions change over time; future cohorts of 'Asian' older people, for example, will be seen somewhat differently from today's communities.   `

The three models or images of ageing are an attempt to show how older people are perceived, and in particular how those in minority communities are viewed. The 'minority within a minority' experiences of older Afro-Caribbean and Asian people are instructive. Becoming old means, to a greater or lesser degree, adding to the loss of power and the uncertainties that go with minority status. What the minorities illustrate particularly well, therefore, is the importance of power in the relationship between a dominant ethnic and racial majority (which defines the 'acceptable' ways of growing old and, among other things, the kinds of social or health services available for older people) and subordinate minority groups. One of the main questions to ask about the ageing process is how far minority groups will be able to challenge or replace the 'acceptable' patterns, and how far they will be able to maintain alternative ways of growing old.

Note

1. Of 110 leading articles in most, but not all, issues of *Ageing and Society*, 1982–92, only nine dealt with comparative questions of ethnicity and culture.

References

Beevers, D.G. (1981) 'Ethnic differences in common diseases', *Postgraduate Medical Journal*, 57: 744.
Bhachu, P. (1985) *Twice Migrants: East African Settlers in Britain*. London: Tavistock.
Blakemore, K. (1985) 'Ethnic inequalities in old age: some comparisons between Britain and the United States', *Journal of Applied Gerontology*, 4: 86–101.
Blakemore, K. and Boneham, M. (1993) *Age, Race and Ethnicity: a Comparative Approach*. Milton Keynes: Open University Press.
Driedger, L. and Chappell, N. (1987) *Aging and Ethnicity*. Toronto: Butterworths.
Fenton, S. (1986) *Race, Health and Welfare: Afro-Caribbean and South Asian People in Central Bristol*. Bristol: Department of Sociology, University of Bristol.
Gelfand, D.E. and Kutzik, A.J. (eds) (1979) *Ethnicity and Aging*. New York: Springer.
Jackson, J.A. (1963) *The Irish in Britain*. London: Routledge.
Johnson, C.L. (1985) *Growing Up and Growing Old in Italian-American Families*. New Brunswick, NJ: Rutgers University Press.

Markides, K. and Mindel, C.H. (1987) *Aging and Ethnicity*. Newbury Park, CA: Sage.

Nanton, P. (1992) 'Official statistics and the problem of inappropriate ethnic categorisation', *Policy and Politics*, 20 (4): 277–86.

Rex, J. (1986) *Race and Ethnicity*. Milton Keynes: Open University Press.

Rowland, D. (1991) *Pioneers Again: Immigrants and Ageing in Australia*. Canberra: Australian Government Publishing Service.

Saifullah Khan, V. (1982) 'The role of the culture of dominance in structuring the experience of ethnic minorities' in C. Husband, (ed.), *'Race' in Britain*. London: Hutchinson, pp. 197–215.

Stone, J. (1985) *Racial Conflict in Contemporary Society*. London: Fontana/Collins.

Wallman, S. (ed.) (1979) *Ethnicity at Work*. London, Macmillan.

15

The health of older Asians

Liam Donaldson and Marie Johnson

Elderly Asian people, in keeping with other age groups within the Asian communities of the United Kingdom, have been much less studied, as a population, than their non-Asian counterparts. Moreover, many people from the majority population will have never had prolonged direct contact with elderly people from the Asian community.

It is in these circumstances, of paucity of research data and the absence of widespread direct experience on the part of the indigenous population, that quite stereotypic assumptions develop. For example, it is widely believed that old age is a greatly revered state within the Asian community, and hence an elderly person will enjoy the warmth, support and care of an extended family, so that little priority needs to be given to policy-making to meet the needs of the elderly. [. . .]

There is also the view that characteristics attributed to minority groups, such as strong kinship bonds, which are thought to be a cultural characteristic, may, where they are found, be a response to living in a hostile environment where kinship and other forms of mutual aid are reinforced because of reduced access to the rewards and services of the wider society (Colen and McNeely, 1983).

In contrast to the roseate view of the extended Asian family, a body of literature has emerged which makes much of the potentially serious problems and disadvantages faced by people who are not only old, but also bear the additional burdens of discrimination which accompany non-white status (so called 'double jeopardy'); to this has been added the 'triple jeopardy' of perceived lack of access to services (Norman, 1985), and even the 'quadruple jeopardy' of being non-English-speaking (Lum, 1983).

While it has been quite justifiably argued that studies of the health

Originally published as 'Elderly Asians', in B.R. McAvoy and L.J. Donaldson (eds), *Health Care for Asians*. Oxford: Oxford University Press, 1990, Chapter 14, pp. 237–49 (abridged).

of the Asian population have placed too much emphasis on the differences from the majority population, rather than the similarities (Bhopal, 1988), it would seem to be the case for Asian elderly people, more so than for other age groups, that they have significantly different life experiences from the indigenous elderly. They are, after all, a group who have experienced migration, marked cultural change and racial prejudice. They are minority members of a minority group, often poor and politically weak. [. . .]

[. . .] Reviewing and improving services for Asian elderly people should be seen as part of the effort to ensure that welfare services are sensitive to the needs of all of Britain's culturally diverse society:

> Indeed, one of the questions which the whole issue of care for older people with particular ethnic characteristics forces us to face is the appropriateness and efficiency of our services for *all* elderly people. (Norman, 1985: 2)

The size of the elderly Asian population

[. . .] It is clear [. . .] that elderly people represent a relatively small proportion of the Asian population of the UK today, markedly so when compared with the elderly in the white population (Table 15.1).

Another factor of particular importance will be the point at which those Asians who were born in the UK start to form increasingly higher proportions of the elderly population. This will have a numerical impact, as the Asian population starts to resemble the age-

Table 15.1 *Percentage of elderly people within different ethnic groups: Great Britain 1985*

Ethnic group	Percentage who were elderly[a]
White	19
Total non-white	3
West Indian or Guyanese	4
Indian	3
Pakistani	1
Bangladeshi	1
Chinese	4
African	1
Arab	2
Mixed	2
Other	4
Not stated	14
All ethnic groups	18

[a] Men aged 65 years or over and women aged 60 years and over.

Source: OPCS, 1986

structure of the white population; but it will also be of importance because this group is likely to have different life experiences and cultural expectations from those of their parents and grandparents who migrated to the UK. [. . .]

Health problems of elderly Asian people

There has been criticism of studies of the health of Asian people which have concentrated on those conditions which are unusual in the majority population, but present in the Asian population. The effect is that a disproportionate amount of emphasis may be put on the possibility of Asian people suffering from these conditions. The fact is that the Asian population suffers many of the health problems which also affect the majority population [. . .]. While the greater incidence of some conditions such as tuberculosis or intra-hepatic bile-duct cancer among the Asian population cannot be ignored, their absolute frequency should mean there is not overemphasis on such illnesses among Asian people at the expense of the common causes of illness and death.

Ethnic diversity

The term 'Asian' has been adopted to refer to people resident in the UK who themselves originated, or whose parents and grandparents originated, from the Indian subcontinent. Use of this term by the majority population, social scientists and caring professionals does tend to mask the ethnic diversity found among Asians living in the UK today. [. . .] Asian people are diverse in terms of language, religious affiliation, caste, class, and place of residence prior to migration to the UK. It is equally inappropriate when considering older members of the Asian community to regard them as a homogeneous, undifferentiated social group. [. . .]

In addition to the likelihood that their personal history prior to arriving in the UK will have been very diverse, elderly Asians' experience of life in this country may also be quite varied. For instance, living in contact with a group of people sharing the same ethnic identity may mean for the elderly person that there are local-level networks which provide support. On the other hand, if they are separated from other people sharing their ethnicity old people may lack such support and sources of information. Moreover, if Asians are a significant presence in a locality, service-providers may have, through direct experience, more awareness of the needs of elderly Asian people, and there may be local pressure-groups which have worked to ensure a more sensitive approach to assessing and providing for the needs of elderly people from the different ethnic groups.

Facility in English

[. . .] In many health settings an elderly Asian person will have to rely on knowledge of written and spoken English. In a survey carried out in Leicester over one-fifth of people said they could speak English but there was a marked difference between the sexes (Donaldson and Odell, 1986).

In a range of everyday situations which called for a certain degree of fluency, in three out of six situations more than half the elderly Asian people interviewed felt they would have difficulty in communicating without an interpreter, while in the remaining situations this was so for a substantial minority [. . .]. Overall 35 per cent could not read in any language, and this proportion was much higher for women than men: 63 per cent compared to 11 per cent.

There is also evidence that older Asians, particularly women, are not able to read in their first language, and therefore, while providing health leaflets in Asian languages is to be encouraged, it should not be assumed that this solves the problem of communicating information to the elderly population. Younger generations may read Asian-language leaflets for their older relatives; but audio cassettes or videos may in fact be a much more efficient way of reaching this population.

Household patterns

Acknowledging the problem of simply accepting the cultural stereotype of elderly people inevitably being cared for within the community, Asian people do tend to live in extended households [. . .].

The households that many elderly Asian people live in also tend to be multigenerational ones. In the Leicestershire survey nearly three-quarters of the people in the sample had four or more grown-up children alive, and over 70 per cent had at least one grown-up child living in the same household as themselves.

The most frequent household configuration for elderly Asian people seen in this study was multigenerational [. . .] – usually the elderly person, their children, and their grandchildren. Of those who did not live in multigenerational households over three-quarters had children living elsewhere in the city, and over half, elsewhere in the UK. This pattern was common to the three main religious groups (Donaldson and Odell, 1986). [. . .]

Clearly living within a multigenerational household potentially provides considerable social support for an elderly person; but there may also be disadvantages in this situation, particularly as British domestic architecture is not on the whole designed for these types of domestic arrangement. For example, in the Leicester Survey 22 per cent of those old people interviewed shared a bedroom with someone else, most commonly a grandchild. [. . .]

Status within the household can be an important factor. In Leicester, elderly Asian women played a prominent role within the household in relation to domestic tasks; but elderly Asian men played relatively little part in these activities, although more than half helped with shopping. [. . .]

As might be expected, time spent outside the home was related to age, but, notwithstanding this effect, there was a striking difference between the sexes: for example, 45 per cent of elderly women had not been out on any morning during the previous week, compared with 13 per cent of elderly men. It is not uncommon for it to be understood that elderly Asian men will spend much of the day outside the house; and this can lead to them spending a great deal of unstructured time outdoors, even in bad weather.

While many elderly Asian people live in extended, multigenerational households, there are those who live independently or with others than their kinsfolk, for a variety of reasons. There are those referred to above who formed one of the early groups of migrants to this country, the single male seamen who led an independent, peripatetic life, and in their old age are settled in this country, often without close kinship ties. Those Asians who came to this country when they were expelled as refugees from East Africa often find themselves without the type of communal support they were familiar with in Africa (Norman, 1985). Such people are sometimes lodgers with other families; and in this situation it cannot be assumed that they receive the support or have the high status within the domestic setting which is often considered as typical of Asian culture.

Knowledge and use of welfare services

Research has shown that Asians and other members of ethnic groups do tend to be registered with GPs. A study in 1981 of 2000 households (but one that excluded those over 60 years old) showed that 96 per cent of Asians were registered with a local GP, and the remaining 4 per cent with a GP elsewhere. Two-thirds of these people were registered with a GP of Asian origin, and a further 10 per cent at a practice with an Asian doctor (Johnson, 1986).

The research also showed that Asians were likely to have visited their GP in the previous year, and more frequently than either whites or Afro-Caribbeans. This pattern was confirmed by a study of elderly people from similar ethnic groups in Birmingham (Blakemore, 1982). It is not possible to be categorical about the reasons for the relatively frequent use of the GP service by Asian people, but among the relevant factors may be cultural expectations of the type of role the GP has, higher rates of disease and illness engendered by their socio-economic circumstances prior to migration and since arrival in the UK, and the stress which may be experienced by elderly people who have had to adjust to an alien society.

The figures for registration and use of the services do not in themselves demonstrate that elderly Asian people find their interaction with their GPs easy, even if the GPs are of Asian origin themselves. As has already been emphasised, the ethnic diversity of Asian Britons means that the patient and doctor may not necessarily have language, religion or other characteristics in common. However, these data do underline that GPs have a major role in ensuring that elderly Asian people obtain appropriate care and facilities from the health and social services, because they are the representatives of the caring professions most likely to have frequent contact with older members of the Asian community.

While there have been initiatives to ensure uptake of community services by the Asian population, in general there seems to be a low utilisation of the services provided by community-based NHS staff. Improving elderly Asians' use of these services is not simply a question of letting them know that they exist, but also ensuring that they are of an appropriate type; making sure, for instance, that full use is made of community nurses and health visitors from the Asian community, and approaching the community through the traditional meeting places, such as temples, mosques and community centres. Utilising the local institutions and networks set up by the Asian population is one of the most constructive ways of disseminating information about services currently available, and learning what the needs of the community are.

Consideration has to be given to setting up residential homes and day centres specifically for Asian elderly people. Facilities where the large majority of clients, residents and staff are white, and where the sexes are mixed, may not be seen as an attractive option for an elderly person from the Asian community.

In response to the need for sheltered accommodation for elderly Asian people, [. . .] a number of initiatives have been taken to provide housing for elderly Asians [in] London [. . .] Leeds, Birmingham and Leicester. [. . .]

Improving the sensitivity of hospital-based services in very much the responsibility of the District Health Authorities; but GPs have to be aware of how potentially alienating hospital services are to elderly Asian people. Concerns about lack of signs in community languages and of opportunities for religious observances, about whether food will conform to religious dietary norms, and whether personal hygiene preferences will be respected, can all ensure that the perception of services is poor and uptake low. Being able to give reassurance and information about these aspects of the health service can have a strong influence on whether elderly Asian people take up the services and get the best out of them.

Cultural attitudes to illness and health care

Those writing on Asian attitudes to illness and health care have tended to concentrate on the extent to which the systems of medicine in the Indian subcontinent, the *Tibe-Unani* and Ayurvedic systems, are used in this country. [. . .] In the Indian subcontinent these two systems co-exist with homeopathy, which established itself well there, and with allopathic medicine. The *Tibe-Unani* and Ayurvedic systems take a holistic approach, and involve the understanding of personality humours, and life-style in the causation and treatment of conditions. Practitioners called *hakims* (*Tibe-Unani*) and *vaids* (Ayurvedic) are trained in schools for traditional medicine, and are registered by the governments of India and Pakistan.

Reports vary on the extent to which *hakims* and *vaids* are active in the UK, and the amount of use made of them by British Asians. Mays (1981) quotes a report to the DHSS which suggests that traditional practitioners are to be found in all the main Asian communities in the UK, and that it is common for patients to consult both a traditional practitioner and a GP about their condition. [. . .] In contrast Johnson (1986) found [. . .] only 2 per cent of respondents in his survey had consulted a *hakim* or a *vaid* in the previous year. Bhopal (1986) similarly found a low rate of consultation of traditional healers in Glasgow [. . .].

The way in which Asian knowledge of traditional systems and medicine may be most significant to the GP is that these approaches are of a general, holistic nature, and predispose the patient to expect the practitioner to take an interest in their total condition, and to spend time and care over consultation. The fact that this type of approach is not axiomatic under the NHS may cause patients to doubt the efficacy of the treatment and remedies they are being prescribed. [. . .]

Providing welfare services which are sensitive to cultural diversity, but do not treat the individual elderly person as a cultural stereotype, is one route to ensuring proper health care for all citizens.

References

Bhopal, R.S. (1986) 'The inter-relationship of folk, traditional and western medicine within an Asian community in Britain', *Social Science and Medicine*, 22: 99–105.

Bhopal, R.S. (1988) 'Health care for Asians: conflict in need, demand and provision', in *Equity: a Prerequisite for Health*. London: Proceedings of 1987 Summer Scientific Conference, Faculty of Community Medicine and WHO. pp. 52–6.

Blakemore, K. (1982) 'Health and illness among the elderly of minority ethnic groups living in Birmingham: some new findings', *Health Trends*, 14: 69–72.

Colen, J.L. and McNeely, R.L. (1983) 'Minority aging and knowledge in the social professions', in R.L. McNeely and J.L. Colen (eds), *Aging in Minority Groups*. London: Sage, pp. 15–23.

Donaldson, L.J. and Odell, A. (1986) 'Health and social status of elderly Asians: a community survey', *British Medical Journal*, 293: 1079–82.

Johnson, M. (1986), 'Inner city residents, ethnic minorities and primary health care in the West Midlands', in T. Rothwell and D. Phillips (eds), *Health, Race and Ethnicity*. London: Croom Helm.

Lum, D. (1983) 'Asian-Americans and their aged', in R.L. McNeely and J.L. Colen (eds), *Aging in Minority Groups*. London: Sage, pp. 85–94.

Mays, N. (1981) 'The health needs of elderly Asians', *Geriatric Medicine*, 11: 37–41.

Norman, A. (1985) *Triple Jeopardy: Growing Old in a Second Homeland*. Centre for Policy on Ageing.

OPCS (Office of Population Censuses and Surveys) (1986) *OPCS Monitor Reference LFS 86/2 Labour Force Survey 1985: Ethnic Group and Country of Birth*. London: HMSO.

16

Osteoporosis in women

Jean Shapiro

Osteoporosis[1] is a vital women's health issue because we develop the condition more frequently than men. The condition leads to loss of teeth and wrist fractures, usually starting in our fifties, spinal crush fractures when we are between 55 and 75, and hip fractures in our seventies and eighties (National Institutes of Health, 1984). [. . .]

Our bones are made up of living cells in a state of constant breakdown and repair. Except for the skin, no other substance in the body has such excellent regenerative powers as bone. As new bone is produced, it is actually laid down on the solid outer shell (cortical bone). Old bone disappears from the softer, less dense substance inside (trabecular bone) where calcium can enter and leave. Normally, our body balances the two processes of building new bone and removing old bone so that our bones remain strong. This continuous building process is called remodelling. When new bone formation no longer keeps up with bone loss, bones begin to thin and weaken.

We lose a certain amount of lean muscle tissue and some bone cells as a natural result of the ageing process, although most of us will not develop osteoporosis. Bone loss starts in women a few years after bone density peaks at about age 35. The loss increases slightly in the four to five years following menopause (Raab and Smith, 1985). There are large differences in the rate and amount of thinning among individuals (Parfit, 1984).

In addition, calcium can be leached out of the bones if the level of calcium in the blood drops below normal. Through an intricate process, the level of calcium in the blood is kept within a very precise, narrow range (Kamen and Kamen, 1984) necessary for muscle contractions, transmission of nerve impulses and blood clotting. If the level of calcium in the blood is higher than necessary, the body excretes whatever cannot be absorbed.

Osteoporosis is a complex condition that usually takes years to advance to the stage where it can be detected. Many interrelated

From *Ourselves Growing Older: Women Ageing with Knowledge and Power*. London: Fontana/Collins, 1989, Chapter 19, pp. 342–66 (abridged).

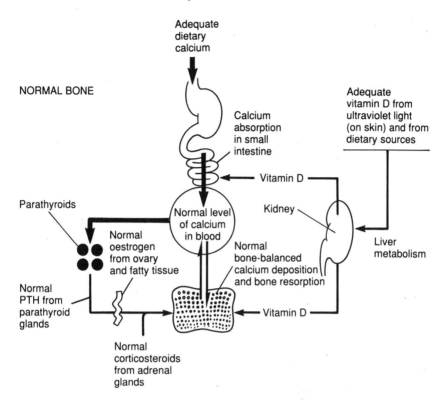

Figure 16.1 *Multiple factors affecting the condition of bone*

factors affect the exchange of calcium between the blood and the bones (see Figures 16.1 and 16.2). These factors include the amount of calcium in the diet, how efficiently our bodies absorb it, hormonal balance, and our level of physical activity. Lowered oestrogen level after menopause is only one factor – often over-emphasised in the mass media and medical literature – that contributes to the development of osteoporosis. We can understand these factors and make changes that will slow bone loss and improve bone remodelling.

For example, when we are young, diet is our chief source of calcium. Vitamin D is often added to babies' milk because it helps the body absorb calcium from the small intestine and also promotes the transportation of calcium into bone. The level of calcium in the blood, in turn, controls the amount of hormone secreted by the parathyroid gland (parathyroid hormone, or PTH). If the level of calcium in the blood decreases, more PTH, which triggers leaching of calcium from the bones, will be produced to correct the deficit in the blood. Other hormones also play a role – normal oestrogen levels protect women from producing too much PTH; cortisone-like products (corticosteroids)

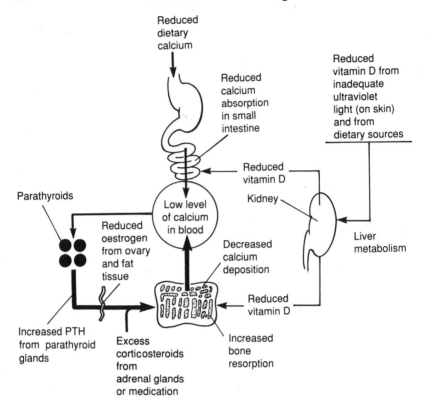

Figure 16.2 *Some factors contributing to osteoporosis*

can increase PTH production, leading to excessive loss of calcium from the bones.

It is also important to understand how activity, or the lack of it, affects bone strength. Bone mass will increase or decrease according to the demand placed on it. The total amount of calcium in the body increases with exercise, but muscle strength, bone-mineral content and specific bone mass will vary depending on activity patterns. For example, tennis players have thicker bones in their dominant arms. Demand in an active part of the body will pull bone mineral away from inactive parts. In one study, women aged 35 to 65 in an aerobic movement programme showed loss of mineral in upper-body bone, which was regained when upper-body resistance exercises were added (Raab and Smith, 1985: 37). Exercise physiologists have known the value of motion and the pull of muscles on bones (not just weight-bearing) since the 1890s, but knowledge is forgotten and the research in one field is not always read by other specialists. [. . .]

All these factors – reduced activity, reduced calcium absorption in our intestines and reduced levels of oestrogen to counteract the effects of PTH – result in increased calcium loss as we age.

Symptoms

[. . .] Early warning signs of osteoporosis include wrist fracture following a simple fall or blow, and muscle spasms or pain in the back while at rest or while doing routine daily work such as making a bed or picking up an object from the floor. This pain comes on suddenly; most women can recall the exact moment it began. It is often caused by the spontaneous collapsing (a spinal crush fracture) of small sections of the spine that have been severely thinned or weakened. These compression fractures can lead to 'dowager's hump', which shortens the chest area and makes digesting food more difficult. Because compression fractures do not always cause prolonged, severe pain or disability, some women are not aware that they have this condition, although 20 per cent of women do by age 70.

Loss of height is another early sign of spinal crush fractures and osteoporosis. [. . .] In extreme cases, women can lose as much as 8 inches of height, all from the upper half of the body (Notelovitz and Ware, 1982: 32).

Risk factors and self-help

Biological risk factors

Women are at greater risk of osteoporosis than men because men have 30 per cent more bone mass at age 35 than women, and they lose bone more slowly as they age. If you are black, the chances of your developing osteoporosis are rare. Black women have 10 per cent more bone mass than white women, and may have more calcitonin, the hormone that strengthens bones (Notelovitz and Ware, 1982: 53). If you are of Hispanic, Mediterranean or Jewish ancestry, the risk seems to fall between the low risk for blacks and the high risk for Northern European white women and Asian women. The fairer your complexion, the greater your risk.

A person's risk of hip fracture doubles approximately every six to seven years, regardless of sex or race. At any age, the risk for white women is approximately double that for men, regardless of race, and also double that for black women (Farmer et al., 1984). [. . .] Therefore, if you are white, slender, short, and of Northern European descent, although you cannot change these biological factors, you can make a special effort to prevent osteoporosis by starting early in life, or starting now, to eat a calcium-rich diet, and also by exercising. [. . .]

Women who have never had a child or breastfed an infant have missed out on the temporary surges of oestrogen that accompany pregnancy and follow breastfeeding and help protect us against osteoporosis in later life. Although oestrogen levels temporarily drop during lactation and calcium leaves bones to go into milk formation, as soon as you stop breastfeeding your oestrogen level rises again. This helps strengthen the bones in preparation for another pregnancy (Greenwood, 1984: 55).

A nutritious diet during pregnancy will help bones get stronger. If you are not on a nutritious diet, pregnancy and breastfeeding can actually draw calcium out of the bones – hence the adage about losing a tooth for each child. Many British women now in their sixties and seventies may have been poorly nourished when pregnant during the Second World War. It was not until 1942 that the need for special rations in pregnancy was recognised. When the mother's own bones are not fully formed, adequate calcium is especially necessary. The adolescent mother can suffer as much as a 10 per cent loss in bone content after four months of breastfeeding (Chan et al., 1982). [. . .]

Medical research in the US reports that women experience increased bone loss four to five years following the onset of the menopause (Lindsay et al., 1976; Meema et al., 1976). If you have an early natural menopause, before age 40, you are at risk for osteoporosis because the cessation of menstruation causes oestrogen levels to drop. [. . .]

Medical risk factors

In addition to biological factors, certain diseases or chronic conditions can make us vulnerable to excessive bone loss. Women with anorexia, for example, may develop osteoporosis as early as age 25 – even to the point of having spinal crush fractures, which are usually seen only in elderly women (Foreman, 1984). Extremely strenuous exercise, as a result of which the percentage of body fat drops so low that menstruation stops, can also lead to osteoporosis. [. . .]

If you have diabetes, you have to contend with frequent urination, which causes excessive loss of calcium, and high blood acidity, which interferes with the absorption of vitamin D. If you have kidney or liver problems, the calcium in your food is not efficiently absorbed; kidney dialysis adds to calcium deficiency.

Certain surgery can also put you at risk for osteoporosis. Surgical removal of the ovaries, especially before, but even at the time of, the menopause, reduces oestrogen production more rapidly and for a longer period of time than a normal menopause. If you undergo this surgery, you need to take special care to maintain an adequate calcium intake and exercise programme. Many researchers report a high rate of osteoporosis if hormone replacement therapy isn't started soon after removal of premenopausal ovaries (Aitken et al., 1973; Lindsay et al., 1976). But we believe that each woman has to decide for herself if she wants hormone replacement therapy, based on a careful evaluation of her individual situation. [. . .]

It's also necessary to consider medications often taken for chronic health problems, such as cortisone for severe arthritis, thyroid for hypothyroidism, phenobarbitol or phenytoin (Epanutin) for seizures, aluminium-containing antacids for ulcers or heartburn. Exercise and a nutritious diet are a must if you take these drugs, because they all interfere with the body's ability to absorb calcium from food and calcium supplements.

Life-style risk factors

[. . .] Most of us can take immediate steps to slow down bone weakening by changing our daily habits.

Nutrition, for example, plays a major role in preventing and treating osteoporosis. [. . .] The amount of phosphorus (which aids in the development and maturation of bones: Raisy and Kream, 1983) we consume should be equal to the amount of calcium we consume. Most of us, however, probably take in too much phosphorus from eating red meat, processed cheese, baked goods that contain phosphate baking powder, cola and other soft drinks, instant soups and puddings, bread and phosphate food additives. High amounts of phosphorus are absorbed very efficiently; high amounts of calcium, on the other hand, are absorbed less efficiently. Dried skim milk is very high in phosphorus [. . .] so if you add powdered milk to soups or casseroles for extra calcium, take care to cut out other unnecessary sources of phosphorus.

We also need magnesium for strong teeth and bones. The amount of magnesium we consume should be at least half the amount of calcium we consume – perhaps equal to it (Porcino, 1983: 233). If magnesium intake is too low, the body is not able to utilise calcium or vitamin D, even if a sufficient amount of those substances is available. There is a rich supply of magnesium in nuts, whole grains, sprouts, beans, fresh vegetables and fruit.

It's also important that we get enough zinc and manganese, because calcium added to the diet decreases their absorption. Zinc is found in whole-grain breads and cereals, nuts and seeds. Manganese is found in sunflower seeds, nuts, rice, barley, oats and blueberries.

Vitamin D is a vital factor in the body's use of calcium. In order for vitamin D to aid in calcium absorption, it has to be converted into a hormone in the liver and in the kidneys. Osteoporosis may occur when the conversion is not taking place, and hence may be a symptom of liver and/or kidney disease. In addition, vitamin D can't be converted to its active hormone form when the blood is too acid due to stress, diabetes or fasting, or if you have a magnesium deficiency. Certain medications such as anticonvulsants, laxatives, cortisone and mineral oil can also interfere with the absorption of vitamin D.

A summer holiday in the sun allows us to store vitamin D for prolonged periods of time. Half an hour in the sun with 30 per cent of the body exposed several times a week is fine too. This is especially important if we live in the North, in overcast areas, or are confined indoors. But be sure to avoid excessive exposure to the sun.

Foods rich in vitamin D are egg yolk (if hens are allowed outside), certain fish, fish liver and butter. Fortunately vitamin D is added to margarines and some milks. [. . .] Our bodies have a decreased capacity to absorb and convert vitamin D as we get older, which may be a significant factor in osteoporosis. You can take a supplement [but] amounts over 1000 International Units a day interfere with calcium absorption and, because vitamin D is stored in the body for long periods of time, higher amounts can be toxic.

Prolonged dieting and fasting are common in our society because of its obsession with slenderness. If you habitually eat little, your daily requirements for calcium and related nutrients are not met, so that calcium has to be taken from your bones. Adequate weight and fat tissue offer protection from osteoporosis. The weight on the bones makes them work to produce new bone tissue, and the fat tissue helps to maintain some oestrogen in the body after the menopause. The ovaries continue after the menopause to produce a little oestrogen of the type seen in menstruating women and the adrenal glands continue to produce androgens, which are converted to another type of oestrogen in fat tissue.

Other life-style factors, such as alcohol and caffeine abuse, can also contribute to bone loss. Both caffeine and alcohol act as diuretics that can cause loss of calcium and zinc in the urine. Alcohol damages the liver, interfering with vitamin D metabolism. However, one or two cups of coffee or tea, a beer or a glass of wine, or $1\frac{1}{2}$ ounces of spirits daily probably do no harm.

Smoking is a known risk factor in osteoporosis. It is directly toxic to the ovaries. Women who smoke often experience the menopause up to five years earlier than non-smokers, and thus have lower oestrogen levels for a longer period of time. Smoking may also interfere with the body's metabolism of oestrogen, and may affect bone remodelling in other ways (Baron, 1984). Smoking often accompanies high alcohol or caffeine use. [. . .]

Lack of exercise is another major risk factor [. . .]. Part of the geographical and racial differences among women relative to the incidence of osteoporosis may be due to differences in physical activity (Chalmers and Ho, 1970). In the past, middle-class women didn't exercise vigorously. To sweat was unfeminine, and our society equated femininity with a small frame, low weight and a passive attitude toward life; certainly there was no approval of a female 'athletic' type. Fortunately it's never too late for us to start exercising. Weight-bearing exercises such as walking, jogging, skipping and dancing all make our bones work harder and strengthen the muscles and ligaments supporting the skeleton. One researcher reported that weight-bearing exercise that excluded upper-body activity resulted in a 3.5 per cent increase in spinal bone during an 18-month period, but a 3.6 per cent decrease in wrist bone (Pollner, 1985). It is important to make our arms work also, by swimming, wearing weights on them as we walk, carrying equally-distributed shopping bags, doing push-ups, or other arm exercises.

Prolonged inactivity, such as bed rest, can speed up the rate of bone-density loss.

Environmental risk factors

Fluoridation of drinking water has been successful in the prevention of tooth decay – and it may also prevent bone fragility and osteoporosis (Bernstein et al., 1966). [. . .] Levels as low as one part fluoride to one million parts water are reported to reduce osteoporosis by up to 40 per cent (Division of Dental Health,

---

FACTORS THAT INCREASE YOUR RISK OF OSTEOPOROSIS

Biological Factors
- Being female
- Having a family history of osteoporosis
- Having Northern European ancestry
- Being thin and short
- Having fair skin and freckles
- Having blonde or reddish-coloured hair
- Early natural menopause
- Childlessness
- Lactose intolerance
- Teenage pregnancy
- Scoliosis

Medical Factors
- Oophorectomy (removal of ovaries)
- Anorexia
- Coeliac disease
- Chronic diarrhoea
- Diabetes
- Kidney or liver disease

- Use of certain prescription and over-the-counter drugs
- Extended bed rest or immobilisation
- Surgical removal of part of the stomach or small intestine

Life-Style Factors
- Lack of exercise
- Smoking
- High alcohol intake
- Low-calcium diet
- Vitamin D deficiency
- Prolonged dieting or fasting
- High caffeine intake (over five cups a day)
- High salt intake

Environmental Factors
- Inadequate fluoride level in the water supply
- Living in a northern climate
- Being confined indoors

Figure 16.3 *Factors that increase your risk of osteoporosis*

1986). [. . .] Individual [. . .] supplementation by fluoride tablets can lead to medical problems such as inflamed joints and gastric troubles however (Riggs et al., 1985).

Conclusion

If you have several of the above risk factors, or just feel you want further information, you can seek out a doctor who is knowledgeable about osteoporosis. Nutritionists can be extremely helpful in planning a preventive diet to your liking; exercise instructors can tailor a regimen that will strengthen the muscles and ligaments supporting your bones (Yeater and Martin, 1984); nurses and health visitors can help you establish osteoporosis-prevention habits (Colls, 1983; Mines, 1985; Palmason, 1985) and understand the politics of the current osteoporosis controversy (MacPherson, 1985); doctors can order screening (if available) and medication for osteoporosis. [. . .]

Note

1. *Osteoporosis*: from 'osteo', referring to bones, and 'porosis', full of holes. In this condition, the actual bone is normal – there is just not enough of it. When osteoporosis exists, certain bones become so thin that they are likely to fracture or become compressed as a result of even a minor fall, or making a bed, or opening a door.

References

Aitken, J.M., Hart, D.M. and Lindsay, R. (1973) 'Oestrogen replacement therapy for prevention of osteoporosis after oophorectomy', *British Medical Journal*, 8-18 September: 515.

Baron, J.A. (1984) 'Smoking and estrogen-related disease', *American Journal of Epidemiology*, 119 (1): 9–22.

Bernstein, D.S., Sadowsky, N., Hegsted, D.M., et al. (1966) 'Prevalence of osteoporosis in high and low fluoride areas in North Dakota', *Journal of the American Medical Association*, 196: 85–90.

Chalmers, J. and Ho, K.C. (1970) 'Geographical variations in senile osteoporosis: the association with physical activity', *Journal of Bone and Joint Surgery*, 52B: 667–78.

Chan, G.M., et al. (1982) 'Decreased bone mineral status in lactating adolescent mothers', *The Journal of Pediatrics*, 101, November: 767–70.

Colls, J. (1983) 'Osteoporosis protocols'. Developed for Inservice Education for the Nurses' Association of the American College of Obstetrics and Gynecology.

Division of Dental Health (1986) *Fluoridation, Nature's Tooth Protector*. Massachusetts Department of Public Health, January.

Farmer, M.E., et al. (1984) 'Race and sex differences in hip fracture incidence', *American Journal of Public Health*, 74, December: 1374–9.

Foreman, J. (1984) 'Study, anorectic women may have osteoporosis', *The Boston Globe*, 20 December.

Greenwood, S. (1984) *Menopause Naturally*. San Francisco, CA: Volcano Press.

Kamen, B. and Kamen, S. (1984) *Osteoporosis: What It Is, How to Prevent It, How to Stop It*. New York: Pinnacle Books.

Lindsay, R., et al. (1976) 'Long-term prevention of post-menopausal osteoporosis by oestrogen', *The Lancet*, 1, 15 May: 1038f.

MacPherson, K.I. (1985) 'Osteoporosis and menopause: a feminist analysis of the social construction of a syndrome', *Advances in Nursing Science*, 7, July: 11–22.

Meema, S., et al. (1976) 'Preventive effect of estrogen on post-menopausal bone loss', *Annals of Internal Medicine*, 135: 1436–40.

Mines, A. (1985) 'Osteoporosis: a detailed look at the clinical manifestations and goals for nursing care', *The Canadian Nurse*, 81, January: 45–8.

National Institutes of Health (1984) *Osteoporosis Consensus Development Conference Statement*, 5(3), Washington, DC: US Department of Health and Human Services, Office of Medical Applications of Research.

Notelovitz, M. and Ware, M. (1982) *Stand Tall! The Informed Woman's Guide to Preventing Osteoporosis*. Gainsville, FL: Triad Publishing Co.

Palmason, D. (1985) 'Osteoporosis: catching the silent thief', *The Canadian Nurse*, 81, January: 42–4.

Parfit, A.M. (1984) 'Definition of osteoporosis: age-related loss of bone and its relationship to increased fracture risk'. Paper presented at the National Institutes of Health Consensus Development Conference on Osteoporosis, 2–4 April. Bethesda, MD: National Institutes of Health.

Pollner, F. (1985) 'Osteoporosis: looking at the whole picture', *Medical World News*, 14, January: 38–58.

Porcino, J. (1983) *Growing Older, Growing Better: a Handbook for Women in the Second Half of Life*. Reading, MA: Addison-Wesley.

Raab, D.M. and Smith, E.L. (1985) 'Exercise and aging effects on bone', *Topics in Geriatric Rehabilitation*, 1 (1), October: 31–9.

Raisy, L.G. and Kream, B.E. (1983) 'Regulation of bone formation, part II', *The New England Journal of Medicine*, 309: 83–9.

Riggs, B.L., et al. (1985) 'Effect of the fluoride/calcium regimen on vertebral occurrence in postmenopausal osteoporosis', *The New England Journal of Medicine*, 306 (8): 446–50.

Yeater, R.A. and Martin, B.R. (1984) 'Senile osteoporosis: the effects of exercise', *Postgraduate Medicine*, 75, 1 February: 147–58.

17

Depression in later life

Elaine Murphy

Depression in the medical sense [. . .] means something very different from just feeling understandably low spirited or fed up. The more severe forms of depression are real illnesses and are characterised not only by low 'mood' but also by certain specific physical symptoms. These more serious forms of depression are referred to by psychiatrists as 'depressive illnesses' or 'depressive disorders'. Depressions of this kind cause an enormous amount of suffering to the afflicted person and their family. [. . .]

How common is depression in elderly people?

[. . .] The vast majority of elderly people are not depressed or miserable at all and no more of them suffer from depressive illnesses than do younger people. It is nevertheless important to remember that a significant minority, perhaps one in ten, of the population do suffer from depression [. . .].

It is extremely important to spot when someone is depressed because depression is *treatable*, by a variety of means. Severe depression usually gets better when treated with the right medicines, and there is a great deal that family and friends can do to help. [. . .]

Old people living in old people's homes or nursing homes are more likely to suffer from depression than people living in their own homes. As many as one-third of the residents of such homes in Britain are suffering in this way. We do not know if the environment and quality of life in these institutions are the cause of the problem. [. . .]

Incontinence, inability to walk unaided and bad-tempered or aggressive outbursts towards other residents and staff may all be symptoms of depression. Complaining, hypochondriacal and irritable elderly people are frequently suffering from depression.

Originally published as 'Depression', in *Dementia and Mental Illness in Older People*. London: Macmillan/Papermac, 1993, Chapter 9, pp. 158–76 (abridged).

Signs that a person has depression

[. . .] Depression affects every part of the person's thinking, feeling, conversation, behaviour and physical health. Specific symptoms often give the clue to the diagnosis. The main clue to look for is a definite *change* over the course of days or weeks from being an active, coping and competent person to being a different sort of personality. It may take weeks or months for family and friends to appreciate the great change that has come about in their relative. It is easy to attribute the change to 'just old age'. If someone's personality appears to change for the worse, and the change persists for several weeks, then professional help should be sought.

Turning now to individual symptoms, it is worth noting first that there is an enormous variation from one depressed person to another, and the symptoms will not all be present at once.

Mood

Feelings of depression are *unpleasant*. Although sometimes there is a straightforward feeling of being sad, low and dispirited, more often the mood is one of being keyed up, tense and extremely *anxious* for no apparent reason. Depressed people feel fatigued and generally unwell. Waves of panicky fear sweep over them, and there is a foreboding of impending catastrophe without any identifiable cause. Some people feel dreadfully ill and worn out all day. *Feeling ill and anxious makes people very irritable.* They snap at other people, complain about noise and feel constantly 'on a short fuse'. The fearfulness of depression makes them cling to other people and constantly seek help and reassurance. This anxious, clinging behaviour can be extremely annoying for those around them, and most relatives and friends find it difficult to feel sympathetic towards a depressed person.

Someone with a serious depressive illness usually feels much worse first thing in the morning, but then brightens up a little as the day wears on. However, others may feel progressively more despondent and worried with every passing hour and quite worn out by the end of the day.

Depressed thoughts

Depressed people feel as though they are looking at the world from the bottom of a dark pit from which they can never escape. The future appears hopelessly gloomy; they feel they will never recover. Thoughts of death intrude in an unpleasant way, and most depressed people at some point wish they were dead. [. . .]

Depressed people interpret everything they hear or observe in a gloomy way. They feel inferior to other people and that they are worthless, no good to anyone. Some sufferers tend to blame other

people for their problems and act in a suspicious, unfriendly and
hostile way. Others feel deeply ashamed and guilty for no apparent
reason. They feel they have a responsibility for some 'catastrophe' due
to a previous misdeed. [. . .]

Depressed people are so preoccupied with their own gloomy
thoughts that they find it hard to take an interest in things going on
around them. This makes them appear lazy and selfish to other people.
They lose interest in their family, friends and home and yet at the
same time desperately want someone to be with them.

Activity

Depression brings tiredness, fatigue and a feeling of being lethargic
and lacking in energy. This 'slowing down' makes people withdrawn
and uncommunicative. They speak more slowly than usual and in
short, uninformative sentences. A depressed person may be so 'slowed
up' that they appear to lack understanding. It is almost as if they were
suffering from dementia. On the other hand, depressed people can be
extremely restless and agitated. Depressed elderly people sometimes
find it impossible to sit still for any length of time and feel unable to
concentrate on anything – their mind jumps from one worry to the
next. Losing the ability to concentrate makes sufferers feel as if they
are losing their memories, and they often wonder if they are losing
their minds and becoming demented. No wonder that it is sometimes
difficult for both relatives and professionals to tell the difference
between depression and dementia. [. . .]

Sleep

Elderly people often sleep less at night than younger people. They tend
to catch up during the day through cat-napping for short periods.
Elderly people today also tend to belong to a generation that
traditionally started work early in the morning, so it is not unusual for
the habit of rising at six o'clock or earlier to persist long into
retirement. However, depressed people have great difficulty getting off
to sleep; they tend to wake frequently through the night and then
wake early in the morning feeling unrefreshed and still tired. Waking
regularly at three or four in the morning feeling frightened and
despairing is a particular sign of serious depression.

Appetite

Some people with mild depression keep eating the same as usual
although they may have lost enjoyment in their meals. But most
depressed people lose their appetite. It is not just that they do not feel
like eating, but taking food itself becomes unpleasant, and it becomes
difficult to get it down. Food seems to stick in the throat or give an

unpleasant over-full feeling. Consequently one of the key signs of depression is *weight loss*. This can sometimes be very dramatic, and a loss of a stone or more over the course of a few weeks is not uncommon. [. . .]

Bowels

Constipation is almost universal in depression. An overall slowing down and loss of appetite lead to a slowing of the bowels too. Some people become so preoccupied with their bowel function that they can think and talk of nothing else, an irritating symptom for those who have to listen to 'blow-by-blow' accounts of bowel actions every day.

Other physical symptoms

Increased tension in the body muscles leads to numerous aches and pains. Severe headaches, which feel like a tight band round the head or a weight on top of the head, neck-aches and back-aches are all common. Anxiety leads to episodes of dizziness, giddiness, churning stomach, cold sweats and breathlessness. These symptoms can be very hard to distinguish from real physical disease, and it is not surprising that sufferers frequently interpret them as being caused by physical illness. [. . .]

One of the most important causes of depression is long-standing poor physical health. Chronic pain, immobility and feeling 'under the weather' are understandable causes of depression. Someone who is taking a lot of tablets for heart and chest problems or arthritis often feels permanently 'off colour'. Serious depression can nevertheless come quite suddenly, with no apparent cause at all. We do not know why some people are liable to develop depression of this kind, but it is possible that changes in the biochemistry of the ageing brain predispose some individuals to developing depression.

What can be done?

The most important thing that a friend or relative can do for a depressed person is to *spot* that the person has become depressed and ask the family doctor to assess whether or not they need medical treatment with antidepressant medication or other physical treatments. [. . .]

Depressive illness is associated with an upset in the brain's metabolism. Medication can reverse this upset and return the person to normal. Medication cannot reverse normal unhappiness, of course, or control the normal grief of bereavement, but it can help in those cases of serious depression where appetite and sleep are affected or where the person has become very agitated or slowed down. [. . .]

Antidepressant drugs take at least ten days and sometimes as long as three to four weeks before they begin to work. It can be very tedious taking tablets regularly every day when no benefit is detected. Plenty of perseverance is required of the patient. Relatives can help considerably by encouraging the person regularly. A small dose is usually prescribed first and then the dose is built up over the course of a week. Like all medication, antidepressant drugs may have unpleasant, unwanted effects that can be troublesome and need watching out for. But it is worth persevering because they really can help enormously.

Antidepressant drugs are *not addictive* and can be stopped after the end of the course of treatment without unwanted effects. A course of antidepressant drugs lasts from six months to two or three years, and is usually continued after the symptoms of depression have lifted. This is because depression in elderly people tends to recur within a few months if the medication is withdrawn early.

Side-effects of antidepressant drugs. The list of unwanted effects is long. Most people experience the less serious ones very mildly, but it is as well to be aware of them.

1 Dizziness, especially when rising from a chair or getting out of bed.
2 Difficulty in starting the stream when passing urine.
3 Dry mouth.
4 Constipation.
5 Difficulty in focusing the eyes.
6 Sleepiness: this can be put to good effect by taking most of the tablets at night.
7 Mental confusion: this occurs in some vulnerable elderly people and is an indication that the medication should be stopped immediately and a doctor consulted. He may wish to restart the drug at a lower dose.

Most antidepressant medicines are dangerous if taken in overdose. There is a danger that a depressed person will take them as a means of suicide. If someone has expressed suicidal ideas, however fleeting or seemingly unimportant, they should never be left to supervise their own medication. A relative or friend should keep the bottle of tablets and give only one or two day's supply at a time. The person should be told why this is being done and will often be relieved of the burden of having an easy means of self-poisoning in the house.

How else can relatives and friends help?

One important fact is worth remembering: *nearly all depressed people get better in time.* Treatment speeds up the process, but nature will eventually heal the problem. During the period of depression, relatives can help enormously by continually reminding the person that they will feel better in time and of the good and successful things in their lives. Relatives and friends should also remember to tell the sufferer that someone cares about them.

It is easy to fall into a pattern of behaviour with a depressed person that is rejecting and unhelpful. When someone is irritable, rude and complaining towards you when you visit, for example, it is tempting to visit less frequently in future and to ignore the person, hoping they will appreciate you more following an absence. But this will make a depressed person feel even more rejected and isolated. [. . .]

Dissuade a depressed person from making major decisions during the course of the illness. This is not the time to decide to enter an old people's home, change a will, sell the house or move in permanently with a relative. The individual concerned often later regrets decisions made in haste while feeling depressed.

During the course of a depression it is difficult to tackle any underlying problems of isolation and loneliness because the illness itself prevents the sufferer from being able to benefit from increased social contact by forming new acquaintances and friendships. However, when someone is beginning to recover they may be more receptive to the idea of joining a club or attending a day centre to expand their social horizons. This possibility can be investigated by contacting the local area social services office.

Elderly people often lose their family contacts and friendships during the course of a depression because people lack understanding as to why the depressed person is behaving in such a difficult way. Supporting someone through a depression is a taxing and difficult business but very rewarding when the depression finally lifts and the person returns to their former self.

18

Frames of reference for an understanding of dementia

Tom Kitwood

One of the most hopeful signs of the present time, in relation to old age, is that attitudes to the dementing illnesses are undergoing radical change. Not many years ago, pessimism perfused the whole domain; dire images such as that of 'the death that leaves the body behind' prevailed. Now, however, the dementia sufferer is being reinstated as a person: one who carries certain handicaps, rather than the victim of a psychiatric illness. The special skills and insights needed in working with those who have dementia are increasingly valued and respected. The prospects for long-stay care are coming to be viewed much more hopefully, as the consequences of excellent care practice are being acknowledged.

Despite many obstacles, and a pitiful insufficiency of provision, a slow revolution is occurring.

Framing illness

We may make a distinction between two possible ways of framing human ill-being, whether of body or of mind: the technical and the personal (Kitwood, 1988). Those who adopt a technical approach see illness very much in the way that a mechanic might look at the breakdown of an automobile, or an electronics engineer the malfunction of a computer. Medical science in the West is strongly committed to this approach, which has indeed yielded some remarkable victories.

In the case of dementia in old age a technical frame has long held dominance, tending to force other frames into the background. The basic assumption, although rarely made explicit, may be summed up in a simple, linear causal sequence:

$$X \longrightarrow \text{neuropathic change} \longrightarrow \text{dementia}$$

In the case of multi-infarct dementia the factor X is fairly well understood. In the case of so-called Alzheimer's disease (in reality a cluster of 10 or so neuropathologies that are now beginning to be differentiated), X remains mysterious. It is likely to be many years before the causes of the degenerative processes are fully elucidated.

For medical science, and hence for a psychiatry that looks to medical science as its main tutor, the inferences from the technical framing are clear. The brain is failing: discover, then, precisely what is going wrong, with the hope of eventually uncovering and controlling the causal process. But for the person, in the short term, almost nothing can be done.

The technical frame and the taken-for-granted world

Why has one particular theoretical approach to dementia received such prominence, while the 'silent epidemic' has been advancing? Why is it that, until recently, frames that put the person at the centre have been largely excluded? Very speculatively, it may be suggested that there has been a convergence of interests in adopting a purely technical frame; and that as research within it gathered momentum, clearly achieving results, other approaches came to appear irrelevant or absurd.

Most significantly, perhaps, medicine in the West has tended more and more to view human illness by analogy with problems in engineering. Also, as high technology has become available to medical science, those carrying out research have often been lured by what is 'technically sweet'. Their good faith is not in question here. The point is that their milieu, the world with which they are familiar by training and experience, is one deeply impregnated by technology and natural science, and the objectifying mode that accompanies them. The skills of interpersonal understanding, on the other hand, belong to another milieu, which only a minority of health professionals have entered. The technical framing of dementia, it need hardly be added, has had powerful support from some drug companies, which could then produce specific sedatives and palliatives; and even, in certain instances, complete schedules for the assessment and management of the dementing illnesses. Alongside this there has been a powerful lobby from neuro-scientists, eager to obtain grants and recognition for their research (Fox, 1989).

The technical frame can make a strong appeal to those who control the funding of dementia care, whether as guardians of meagre allocations of public money, or as private entrepreneurs. Forms of caring that attempt to meet psychological needs are labour-intensive, and hence expensive. Grounds for low levels of staffing, however specious, are all-too-easily accepted. At times technical means, particularly the use of tranquillising medication, are seen as more cost-effective than human interaction. In the most extreme instances the technical frame becomes an ideology used to justify neglect. 'The brains of these people are virtually dead. All they need now is quietness and basic physical care.' This was the account given to me by a senior manager in justifying a care situation that, from a personal-centred point of view, amounted to near total neglect.

Clinical psychologists, nurses, and those who are employed as direct careworkers often find themselves in a deeply paradoxical situation. The theory of dementia which they have absorbed through their training is strongly and uncritically committed to the technical frame. Their lived experience, however, inclines them to another view, in which the dementia sufferer is genuinely acknowledged as a person. So they operate on the basis of a kind of 'doublethink'. In good times, and when resourcing is sufficient, the personhood of those they care for is acknowledged. In bad times, on the other hand, when they are close to exhaustion, disillusionment or burn-out, the technical frame provides a kind of distancing. It helps to rationalise the impossibilities of their working life, and to justify a level of care provision over which they have no control.

But we must consider also the predicament of relatives and, in some cases, friends. For them, too, the technical frame may seem helpful, for it enables them to cope with the feelings of grief, anger, guilt and inadequacy in which they are often enveloped. Also, it can give grounds for an apologia, since it is far easier to describe the afflicted person as 'having' Alzheimer's disease or some other condition than to express matters in everyday terms. Morever, by adopting the technical frame carers can avoid facing the immensely threatening possibility that there might have been, and might still be, psychologically malignant processes at work within the family, including even their own relationship to the dementing person. Perhaps this is why the associations of carers contain people for whom the technical frame virtually provides a mythology, and why some of their own written contributions express a touching yet tragic combination of sentiment and subservience to the technical view. The truth, surely, is that family carers are often left desperately unsupported. They are generally forced into an intense preoccupation with survival from day to day – there is no space for a therapeutic 'working through' of their grief and conflict. A defensive posture may be all that is possible when society lays such burdens upon them.

There may, too, be a larger psychological investment in the technical framing of dementia, within a culture that makes so great a fetish of youth and beauty, while being so reticent about its fears of frailty and mortality. To view dementia as a problem in neurological or biochemical engineering provides a small consolation, insulating people from a disturbing truth which at some level they do not wish to know. This truth is that any of us may at some point suffer from a dementing condition, and die without full possession of our mental powers. The technical framing of dementia, then, contributes to a widespread collusion. It is part of that technical framing of personal anguish, frailty, ageing and death which helps a society committed to a shallow materialism to bear its existential plight.

Social psychology and the dementing process

A good care practice for dementia, informed by real understanding, requires a theoretical frame which acknowledges personhood fully. Also, of course, it must be compatible with the established findings of neuropathology and the related sciences. Such a frame might point to five factors as crucial in any manifestation of a senile dementia.

The first is *personality*: that which each individual has constitutionally, overlaid with all the outcomes of social learning. Included here are such aspects as styles of coping with crisis, loss and change; defences against anxiety; and openness to help proffered by others. The second factor is *biography*, and in particular the effects of the vicissitudes of later life. Some individuals embark on a dementing illness with most of the structures that formerly supported them still intact; others, however, have undergone a succession of destabilising and demoralising life-changes, and with their personal resources already dwindling to zero. The third is *physical health status*, including the acuity of the senses. The bearing of this on mental functioning is not controversial, although many of the subtler effects still elude scientific inquiry. The fourth factor is the *neurological impairment* itself; according to its location, type and intensity, reducing the capacity for storing and processing information, executing 'plans', etc. Finally, there is the *social psychology* which makes up the fabric of everyday life: and in particular, whether it enhances or diminishes an individual's sense of safety, value and personal being.

Of these five factors, three are already 'given'. Personality has largely been formed, and the main changes that will ensue are those of deconstruction. The greater part of biography has now been written; nothing can change the life-events that have taken place. Neurological impairments are already present, and tending to advance; biomedical interventions can do virtually nothing to arrest or reverse them. Only the other two factors still remain as key variables. Physical health may often be improved, with corresponding recoveries in mental functioning. But also, and crucially, there is the social psychology; its significance has, until fairly recently, passed largely unnoticed in dementia research. It is only when this is brought fully into the frame that we can begin to conceptualise the consequences of good and bad care practice.

The dialectics of dementia

A few years ago, I spent a good deal of time looking at what might be called the 'malignant social psychology' surrounding the dementing process. The method involved collecting vignettes from everyday life, and putting these into 10 categories, as follows:

- *Treachery*: the use of dishonest representation or deception in order to obtain compliance.
- *Disempowerment*: doing for a dementia sufferer what he or she can in fact do, albeit clumsily or slowly.
- *Infantilisation*: implying that a dementia sufferer has the mentality or capability or a baby or young child.
- *Condemnation*: blaming; the attribution of malicious or seditious motives, especially when the dementia sufferer is distressed.
- *Intimidation*: the use of threats, commands or physical assault; the abuse of power.
- *Stigmatisation*: turning a dementia sufferer into an alien, a diseased object, an outcast, especially through verbal labels.
- *Outpacing*: the delivery of information or instruction at a rate far beyond that which can be processed.
- *Invalidation*: the ignoring or discounting of a dementia sufferer's subjective states – especially feelings of distress or bewilderment.
- *Banishment*: the removal of a dementia sufferer from the human milieu, either physically or psychologically.
- *Objectification*: treating a person like a lump of dead matter; to be measured, pushed around, drained, filled, polished, dumped, etc.

The effect of this malignancy, together with the fact of continual neglect, must surely be included in any explanation of the dementing process that aspires to scientific truth.

When the social psychology is taken into account, the dementing process can be seen in dialectical terms: that is, as arising principally from an interaction between the neurological impairments and those interpersonal processes which destabilise and undermine the sense of self (Kitwood, 1990). This is illustrated in Figure 18.1. The details, of course, will be unique to each individual. There is variation between persons in the relative contributions made by the neurological and social-psychological components, in the nature of each, and in the stages of the process where they come into play.

Developing good care practice

When dementia is framed in a way that puts personhood at the centre, a rich and challenging agenda is set for care-giving. The prime task is that of doing positive 'person-work', so as to enable the dementia

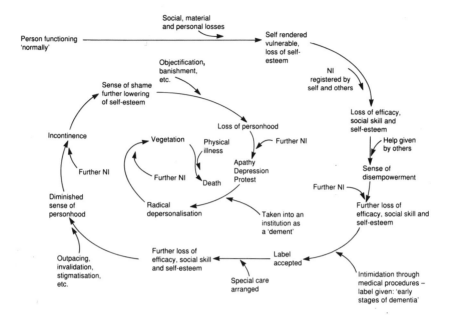

Figure 18.1 *The dementing process (NI = neurological impairment)*
(Kitwood, 1990: 187)

sufferer to be and remain a full participant in our shared humanity. One aspect of this work is 'validation': actively acknowledging the reality and subjective truth of the dementia sufferer's frame of reference (Feil, 1982). Another aspect is 'holding': providing a safe space when emotions such as fear, rage and grief can be experienced and worked through. Another is 'facilitation': filling out gestures or part-actions so that they become completed social acts (Kitwood, 1993). As practices such as these become widespread we may confidently expect much higher levels of personal well-being in dementia, even among those who have very severe cognitive impairments (Kitwood and Bredin, 1992). Increasingly, then, it is being realised that a purely technical frame has had its day.

References

Feil, N. (1982) *Validation: the Feil Method.* Cleveland, OH: Edward Feil Productions. (Now available from Winslow Press, Bicester.)

Fox, P. (1989) 'From senility to Alzheimer's disease: the rise of the Alzheimer's disease movement', *The Millbank Quarterly,* 67 (1): 58–101.

Kitwood, T. (1988) 'The technical, the personal and the framing of dementia', *Social Behaviour,* 3: 161–80.

Kitwood, T. (1990) 'The dialectics of dementia: with particular reference to Alzheimer's disease', *Ageing and Society*, 10 (2): 177-96.

Kitwood, T. (1993) 'Towards a theory of dementia care: the interpersonal process', *Ageing and Society*, 13 (1): 51-67.

Kitwood, T. and Bredin, K. (1992) 'Towards a theory of dementia care: personhood and well-being', *Ageing and Society*, 12 (3): 269-87.

19

Love, sex and aging

Edward M. Brecher

The 1844 women and 2402 men aged 50 or over who participated in [the] Consumers' Union study [detailed in *Love, Sex and Aging*] have provided us with a panorama of life experiences and of sexual likes, dislikes, satisfactions, frustrations, yearnings and memories.

In a study of this kind, statistical data may consign respondents to one group or another; this grouping is valuable mainly as the necessary access to generalizations. Members of such a group may be alike in one or several respects, but they also invariably differ in many other respects. From our statistical data, and equally important, from our respondents' comments and life stories, a central truth emerges again and again: contrary to the stereotype, older people are not alike, nor are they asexual; they differ widely in many characteristics, and their sexuality is manifest in the high proportion of those who are sexually active, and in the quality, quantity, variety and enjoyability of their sexual activities.

What have we learned from our 4246 respondents?

They are very much the marrying kind: all but 3 per cent have been married at least once, and close to three-quarters of them are married now. These 3140 wives and husbands are overwhelmingly happy with their marriage: 87 per cent are happily married. Their marriages are remarkably durable: 80 per cent of our wives and almost three-quarters of our husbands are married to their first and only spouse. Nearly three-quarters of our wives and two-thirds of our husbands have been married for 30 years or more. Five per cent have celebrated their golden wedding anniversary, and some are still as sexually turned on to one another as lovers in a romantic novel.

But other respondents who have remained married through the decades are not happily married, and some report their marriage sexually unrewarding from the very beginning. Still others have secured divorces.

We reviewed 15 *nonsexual* factors in relation to our happily and

From *Love, Sex and Aging: a Consumers' Union Report*. Boston, MA: Little, Brown and Company, 1984, Chapter 10, pp. 403–8.

unhappily married respondents. We found that the wives and husbands most likely to be happily married after age 50 are those who maintain 'excellent' or 'very good' communications with their spouse. The relationship of the remaining nonsexual factors with marital happiness varied from small to negligible to none – and not always in accordance with the conventional wisdom. Family income, for example, seems to have only a modest and inconsistent effect on marital happiness. Wives and husbands with high incomes are no more likely to be happily married than those with low incomes. Happy marriages are reported slightly more often by respondents with an 'empty nest' – that is, without dependent children at home – than by those who still have children living at home.

Among the interesting byproducts of our review of nonsexual factors, a remarkable finding was revealed concerning attitudes toward retirement, before and after the fact. Most employed respondents, married and unmarried alike, are troubled by the prospect of retirement; but most retired respondents are quite pleased with their retirement.

Our review of 10 *sexual* factors associated with marital happiness found that respondents most likely to be happily married after 50 are those who enjoy having sex with their spouse. Among other factors almost as important were satisfaction with frequency of marital sex and comfort in discussing sex with one's spouse. The vast majority of our husbands, both happily and unhappily married, consider the sexual side of their marriage to be important, and this is true for our happily married wives as well. Among our unhappily married wives, however, most consider the sexual side of their marriage to be of little importance. This is the most powerful predictor of marital unhappiness for wives in our study.

While lifelong marital fidelity is the prevailing pattern among our wives and husbands, 8 per cent of our wives and 23 per cent of our husbands report one or more adulterous relationships or encounters since age 50. We don't know how many others engaged in adultery and then were divorced; our data are for those who stayed married despite adultery. Most of the adultery reported is 'cheating' – outside sex without the spouse's knowledge. But some wives and husbands report adultery with the spouse's knowledge, and perhaps with his or her consent; a few engage in 'swinging' – adultery as a mutual enterprise engaged in by wife and husband together. Here, too, the panorama is broad.

We have noted that our 925 unmarried respondents live in a society in which after age 50 unmarried women outnumber unmarried men by 2.7 to 1; when we consider the numbers of unattached heterosexual women and men in this age group, the ratio looks close to 5 to 1. This gender imbalance affects the lives of the unmarried in many important ways. More of our unmarried men than women, for example, have found close friends of the opposite gender. More men report ongoing sexual partners of the opposite gender. More men are living with a sexual partner of the opposite gender, and more of them report one or more casual sexual partners during the past year.

Despite the gender imbalance, however, a substantial minority of our unmarried women have also found sexual partners of the opposite gender. Most of the men with whom they are involved are either married to someone else or are much older. A surprising proportion of our women with men partners, moreover, have men much younger than they are. Some unmarried women discuss entering into a sexual relationship with another woman as a solution to the dearth-of-unmarried-men problem; but only a very few have taken that course.

Many unmarried women, like unmarried men and some wives and husbands, remain sexually active through masturbation; and some unmarried women with sexual partners - like unmarried men with sexual partners and like some wives and husbands - engage in masturbation in addition to sex with a partner, as an added form of sexual enjoyment. Unmarried women and men whose only form of sexual activity is masturbation are more likely to report high enjoyment of life than the sexually inactive; but those who have a sexual partner are even more likely to report high life enjoyment. A smaller proportion of our unmarried respondents than of our wives and husbands report high enjoyment of life.

The overwhelming majority of our respondents are primarily heterosexual. Quite a few, however, report pre-adolescent or adolescent sexual encounters with others of their gender (with little or no harm reported); and quite a few essentially heterosexual women and men report one or more homosexual partners or encounters after 50. These respondents seem to view such homosexual contacts as an additional, rather than an alternative, form of sexual activity.

, In this as in prior human sexuality surveys, more men than women report homosexual experiences; but - and this is an unprecedented finding - more of our women than men report that they have been sexually attracted to someone of their gender. [. . .]

Almost all of our respondents were raised within the constraints of what many of them refer to as their Victorian upbringing. We explored our respondents' attitudes toward five Victorian sexual taboos - masturbation, sex without marriage, sex without love, pornography and homosexuality. We found that some respondents still cling firmly to Victorian views on these five topics, but substantial majorities have abandoned the Victorian position on most or all of them. In opinions as well as behavior, older people are not all alike.

We have found that impaired health has an adverse impact, but only a modest one, on sexual activity, sexual frequency and sexual enjoyment. Both women and men continue to engage in sex, and to enjoy sex, despite health barriers, some of which to others might seem insuperable. Substantial proportions of respondents who have had a heart attack remain sexually active and continue to enjoy sex. The same is true of respondents who are taking anti-hypertensive medication, those with diabetes, and those who have had a hysterectomy, ovariectomy, mastectomy or prostate surgery.

We explored a highly controversial topic: estrogen replacement therapy for postmenopausal women. We stress the fact that many postmenopausal women do not need estrogen because their body continues to produce enough of it. [There are] four reasons why postmenopausal women who need estrogen may wish to take it: to prevent or minimize the hot flash syndrome; adverse vaginal changes, including vaginal dryness and vaginal atrophy; urinary tract problems; and to forestall bone changes and possible bone fractures due to osteoporosis. [There are] risks – including the risk of endometrial cancer – associated with estrogen replacement therapy, [but also] possible ways in which postmenopausal women taking estrogen can minimize those risks.

We have traced the impact of aging on sexuality among our women and men in their fifties, sixties, and thereafter. Decade by decade, respondents report declines in many aspects of sexual function: in sexual desire, ease of sexual arousal, and enjoyment of sex; in the proportions of respondents having sex with a partner, in the frequency of sex with a partner, and in the frequency of orgasm during sex with a partner; in the proportions of respondents who masturbate, in the frequency of their masturbation and frequency of orgasm during masturbation; and in other respects. We have presented our reasons for believing that these changes are much more frequently due to aging per se than to declining health or other factors.

We have also noted, however, that despite these progressive declines, large proportions of our respondents still report being sexually active and enjoying a wide variety of sexual activities. Indeed, this is true for a number of women and men in their eighties, including some who report continued sex with a partner and orgasm during sex with a partner.

Finally, we have described how the majority of our women and men have managed to surmount the rising barriers to sexual fulfillment posed by advancing age and by health impairments, and to maintain and in some cases enhance sexual enjoyment in their later years. The physiological and psychological methods for surmounting these barriers employed by our respondents are numerous and varied; describing and explaining them may well be the greatest single contribution our respondents have made to the well-being of other older women and men, and to the concerns of younger women and men as they approach their older years.

Both our statistical data and the written comments of our respondents provide an impressive testimonial to the capacity to enjoy life, often under the most adverse circumstances. We salute the women and men aged 50 to 93 who invested so much of their time and psychic energy in telling us how things are with them, and we again thank them for their contributions. We feel very sure that readers of this report will thank them with equal fervor.

20

Age discrimination in health care

Melanie Henwood

[. . .] Two major theoretical issues underlie the reality of health care provision for older people. The first concerns the limits to intervention for individual patients; the second concerns the relative claims of older people and other citizens. These two areas are not entirely distinct, but it may be useful to examine them separately.

A contributor to a recent American volume on the ageing population described health care in an ageing society as 'a moral dilemma'. He argued that 'experience is teaching us that medicine can keep some elderly people alive for longer than is of any benefit to them'. There is, he suggested, 'the increasing necessity to make painful moral choices in the care of the dying elderly as a class, particularly among that growing number who end their days incompetent, incontinent, and grossly incapacitated, more dead than alive' (Callahan, 1986). The maxim that life should not be extended at the cost of worsening it has an obvious appeal: it is also a gross over-simplification. The optimal moment for ceasing medical intervention is rarely this clear-cut, but obviously there are tensions between attempts to prolong life, and the quality of life in the extra days attained. Issues about 'dignity in death' are complex and rarely fully aired. Many states in the United States recognise the authority of a 'living will', which gives prior authorisation for the cessation of life-prolonging medical intervention in the event of terminal illness or irreversible brain damage. In Britain, such a declaration has no legal status, and decisions about continuing heroic treatments, even where there is no prospect of recovery or benefit, are left very much to clinical judgement (Age Concern Institute of Gerontology, 1988).

The second major issue concerns both implicit and explicit discrimination against elderly people, both as individuals and as a group. While life expectancy has extended, it appears to have been at the price of a longer period and a greater proportion of life being spent in chronic sickness. At the same time, within the National Health

Originally published as 'No sense of urgency: age discrimination in health care', in E. McEwen (ed.), *Age: The Unrecognised Discrimination*. London: Age Concern England, 1990, pp. 43–57 (abridged).

Service, it has been acute and curative services which have been developed, despite attempts to shift the balance towards preventive and caring services directed at chronic conditions. Older people are not the only group to be disadvantaged by such trends. The phrase 'Cinderella services' was coined to describe the relative paucity of care for the mentally ill, people with learning difficulties and people with physical disabilities as well as elderly people. These groups share the characteristics of having long-term and chronic needs. Because of the scale of increase in the older population, however, it is the very old and frail who are seen to represent the greatest challenge to the health and community care services.

Services for people with disabilities have been a low priority over many years, and the inadequacy of provision – both in quantity and in quality – is well known. Older people are particularly disadvantaged by this situation because of their greater likelihood of disability. It has been suggested that 'aids and equipment supply is the single most confused area of service provision for disabled people'. Health authorities have responsibility for nursing aids, and social service departments are responsible for aids to daily living. In practice, these distinctions are rarely so clear, and many severely disabled people will have needs for multiple support which cross these agency boundaries. The result is 'a complex, time-consuming and often frustrating business for people with disabilities'. Long delays in the supply of equipment are commonplace, and poor assessment frequently leads to inappropriate or inadequate aids being supplied (Beardshaw, 1988).

Moreover, failure to provide adequate services means that less is being achieved for many elderly people than is possible. Improved rehabilitation techniques, for example, mean that many elderly stroke patients can now achieve greater functional improvement than was previously thought possible. However, shortage of physiotherapy and other services, together with rapid hospital discharge, militates against such results being achieved.

The 1979 Royal Commission on the National Health Service estimated that an annual growth of 1 per cent in public expenditure was required simply to keep pace with demographic pressures. Recent public expenditure White Papers have allowed an annual 2 per cent for such changes as well as to take account of the increased costs of technological progress, but the adequacy of this allowance is in doubt. The Social Services Committee of the House of Commons continues to stress that 'the Government should acknowledge that improving health services and expanding services as dictated by the twin demands of demography and technology will not be cheap' (1988: para, 217).

The domination of acute services and the parallel increases in high-tech medicine have considerable influence on people's expectations of what is appropriate and possible in health care. Dramatic life-saving techniques, organ transplants and similar developments have popular appeal. They are also more likely to be directed at people below retirement age; indeed, the latest challenge in micro-surgery appears to be successful operations on ever younger patients. At the beginning of 1990, for example, there was a much publicised case of heart surgery carried out on an infant still in the womb. The baby subsequently died in intensive care.

The need to ration health care resources is a fact of life for the National Health Service, as for any modern health care system. Questions about *how* care is rationed, however, are crucial. If services were to be provided on purely egalitarian terms, all people who might benefit from any given treatment would be able to do so. However, given finite resources, concepts of effectiveness and efficiency must be considered alongside concepts of need. In other words, the principle is that 'within a fixed budget, health care resources should be allocated so as to achieve the greatest aggregate of well-being for patients' (Jennet and Buxton, 1990). However, how such a judgement can be made is controversial. The view expressed by health economists such as Alan Maynard (1988) is still one which is rarely articulated quite so starkly: 'We have to demonstrate much more clearly that the spending involved in care for elderly people is spending which is efficient. Until we demonstrate that, the case for increasing expenditure on elderly people has to be very modest, and related to what evidence we have about whether it will improve their welfare.'

One concept which has been the focus of much debate in evaluating efficiency is that of the 'Quality Adjusted Life Year' or QALY developed by the health economist Alan Williams. An attempt is made to value the resources required for a given treatment against the years of better quality of life it will produce. Whatever the limitations intrinsic to the QALY approach, the approach itself is inherently discriminatory. A report of a working party on the ethical dimension of choice in health care observed that 'any procedure that includes counting extra years of life as part of the benefit of medical procedures will risk shifting resources away from the elderly and towards younger age groups' (Weale, 1988).

The QALY approach is formally egalitarian, but its application introduces bias against older people. There will generally be fewer life years added by the treatment of older people and, similarly, those with a low quality of life – predominantly older people – will be disadvantaged by a QALY approach to life-saving measures.

The respective rights of young and old – whether for health or welfare and income support – have not generally been articulated as sharply in this country as they have in the United States. The prevalence of 'burden of dependency' attitudes to old age are, however, reflections of a similar perspective. One American commentator has expressed the following view: 'the skewing effect of an aging society is that the economic imbalances caused by the provision of health care for the elderly potentially threaten the welfare of younger generations and of society as a whole . . . the stage is set for a profound confrontation' (Callahan, 1986).

Such 'a profound confrontation' has not yet occurred in Britain, perhaps in part because issues of cost and economics have been more easily concealed within a universal health care service such as the National Health Service, than they are within more market-driven systems. Questions of cost, however, are likely to become more explicit in the 'internal market' being developed within the National Health Service in the 1990s.

Discrimination in screening

If rationing or discriminatory decisions in health care are rarely made explicit within the National Health Service, such judgements are none the less made, and have typically been left to individual doctors. In some areas, however, guidelines *are* more explicit. The field of screening is one example. Despite the obvious appeal of the 'prevention is better than cure' maxim, the matter of screening apparently healthy populations for hidden or unreported disease is controversial. Much screening is experimental in nature, and of dubious – or unproven – benefit. There has, however, been considerable work in developing the concept of 'opportunistic' case-finding, which for older people means identifying those likely to need help or to develop health care problems. Such case-finding, it is suggested by some, should be applied annually to all people aged over 65. The belief underlying such proposals is that many older people are only referred for treatment at a late stage of dependency when treatment is less effective and more expensive. However, evidence suggests that such general screening may be inappropriate.

A review of screening and preventive care of older people by the Royal College of General Practitioners published in 1987 indicated particular 'high risk' groups for whom screening might be targeted. These risk indicators took account of both social and medical variables – for example, elderly patients receiving repeat prescriptions, or those recently widowed (Taylor and Buckley, 1987).

A 1986 report from the British Medical Association also suggested that universal screening is 'probably not justified', and that it could 'alarm some elderly people unnecessarily'. None the less, it was also pointed out that screening *could* be effective in uncovering treatable conditions which sufferers were otherwise likely to put up with as simply the inevitable consequence of old age. An attempt at geriatric screening in general practice in 1979, for example, found 145 patients aged over 70 with 400 conditions between them. More than a third of these conditions had been previously undetected, and two-thirds of the illnesses were manageable, while half of them were totally cleared up by treatment (British Medical Association, 1986).

The new contract for General Practitioners now stipulates that all patients aged over 75 should be offered an annual check-up and home visit where, if possible, assistance can be offered to cope with any undetected functional handicaps. The functional rather than case-finding approach to this screening raises different issues. It does offer some opportunity to counteract the disadvantage many older people experience in access to health services, and in the reluctance of doctors to make home visits.

There are strong arguments, however, for case-finding screening for particular conditions. Osteoporosis is one example. The Office of Health Economics (1990) observe that 'osteoporotic fractures in the elderly present a major health care and social problem which is largely preventable. The consequences of these fractures are enormous both socio-economically and as regards morbidity and mortality.' More than 46,000 people in England and Wales suffer hip fractures each year – 60 per cent of them are women aged at least 75. About a quarter of these people die as a result of their injuries and complications, and many more fail to regain full mobility. As well as the extreme distress and loss of life this condition can cause, the hospital costs of dealing with the fractures are some £160 million a year, and a fifth of orthopaedic beds are occupied by such cases (Royal College of Physicians, 1989).

The risk factors for osteoporosis are well known, yet despite its prevalence – perhaps 25 per cent of women are at risk of osteoporotic fractures – and the severe consequences of such fractures, little priority is currently attached to developing preventive and screening approaches to this condition. Such apathy is indicative of the generally low emphasis and under-investment in health education and preventive medicine in Britain (Whitehead, 1989). Without such a preventive drive, the cost will rise dramatically with the growth of the very elderly population. The Royal College of Physicians (1989), for example, calculate that if present trends continue, the incidence of hip fracture will increase to an annual 94,000 by 2006. This state of affairs is an example of discrimination against the needs of older people; it causes not only great suffering but also unnecessary economic costs.

The logic of any screening method is two-fold. First, that it detects the affected or at-risk groups, and second that these can then be referred for suitable treatment. In the case of osteoporosis there *are* preventive therapies, but insufficient research has been undertaken into the costs and benefits of hormone replacement therapy (HRT), calcitonin therapy and mineral supplements. The Office of Health Economics (1990) suggests that the benefits to be gained from HRT 'are far in excess of any known risks associated with its use'. The hospital cost alone of hip fractures in England and Wales was £128 million in

1985. In 1988 the total cost to the National Health Service of all osteoporotic fractures was an estimated £500 million. It is likely that HRT for post-menopausal women would reduce hip fractures by 50 per cent.

The example of osteoporosis helps to illustrate that it is not simply older *people* who suffer from inadequate and discriminating health care, more specifically it is older *women*. Because women generally outlive men, most very elderly people are women (almost 70 per cent of those aged over 75 and 75 per cent of those over 85), and it is conditions affecting older women where questions about equity in health care are particularly obvious.

If osteoporosis is one area where people suffer particularly because of inadequate attention to screening methods, cervical cancer provides an example of where screening processes *do* exist, but specifically exclude older citizens. Some 40 per cent of deaths from cancer of the cervix in England occur in women aged 65 or over. Department of Health guidelines, however, exclude screening or regular follow-up of women over 65, and none of the 94 per cent of district health authorities with a recall system includes women of this age. A recent analysis of such practices in *The Lancet* concluded that 'there seems to be no reason to exclude older women from regular screening for cancer of the cervix. On the contrary, since a high proportion of this age group have never had a smear or no recent smear, screening of this age group would have substantial benefits' (Fletcher, 1990). It cannot be assumed that women over 65 would have had an adequate screening history and therefore can be forgotten, or that there is no point in regular follow-up of older patients. In fact the screening rate of women in the excluded group has been low over the last 20 years – some 50–80 per cent of older women have never had a smear. The natural history of cervical cancer among older women is uncertain, but 'that little is known about the natural history of cancer of the cervix does not seem to have been an obstacle to the introduction of screening programmes for younger women' (Fletcher, 1990).

Opportunistic screening would, it is believed, identify more cases at an earlier stage. Women aged over 65 would benefit most, with a 63 per cent improvement in five-year mortality. To deny older women access to routine screening is both contra-indicated and explicitly discriminatory.

Sometimes screening which is not available to older women may not have proven effectiveness for the group to whom it is offered. Screening for breast cancer is usually offered to women aged 50–64. It is generally assumed that it is not cost-effective to screen either younger or older women, but the achievements of *any* screening in this area are unclear. Maureen Roberts (1989), the late Director of the Edinburgh Breast Screening Project, observed that screening 'is not offering any certainty of cure or normal life to the women who attend, merely a prolongation of years for a few. Not only that: we cannot predict who will have those extra years.'

Breast screening is a politically sensitive issue. Considerable resources are expended on screening and evaluation programmes. Yet it seems likely that resources would actually be better used in other prevention programmes. Such programmes should be directed at life-style rather than disease detection, and targeted at improving the health of women of all ages.

Discrimination against elderly people, however, appears to be a general feature of cancer treatment. About half of all new malignancies occur in people aged over 70, yet such cancers are often poorly treated and little understood. A recent paper in *The Lancet* observed that people aged over 70 are excluded from almost all clinical trials of cancer treatment, with the result that elderly patients 'receive either untested treatments, inadequate treatments, or even none at all, at the whim of their clinician' (Fentiman et al., 1990).

Many erroneous assumptions are made both about the nature of cancer in older people and the response to treatment. The under-treatment of cancer in older people means that many tumours which could be controlled or cured are not. The authors of the paper do not suggest ignoring the age of the patient, quite the reverse: 'criteria appropriate for younger patients may not be suitable in the elderly, for whom effective stabilisation of disease, a partial remission, or a complete remission of short duration may be sufficient to achieve worthwhile prolongation of life with an acceptable quality of life'. They argue that the same rigour should be applied to the study of older patients with cancer as for younger – 'only then will we see strikingly reduced population mortality and improved quality of life for older patients with cancer' (Fentiman et al., 1990). [. . .]

References

Age Concern Institute of Gerontology (1988) *The Living Will: Consent to Treatment at the End of Life, a Working Report.* London: Age Concern Institute of Gerontology and Centre for Medical Law Ethics.

Beardshaw, V. (1988) *Last on the List: Community Services for People with Physical Disabilities.* Research Report No. 3. London: King's Fund Institute.

British Medical Association (1986) *All Our Tomorrows: Growing Old in Britain.* Report of the British Medical Association's Board of Science and Education, London.

Callahan, D. (1986) 'Health care in the aging society: a moral dilemma', in A. Pifer and L. Bronte (eds), *Our Aging Society: Paradox and Promise.* London: W.W. Norton.

Fentiman, I.S., et al. (1990) 'Cancer in the elderly: why so badly treated?', *The Lancet*, 28 April, 335: 1020–2.

Fletcher, A. (1990) 'Screening for cancer of the cervix in elderly women', *The Lancet*, 28 April 335: 97–9.

Jennet, B. and Buxton, M. (1990) 'When is treatment for cancer economically justified?' Discussion paper, *Journal of the Royal Society of Medicine*, January, 83: 25–8.

Maynard, A. (1988) 'What can we afford?' Paper delivered at the 1988 MSD Foundation Symposium Review on *Health Care in Old Age: Choices in a Changing NHS*, London, November.

Office of Health Economics (1990) *Osteoporosis and the Risk of Fracture*. London: OHE.

Roberts, M.M. (1989) 'Breast screening: time for a re-think?', *British Medical Journal*, 4 November, 299: 1153–5.

Royal College of Physicians (1989) *Fractured Neck of Femur: Prevention and Management*. London: Royal College of Physicians of London.

Social Services Committee (1988) *Fifth Report on the Future of the NHS (Session 1987–88)*. London: HMSO.

Taylor, R.C. and Buckley, E.G. (eds) (1987) *Preventive Care of the Elderly: a Review of Current Developments*. London: Royal College of General Practitioners.

Weale, A. (ed.) (1988) *Cost and Choice in Health Care: the Ethical Dimension*. London: King Edward's Hospital Fund for London.

Whitehead, M. (1989) *Swimming Upstream: Trends and Prospects in Education for Health*. Research Report No. 5. London: King's Fund Institute.

21

Does group living work?

Julia Johnson

The potential for institutional living to deprive residents of autonomy and privacy and to induce dependency and apathy has been well documented over the last 30 years. The need to develop more resident-oriented regimes in residential care is now established. Indeed, over 20 years ago, the revised Local Authority Building Note (DHSS and Welsh Office, 1973) on the design of residential homes for older people advocated the concept of group living as a way of promoting more autonomy and control on the part of residents. This was supported by research which reported positive outcomes of group living (Hitch and Simpson, 1972; Lipman and Slater, 1977; Marston and Gupta, 1977; Wyvern Partnership, 1979). But how is successful group living achieved?

Arden House and Parkview[1]

I first visited Arden House in 1973. It was lunchtime and I anticipated a dining-room full of residents with walking frames and staff bustling around, the clatter of pots and pans in the kitchen and the inevitable music in the background. To my surprise, I found none of these things on my arrival. What might have been the dining-room was empty, there were no sounds of catering and no staff rushing about. I was met by a member of staff who was quiet and relaxed, and who invited me to sit down to a cup of coffee. Yes, the residents were eating lunch in their own lounges. And where were the staff? They were having their own meal in the staff room at the end of the corridor.

I was to find out much more about Arden House over the next few weeks. But, I was also to discover Parkview. This home was run by the same local authority using identical admission criteria, had opened within three months of Arden House, was architecturally identical and had the same fittings and furnishings, even down to the cups and saucers. Despite these similarities, entering Parkview was a completely different experience. It was exactly what I had first anticipated and feared. How could such a different world have been created in an identical physical environment?

Nearly 10 years later, I spent six months in each home, making daily recordings of the words and deeds of both the staff and the residents. For this, I used structured observation schedules (Evans et al., 1981) which enabled me to gather a rich fund of both qualitative and quantitative data. A full account of the way in which this study was undertaken and of its findings can be found elsewhere (Johnson, 1982). In this chapter, I shall describe something of what I learned, through comparing these two homes, about how group living can work. For, it is through detailed observation of organisation and behaviour that we can begin to understand process as well as outcome.

The building

Each home accommodated 42 residents. The homes were purpose-built for a traditional form of residential care where meals would be taken in a central dining-room and served through a hatch from the adjoining kitchen. Parkview was used in this way. Residents took all their meals in the central dining-room, they were each allocated to one of the five lounges for sitting in during the day, and hairdressing or medical appointments were conducted in the medical room. At Arden House, on the other hand, some inexpensive but crucial changes had been made at the instigation of the officer-in-charge. For example, the sluices at the end of each corridor had been removed and converted into kitchenettes, and dining tables had been redistributed from the central dining room to nine small dining areas created in various ways around the home. In effect this meant that nine separate groups of four or five residents ate together in their own dining areas, each having access to their own kitchenette for washing up. Each group was supplied with a small refrigerator, kettle, crockery and cutlery so that residents could make their own breakfasts, tea or coffee. Also a trolley was supplied to each so that they could collect lunch and dinner for their group from the main kitchen.

Arden House had, therefore, used the building to create discrete and manageable living areas for small groups of residents. These living areas had all facilities close at hand – dining areas, living-room, bedroom, kitchen, toilet and bathroom. Distances to be covered were small and more manageable therefore for the less able-bodied.

A critical feature of Arden House was the composition of these small groups. The Crichton Royal Behavioural Rating Scale (CRBRS) measurements showed that each group at Arden House was composed of a variety of residents ranging from severely disabled (either physically or mentally) to quite able. Hence, the more able residents could assist the less able where necessary. At Parkview, however, residents had been categorised and grouped so that 'the confused' occupied one of the two downstairs lounges and 'the immobile' the other. Here they could be easily monitored by staff and conveniently attended to. The upstairs lounges contained more able residents whose demands upon staff time were less. Unlike Arden House, where a resident slept was not necessarily close to where her daily lounge was. As a result a day-time journey from lounge to bedroom at Parkview might be impossible without aid.

Organisational routines and practices

Table 21.1 indicates an astonishing difference in levels of staffing between the two homes, Parkview consuming near twice as many staff hours as Arden House.

Table 21.1 *Staffing at Parkview and Arden House*

Staff category	Parkview		Arden House	
	Staff numbers	Weekly hours	Staff numbers	Weekly hours
Supervisory	5	143	4	145
Care assistants	10	244	8	123
Domestics	6	129	2	23
Cooks	3	56	2	39
Night care assistants	7	128	3	70
Total	31	700	19	400

The daily routine at Parkview dictated the need for more staff. For example, all 42 residents had to be assembled in the central dining-room four times a day. Ensuring that all were thus assembled put enormous pressure on staff, particularly in the mornings. Many residents had to be assisted with washing and dressing to ensure that deadlines were met, and then escorted on long journeys to the dining-room. The 'block treatment' of residents, therefore, was extremely consuming of staff time and effort. This had the added effect of stripping many residents of their independence and competence by preventing them from being able to manage for themselves in their own time.

All snacks and meals at Parkview were prepared in the central kitchen by domestic staff, served to residents by staff, cleared away and washed up by staff. This also demanded staff hours and meant that for large parts of the day the kitchen was buzzing with activity. In contrast, at Arden House, breakfast, tea and coffee were prepared and cleared away by residents according to their own individual schedules. Main meals were prepared by the cook, collected from the kitchen by the residents, and cleared away and washed up by the residents in their own kitchenettes. Clean serving dishes were then returned to the main kitchen by the residents for the next meal. Hence for large parts of the day the central kitchen was empty and spotlessly clean.

These contrasting daily routines had a fundamental effect on the way in which staff worked. The routine at Parkview produced a predominantly 'doing for' style, whilst that at Arden House produced more of a 'doing with' or 'maintaining a discreet distance' style. Over two and a half times as many staff hours per week were given to 'functional' care (i.e. doing for) at Parkview as compared to Arden House.

Staff activity

The larger number of staff at Parkview created clearer divisions of labour between different categories of staff. The supervisory staff focused mainly (but not exclusively) on administrative work and were to be found frequently in the office. It was here that they had their tea breaks too, served to them by the kitchen staff. The care assistants focused mainly on physical care activities – helping residents to the toilet, bathing, dressing and so on. Their shifts included unpaid tea breaks which were taken in the staff room together with the domestic staff, whose activities centred on cleaning, food preparation and washing up. There was, of course, some overlap between the work undertaken by different categories of staff but demarcation lines were fairly clear, and all care and domestic staff belonged to a trade union.

At Arden House there were fewer members of staff and the division of labour was more flexible. It was not unusual to find the officer-in-charge wielding a vacuum cleaner and the office was more commonly locked than open and occupied. A staff shift rarely involved more than one supervisory member of staff and one care assistant, and tea and meal breaks were taken together in the staff room. None of the care and domestic staff belonged to a trade union. In effect, a less conflictual and hierarchical system prevailed at Arden House and the exchange of information about the care of individual residents was less complicated and more direct.

Staff/resident interaction

Significant differences in the nature of communication between staff and residents were found in the two homes. At Parkview, there was a higher proportion of purely instrumental verbal communication by staff, such as instructing a resident to go to the toilet without any further verbal elaboration. Furthermore, when a staff member was observed in interaction with a resident, the response of the resident was, on 35 per cent of occasions, completely passive. This compared to only 6 per cent of such occasions at Arden House. Since there were more staff per shift at Parkview, residents were far more likely to be interacting with more than one member of staff at any one time. This of course increased the danger of a resident being 'talked over' and decreased her chances of equal and active engagement. One to one staff/resident interactions were observed on only 38 per cent of occasions compared to 92 per cent at Arden House.

All residents at Parkview were called by their first names. Pet names, other terms of endearment and infantilising words were sometimes employed. One resident was observed requesting, and being rewarded with, a sweet for 'being a good girl'. They were often treated, and behaved, like children and frequently resorted to staff to resolve arguments with other residents. At Arden House, titles such as Mr and Mrs were used by staff to address residents who, with one exception, never requested to be addressed otherwise. Residents here tended to resolve their own disputes, and indeed many other daily problems.

Resident activity and interaction

The pattern of interaction among residents was significantly different. Observing individual residents in their lounges, during waking hours, was a relatively easy matter at Parkview because, apart from meal times, residents tended to be gathered together in their lounges. At Arden House, however, this was not so simple because, apart from meal times, residents were rarely gathered together. Generally speaking, only two or three might be in the lounge while others in the group were elsewhere – most often in their own room. This suggests that residents at Arden House claimed more individual privacy than those at Parkview and engaged in more individual action. Residents at Parkview were discouraged from using their own rooms in the day time – apart from two, who spent all their time in their rooms.

More time was spent engaged in daily living activities (e.g. making tea, washing up) as opposed to social recreation (e.g. chatting or watching television) by residents at Arden House. The converse applied at Parkview. Over half the residents at Arden House were actively involved in domestic routines on a regular basis, and physical limitations or mental confusion did not preclude such involvement.

Residents at Arden House were less likely to rely upon staff assistance with dressing or moving around than at Parkview, and the use of walkin... ds was markedly lower. A culture had developed at Arden House wh...e... y those who arrived at the home with a zimmer frame might become inclined to give it up. One resident told me,

> I can't walk very well. I used to have a frame but I gave it up the day I came here because I wanted to walk and it was in the way. Nobody suggested that I shouldn't use it – but at the hospital, where I was before, I wasn't allowed to be without it.

Residents were actively encouraged to make use of the handrails from the start. Commenting upon the admission of Miss Webb, a new resident to the home, the officer-in-charge said,

> Pointing the resident to the handrail is much more important than propping her up personally. If the staff make this early mistake, Miss Webb will always be looking to staff for assistance. It is all too easy to create dependence within the first few hours.

The benefits of the trolley were also promoted,

> How much better is the trolley, with things on it, than a zimmer, because the trolley means you are going somewhere to do something.

In contrast, the use of walking aids was encouraged at Parkview. I observed one new resident, on the day of her arrival from hospital, having her familiar stick replaced by a walking frame, despite clear indications that she did not need it or want it. In my view, the staff saw the provision of such an aid as therapeutic and indicative of their own expertise in matters of 'rehabilitation'. The same resident was also informed that she would neither have to, nor be able to, use the lift on her own. In contrast, Miss Webb was shown into the lift and used it, on her own, within minutes of her arrival at Arden House.

Discussion

In the early 1980s, Willcocks et al. (1987) conducted a survey of 100 local authority homes. Only 11 of these were run along group living lines. Although positive outcomes of group living were reported, staff in these homes felt that it was 'more work and more worry' and required more staff (1987: 131). In addition, staff expressed anxieties about 'personality clashes' between residents, individual residents becoming isolated, and particular individuals dominating others. Overall, the researchers' impression was that staff in these homes were reluctant to relinquish control. Dixon (1991), in her attempts as an action researcher to help staff to develop more resident-oriented practices, also found attitudes to be the biggest stumbling block: in truth, she commented, staff saw residents as 'less than whole people'.

Booth, in a study of 175 homes, reported somewhat negatively on group living (Booth, 1985; Booth and Phillips, 1987). He conceded, however, that the design and methods of his study precluded an examination of the relationship between group living and the subjective well-being of residents, or a test of the argument that group living reduces loneliness and passivity and increases interaction and self-esteem. Most significantly, he acknowledged that the findings of his research might not point to flaws in the principles of group living so much as to failures in their implementation.

I concluded from my study that group living can work. The residents of Arden House were more active, confident and competent and less reliant upon staff for assistance. They exercised more choice over their daily lives and claimed more privacy for themselves. This was due to a subtle combination of factors related to physical surroundings, staffing levels, shift systems, daily routines and staff attitudes and actions.

Perhaps fundamental to this regime was the belief of the officer-in-charge that residents wanted and were able to continue to involve themselves in ordinary and familiar activities. From the start, she had been able to select staff who she thought could share and implement her convictions and, thereby, develop a non-intrusive style of working. The conclusion that the leadership of the officer-in-charge is critical has recently been supported by the research of Gibbs and Sinclair (1992) into homes in the private sector.

The comparatively low numbers of staff at Arden House, combined with the decentralised arrangements, contributed towards achieving privacy and self-reliance for the residents. However, to advocate low staff ratios may be dangerous. There is a world of difference between a small, committed, vigilant, well-trained and supervised staff team and a small group of inadequately paid, inadequately supported and inexperienced staff.

In 1993, the direct provision of residential care by local authorities is diminishing and a mixed economy of care has evolved. It is suggested that local authorities may be providing increasingly for the most disabled older people. The establishment of 'high dependency' and 'elderly mentally confused' units within homes is not uncommon. Other developments include the increasing division of labour within a home between managerial and administrative staff, senior care staff, care staff and domestics, together with an emphasis on 'key working' and 'individual care plans'. The study of Arden House shows that group living can work. But to what extent are current developments compatible with its principles and successful implementation?

Note

1. The names 'Arden House' and 'Parkview' are both fictional substitutions for the names of the residential homes discussed here.

References

Booth, T. (1985) *Home Truths: Old People's Homes and the Outcome of Care.* Aldershot: Gower.

Booth, T. and Phillips, D. (1987) 'Group living in homes for the elderly: a comparative study of the outcome of care', *British Journal of Social Work,* 17: 1-20.

DHSS and Welsh Office (1973) *Local Authority Building Note No. 2: Residential Accommodation for Elderly People.* London: HMSO.

Dixon, S. (1991) *Autonomy and Dependence in Residential Care.* London: Age Concern Institute of Gerontology.

Evans, G., Hughes, B., Wilkin, D. with Jolley, D. (1981) *The Management of Mental and Physical Impairment in Non-specialist Residential Homes for the Elderly.* Research Report No. 4. Manchester: University Hospital of South Manchester, Psychogeriatric Unit Research Section.

Gibbs, I. and Sinclair, I. (1992) 'Residential care for elderly people: the correlates of quality', *Ageing and Society,* 12 (4): 463-82.

Hitch, D. and Simpson, A. (1972), 'An attempt to assess a new design in residential homes for the elderly', *British Journal of Social Work,* 2: 481-501.

Johnson, J. (1982) 'Two residential homes for the elderly: a comparative study'. Unpublished MA thesis, University of Keele.

Lipman, A. and Slater, R. (1977) 'Homes for old people: toward a positive environment', *The Gerontologist,* 17 (2): 146-56.

Marston, N. and Gupta, H. (1977) 'Interesting the old', *Community Care,* 16 November.

Willcocks, D.M., Peace, S.M. and Kellaher, L.A. (1987) *Private Lives in Public Places: a Research-based Critique of Residential Life in Local Authority Old People's Homes.* London: Tavistock.

Wyvern Partnership/Social Services Unit, University of Birmingham (1979) *An Evaluation of the Group Living Design for Old People's Homes.*

22

A holistic approach in the ward

Helen Passant

The practice of holistic care in my ward originated from the practice of primary nursing. Let me explain.

I came to the Churchill Hospital in Oxford during an informal visit to Sir Michael Sobell House for the care of the dying, as they wanted another sister. I was delighted by what I saw – flowers and plants everywhere, attractive decor and new furniture. This is it, I thought; this is where I should like to nurse, and decided to apply for the post.

As I was walking to the office to get the necessary papers for my application, the nursing officer said: 'We have another ward without a sister. Would you like to see it?' My mind was on Michael Sobell House, but I did not want to appear rude by refusing her offer. Therefore I said yes, and she took me through a door off the main corridor into Ward 8 for the continuing care of the elderly, known as the geriatric ward.

What I saw dismayed me. It was a ward for very elderly frail and disabled women; the chairs were tattered and old, the decor dull and dirty. The nursing officer introduced me to an old woman sitting in a wheelchair, her feet elevated on a wooden stool. She clutched my hand tightly and lifted it to her mouth and kissed it, whispering to me: 'Are you going to be our new sister?' I whispered back: 'Yes.'

Primary nursing was still in its infancy then; concepts were being discussed, models of nursing and care plans tentatively approached, but a true understanding of the philosophy of care was not yet fully realised. We were short of staff on Ward 8 as usual, but decided we wanted to move in the direction of individualised nursing care. So I became, as well as the ward sister, a primary nurse to four patients and an associate nurse for another four, as well as being co-ordinator for the whole ward.

Being a primary nurse was in many ways very fulfilling, yet I remained dissatisfied. My patients were bathed and washed, dressed neatly, fed and hydrated, given medication to ease aches and pains;

From *Nursing Times*, 86 (4), 24 January 1990, pp. 26–8.

they played bingo and received visitors. It did not seem like nursing to me – and certainly my patients were not living to the full.

I began to look outside conventional methods of care – at complementary therapies which would enhance our nursing. I attended a conference on holistic medicine and participated in a workshop in massage. It was a revelation. I could not wait to get back to share my experiences with my patients – or get properly trained. Later that year I studied massage and healing techniques, as a result of which I began to massage my patients, using herbal oils, and taught my staff to do likewise. The oils strengthened elderly skin, making it more elastic, thus preventing bruising and damage to the tissue.

We also began to use essential oils to enhance the effect of massage and discovered that we were able to reduce conventional sedative drugs to a minimum. A bath with essential oils followed by massage plus a few drops of oil on the pillow induced peaceful sleep. We used the oils intuitively. Lavender and rose geranium were used for patients suffering from dementia; cedarwood for mood swings and chest problems; cardamom for memory; lavender for headache and muscular pain; and so on.

Massage brought many benefits to our patients. Touching in this beautiful and asexual way opened the doors to a closer relationship with us, allowing patients to speak of their dreams and hopes, of their fears and pleasures. To relieve stress and pain on all levels was something I had not thought possible – but it is.

I began to investigate the herbs that had been used in ancient times for healing. As a result, we used remedies such as garlic, in ointment form, for fungal infections, comfrey for bruises, abrasions and sores, chickweed for itchy skins, rosemary for problems of the scalp and eyebright for minor eye infections.

We had great success with our herbal preparations. Patients with skin problems, who had been treated for years with steroid creams, were now treated by us with garlic ointment and were healed. Skin massaged with comfrey oil each day became strong and elastic, able to withstand pressure.

Our consultant gave us support and, when I asked if I could use a herbal preparation for people with a persistent skin problem, he inquired: 'What do you want to use?' 'Garlic,' I answered. His moustache twitched. 'At least it will keep the devils away. Sister,' he said.

I used the garlic, and the patients' skin became soft and pink and started to heal. The consultant wrote in his notes the remedy that had been used. Working with doctors in this way was new and brought us closer together as a team.

Our consultant observed that we used fewer laxatives and sedatives in the ward and that, overall, there was less drug-prescribing. The professor of geriatric medicine was also very supportive and always included any herbal remedies used on the drug c rts anu notes. The pharmacists were very helpful and our supply of comfrey came from them.

I had suffered for many years from arthritis and had tried everything, including herbal medicine. Nothing really provided relief of pain, until I tried dietary therapy. After 20 years of pain, swollen joints and disfigurement, I decided I had nothing to lose. With my new diet the pain went and I was able to move about easily. My energy increased and I was overjoyed - but how did it work?

I took a diploma in nutrition to discover the effect of food on the body and began to look at the effect of food and food additives on our patients. It was one of the most exciting discoveries I have ever made. The staff looked at behaviour problems and compiled charts monitoring such things as food intake, behaviour before and after food, before and after patients had visitors, during the night, after elimination, with and without medication. We discovered that some patients' problems were due to certain foods, combination of foods - or food and drugs that work in opposition - and so we began our nutritional regime.

We also played music and sounds of a healing nature in the ward. We selected pieces for different disorders; for example, for someone who appears lethargic and listless the sound of the flute may bring about curiosity; for someone restless in body and mind sounds of nature will often quieten them; birdsong and water sounds may bring peace; in the evening, music that is enchanting and haunting in melody may bring rest.

Sometimes we sit together, staff, patients and relatives, holding hands as we use visualisation techniques to take a walk in bluebell woods or through spring rain, float down a river to the sea or soar into space. I teach patients that the mind can move anywhere, even though the body may be immobile. Visualisation can be used for pain control. For example, you can imagine away a red-hot pain in the knee by making it travel slowly from the joint down the leg and out of the tip of the big toe. This visualisation can be done with the co-operation of the patient. My hands will rest on the knee, and we visualise the pain - red in colour, as the patient describes it - and then slowly I move my hand down the inside of the leg very gently, down the side of the foot and out of the big toe. We visualise a hot, red ball of fire leaving the toe and disappearing into the air. And it works!

Our patients come to us shattered, angry, full of pain, not just physical pain but the pain of separation from loved ones, a lifetime spent building relationships, homes and families. Now all they have is a hospital bed and a locker, living with noises and smells they have never encountered before. What can be done? We work together to bring peace and harmony to body and mind.

The past few years have not always been easy. My ward closed and

I had to start again. Nursing union representatives sometimes questioned our care, and we were sometimes ridiculed by colleagues. But we held fast – holistic care, by its very nature cannot be denied if we are to nurse the sick properly and care for one another.

I visit hospitals talking to nurses about holistic care, teaching holistic massage and giving workshops in nutrition. In addition, I encourage my staff, who tirelessly raise funds for essential oils, supplementary fresh fruit and vegetables and so on, to write about what we are doing. It is important to spread the word.

23

Elderly people: their medicines and their doctors

Drug and Therapeutics Bulletin

We last discussed the special needs and problems of medication for elderly patients [in 1984][1] after a Royal College of Physicians (1984) report on the subject. This article takes its title from a large descriptive survey undertaken shortly after (Cartwright and Smith, 1988).

Between 1977 and 1985 Department of Health prescribing data showed several important trends, including a 27 per cent increase in the average number of prescription items per person of pensionable age, compared with a 6 per cent decrease in younger patients. Total prescriptions for all ages of 'sedatives and tranquillisers' decreased by 35 per cent while those for cardiovascular drugs increased by 37 per cent. Prescribing practice and patients' compliance with prescribed regimens, as well as the effects of age on the pharmacokinetics and pharmacodynamics of drugs, make older patients more vulnerable to adverse drug reactions. The survey examined these practical aspects and drew a number of important conclusions.

The survey

Data were obtained from 78 per cent (805/1032) of a structured random sample of people aged 65 or over drawn from electoral registers in 10 parliamentary constituencies in England. [. . .] Despite a 22 per cent failure to interview rate, the sample remained representative compared with official (OPCS) national data. Information was also sought from the patients' general practitioners. Only 55 per cent responded to a general questionnaire about their prescribing for the elderly. Where patient and doctor agreed, doctors were also asked about individual patients. This provided information on 39 per cent of the patients interviewed. [. . .]

From *Drug and Therapeutics Bulletin*, 28 (20), 1 October 1990: 77–9 (abridged).

Main findings

Prescribing pattern

Seventy per cent of the people interviewed had been prescribed medication. Sixty per cent had taken one or more prescribed drugs within the previous 24 hours. An average of 2.8 drugs had been prescribed per patient. Those most commonly prescribed were for the heart and circulation (32 per cent), the central nervous system (24 per cent including aspirin and analgesics), for musculoskeletal and joint diseases (10 per cent), for gastrointestinal (8 per cent) and respiratory problems (7 per cent).

Specific drug categories

The most widely used drugs, which together accounted for 45 per cent of total prescribing in the survey, were, in decreasing order of frequency: diuretics; analgesics; hypnotics, sedatives and anxiolytics; antirheumatic drugs and β blockers. Some of these have been singled out before as prone to excessive or inappropriate use in the elderly.

The extensive use of *diuretics* (25 per cent of the survey sample) suggests some inappropriate use, such as for uncomplicated gravitational oedema or 'maintenance' after resolution of mild congestive cardiac failure. Careful withdrawal of diuretics in selected patients should be considered in view of the risks of these drugs, which include postural hypotension and incontinence, hypokalaemia and hypomagnesaemia and disturbances of renal function, urate metabolism and glucose homeostasis. There are adverse effects on cardiac output if doses are excessive. Hyponatraemia especially when combined with a thiazide or loop diuretic and hyperikalaemia can occur with potassium-sparing preparations (one third of diuretic prescriptions in the survey).

Six per cent of those interviewed were taking a *cardiac glycoside*. The prevalence of atrial fibrillation (AF) in those at home is 2 per cent in the age group 65–74 and 5 per cent in the over 75s (Campbell et al., 1974). In many, the ventricular rate is not fast and so does not require treatment. This scale of prescribing therefore suggests some inappropriate long-term use of digoxin in elderly patients in sinus rhythm or slow AF.

The extensive use of β blockers (11 per cent of those on medication) might also be debated now since alternatives can be used for both hypertension and angina in older patients.

The extent of prescribing specifically for *hypertension* does not emerge from the data, mainly because the BNF (British National Formulary) does not classify β blockers and diuretics as antihypertensives. Treatment has benefits (European Working Party, 1985) but caution is still necessary because of the frequency of unwanted effects from antihypertensive medication in old age. Over the age of 80 the risk/benefit ratio increases sharply and is still ill defined (European Working Party, 1986).

Between 15–20 per cent of those interviewed were taking a *non-steroidal anti-inflammatory drug* (including aspirin). The risks of peptic ulceration, serious gastrointestinal haemorrhage and nephrotoxicity are known to be age related (Bailey, 1988; Langman, 1986)[2] and one wonders how many older patients receive a satisfactory trial of regular analgesic use (e.g. paracetamol or in some cases local injection) before using an NSAID.

The findings with *sedatives and anxiolytics* (15 per cent of those interviewed; 90 per cent of recipients started outside hospital) highlight potential problems of over-consumption and dependence. Enhanced sensitivity in the elderly increases the risk of hangover sedation, postural instability and cognitive and psychomotor performance impairment (Swift, 1982).

Duration and review of therapy

Fifty-nine per cent of prescriptions had been given for more than two years, 32 per cent for more than five years and 16 per cent for more than 10 years. Eighty-eight per cent of these were by repeat prescription and 40 per cent had not been discussed with the doctor for at least six months (especially hypnotics and anxiolytics).

Appropriateness

A number of assessments were made by pharmacists working with a clinical pharmacologist. Inappropriate dosage was identified for some drugs (e.g. in 36 per cent of hypnotic prescriptions the dose exceeded the manufacturer's recommendation). The prescribed regimen was considered 'pharmacologically open to question' in 31 per cent. Such assessments of appropriateness do not supercede clinical judgement, but the finding that 4 per cent showed duplication (e.g. Inderal plus propranolol, Indocid plus Butazolidin) and 17 per cent potentially harmful interactions, suggests the need for greater vigilance by individual prescribers. The survey preceded the introduction of the Limited List.[3]

Adherence of patients to prescribed regimens

Comprehension

The elderly people claimed to take most (75 per cent) of their prescribed drugs as advised. Comprehension of the purpose and nature of the regimen were strikingly high, only 4 per cent being assessed as having no knowledge and 5 per cent erroneous knowledge (17 per cent over the age of 90) of the reasons for their medication.

Twenty per cent of patients had understood their prescribers' personal instructions on the regimen to be different from those given on the label. The issue was usually between 'as required' and regular use. Written instructions were generally of poor quality, over 20 per cent of containers being labelled 'as before' or 'as directed', 31 per cent being hand-written and 14 per cent undated. The introduction of mandatory typed labelling by pharmacists will since have improved legibility, but prescriber and pharmacist remain jointly responsible for the content and quality of written instructions – of undoubted importance in drug compliance – and communication between them must be effective.

Concordance between patient and prescriber

Twenty-eight per cent of prescribed medicines identified by the GPs were unreported by the corresponding patients, while 36 per cent of medicines were reported by the patient but not the doctor. Such discrepancies have been found in previous studies (Gibson and O'Hare, 1968; Price et al., 1986). Inaccurate general practice and hospital records (70 per cent of one series of 59 patients seen with their medicines: Price et al., 1986) and the independent prescription of some medicines directly from hospital (7 per cent of all medicines reported only by the patient in this study) appear to contribute. The drugs involved included potentially toxic ones in the categories most commonly prescribed as well as topical corticosteroids and oral hypoglycaemic drugs.

Other data on doctor/patient contact caused concern. Of one third of patients living alone, their GPs were unaware of this. GPs did not know the alcohol habits of two-thirds, whether or not they drove for half, or of adverse drug reactions (ADRs) reported for 15–30 per cent. Between 30–40 per cent of patients were agreed to have had only one or no consultations within the previous 12 months. Some of the above (such as doctor/patient discrepancy, numbers of potentially interacting preparations and the percentage of long-term repeat prescriptions) occurred whether or not the practice used repeat prescription cards. Data on practices with and without computers were insufficient to assess any impact. Although 61 per cent of practices had a stated policy on repeat prescriptions, many had not yet successfully implemented it.

Conclusion and recommendations

- The impact on the elderly of general trends in prescribing has again been emphasised.
- Every general practice and hospital department concerned with

elderly patients should audit its prescribing for the elderly at regular practice/departmental meetings.

- Prescribers should take particular note of the manufacturers' data sheet recommendations for elderly recipients. These are mandatory for all new products and widely available for established ones.
- Prescribers should document prescribing much better to ensure continuity between hospital and community (e.g. facsimile, computer-readable cards carried by the patient). Risk factors, such as social isolation, alcohol consumption, use of over-the-counter medication and the occurrence of ADRs need reliable documentation.
- Prescribers should inspect patients' drug supplies at every consultation to avoid confusing discrepancies. Screening under the new GP contract may facilitate this, and community nurses and pharmacists should have important roles in helping to monitor drug compliance.
- Every practice/department should establish its own defined mechanism for reviewing prescriptions for elderly patients regularly with particular reference to continued indication, duration of therapy, total number of medicines prescribed, possible duplication or interactions and likelihood of compliance.

Notes

1. *Drug and Therapeutics Bulletin*, 22, 1984: 49–52.
2. See also *Drug and Therapeutics Bulletin*, 25, 1987: 81–4.
3. Editors' Note – Two-fifths of the prescribed medicines that were 'pharmacologically open to question' were not available under the NHS after the introduction of the Limited List.

References

Bailey, R.R. (1988) *Adverse Drug Reaction Bulletin*, 131: 492–5.
Campbell, A., Caird, F.I. and Jackson, T.F.M. (1974) *British Heart Journal*, 36: 1005–11.
Cartwright, A. and Smith, C. (1988) *Elderly People: Their Medicines and Their Doctors*. London: Routledge.
European Working Party on High Blood Pressure in the Elderly Trial (1985) *The Lancet*, 15 September, 1: 1349–54.
European Working Party on High Blood Pressure in the Elderly Trial (1986) *The Lancet*, 13 September, 2: 589–92.
Gibson, I.I.J.M. and O'Hare, M.M. (1968) *Gerontologia Clinica*, 10: 271–80.
Langman, M.J.S. (1986) *Adverse Drug Reaction Bulletin*, 120: 448–51.
Price, D., Cooke, J., Singleton, S. and Feely, M. (1986) 'Doctors' unawareness of the drugs their patients are taking: a major cause of overprescribing?', *British Medical Journal*, 11 January, 292 (6513): 99–100.
Royal College of Physicians (1984) 'Report on medication for the elderly', *Journal of the Royal College of Physicians*, 18: 7–17.
Swift, C.G. (1982) 'Hypnotic Drugs', in B. Isaacs (ed.), *Recent Advances in Geriatric Medicine*, Vol. 2. London: Churchill Livingstone. pp. 123–46.

24

Assessing risk

Alison Norman

Losing your home

It is not sufficiently realised that the loss of one's home – however good the reasons for leaving it – can be experienced as a form of bereavement and can produce the same grief reaction as the loss of a close relative. Peter Marris (1974) in his book *Loss and Change* quotes a study of the reactions of families moved from the West End of Boston under an urban renewal scheme in which it was concluded that

> for the majority it seems quite precise to speak of their reactions as expressions of *grief*. These are manifest in the feelings of painful loss, the continued longing, the general depressive tone, frequent symptoms of psychological or social or somatic distress, the active work required in adapting to the altered situation, the sense of helplessness, the occasional expressions of both direct and displaced anger, and the tendencies to idealise the lost place. At their most extreme, these reactions of grief are intense, deeply felt and, at times, overwhelming. [. . .] (Marris, 1974: 43)

[For] old people who are moved into sheltered housing or residential care [. . .] the sense of loss must surely be equally great [. . .]. Indeed it may be greater if, in the process, they have to sacrifice not only a home and neighbourhood but the greater part of the possessions of a lifetime. It must also be true that they are likely to work through the loss only if they make a positive identification with their new life. If they are being moved in conformity with ruling social values which are offended by letting them stay where they are, or are forced to go by the physical duress of having no viable alternative, they are still less likely to recover from the loss.

A good deal of research data [. . .] supports such a conclusion, and it is clear that the loss of a home may be particularly serious for those who are mentally impaired, physically ill, or depressed and thus unable to make a positive effort to identify with the new life. [. . .]

'Losing your home' from *Rights and Risk*. London: Centre for Policy on Ageing, 1980, pp. 14–28 (abridged); 'Dangers and advantages' originally published as 'Risk', in B. Gearing, M. Johnson and T. Heller (eds), *Mental Health Problems in Old Age*. Milton Keynes: Open University Press, 1988, pp. 82–6 (abridged).

M.A. Lieberman (1974), in an important paper on relocation and social policy, [. . .] concludes that [. . .] 'Relocation is a risk to the individual not because of the symbolic meaning that such transitions imply, but because it entails radical changes in the life space of an individual that require new learning for adaptive purposes. Over and over again, studies on relocation report findings that physical status, cognitive ability and certain other characteristics of personality are powerful predictors to the outcome of relocation.' In other words, those who need institutional support the *least* are those who are most likely to survive the move into it, and 'it is often the very people who require supportive services that can be shown to entail the greatest risk'. [. . .]

A study of fatal home accidents made [. . .] by the Tavistock Institute of Human Relations on behalf of the Department of Prices and Consumer Protection (Poyner and Hughes, 1978) also suggest that old people are not necessarily safer when they are 'in care'. The authors found that out of 133 fatal accidents studied in the 65 and over age group (75 per cent caused by falls) 35 per cent were in institutional care, although only 4.8 per cent of this age group live in institutions. They comment 'Even considering that residential institutions contain a higher proportion of the infirm, the difference in accidental deaths high.'

It would seem to follow [. . .] that if avoidance of 'risk' is indeed a prime objective, moving people out of their homes may not be the best way of achieving it, and that the more they appear to be at risk where they are, the worse will be their prognosis if they are moved. Yet this is a factor which is so seldom taken into consideration when considering transfer into residential care, and still less is it taken into consideration when deciding on hospital admission. [. . .]

[Often] it is much easier for an elderly person to become a hospital patient than to cease to be one. There are a number of reasons for this. The 'social space' in which the person has been living may close behind him on admission, so that he cannot get back. A family may heave a sigh of relief, having realised, perhaps for the first time, what a burden it has been carrying and say 'he's not coming back here'. A landlord may take the opportunity to re-possess his house, or the warden of a sheltered housing complex say 'He needs too much nursing now, I can't cope.' Ironically, it is often the person who would appear to be most at risk, who lives alone in his own home, who is in least danger of having his social space close up on him.

It is also often the case that if a person has only just been coping with independent life, hospital admission breaks a tenuous level of confidence which can only be restored with time, care and skill. Elderly people who are suffering from some degree of dementia are especially at risk because the experience of admission to a totally strange and unfamiliar environment is likely to increase confusion and generate problems such as falling and incontinence which may not have been present before.

Another possibility is that hospital 'investigation' may show up undiagnosed diseases which a person has been living with for years, but which, once diagnosed, the hospital may feel compelled to treat. Observation after a fall may then become treatment for something quite different, so that the person is confirmed in his patient status. Moreover, if the person is being treated in an acute ward, the nursing staff may not have the time, interest or training to help the patient to retain independence and mobility [. . .]. A period of treatment in an acute ward may therefore mean that an elderly person requires a prolonged period of rehabilitation in a geriatric ward before he can recover his skills sufficiently to manage at home again – and the longer the period in hospital, the more likely it is that the 'social space' at home will have closed up.

For all these reasons, hospital admission – which can undoubtedly be 'life-saving' – may also be dangerous to elderly people, and the dangers need to be weighed against the advantages when deciding whether or not to admit someone to hospital.

Many of the comments made above about the way in which elderly people become patients apply with equal force to the way in which they become residents in old people's homes. Indeed, in some ways the process appears often to be an even more arbitrary response to social fears and pressures, or the failure of social support, rather than to be a carefully thought-out assessment of alternatives. [. . .]

[One] fault in the usual procedure for deciding that admission to residential care is necessary is that there is seldom a medical assessment to check whether the mental or physical condition which is causing concern can be remedied. For example, whether confusion might be caused by 'drug cocktails', or self-neglect by depression. [. . .]

Medical assessment may be inadequate for those moving from their own homes into residential care but there is also uncertainty about the adequacy of social assessment when people are discharged from hospital into a home. This is a very common route into residential care [. . .] and it seems likely that at least some of these cases arise because hospital staff are too anxious to allow the patient to try out his independence at home and (perhaps partly because of staff anxiety) the patient has lost confidence in his own ability to cope. Further, as has been noted, admission to hospital may cause a patient's social space to close behind him [. . .]. In these circumstances, homes may resist admitting ex-hospital patients who really are dependent and need residential care because they are considered to be 'nursing' cases, while accepting those who, given sufficient and proper accommodation could perhaps manage in the community.

If assessment procedures are inadequate for the very serious step of taking someone from his own home for the rest of his life, the way in which application is discussed with the potential resident, and the actual admission procedure, may also leave a great deal to be desired. [One] study (Shaw and Walton, 1979) found that 19 (35 per cent of their sample of 55) said that they had not wanted to become a resident (almost all these were people referred by officials or by relatives) and only 14 felt completely happy with the prospect, the remainder suffering 'greater or less unhappiness in contemplating the future'. Yet the social workers concerned were not felt by the respondents to have given any very clear idea of the practical consequences of entering a home, what the life there would be like, or what alternatives there might be. 'There was a feeling from their replies that the issue of whether or not they were to be admitted is already determined by the time of this interview' and that when life in residential care was discussed it was as an aid to persuasion. 'Talked about how nice the Home was', or 'You would be better off in a Home' were typical recollections. People were sometimes left with the impression that they could change to another home if they wished, or that they could return to their own home later, when this was not true. Only five of the 55 had visited the home to which they were admitted (and some of these had done so because of other contacts, not because of their own impending admission). Only one had been visited by a staff member. When a vacancy became available, a very short period was sometimes given to make a decision and move in, and the prospective residents were often informed indirectly of the vacancy (via relatives or hospital staff) so that there was no opportunity at that stage to discuss their final decision to accept or refuse the place. Ten of the sample were left to enter the home unaccompanied by anyone – regardless that it was likely to be one of the most traumatic moments of their lives.

Nothing has yet been said about the part which relatives may play in the process of losing independence. This would seem to be a crucial area about which too little is known. It is, of course, very common, and socially approved, for a married son or daughter to invite an elderly parent to give up his own home and live with them, and if there is sufficient space, and sufficient physical and financial resources for the family to cope, this may work out very well. However, there are a number of inherent dangers in this course which may not be fully appreciated: first, the old person is still losing his *own* home, even if he is not going to an institution and the sense of psychological loss and need for personal adaptation can be as severe as if he was going into institutional care. This is especially true if the neighbourhood is different so that the contacts and customs of a lifetime are also lost. Second, it can never be certain that the family will be able or willing to continue to cope and in that case, the old person, having lost his own home, has no alternative to institutional care since it is likely to be almost impossible to set himself up again in independence. (The possible use of sheltered housing for situations of this kind needs to be explored.) Third, it is almost impossible for the caring relative to resist taking over from the old person, both physically and mentally – what might be called the 'I'll do it for you' syndrome. Traditional role playing has an interesting effect on this tendency. A study of elderly people living with single adult children has shown that severely disabled mothers living with sons will continue to cook and look after the house when less disabled mothers living with single daughters relinquish almost all household activity (Wright, n.d.).

It would seem that there is a need for much more public education about the advantages and disadvantages of taking an old person into one's home and about the danger of meeting the *relative's* anxieties and guilt feelings by this means, rather than looking objectively at what the old person himself really wants and needs.

The same is true of situations where relatives try to persuade an old person to go into a home, or put pressure on the local authority, or GP to arrange this. [. . .] Often the relatives may take this action because they are afraid that they will incur criticism if an accident occurs and the old person is living alone, but this guilt can be assuaged if a social worker or doctor suggests to them that the old person has a right to live as he likes and that if he wants to take risks it is up to him. One experienced social worker told the writer that elderly people themselves do not need social work – but their relatives do. [. . .]

Dangers and advantages

[. . .] To try to illustrate some of these points let us take as an example an imaginary lady called Mrs Jones. She lives on the ground floor of a block of council flats and is a widow with one daughter who lives a complicated bus journey away. The daughter is the breadwinner for her own household and has a husband who is long-term sick and is unemployed. Her only child has left home, so she has a spare room. Mrs Jones is suffering from a long-standing and increasingly severe dementia with consequent serious neglect of herself and her flat and some nuisance to her neighbours. She is reluctant to accept the help of anyone except her daughter and will not eat meals-on-wheels though she seems to keep quite healthy on a diet of bread, cheese and tea. A small fire which was caused by airing her clothes too close to the heater has brought the neighbours up in arms saying that *Something must be done!* Mrs Jones is fiercely independent and does not want to leave her home but she retains a deep respect for the authority of officialdom and would not actively resist being moved. The choices are:

Table 24.1

STAYING AT HOME		MOVE TO DAUGHTER		MOVE TO RESIDENTIAL CARE	
Danger to Mrs Jones	**Advantages to Mrs Jones**	**Danger to Mrs Jones**	**Advantages to Mrs Jones**	**Danger to Mrs Jones**	**Advantages to Mrs Jones**
Painful death by fire or accident	No traumatic change	Anger at forced move	Increased physical safety	Anger	Safety
Slow death by malnutrition and neglect	Stays in a familiar place	Disorientation	More social contact	Disorientation	Social contact (if it is a good home)
Increasing mental isolation and bewilderment at inability to understand and control environment	Minimal loss of identity	Loss of independence and self-care	Better diet, warmth, etc.	Loss of self-care skills	'Not being a burden'
Development of paranoid fears	Wishes respected	Possible antagonism from family members		Reduced family contact	Warmth and diet
Antagonism from neighbours				Possible antagonism from residents	No conflict with family/neighbours
Danger to daughter	**Advantages to daughter**	**Danger to daughter and family**	**Advantages to daughter and family**	**Danger to daughter**	**Advantages to daughter**
Guilt	Does not have to share her home	Lost earning power	Relief from guilt and anxiety	Guilt	Home and life-style unchanged
Increased strain and cost from travelling to give care in a deteriorating situation	May transfer guilt by blaming SSD for the decision	Lost privacy and freedom	Less travelling	Resulting family conflict	No anxiety about safety
Repercussions of this on the family	Can still give help – as opposed to an institutional situation	Marital relationships might suffer		Little opportunity to give personal care	
Possible blame from family members for 'not taking mother to live with her'		Potentially very long-term responsibility of increasing severity		Possible dissatisfaction with home	
Danger to social services	**Advantages to social services**	**Danger to social services**	**Advantages to social services**	**Danger to social services**	**Advantages to social services**
Extensive domiciliary services will be needed	Respects self-determination and independence	Possibility of breakdown in daughter's care, with institutional care then the only solution left	Socially acceptable, cheap solution (at least in the short term)	Residential care place used up	Safety
Pressure from neighbours, GP, etc.	Other solutions possible later	Cost of giving the daughter appropriate support		Self-determination not respected	Flat freed
Possible fire or accident with resultant bad publicity	Residential care place available for another client			Home may be reluctant to go on coping	Resources not used on domiciliary care
					Neighbours happy

Source: Norman, 1987: 17–18

1 To keep her at home and make a real effort to provide supportive services.
2 To tell her she must go and live with her daughter and put moral pressure on the daughter to accept this.
3 To take her into residential care.

One might (in very simplified terms) weigh up the situation as in Table 24.1.

Of course, in any of these possible scenarios the nature and quality of the resources available have to be taken into account. It will be much more possible to maintain Mrs Jones at home, at least for a time, if an intensive support scheme and flexible 'care packaging' can be provided. The previous relationship between Mrs Jones and her daughter, the daughter's own view of her responsibilities, her own mental and physical health and the attitude of her husband will be key factors in assessing the possible dangers and advantages of a move to the daughter's care. The availability, cost and quality of residential care also need to be taken into account. Above all, the process of decision-making needs to be honest and open, involving a fair discussion of the risks to, and the rights of, everyone concerned and taking into account psychological as well as physical danger. Is such a model of 'risk weighing' too much to ask? [. . .]

References

Lieberman, M.A. (1974) 'Symposium – Long-term care: research, policy & practice', *The Gerontologist*, 14 (6), December.

Marris, P. (1974) *Loss and Change*. London: Institute of Community Studies/ Routledge & Kegan Paul.

Norman, A. (1987) *Aspects of Ageism*. London: Centre for Policy on Ageing.

Poyner, B. and Hughes, N. (1978) *A Classification of Fatal Home Accidents*. (Report to the Department of Prices and Consumer Protection). Tavistock Institute of Human Relations.

Shaw, I. and Walton, R. (1979) 'Transitions to residence in homes for the elderly', in D. Harris and J. Hyland (eds), *Rights to Residence*. Residential Care Association. London.

Wright, F. (n.d.) 'Care of elderly disabled parents in the community by single sons and daughters'. Social Research Unit, Bedford College (preliminary findings).

25

Vulnerable to abuse

Olive Stevenson

Because we are more dependent and more vulnerable in later years, there has rightly been concern about what may be termed 'old age abuse' [. . .]. The research literature, mostly emerging from the USA, has many parallels with earlier writing on the subject of child abuse. There are the same problems in estimating incidence, in defining the phenomena and in defining the characteristics of the abuser or the situations which give rise to abuse.

There seems little point in wasting research time on the incidence of old age abuse; as with child abuse, it can lead to a kind of spurious precision, in which figures are cited which will not bear scrutiny for three main reasons. First, unless and until definitions are agreed, we may be attempting to compare the incidence of different phenomena. Secondly, the estimates are based on *reported* abuse, which is dependent on the highly variable practices of agencies and practitioners. Thirdly, by its very nature, abuse is likely to be 'hidden' and difficult to discover (except in its grossest forms), with the abused person, as well as the abuser, having a stake in keeping it secret. However, what is needed on the part of practitioners is a raised level of awareness of the problem and a willingness to entertain the possibility that it exists. In this we have much to learn from child abuse. One of the most striking and curious aspects of the social history of child abuse is the way in which it was denied and ignored by the professionals, notably doctors. Physical abuse was 'discovered' in the 1960s. It is now almost impossible to imagine how doctors did not diagnose it before. We are now confronting a similar situation with regard to child sexual abuse. The flood of referrals now reaching health and social services does not, of course, mean that a new evil is stalking the land. It means that public awareness has been raised and that professionals are (more or less) willing to entertain the possibility of its occurrence. Such social processes make us aware how immensely powerful are the mechanisms of denial, the psychological capacity to shut our eyes and ears to

Originally published as 'The emotional and social significance of dependence in old age' in *Age and Vulnerability: A Guide to Better Care*. London: Edward Arnold, 1989, Chapter 2, pp. 15-29 (abridged).

matters which are too painful to be contemplated and which create for practitioners ethical and professional dilemmas which are hard to resolve. It seems clear that we face a similar (though not identical) situation with regard to old age abuse. It remains to be seen whether we can learn by analogy. Meanwhile, rather than trading figures, the need is for openness to the idea. It should come as no surprise that, in a society with increasing numbers of very old people, proportionately and absolutely, a substantial proportion of whom have a serious degree of mental infirmity, a significant number will suffer abuse.

As with child abuse, defining old age abuse is a problem for those who wish to undertake research. There are various suggested categories: direct physical or sexual abuse; physical neglect; psychological abuse, such as verbal threats; material abuse, such as theft of money; and violation of rights, such as forcing an old person into a home against their will (Sengstock and Liang, 1982). Obviously, some or even all of these may be present in one case. Psychological abuse probably poses the greatest difficulty in trying to decide what is beyond the bounds of socially acceptable behaviour towards an old person. Important as it is to recognise that the notion of abuse has wider connotations than the physical, not much purpose seems to be served by struggling to define more precisely such elusive matters as emotional interactions. Rather, it seems preferable that, in making a general assessment of the quality of life of a particular old person, some attempt be made to examine the negative and positive aspects of the relationships which they presently experience.

Research and writing on this subject has concentrated almost exclusively on abuse by family members and most of it occurs in the domestic setting. Yet it is self-evident that it may occur in other situations, most particularly in institutional care. Where such establishments are subject to careful 'quality control', one would hope not to find physical abuse or neglect in their grosser forms. Yet it should never be forgotten that some of the disquiet felt about institutional care [. . .] has arisen from the 'scandals' of chronic wards in hospitals, in which long-term patients were, on occasion, subjected to degrading treatment. At the present time, there are grounds for similar concern about both the public and the private sector. It is clear that mechanisms for quality control are not adequate.

Why then are old people abused by those who look after them? [. . .] First we must link the problem to attitudes to old people generally [and to] the prevalence of ageism. Inherent in such attitudes is denigration of old people. There is a terrifying slippery slope in the process, by which old people come to be regarded as less than fully human and are therefore not treated as persons deserving equal respect. This may be exacerbated by their mental frailty or by their neglected appearance (a vicious circle in this context) or by sensory deficits such as deafness.

Secondly, in family abuse, the history of the relationships may be of great significance in current abuse. On occasion, current behaviour is simply a repetition of long-standing family patterns, as for example when there has been marital conflict expressed in physical violence or where a mentally ill son or daughter has had periodic outbursts of physical aggression. In such cases, the physical frailty of the old person may be the only element in the situation which has changed.

Whether or not there has been any history of violence, the association between the past and the present is bound to be significant in understanding present abuse within the family. It is in this area that more clinical research might most profitably be done, for these are complex psychological phenomena about which we have little certainty. For example, it has been suggested that sons or daughters may resent a situation in which they find themselves forced to be 'in charge' of a formerly dominant parent. Or there may be an element of retaliation for past suffering.

Thirdly, both in families and institutions, sadism is occasionally encountered. Sadistic people derive perverse pleasure from the suffering of others and may seek out situations in which they can inflict this. Again, it has been suggested that this is associated with past experiences of violence on the part of the abuser. Although it is important to seek to understand the roots of sadism if one is to help the person to change, those who care for elderly people will be primarily concerned to protect them. In institutional care there should be no place for such people. When the old person is in a family, complex and as yet unresolved issues are raised concerning the introduction of legal powers which would enable the abused person to be removed. [. . .]

Acknowledging that ageism, family discord and psychopathology all play their part in abuse, it is situational stress which is probably the most significant factor in those many episodes which fall short of systematic and gross abuse but which nevertheless cause great distress and suffering. It is also the factor most likely to be remediable by practitioners. [. . .]

Increased understanding of the burdens which [carers, paid and unpaid,] carry should lead us to greater awareness of the strain under which they are so often put. There are two matters which merit particular attention in relation to abuse. One concerns their reaction to 'mess'. The physical care of frail old people necessarily involves much attention to food and to toileting. Old people, perhaps mentally infirm, who spit out food when it is given, or who lose the capacity to eat tidily and whose bowel and bladder functioning is impaired, may rouse deep feelings of revulsion in carers, of which they were quite unaware until confronted with the behaviour. This is particularly likely to provoke hostility when it is believed that there is an element of wilfulness in the old person's responses. For example, it is not uncommon to hear that the carer 'cracked' when a parent is incontinent immediately after leaving the toilet. It is interesting to contrast this with similar descriptions in child abuse in which, for example, a baby is punished for being dirty, the expectations of the parent being quite unrealistic. The extent to which particular old people can control their behaviour and to which certain actions are an expression of hostility is problematic. But if it is experienced as hostile, it may provoke the carer into actions which are atypical and frequently followed by remorse and guilt. People vary greatly in their tolerance of 'mess', which no doubt is rooted in their own personality and childhood experiences.

A second element in much situational stress arises in the care of those suffering from severe dementia. Such old people customarily exhibit behaviour which is extraordinarily difficult to tolerate and which raises a high level of anxiety. Carers are ever conscious of danger and often of restless and agitated behaviour which pervades the household. Small wonder, then, that restraint on occasion gives way to abuse, especially given the failure of our formal systems to offer adequate support.

Whilst these problems arise acutely for family carers, who are so often grievously isolated socially, they are also salient to care staff in institutions, especially when staffing levels are inadequate. Unacceptable practices which have an abusive component, such as tying old people to commodes, are much more likely to arise when there are insufficient numbers of staff to complete the ascribed tasks.

Situational stress, however, is not only related to the actions or behaviour of the person being cared for. It is bound up with the family as a whole. An approach to family functioning which emphasises the interactions of each upon the other and their cumulative impact is essential if we are to understand adequately the position of an old person at a given time. This applies not only to the small number of the very old who live in three-generational households, although that throws up some particular issues and problems, it is equally relevant when there are triangular interactions, such as husband, wife and old person, or to situations when the old person lives alone but is closely supported by kin. It has further been suggested by Sengstock and Liang (1982) that abuse frequently occurs at times when other problems, both practical and emotional and not specifically connected with the old person, are occuring in the family. It would not be surprising to find that material and social deprivation play a part in increasing stress and propensity to abuse, especially when associated with isolation. [. . .]

Reference was made earlier to financial abuse. There are matters here which are of great social concern and which [have been] excellently discussed by Greengross (1986), in *The Law and Vulnerable Elderly People*. These concern the confused and inadequate systems which at present exist to protect old people's money and property. They cannot be adequately explored here, but practitioners are urged to read Greengross' book and to consider the position of old people with whom they work.

Practitioners concerned about suspected or actual abuse of old people will often be perplexed as to the best course of action. Where carers admit that abuse has occurred, or are fearful that it may, the worker may have the opportunity to work with the carer (and where possible, the old person) on a future strategy. This may be focused on support to relieve stress, the modification of certain behaviour or interactions, or the need for the parties to separate. The last is usually to be regretted but there have been occasions when long-standing marital unhappiness was resolved by admission to residential care in the last years. More often, of course, separation involves a younger carer giving up the role, about which there is often profound ambivalence. The manner in which people are helped with those confused and painful feelings may have considerable significance for their future mental health.

There will be other situations in which abuse is not admitted. Where the evidence seems incontrovertible, it may sometimes be desirable to confront the persons concerned, even to the point of suggesting that a referral to the police might be made. Some social workers have found that such directness produced an admission which enabled some honest work to take place and help to be offered. But that is clearly a radical step, only likely to be taken when very serious abuse is involved.

A central problem in working with such cases concerns the position of the old person in question, who has been abused. Their wishes and feelings are, or should be, of primary concern. They are adults, not children, which places practitioners in a different relationship to them, in which their rights to determine their own lives are accepted, unless they are 'incompetent' to do so. It is common for old people to play down the extent of the abuse and it is not easy to gauge how far their reluctance to discuss alternative care is due to fear of the unknown rather than acceptance of the situation. Furthermore, decisions as to 'incompetence' are highly complex. On the one hand, it may well be felt that an old person's wish to stay with a carer should be respected unless their mental state is so gravely impaired that they literally do not know what they are doing. On the other hand, fear of the unknown, shame at admitting that relatives have harmed them, and fear of retribution may create a kind of mental and emotional paralysis which is not the same as a positive wish to stay at home. [. . .]

As things stand, a dilemma of this kind can only be resolved through the use of cumbersome legal machinery which is not appropriate to the situation. There are two relevant statutes. One, Section 47 of the National Assistance Act 1948, allows for the forcible removal from their own homes of elderly people who are not mentally ill. This provision has been the subject of wide-ranging criticism (Greengross, 1986; Norman, 1980). [. . .]

The second relevant statute concerns guardianship under the Mental Health Act 1983. [. . .] In cases of abuse, two problems may arise. First, the old person must be clinically diagnosed as mentally ill. Secondly, if the nearest relative objects an order can only be made by application to the county court, which would complicate and delay the process.

If an offence has been committed against the person, the police can of course bring charges and, under certain conditions, make an arrest. However, the granting of bail is the most likely outcome. [. . .] It seems clear that, with careful safeguards, we need some legal machinery, similar to the provision of Place of Safety Orders for children, by which an old person could be received into residential care for their own protection, at least for a limited period of time, which would afford a breathing space for all concerned and enable a proper assessment to be made of the situation – including the wishes of the old person once they were out of the violent or neglectful environment. Greengross (1986) has suggested that an 'intervention order' might be granted by a magistrate in these circumstances. She points out that at present local authorities have no duty to investigate alleged abuse, as in child abuse, and suggests this should be remedied. [. . .]

While the need to protect old people and their carers from unwarrantable intrusion is of great importance, it would seem that there is a strong case for new legal provisions to afford better mechanisms for protecting old, abused people, in the community and in residential care. It is to be hoped that we will not need a scandal to bring it about. [. . .]

To separate consideration of old age abuse from the range of powerful emotions, positive and negative, which are present in those who depend and those who care, and which affect all interactions, is both limiting and stigmatising. The dangers of such an approach have been seen in comparable work with children and families. That is not to say, however, that we should collude in a denial of the phenomenon. Hence the attention that it has been given here.

Will we see scandals, even inquiries, in future concerning old age abuse, as we have seen them with children? Sadly, there must be some cause for them. Does the general public care less about the plight of some old people than it does about children? Will greater professional awareness raise public consciousness? These are matters on which we must ponder. [. . .]

References

Greengross, S. (1986) *The Law and Vulnerable Elderly People*. Mitcham: Age Concern England.
Norman, A. (1980) *Rights and Risk*. London: Centre for Policy on Ageing.
Sengstock, M. and Liang, J. (1982) *Identifying and Characterizing Elder Abuse*. Institute of Gerontology, Wayne State University, Michigan.

Further reading

Decalmer, D. and Glendenning, F. (eds) (1993) *The Mistreatment of Elderly People*. London: Sage.
Phillipson, C., Biggs, S., Griffiths, A. and Roberts, G. (1992) *Understanding Elder Abuse: a Training Manual for Helping Professionals*. Harlow: Longman.
Pritchard, J. (1992) *The Abuse of Elderly People: a Handbook for Professionals*. London: Jessica Kingsley.

26

Baffle locks: in whose best interest?

Grainne Sheridan

[. . .] In my district there is no written policy for the locking of wards or the use of security doors. All wards in psychiatric hospitals in this district, apart from those for the elderly, are open. Wards for the over-65s which do not use security doors tend to be for people with a functional psychiatric disorder.

In Norman's (1987) discussion about the rights of the elderly, she includes their right to take risks and asks whether our attitudes to the elderly are generally 'ageist'. While I understand and share nurses' anxieties about patients leaving the ward unaccompanied, the use of security doors does not take into account the individual patient's observation needs.

Other areas of psychiatry, particularly acute admission wards, have written observation policies. Each patient is assessed individually and the degree of observation required is recorded in the nursing and medical notes. As this is a written policy, each member of staff is aware of what each category of observation entails. This ensures that the patient's observation needs are met, without infringing the rights of other patients to leave the ward. In care of the elderly wards I believe this is generally not the case.

Another point made by Norman is that continuing care areas tend to have low staff levels and generally low funding, making it more difficult for staff to cope without security doors.

Most direct reference to security doors has been made in American articles, in which restraint in care of the elderly units is seen as normal. Gaffney (1986) and Fennelly (1985) describe a buzzer system that alerts staff when ward doors are opened, instead of having locked doors or security doors. These authors accept that some form of restraint is necessary when caring for elderly people, and suggest that the main motive for its use is concern about the unit's reputation among patients' relatives and the wider public.

Another American article (Harris, 1985) suggests that the motives behind using forms of restraints, such as buzzer systems and cot sides,

From *Nursing Times*, 85 (22), 31 May 1989: 69–70 (abridged).

centre on the liability of staff if patients come to harm. Therefore, staff tend to use restraints to protect themselves against allegations of neglect.

The RCN booklet, *Focus on Restraint* (1987), discusses the use of security doors, using the term 'baffle locks', and suggests the use of individualised assessment and planning as alternatives to these doors. It also includes guidelines for good practice.

The Mental Welfare Commission for Scotland (*Report of the Mental Welfare Commission for Scotland*, 1985) surveyed 150 locked wards and commented that many people over the age of 60 are nursed in locked wards. The commission found this unsatisfactory because some informal patients were detained in these wards. The report does not say what constitutes a locked ward, but the inference is that this involves more than security doors.

Little research appears to have been done on observation policies for elderly people in psychiatric wards, or to determine how many of them use security doors.

I compiled a questionnaire to find out which wards had security doors, the legal status of patients in such wards, and the existence of observation policies. Also included in the study were staff/patient ratios and attitudes of staff to patients being allowed to leave the ward. Continuing care and assessment wards were included in the research.

The method used was not suitable for drawing definite conclusions, but some interesting information emerged.

Staffing in all 14 wards surveyed was low; the best staff/patient ratio being 1:4. The biggest ward had 28 beds, yet it had only fractionally more staff then the smallest ward with 16 beds. Most wards had more staff in the mornings; after this the numbers decreased and the night staff/patient ratio was, on average, 1:10. With staffing levels like this, it is difficult for nurses to give individualised care – particularly when considering the needs of patients in elderly continuing care and assessment wards.

Security doors were seen as an essential aid to nursing care. One of the benefits reported was that patients could wander freely in the ward, without nurses continually having to make sure they were not walking out of it.

Although the questionnaire responses indicate that not all of the wards have these doors, this is not the case; all of the wards included in the project do have some form of security door. Wards which had a buzzer system tended to use this if they had restless patients or if staffing levels were low. There were some comments that security doors were not always effective as certain patients could open them.

The main worry about patients leaving the ward unaccompanied was that they might be involved in accidents, so the security door was seen as in the patients' best interests. Judging by the low staffing levels, opportunities for taking patients off the ward must be quite rare.

The legal status of patients in most of the continuing care wards was informal.[1] It would seem that few of the patients were detainable, or, that it is not considered necessary to hold people on sections[2] in these areas. I do not suggest that people who are legally detained should necessarily be in locked wards, but it seems to be an accepted fact that informal patients over 65 are effectively locked in.

The observation policies described on the returned questionnaires generally consisted of the same procedure – a policy of observation for a group of people, meaning that a nurse must be in patient areas at all times. While this ensures patients are observed, it is not an individualised policy and it is not a written policy.

Only two respondents described a procedure for assessing patients individually, but this was not part of a written ward policy for observation. Therefore, the use of security doors would seem to affect observation policies on psychiatric care of the elderly wards: staff rely on the doors to assist them in protecting patients from coming to harm.

I would recommend:

- Distribution of the RCN publication *Focus on Restraint* to all elderly care areas to increase staff awareness of the forms of restraint commonly in use, and encourage wider discussion of our attitudes to elderly patients and the care we give them
- Individualised planning of observation needs
- Increased awareness of the needs of this client group and appropriate funding
- The establishment of a local working party to look into the use of restraints and to discuss workable alternatives
- That more nurses are encouraged to participate in interest groups in caring for elderly people.

Obviously, this will all depend on funding being made available to develop the service but we who work in this area need to highlight these needs.

Notes

1. Editors' Note – The term 'informal' means that the patient has not been compulsorily detained in hospital and is free to discharge herself at any time.
2. Editors' Note – A 'section' refers to one of several possible sections of the Mental Health Act, 1983, whereby a patient can be compulsorily detained in hospital and is not free to discharge himself while the section is in force.

References

Fennelly, A. (1985) 'Making it safe for the patient to wander', *American Health Care Association Journal*.

Gaffney, J. (1986) 'Towards a less restrictive environment: nursing staff devise a system that safeguards wanderers', *Geriatric Nursing*, March-April: 94–5.

Harris, S. (1985) 'The use and misuse of restraints', *American Health Care Association Journal*, 8 December: 45–6.

Norman, A. (1987) 'Overcoming an old prejudice', *Community Care*, 29 January, 14–15.

Report of the Mental Welfare Commission for Scotland (1985) Edinburgh: HMSO.

Royal College of Nursing (1987) *Focus on Restraint*. London: RCN.

27

Freedom to wander

Peter Blackburn

Caring for elderly mentally infirm (EMI) patients in a ward that is part of a complex district general hospital site can give rise to many problems. One of these is how to care for the confused wandering patient without unduly restricting his movements.

The staff in the ward are responsible for administering prescribed treatments to the patient, but they are also responsible for the patients' physical safety. These two areas alone can cause a moral conflict. Do you allow the patient to wander freely in the ward with the certain knowledge that some of the patients will wander off into unsafe areas? Or do you restrict the movement of the patients and keep them under close observation? Whatever direction you take you will be wrong! Legally, a nurse cannot restrict the movements of informal patients, and allowing them to wander freely and unobserved would be contrary to the nurses' professional, moral and ethical responsibilities.

Tulliver Ward [. . .] at George Eliot Hospital, opened in December 1986, Figure 27.1. It was designated as an EMI ward, caring for short-term and respite care patients, and because of the nature of the ward it had a high percentage of very confused, wandering patients. Not long after the ward opened, a member of the regional nursing department received details of a patient monitoring system (PMS). The PMS appeared to offer potential benefits in EMI wards.

Discussions took place between regional officers, staff from North Warwickshire Health Authority and Knogo UK Limited (makers of the PMS). The outcome was an agreement that the mental health unit of North Warwickshire Health Authority would evaluate the system for the West Midlands regional health authority, in Tulliver Ward.

In order to get a full and valid evaluation of the system we needed a protocol for the trial and a base line for comparison of the pre- and post-trial information. The aims of the trial were as follows:

- to assess the potential of the system over a six-month period to

From *Nursing Times*, 84 (49), 7 December 1988: 54–5.

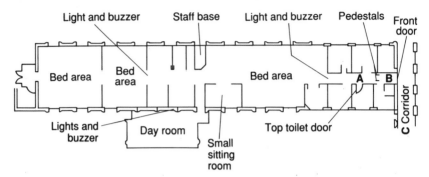

A = Patient beyond the top toilet door and
needing to be diverted to prevent him going
to the door

B = Patient attempting to leave the ward,
therefore trying the handles on the main
door

C = Patient leaving the ward

Figure 27.1 *Map of Tulliver Ward showing coding category of patient
movements*

assist staff in allowing maximum flexibility of patient movement by
minimising the risk of the patients wandering off the ward;
• for staff to assess the system positively in the ward using an agreed
procedure;
• to show patients, staff and relatives factual evidence for or against
the system's benefits at the end of the trial.

To set the base line, we agreed to collect information for three
months before installation of the system. This comprised patient mix,
age, sex and dependency levels; identifying the risk factor (wanderers);
noting the staffing levels per shift; and monitoring the potential and
actual incidents of patients leaving the ward. The other area we felt
was important was to try to find out the anxiety levels of the staff with
regard to patients wandering off.

The method of recording all the information needed to be as simple
as possible in order to minimise staff time used in collecting it. We
noted the main records daily in a ward diary and we recorded the
number of at-risk patients' incidents on a white board located by the
main door that would need a tick only if the patient came into
category A, B or C (Figure 27.1).

The system used was a Knogo retail store system adapted for
hospital use. It consisted of two pedestals and a monitoring device the
size of a small wafer.

Before installation of the system, patients had to be closely
observed, even as far as giving one-to-one nursing for the very

Table 27.1   *Results of the first stage of the evaluation*

		Number of incidents	
Admissions	29	Category A	93
Discharges and deaths	26	Category B	167
Occupancy rate (%)	68.5	Category C	121
Turnover rate (%)	89.65	Total ABC	381

Table 27.2   *Results of the second stage of the evaluation*

		Number of incidents	
Admissions	48	Category A	278
Discharges and deaths	41	Category B	53
Occupancy rate (%)	85.2	Category C	37
Turnover rate (%)	85.42	Total ABC	368

confused. To allow the staff to give more time to patient care meant that the patients would have to be allowed to wander freely and to be observed only from a distance. The staff agreed to do this unless there was a justifiable reason for doing otherwise.

At the end of the pre-installation trial period, information was collected to establish a baseline (Tables 27.1 and 27.2).

Before the installation of the system we assessed the anxiety levels of nursing staff working in the ward in order to ascertain whether there was any change in these levels after the installation of the system. A questionnaire was devised and issued to all members of staff, and weekly ward meetings were held. The results of the questionnaire and the information gathered from the meetings indicated that staff were very anxious about losing patients.

For the trial, the monitoring device was attached to the patients' clothes, either in a pocket or on the inside of an item of clothing. These activated a buzzer and lights at strategic points in the ward when a patient passed between the pedestals by the main door (Figure 27.1). The buzzer could be muted.

For the second part of the evaluation it was necessary to change the procedures slightly. It was decided that only one nurse per shift would be identified to respond to the alarm system so allowing the other staff to concentrate on the remaining patients. The only change in the record-keeping was to record in the patient's case notes a relative's consent for him to take part in the trial. None of the relatives objected once the system had been explained to them.

From a review of the total number of incidents in the two stages of the evaluation, there does not appear to be a great deal of difference (Tables 27.1 and 27.2). It is only by comparing the incidents in each category that any marked difference is noticed. This showed an increase of 299 per cent of patients being diverted beyond the top toilet door, but a reduction of 41 per cent of patients leaving the ward, and a reduction of 62 per cent of patients attempting to leave the ward.

In a ward that on average has only three staff on day duty and two on night duty, effective use of nursing time is very important. It was estimated that before the introduction of the system the average response and return time for a patient leaving the ward was approximately 10 minutes. Two nurses were often involved because the patient could go in either direction and become lost very quickly. During this period it was estimated that up to 40 hours of nurse time was lost, often leaving only one nurse in the ward. Since the ward opened there have been three occasions in which portering and other staff had to chase up wandering patients, but no times have been estimated for these incidents.

After the system was introduced it was estimated that the time taken to respond to a patient was two minutes, and only one nurse was involved. This was because the nurse would be alerted and see the patient leaving. The total time involved for the number of incidents was estimated at 1 hour 15 minutes. If these times are calculated for a 12-month period then the reduction in time lost is 152 hours; a very valuable contribution to a ward averaging three staff on duty during the day.

The trial has highlighted the following benefits:

1 It allows the staff to concentrate on patient care and not to worry about the risk of patients leaving the ward.
2 Nursing staff have longer uninterrupted periods to carry out patient care.
3 The results of a follow-up questionnaire indicated a marked reduction in anxiety levels of the ward staff.
4 The patients seemed to settle more easily into the ward environment when allowed increased freedom.
5 This may lead to a more rapid response to their treatment, but this has not been evaluated.

The major benefits of the system are: a reduction in potentially serious incidents and staff anxiety levels and a more effective use of nursing time.

Some staff will always resist change; initially some were worried that the patients would object to wearing the monitoring device but this was totally disproved. Some of the patients wore them with pride like a badge.

There were two problems with the monitoring devices. One was taken apart by an inquisitive gentleman to find out how it worked, and another one was sent to the laundry. Not surprisingly, both failed when they were tested. These problems can be overcome by heat-sealing the plastic envelopes containing the device.

Since the evaluation began, many other health authorities have shown interest. Relatives have also asked if they can get a system for home use.

28

Obstacles to the development of user-centred services

Tim Booth

One of the main objectives of the raft of reforms outlined in the White Paper *Caring for People* (Department of Health, 1989), and introduced by the NHS and Community Care Act 1990, is to 'give people a greater individual say in how they live their lives and the services they need to help them to do so' (para. 1.8). Here it is argued that little progress in this direction will be achieved by the sort of 'new consumerism' which sees the way forward solely in terms of procedural changes aimed at giving users and potential users more say in the kind of services they want and how they are delivered. Although important in their own right, reforms such as the introduction of complaints procedures or care management will not succeed by themselves in overcoming the tendency for services to turn people into merely passive recipients of care. A fundamental shift in the balance of the relationship between users and providers is also called for; one which challenges the terms on which many services are currently delivered and, in some cases, the nature of the services themselves.

The remainder of this chapter examines the scale of this challenge both in the residential sector and in the field of community care. The general argument presented below is that the main obstacles to the development of more responsive services are precisely those preventing us from listening to their users.

Responsiveness in residential care

Most of those living in old people's homes are put there by someone else. Willcocks et al. (1987) found that only about 14 per cent of the residents in their study had any say in the decision. Likewise, Bland and Bland (1985) report that 82 per cent of their sample of residents claimed entering a home had not been their own idea. When asked, most people say they were not given enough information to make an informed choice (few visit the home beforehand), were not sufficiently consulted, or had been put under pressure to agree to admission (Sinclair, 1990).

Authority figures play a major part in influencing old people to apply for residential care. Evidence suggests that doctors in particular may be responsible for initiating as many as two out of every five applications. A significant minority of applications occur as the result of unsolicited arrangements by professionals. Moreover, decisions are often made in times of crisis, for example following admission to hospital, or at times of emotional stress, such as bereavement. Not surprisingly, research has found that the majority of applicants either shrink from the prospect of living in a home or submit to admission with an attitude of resignation (Evans et al., 1981; Neill et al., 1988; Shaw and Walton, 1979).

The process of admission to care itself devalues the views of old people. Following admission they are identified as no longer capable of managing their own lives, people whose competence and judgement cannot be trusted. From here on they are trained to enact the role assigned to them by the institution: learning to adapt their behaviour to the formal routine of daily living and internalising the expectations of residential staff. The upshot is that residents' views are either regarded as unreliable and treated with suspicion or, when asked, residents themselves are found to have little to say.

Willcocks et al. (1987) encountered the obstacle of institutionalisation when trying to survey residents' opinions in a sample of old people's homes. They found that 'eliciting consumer preferences from those already acculturised by familiar surroundings can prove difficult using traditional methods of interviewing, for the tendency is often to endorse present provision' (Willcocks et al., 1987: 133). The apathy and submissiveness induced by residential life leads to unthinking compliance. Lacking opportunities for expressing individual choice or exercising personal responsibility in their lives, residents submit to inertia and a kind of enforced helplessness which hastens disengagement and leaves under-used skills to atrophy:

> Both mental and physical deterioration often occurs after admission because of the lack of the need to do even simple tasks like dressing, bed-making, or cooking, or to apply the mind to even the simplest of decisions, such as choosing a menu. (PSSC, 1977: para. 4.2)

Evans et al. (1981) observed that the residents in their study 'felt resigned to whatever arrangements staff were inclined to make on their behalf'.

Other factors, too, contribute to the quiescence of residents. Their powerlessness and dependence on staff foster both a fear of retribution should they press a complaint too forcefully and a feeling of indebtedness which makes honest criticism seem more like ingratitude. Speaking out may demand the sort of competence and control which would have prevented their admission in the first place. At the same time, residents' attitudes to staff are essentially of an instrumental kind based on 'gratitude for services received'. It is very difficult to complain if you do not perceive yourself as having any choice, and most residents have very little choice but to be satisfied with their home (Allen et al., 1992).

There is a well-documented tendency for people to register a high degree of satisfaction with just about everything when asked (Gutek, 1978). Users are very hesitant about seeing themselves as qualified to comment on the adequacy or quality of services (Craig, 1981).

People who are inured to their situation, who are powerless to change it, and who do not expect anything different, are not inclined to see themselves as ill-used or deprived (Runciman, 1966). Residents generally have little idea of what to expect before admission. They have few if any opportunities thereafter to compare the quality of care in different homes. And they are unlikely to meet residents from other homes with whom they can compare experiences. Convinced that everyone is treated like themselves, they believe they have no right to more. In this sense, the apparent passivity of residents is fostered by the insularity of residential life.

All these considerations lead to problems in the interpretation of residents' views which any effective approach to user consultation in the residential field must address:

- What weight should be given to residents' reports that they are satisfied and content when observers report widespread boredom, loneliness and frustration?
- If residential life encourages submissive attitudes, can residents' opinions be taken at face-value as a true expression of their real feelings?

The fact is that residential living shapes people's inner worlds as well as their daily routines. Any progress in the residential sector towards more responsive services is dependent on residents feeling free to speak their own minds. Until residents are released from their enforced dependence on staff and secure more freedom of action, their powerlessness and vulnerability will ensure that they continue to defer or comply with the view of themselves and their needs embodied in the routine of residential living and imposed by staff. The tendency will be for them to continue to succumb to the opinions of those who make decisions for them. Consequently, it will be very difficult to treat with confidence what residents say as truly expressing what they think and feel.

Responsiveness in community care

Making residential care more responsive to its users calls for fundamental change in the way homes are run. Such root-and-branch change is now underway in the community care services as local authorities struggle to implement the reforms introduced by the NHS and Community Care Act 1990.

The 1989 White Paper *Caring for People* challenges the assumption that producers rather than users know best. Community care means providing packages of support tailored to individual needs and preferences in order to 'enable people to achieve maximum independence and control over their own lives' (para. 2.2). How is this going to be achieved? Two particular procedural reforms promise to serve as a test bed for user participation in community care.

Care management

Care management has been described by the Social Services Select Committee (1990) as 'the cornerstone of the Government's approach to improving the effectiveness of community care services'. Care management as a process includes assessment and the design, implementation and monitoring of care packages.

The purpose of assessment is to determine the best way of meeting an individual's needs for community care. In the past, assessment has been primarily resource-led, focusing on the user's suitability for some existing service. Under the new needs-led approach, the process starts with the individual with the aim of determining what services are necessary to enable him or her to live as independently as possible.

It has been made clear that assessment should involve the active participation of users and their carers:

> The individual service user and normally, with his or her agreement, any carers should be involved throughout the assessment and care management process. They should feel that the process is aimed at meeting their wishes. Where a user is unable to participate actively it is even more important that he or she should be helped to understand what is involved and the intended outcome. (Department of Health, 1990: para. 3.16)

Assessment procedures must be readily accessible to all potential users and authorities are advised to take positive steps to facilitate the full participation of people with communication difficulties arising from mental incapacity or other disabilities.

Turning these words into actions will not be easy. Three obstacles in particular will need to be overcome if user participation in care management is to become more than a token gesture.

Resources: unless adequate resources are made available for community care, users will continue to experience a mismatch between their own care preferences and the services which care managers can deliver. Assessment of need will still be determined by what can be provided. This will undercut a 'needs-led' approach and nullify the purpose of user involvement.

Incentives: rationing under conditions of scarcity calls for hard decisions. Involving users in these decisions is only likely to make life harder for care workers. As Allen et al. (1992) report, there are 'problems in establishing relationships between consumers, care managers and service providers based on frank and honest discussions of what was possible in the provision of care' (1992: 312). Most social workers and domiciliary care organisers in their study found it too difficult to involve elderly people in decisions, although they regretted the fact that this was how they had to operate. Similarly, the Social Services Inspectorate (1991) have found that staff are reluctant to give information to users about the availability of assessment, the process or outcome of assessment, or what they should do if they are dissatisfied with their assessment. The care workers' main fear seemed to be that involving the users might create a demand for services which they could not guarantee to deliver. There are no incentives to encourage workers to make their job more difficult in this way.

Practice: user participation in assessment runs against the grain of social work practice in which the professional seeks to exert and retain control. Experience with Individual Programme Planning in the learning difficulties field has shown that being included in the process of assessment does not by itself ensure that users get their views across or that the services they receive reflect those views. Meetings can be arranged and conducted so as to effectively exclude the user from the proceedings (Booth et al., 1990). The gap between involvement and participation will only be bridged if professionals can be persuaded to adapt their notions of good practice.

Complaints procedures

Social services departments are required to establish a procedure for allowing service-users or their representatives to complain about the quality or nature of social services. This had to be in place by 1 April 1991. An effective complaints procedure gives some protection for users' interests and rights, and a means whereby the discretion exercised by service providers can be questioned. It also provides a source of users' views on the shortcomings of services. In this sense a complaints procedure increases the scope for users to make themselves heard.

However, making it work in the interests of users entails more than just setting up the system. It also requires that the blocks which prevent people from using it are removed. Two in particular stand out: the need for advocacy and the fear of complaining. Here the omens are not good.

The need for advocacy: in March 1992 the government announced its decision not to implement the first three sections of the Disabled Persons Act 1986 which would have allowed a disabled person to appoint an advocate or 'representative' to act on their behalf in any dealings with a social services department. These sections would have required the local authority to allow advocates to accompany disabled people to meetings and given them access to disabled people in a wide range of accommodation, including private and nursing homes. The disability lobby regarded these sections as a crucial test of the government's commitment to user choice and participation in community care. Without advocacy support in putting their views and pressing their case, vulnerable people are seriously compromised in standing up for their rights.

The fear of complaining: service-users do not generally enjoy the sort of freedom of choice exercised by consumers in the marketplace. The users are often not the people who choose which services they shall consume. Also, they are 'often effectively in the power of their services' (Sinclair et al., 1990). These two facts go some way to explain why older people appear so reluctant to complain. As Allen et al. (1992) report,

> elderly people in the community were anxious about complaining in case the services were taken away, or in case they upset the person providing the services or they were thought to be 'trouble-makers'. Elderly people were afraid of being 'crossed off the list' and thought they should 'best keep in the good books' of those in charge. (1992: 313)

As well as feeling inhibited by their lack of power and control, older users are also held back from complaining by the knowledge that services are scarce and tightly rationed. This encourages low expectations and leaves them feeling lucky to have what they are given and wary of seeming ungrateful.

The government is pursuing its community care reforms on the assumption that the procedural changes outlined in the White Paper will force a realignment of the relationship between providers and consumers so as to create a more responsive and user-centred service. The notion that one will follow from the other is evidenced by the fact that, although the Department of Health has produced a wealth of detailed guidance on the implementation of the reforms, there has been no separate guidance on how to ensure user participation. The argument in this chapter, on the contrary, has been that the reforms are unlikely to meet their objectives, and older people are unlikely to acquire any greater say in the services they receive, until the relationship between staff and users is tipped in favour of the latter. As has been shown, the two key factors which shape this relationship are the scarcity of resources and the unequal balance of power.

Implications for participation

Giving users a say in their own services involves more than just extending the opportunities presented to them for consultation. It means tackling the causes which presently underpin their acquiescence and passivity. Two strategies are suggested by this analysis.

First, the shortfall in services must be addressed. People who are made to feel thankful for the little they get are unlikely to assert themselves, and those with nothing at all are denied a voice. Yet the 'care gap' – between the need for care and the receipt of care – continues to widen. The Audit Commission (1992) has produced evidence of a steady reduction in local authority domiciliary care services over the past decade. For example, there were 80,000 fewer meals-on-wheels per thousand people over 85 in 1989 than in 1979; and the number of home helps and day care places also dropped relative to the size of the older population. Similarly, the 1988/9 OPCS disability surveys found that only 12 per cent of disabled people aged 65–74, who should have been assessed for and provided with help under the Chronically Sick and Disabled Persons Act 1971, were actually registered with their local authority; and only 9 per cent of those aged 75 and over, including only 16 per cent of the people with the most severe disabilities.

Second, initiatives aimed at empowering users must be actively pursued. The concept of empowerment embodies three principles that should form the basis for monitoring the quality of services: a *proactive* principle that focuses attention on the positive qualities and competencies of older people, not just their disabilities, and opposes any form of discrimination on the grounds of age; an *enabling* principle that focuses on validating older people's coping abilities and creating opportunities for self-expression and fulfilment; and an *independence* principle that focuses on meeting needs in ways that promote older people's sense of control over their own lives.

References

Allen, I., Hogg, D. and Peace, S. (1992) *Elderly People: Choice, Participation and Satisfaction*. London: Policy Studies Institute.

Audit Commission (1992) *Homeward Bound: a New Court for Community Health*. London: HMSO.

Bland, R. and Bland, R. (1985) *Client Characteristics and Patterns of Care in Local Authority Old People's Homes*. University of Stirling: Department of Sociology.

Booth, T., Simons, K. and Booth, W. (1990) *Outward Bound: Relocation and Community Care for People with Learning Difficulties*. Buckingham: Open University Press.

Craig, G. (1981) *Review of Studies of the Public and Users' Attitudes, Opinions and Expressed Needs with Respect to Social Work and Social Workers*. London: National Institute of Social Work.

Department of Health (1989) *Caring for People: Community Care in the Next Decade and Beyond*. Cm 849. London: HMSO.

Department of Health (1990) *Community Care in the Next Decade and Beyond: Policy Guidance*. London: HMSO.

Evans, G., Hughes, B. and Wilkin, D. with Jolley, D. (1981) *The Management of Mental and Physical Impairment in Non-specialist Residential Homes for the Elderly*. Research Report No. 4. Manchester: University Hospital of South Manchester, Psychogeriatric Unit Research Section.

Gutek, B. (1978) 'Strategies for studying client satisfaction', *Journal of Social Issues*, 34 (4): 44–56.

Neill, J., Sinclair, I., Gorbach, P. and Williams, J. (1988) *A Need for Care? Elderly Applicants for Local Authority Homes*. Aldershot: Avebury.

PSSC (1977) *Residential Care Reviewed*. London: Personal Social Services Council.

Runciman, W. (1966) *Relative Deprivation and Social Justice*. Harmondsworth: Penguin.

Shaw, I. and Walton, R. (1979) 'Transition to residence in homes for the elderly', in D. Harris and J. Hyland (eds), *Rights in Residence*. London: Residential Care Association.

Sinclair, I. (1990) 'Residential care', in I. Sinclair, R. Parker, D. Leat and J. Williams, *The Kaleidoscope of Care*. London: HMSO.

Sinclair, I., Parker, R., Leat, D. and Williams, J. (1990) *The Kaleidoscope of Care*. London: HMSO.

Social Services Inspectorate (1991) *Assessment Systems and Community Care*. London: HMSO.

Social Services Select Committee (1990) *Community Care: Choice for Service Users*. London: HMSO.

Willcocks, D.M., Peace, M.S. and Kellaher, L.A. (1987) *Private Lives in Public Places: a Research-based Critique of Residential Life in Local Authority Old People's Homes*. London: Tavistock.

29

Rest assured: new moves in quality assurance for residential care

Leonie Kellaher and Sheila Peace

The quality of life of older people living in a variety of non-domestic settings has been a central focus for research in social gerontology. The abstract concept 'quality of life', translated into a variety of forms of measurement, has been used as a way of looking at the outcome of different types of welfare intervention (see Gibbs and Sinclair, 1992; Peace, 1993). In recent years a number of factors have begun to influence this type of research/investigation. During the 1980s we saw the diversification of service provision – particularly long-term care – with the growth of the independent sector; the development of regulatory frameworks through the Registered Homes Act 1984, and the systematic monitoring of institutional and domiciliary services (Social Services Inspectorate, 1991). The NHS and Community Care Act 1990 has brought into sharp focus ideas about people's experiences as recipients of health and social services. Whilst the elements underpinning considerations of quality of provision and quality of life remain constant, the emphasis seems to be shifting, as the person experiencing care is brought into central focus.

Quality control and quality assurance

While the academic researcher talks of quality of life, the terms quality control and quality assurance now find greater currency in everyday practice. Such terms derive from the worlds of business, management and economics rather than the socio-psychological disciplines which generated the paradigms used previously in consumer studies of welfare services. *Quality control* implies quality at a certain level and focuses attention on standards; objective criteria which may be imposed and which outsiders can use to take a 'snapshot' of what is happening. *Quality assurance* implies that the recipients of a service, and the 'public' at large, should in some way be assured of a certain quality of product which meets their needs. It

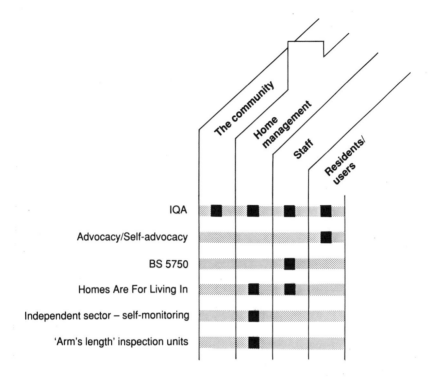

Figure 29.1 *New perspectives on quality care*

is a continuous process and consequently, insiders – 'those who really know' – have to be involved. Both systems should be complementary and feed into each other. The value base which underpins 'quality of life' studies, with its emphasis on personal need for dignity, choice, autonomy, privacy and self-determination, still remains at the heart of both quality control and quality assurance mechanisms. It may be argued, however, that other values such as 'value for money' and 'service efficiency' are now stressed (Pfeffer and Coote, 1991).

In Figure 29.1 we locate a number of systems for demonstrating quality in residential settings that have emerged in recent years. Historically, we have sought to understand services through their administration and organisation rather than from the experiential viewpoint of the user. Today, regulatory bodies, albeit the local authority inspection unit, or the private long-term care sector itself through its professional associations, initiate quality control from the outside. At the other extreme, a programme like Inside Quality Assurance, described below, starts at the centre with those who experience care 24 hours a day.

Two other programmes shown in Figure 29.1 – BS 5750 and Homes Are For Living In (HAFLI) – occupy the middle ground. They involve an understanding of residential life which is organised around staff and inspection officers' perspectives. They are described briefly here.

BS 5750 is a British Standard quality assurance award originally designed by the Ministry of Defence for industrial use. It is a management system designed and set up by staff who develop a 'mission for the whole organisation', and then create a series of check-lists through which every procedure is checked, recorded and monitored. External assessors come in to scrutinise procedures, examine practice and question the workforce. At Napier House in Newcastle, the first residential home to have been awarded BS 5750, a quality manual was developed, which is open to inspection, on every aspect of the 24-hour cycle of residential care (Strong, 1991).

Homes Are For Living In was developed by the Social Services Inspectorate in the North West of England and six north-western local authorities. The main objective of the project team was to develop a model which would help those providing and inspecting residential settings to 'make qualitative evaluations of the performance of residential care homes'. They identified two aspects of 'quality': (a) the care provided by agencies (i.e. what they did and how they did it), and (b) the life as experienced by consumers (i.e. what it was like living in a home) (Social Services Inspectorate, 1989: 6).

In HAFLI, six basic values are put forward as underpinning residents' quality of life: privacy, dignity, independence, choice, rights and fulfilment. A matrix is created using these values alongside dimensions of residential care: physical environment, care practices, staff, staff training, procedures, case records, documents and meals and mealtimes. Within the matrix there are explicit statements about the kinds of practices and resources that are required to achieve the different quality values. For example, issues concerning care practices and dignity include: mode of address; knocking on bedroom doors; dealing with death; sensitivity in handling bathing and toileting.

The document also provides a detailed aide-mémoire for inspectors of homes about each area of the matrix. Information is collected by staff and inspectors through written material, discussion and observation. HAFLI has also proved a useful tool for staff training and development, although at a practical level its procedures take considerable time and expertise.

One of the main differences between HAFLI and Inside Quality Assurance (IQA) is the level of user involvement. In the remainder of this paper we consider the development and use of IQA, which focuses on the everyday experiences of residents. Then we consider some of the questions raised by user involvement.

Inside Quality Assurance (IQA)

The Inside Quality Assurance (IQA) programme was developed by CESSA (Centre for Environmental and Social Studies in Ageing) at the University of North London as one of four programmes within the Department of Health-funded *Caring in Homes Initiative* (Brunel University, 1992), which followed up the central recommendations made in the Wagner Report *Residential Care: a Positive Choice* (NISW, 1988). The programme has been developed through a series of demonstration projects involving some 200 residential care homes from the public, private and voluntary sectors accommodating a range of individuals: children; those with learning difficulties; older people; those with physical disabilities; and people with mental health and alcohol abuse problems. It offers one way of looking at how the views of the organisation and users can be brought more closely together, so that both similarities and differences are revealed (CESSA, 1992).

The stated aim of IQA is to establish a system of review in every residential home which will help create a climate in which individuals have good chances 'to be themselves', whilst living in a setting which has to operate on a collective basis.

Briefly, the IQA system of review is steered by a group – *the quality group* – made up of both insiders and outsiders. It is based upon the two complementary processes which underpin all research, those of collecting, and then organising and analysing information. It is structured by nine progressive steps (see Figure 29.2) which culminate in a *written account* of the home's achievements and intentions for the future.

Seven general topics (from everyone concerned, see Figure 29.3) are the starting-point for collecting information through a guided conversation. People are free to interpret these topics in their own terms and in response to two simple but crucial questions and prompts. The first of these simply asks the informant:

Can you describe . . . [the topic]?

and then asks the person to be a little more precise by saying:

How much do you think it [the topic] needs to be different?

People can say what they think might be done, and they can use a scale which goes from 1 to 9 to show whether they think a lot, or not very much, needs to be different. All of this is optional.

Programmes such as IQA raise a whole series of questions which challenge traditional ways of thinking, not only about how services are run, but also about how we evaluate them. Many of these questions are yet to be answered but some are explored below. Of prime importance is the fact that those *experiencing* care directly see it from a

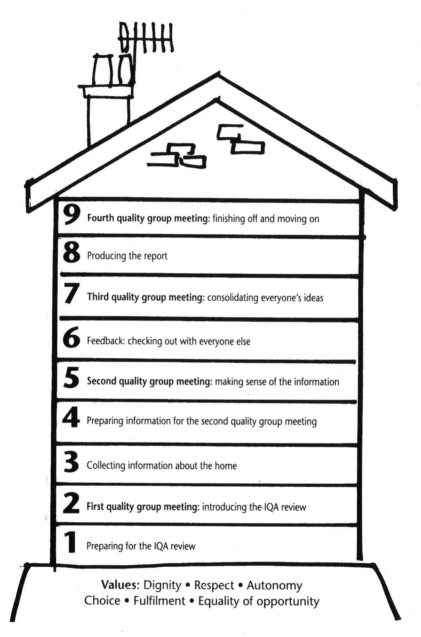

Figure 29.2 *An overview of the steps that make up an IQA review*

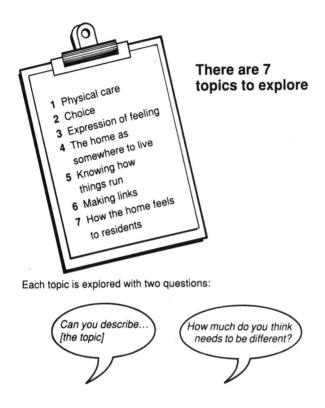

There are 7 topics to explore

1 Physical care
2 Choice
3 Expression of feeling
4 The home as somewhere to live
5 Knowing how things run
6 Making links
7 How the home feels to residents

Each topic is explored with two questions:

Can you describe... [the topic]

How much do you think needs to be different?

Figure 29.3 *Seven general topics to guide an IQA conversation*

unique perspective and often explain it in a *different language* to those who 'manage' care. As a consequence, those who organise care can find what users are saying unfamiliar. They need to be alerted to the differences and helped to understand what people mean, so that valuable information can be brought into the quality equation.

What do users say?

One of the difficulties encountered by researchers is a reluctance on the part of users to say what they think about services. So how may an IQA approach help?

- Users say quite a lot. In response to the invitation to describe, in their own ways, their experiences under a few broad headings, people have plenty to say. Even quite frail people and those with cognitive difficulties can be drawn to suggest their ideas and preferences.

- People make observations about the detail of day-to-day experiences of care.
- Users are frequently well able to focus their remarks on the service under question, the routines and the organisation of service allocation and delivery.
- People make suggestions for changes which generally tend to have low resource implications.
- People say things over and over again but in different ways.
- They don't say many surprising things, and yet staff – front-line staff especially – are surprised, and sometimes shocked or 'thrown', by confronting user comment in a collective form.
- Very occasionally there is a hint that something is being said which needs airing and further exploration, and perhaps urgent action.

How do users say things?

They make comments rather than criticisms:

> . . . *there's a bit of wall-paper torn off and I'm hoping they will be able to fix it . . ..*

When people 'criticise' they compensate or balance with appreciative comment:

> *They work very hard, they are very busy, it would be nice to chat a bit . . ..*

Users often say things 'inside out'; they hint, and they are allusive rather than direct:

> . . . *the staff go home at two o'clock . . ..* [In describing bathing arrangements]

> . . . *the food is alright I suppose . . ..*

> . . . *they can be a bit rough . . ..*

> . . . *some funny things go on . . ..*

What do people mean?

How is this detailed, muted information to be understood? Can we justify making interpretations about what people say, imputing meaning, filling gaps? Researchers working in the area of residential care for old people have often found it difficult to elicit information from resident informers which reflected what could be observed (Booth, Chapter 28, this volume). This suggests that residents of all kinds may be less fulfilled in their residential lives than they would wish to be, and that they are also not fully free to say much about the gaps they may experience.

In the IQA programme one of the crucial aspects is what researchers would call *reflexivity* and which here is called *feedback*. In reporting back to all involved the quality group enables those giving information to consider whether those interpreting it are getting it more or less right. The research strategy known by the term *triangulation* also features in IQA, in that information on the same topics is gathered, using the same questions, from several different sources about one particular setting or service. This method highlights similarities and differences, creating material which can be used to generate greater understanding.

How representative is the user voice?

The point is sometimes made that only the more vocal people speak up, so that the user viewpoint being expressed will be a biased one. The evidence from IQA suggests that where information is collected in a one-to-one personal interview, even the most reticent residents are able to express a view, as can those with a cognitive impairment, if they are given extra help. IQA is based on two principles which have a bearing on representativeness. *First, that any information is better than no information. Second, even if just one resident makes a point, it is worth taking account of.* IQA and quality assurance at this level need not rest upon the application of sampling and survey techniques in their strictly scientific sense.

How reliable is the user voice? What about confidentiality?

Without guarantees of confidentiality it is sometimes argued that residents will not make the criticisms about the service that managers need to hear, and their views may be unreliable. Reservations can be expressed about the likelihood of the source of comments and criticisms being identified by management, with the attendant risk of 'reprisal'. IQA can only go so far in dealing with these dilemmas. In each setting the quality group has to decide on the kind of confidentiality which can be offered. The IQA process, however, aims to collect and share information about residential experiences and this will entail a degree of *openness*. Confidentiality and anonymity can rarely be totally guaranteed. So residents may well be cautious in what they say. Greater confidence in the process may overcome this natural caution, given time.

Can what users say be acted upon by managers? And is it?

Whilst it may be acknowledged that users often have quite a lot to say, there may be reservations about the 'softness' of the kind of data which IQA generates. Even if it were interpreted efficiently, and with sensitivity, would it provide a sound basis for decision-making? How would different, and perhaps opposing, ideas be dealt with? What about demands which would be too expensive or otherwise impossible to implement? There are increasing numbers of people who believe it can contribute. There are others, though, who are doubtful.

Accounts of user and advocate involvement have been emerging which suggest that the user voice can be valuable (Norfolk County Council, 1989). The findings which continue to emerge from IQA suggest that users' views do not run against managerial needs to ration resources, but may well, because users are themselves resource-conscious – not to say resourceful – provide solutions which are both practical and realistic. Examples from the IQA demonstration projects show that things can change. In one home the issue of staff not having much time to talk to residents – especially in the mornings as people were getting up – was tackled by the suggestion that there needed to be two staff 'floaters' at this time. Negotiations led to subsequent shift rearrangements which meant that night staff could stay on to assist day staff with getting people up, thereby releasing a little extra time for talking at what users suggested was a critical time of day.

Conclusions

IQA is just one system of quality assurance, built upon the user view. The value of user input lies in the important perspective it offers. But this perspective is frequently expressed in forms which may be unfamiliar to those with managerial and organising roles and responsibilities. It is important that user opinion and ideas are built into the management of social care provision in ways which preserve the uniqueness of the perspective, and do not convert it to the bureaucratic or administrative form. This means that sensitive interpretation rather than crude translation of the user viewpoint must be the goal, so that both managerial and user aspirations are, at least in part, achieved. Many of the questions raised above have only just begun to be tackled, but at least the process is underway.

References

Brunel University (1992) *Caring in Homes Initiative: Programme Summaries*. Department of Government, Brunel University.

Centre for Environmental and Social Studies in Ageing (1992) *Inside Quality Assurance*. Information Design Unit. Newport Pagnell: University of North London.

Gibbs, I. and Sinclair, I. (1992) 'Residential care for elderly people: the correlates of quality', *Ageing and Society*, 12 (4): 463–82.

NISW (1988) *Residential Care: a Positive Choice* (Report of the independent review of residential care chaired by Gillian Wagner). London: HMSO.

Norfolk County Council (1989) *Tell Us What It's Really Like*. Norfolk Social Services Department, Norwich.

Peace, S.M. (1993) 'Quality of institutional life', *Reviews in Clinical Gerontology*, 3 (2): 187–193.

Pfeffer, N. and Coote, A. (1991) *Is Quality Good for You? A Critical Review of Quality Assurance in Welfare Services*. Social Policy Paper No. 5. London: Institute for Public Policy Research.

Social Services Inspectorate (1989) *Homes Are For Living In*. London: HMSO.

Social Services Inspectorate (1991) *Inspecting for Quality: Guidance on Practice for Inspection Units in Social Services Departments and Other Agencies: Principles, Issues and Recommendations*. London: HMSO.

Strong, S. (1991) 'Home with an official seal of approval', *Care Weekly*, 1 November, 10–11.

30

A powerhouse for change: empowering users

Phyllida Parsloe and Olive Stevenson

The Department of Health (DoH) said in its summary of practice and management guidance that: 'The rationale for this reorganisation is the empowerment of users and carers' (Social Services Inspectorate, 1991). But there is no doubt that various factors, with resource constraints being the main one, may wreck the new community care initiative with even the rhetoric of empowerment becoming suspect. This is especially so when the DoH mentions, in a later extract of the same document, that need is to be defined by the particular care agency or authority.

None the less, we believe it is important to have that principle of empowerment articulated in a central government document. It sets a standard, an objective by which the changes can be evaluated and by which both local authorities and central government can be judged.

For this reason, we chose the word empowerment as the focus of our inquiry into developments in community care. We took empowerment to be both a process and a goal, by which users and carers would have greater power to express their needs and decide how they should be met.

We spoke with a range of people across the country to learn how they were empowering users and carers: those working in the adult care services of Social Services Departments (SSDs), users and carers and, to a more limited extent, people in the voluntary sector. We talked mainly to frontline staff and first line managers, and we met men and women of various ages and races.

We learned that, despite resource problems and political uncertainties, there are social services workers and managers who are finding imaginative and empowering ways to work with elderly people and those with physical and mental disabilities and learning difficulties. The big question, however, remains: can this good practice become the norm for all SSDs and voluntary agencies?

We believe it can, but only if two factors are recognised and

---

From *Community Care*, 18 February 1993, pp. 24–5. A full account of this research can be found in O. Stevenson and P. Parsloe, *Community Care and Empowerment*. York: Joseph Rowntree Foundation, 1993.

acknowledged: the complexity of the task and the need for the whole organisation to change. The attempt at empowerment will fail if it is seen as simple, or as requiring change only in frontline staff.

First, let us consider complexity. Much of the official guidance seems to ignore the fact that empowerment raises profound ethical questions and demands a high level of professional expertise. Workers raised their concerns about how to balance service-users' needs and rights to be empowered with their need and right to be protected.

This is an issue more often explored in child protection work, but in a high proportion of the most complex adult cases it is also of great concern. It is about assessing risk and balancing the need for protection against the right to autonomy. The emphasis on autonomy is welcome and long overdue but it does not remove the moral responsibility to ensure that those who, wholly or partly, cannot look after themselves are looked after by SSD staff.

Ethical dilemmas

The balance between need and autonomy varies not just between individuals, but also between user groups. For example, in the care of frail, old people we are often working with a gradual decline, especially where dementia is involved. Workers are faced with acute ethical dilemmas as they struggle to encourage an ordinary degree of self-reliance, while recognising this is increasingly problematic.

Here, as in old age which has only a physical dependence, we saw staff trying to preserve those areas of autonomy which the elderly people most prized. Discovering and protecting these areas is skilled work, especially when there are racial or gender differences between user and worker.

Other ethical questions arise between the needs of user and carers. The guidance, we believe, does not sufficiently acknowledge that these are not always compatible. Staff operating in the real world of family relationships know this all too well. In the case of young people with learning difficulties and physical disabilities, we heard of acute conflicts between user and carer, with workers seeking to reconcile the two. But compromise may not always be possible and workers will have to throw their influence one way or the other. They are forced to choose between competing values.

Work of this kind needs reflective practitioners who can recognise and weigh up the ethical issues as part of their assessment. Then they need the skills to take action. We were told repeatedly that such assessment, planning and action can take place only within a relationship; then there is a chance service-users and carers will be empowered.

Without a relationship the process, which is about understanding another human being, becomes an impertinent entry into another's personal world. This emphasis on relationships may seem old fashioned to some if they are accustomed to the value for money demands of the market in social care. But rest assured, it is not being introduced by ageing social work professors but by the young, and recently trained, frontline staff whom we met.

Empowering users is emotionally and intellectually demanding work and it needs time. Relationships are not created instantly and a needs-led assessment sometimes takes many hours. It is these facts which mean the whole organisation must change. SSDs must develop a new culture if their own staff and those in provider agencies are to translate the principle of empowerment into day-to-day practice in people's own homes, residential homes and day care centres.

Policies and procedures have to be congruent with users' empowerment, but this is not always the case. We found staff struggling with complicated assessment forms which were intrusive and should have been completed at the first meeting.

Tested for impact

New structures are being created in SSDs which need to be tested for their impact upon empowerment. If budgets are devolved, who should hold them? Is it more empowering for users to argue their needs directly with the budget holder who is also care manager or for the care manager to put their case to a first line manager budget holder? How is the question of empowerment being dealt with when contracts are drawn up with providing agencies? Will they require – and fund – staff training in these new agencies which focuses upon user empowerment? The point is empowerment must permeate the agency.

But this is not enough. Staff are more likely to empower users if they are empowered themselves. Staff supervision and forms of peer consultation, which allow for discussion of ethical and professional matters as well as managerial issues, provide one means of empowerment, but more than that will be required.

Much of the good work we saw took place in teams and centres where the manager had been able to share power with his or her staff, sometimes with similar help from the manager above, but often without it.

Senior managers, along with all their other demands, must take on this task of empowering their staff. If they cannot shift the balance of power in the organisation, then empowered users will remain a rare and endangered species.

Reference

Social Services Inspectorate and Social Work Services Group (1991) *Care Management and Assessment: Managers' Guide.* London: HMSO.

31

Approaches to advocacy

Chris Phillipson

[The] purpose [of] this paper is to try to assess the way forward in terms of understanding some of the problems involved in developing [the idea of advocacy] in working with groups of vulnerable older people.

The development of an advocacy perspective

[. . .] Why has the notion of advocacy come on to the agenda in the UK? Six main reasons [may be cited]:

1 The development of Charters of Rights (particularly in the field of residential care).
2 The pressures facing informal carers (evidence for which came in numerous studies in the 1970s and 1980s).
3 The role of the ombudsman.
4 Sections 1 and 2 of the Disabled Persons Act 1986, which, if implemented, will give disabled people the right to have the views of a representative taken into consideration.
5 Legal areas such as Guardianship, enduring powers of attorney and the role of the Court of Protection.
6 The debate about the political empowerment of older people and the need to combat the social creation of dependency in old age (Phillipson, 1982; Walker, 1981).

We also know [. . .] that advocacy may be important in certain critical transitions which run through the lives of older people. These might be listed as follows:

- deciding on residential care;
- deciding on hospital treatment;
- discharge from hospital;

From M. Bernard and F. Glendenning (eds), *Advocacy, Consumerism and the Older Person*, Stoke-on-Trent: Beth Johnson Foundation and University of Keele, 1990, pp. 30-5 (abridged).

- support in situations where services are being cut back or privatised (the sell-off of older person's homes is clearly a concern in the latter);
- support in situations where professionals exercise undue power.

The Age Concern (1989) monograph on advocacy noted that the advocacy approach emerged from concerns about mentally handicapped and mentally ill people, especially in the United States where advocacy was recognised by the United Nations League of Mental Health as a means of ensuring access to essential services and facilities. At the present time, we are now seeing the advocacy approach being extended to a number of new groups, work with older people being amongst these.

There are a number of reasons for thinking that an advocacy approach would have benefits for work with elderly people. First, it may help restore people's confidence about asserting their rights for services or making new relationships in old age. Secondly, it may highlight injustices in old age; areas which would otherwise remain hidden from view. Thirdly, by restoring the voice of the consumer, this may help to influence an improvement in the quality of services received by older people.

The above perspective suggests to us that advocacy has a vital role in terms of strengthening the rights of people as consumers of essential services, particularly for those who find handling information, consultation and negotiation difficult to achieve. If it is difficult, as many people say it is, to achieve fundamental change for people who are very frail or have dementia, then rather than assert that it is impossible and to deny the rights of these people as we do at present, there is all the more reason to ensure the maintenance of rights which people hopefully have enjoyed earlier in their lives.

Understanding advocacy: critical perspectives

All of the above suggests that we have made some progress in terms of clarifying what is in some respects an ambiguous term. But we need to pursue with a little more rigour what is meant by this notion of advocacy so that we can make clearer how far we have to go in terms of achieving our objectives. The general understanding of advocacy is that it is concerned with the balance of power between the client as a member of a minority or other disenfranchised group and the larger society. From the advocate's point of view, the client's problems are not seen as psychological or personal deficits but rather as stemming or arising from discrimination as regards social and economic opportunities. Therefore, techniques of intervention, rather than focusing solely on the relief of individual clients, should challenge those inequalities within the system which contribute to or which cause difficulties for the older person. (There are obvious parallels here with the political economy perspective on ageing.)

Definitions of advocacy have focused on many of the problems identified in the preceding paragraphs. [Various definitions have been offered:]

1   Someone who defends, promotes or pleads a cause. In this role, the worker acts as a partisan in the social conflict and uses professional expertise in the interests of the older client.
2   An advocate is one who 'organises activity to obtain goods, services, power or other resources for clients'.
3   Advocacy is an attempt by an individual or group to influence another individual or groups to make a decision that would not have been made otherwise and that concerns the welfare or interests of a third party who is in a less powerful status than the decision-maker.
4   Advocacy is a process of empowerment. Elderly people, by virtue of disability, frailty, marginalisation, institutionalisation, financial circumstances or even social attitudes, may find themselves in a vulnerable position where their ability to exercise choice is limited and their ability to exercise their rights or represent their own interests may be at risk. Good advocacy enables individuals or groups of people to have their interests given the same consideration as those of other citizens.

Beyond these general definitions, [we can] identify three additional themes [. . .]:

1   Advocacy as a way of meeting human needs.
2   Advocacy as a way of increasing power and participation.
3   Advocacy as a way of responding to intergenerational conflicts.
     [. . .]

1. Advocacy and human needs

The first argument for advocacy [rests] on the distinction introduced by Michael Ignatieff in his book *The Needs of Strangers*. Ignatieff argues that:

> Modern welfare may not be generous by any standard other than a comparison with the 19th century workhouse, but it does attempt to satisfy a wide range of basic needs for food, shelter, clothing, warmth and medical care. The question is whether that is all a human being needs. When we talk about needs we mean something more than human survival. We also use the word to describe what a person needs in order to live their full potential. What we need to survive, and what we need to flourish are two different things. The aged poor in my street get just enough to survive. The question is whether they get what they need in order to live a human life. (1990: 10–11)

Now this is, of course, a very difficult area: defining the task associated with how to make lives flourish and reach their potential will certainly not be easy. But the idea of advocacy seems to fit extremely well in relation to this objective. At the moment, however, I would suspect that our view of how we see advocacy is much more in terms of guaranteeing basic rights than it is about realising human potential. I suspect this, if only because it seems to me that we are pretty unclear about what is the potential of old age. Many advocacy projects are themselves concerned with the abuse of rights, an important area of concern. But to protect against the loss of rights we also need to be better informed about the wider potential and abilities of older people. How do we know what rights are being abused if we cannot place them within a broader framework of human potential? This is an area which we urgently need to address within the field of work with older people.

2. *Advocacy as a way of increasing power and participation*

It is clearly the case that much of our thinking about advocacy has revolved around the need to increase the participation of older people in the organisation of services. But from a critical standpoint we need to ask how realistic are some of the objectives we have set. The British debate about the potential benefits of advocacy has been somewhat naive in this context, failing to ask whether statutory and voluntary bodies will really welcome an advocacy perspective. One of the problems here has been a lack of recognition of the distinction made by Carroll Estes (1979) between citizen involvement and citizen action. Citizen involvement allows for appropriate input from the client population but is predicated on the acceptance of the agency's viability and rationale. The assumption is that

> the views of responsible citizens will be congruent with those of agency staff and the citizen participants will support agency programs, if only they receive sufficient education. Citizen involvement means 'at the most education and at the least a pretence at consultation . . . [what education there is orients clients] towards professional views based on consensualism'. (Estes 1979: 215)

Citizen action roles, on the other hand, focus on obtaining political power in order to make the system responsible to participants: to their defined needs and demands. Estes goes on:

> While involvement roles focus on obtaining desired services, citizen action roles focus on obtaining political power in order to make the system responsible to participant-defined needs and demands. Underlying differences between involvement and action roles revolve around (1) who defines the problems and needs of the constituency, (2) what procedures are to be employed in making those definitions, and (3) how solutions to problems are to be implemented. (1979: 215)

It is clear that not enough has been made of this important distinction between citizen involvement and citizen action. The consequence of this has been that it is the former rather than the latter which has tended to dominate discussion. The result of this is that we are not sufficiently aware of the barriers to achieving effective advocacy. In her analysis of the Older Americans Act, Estes lists some of these as follows.

First, sponsoring bodies may be unwilling to give real authority to older people or their advocates in respect of policy-making. The older person may still be viewed as essentially a client with all the limited reciprocity which that entails. Secondly, there may be few inducements to organisations to take on board the views of either older people or advocates. These may not be sanctioned or required in any legal sense; they may also be against the grain of what is perceived to be professional responsibility. Thirdly, there may be no inducements to older people or their advocates. Financial remuneration may not be given; it may not be clear that there will be any short-term or medium-term gain for the carer or the older person. Fourthly, neither the older person nor the advocate may have the skills for participation. As Estes points out: 'Poverty, despair and skepticism about whether participation can make a difference are factors that minimise target group involvement in advisory activities' (1979: 219).

None of this undermines the case for attempting to achieve greater participation by older people in the organisation and delivery of care. It does remind us, however, that achieving a consumer-oriented service is likely to be fraught with problems, especially in a context of restrictions on public expenditure and uncertainty about the future of many of the services traditionally received by older people (Godber and Higgins, 1990).

3. Advocacy and intergenerational relations

The final area where we see the force of an advocacy perspective is in the field of intergenerational relations. Here we are seeing a debate in western societies about the share of resources between older and younger generations; ideas that older people will be a burden; and arguments that older people have bought a welfare system for themselves which will prove too expensive for younger generations. I do not want to deal here with the merits or otherwise of these arguments. What is clear is that advocacy can be part of the way in which one generation justifies its particular share of resources. This must, though, involve more direct action than I think we are taking at present. The drift in terms of the value of the state pension has been one of the disturbing features of the 1980s. But this has of course run alongside a period when older people have been increasingly removed from the labour market. Advocacy has not been strong enough in the UK to protect either the incomes or the jobs of the old. This is a rather sobering assessment in terms of the tasks before us. It is certainly a justification for collective action on the part of pensioners, action which has been illustrated by the Sheffield Pensioners' Action Group, for example.

Conclusion

This paper has set out some issues which will need to be tackled in terms of developing advocacy work in the 1990s. Such work will not be easy. First, the changes to community care, consequent upon government legislation, is creating much uncertainty in terms of traditional roles and relationships. Will the advocacy role survive the post-Griffiths age? Will it be submerged within new activities coming from a managerialist welfare state? Secondly, will there be the people there to do the advocacy? In the 1960s and 1970s there was much talk about the shortage of volunteers. Advocacy work is the most demanding of all citizenship roles. Whether the citizens will want to do it remains to be seen. Thirdly, it might be helpful to suggest that we need a lead body to co-ordinate the debate about advocacy for groups such as the elderly mentally ill. The role of the lead body would be to monitor the implementation of [the changes to community care] in terms of [their] effectiveness in giving older people a greater say in respect of the services they receive. Voluntary bodies such as Age Concern might be able to develop this role. On the other hand, individual branches may have problems if they try to be advocates and service providers at the same time. Voluntary organisations have to be careful in assuming that the provider and advocacy roles can be combined. It may be that the voluntary movement needs to accept that its involvement in service provision must be curtailed if it is genuinely to represent those who cannot claim services for themselves. And, finally, what about the customer? What sort of advocacy relationship do they want? Are they 'just' interested in rights or do they want to go further and explore with a concerned individual some of the undefined areas of human potential? These will be important questions to find answers to in the years ahead.

References

Age Concern England (1989) *Guidelines for Setting Up Advocacy Schemes*. Mitcham: Age Concern England.
Estes, C.L. (1979) *The Aging Enterprise*. San Francisco, CA: Jossey-Bass.

Godber, C. and Higgins, J. (1990) 'Care for the infirm elderly', *British Medical Journal*, 300: 555-6.

Ignatieff, M. (1990) *The Needs of Strangers*. London: Hogarth Press.

Phillipson, C. (1982) *Capitalism and the Construction of Old Age*. London: Macmillan.

Walker, A. (1981) 'Towards a political economy of old age', *Ageing and Society*, 1 (1): 73-94.

32

The pensioners' movement: federation, consolidation, fragmentation, 1938–1948

Andrew Blaikie

[. . .] Unlike earlier efforts, agitation during the late 1930s and 1940s owed much to the militancy of pensioners themselves. Reflecting, as an octogenarian, upon the highlights of his sixties, James Birtles, founder president of the National Old-Age Pensions Association, reminisced:

> One of the great joys of my life was when I arrived at the House of Commons in a furniture van, accompanied by that petition. People began to realise that for fourteen long years [1925–1939] the old people had been neglected and forsaken. (Birtles, n.d.)

From small beginnings the Old-Age Pensions Association mushroomed. The Blackburn branch, founded in October 1938 with nine members, grew in numbers to 3500 by February 1940 whilst even small branches, such as Rhymney in South Wales, had 360 adherents by this time. By mid-1940 their mouthpiece, *The Pensioner*, claimed sales in excess of 500 in several branches and reported on the 'phenomenal growth' of the movement – to 600 branches – within its first 16 months. Meanwhile, the Scottish OAPA, formed in February 1937, comprised a total membership of 8000 by the start of 1941 (Birtles, n.d.).[1] The National Federation (NFOAPA), as it became, had grown to 400 branches by June 1942. In August it was remarked in the Commons that, 'Wherever you go now in every constituency you are met by the aged people and their organisations.' By spring 1944 some branches had nearly 10,000 members, many had over 5000 and 'quite a lot, started less than six months ago' had already topped the 2000 mark. In villages like Dearham in Cumberland, with a total population of 1500, 900 were members of the Federation. By 1953 there were 1300 branches in total (Birtles, n.d.).[2]

Such growth owed much to the sense of purpose and national identity gained through petitioning Parliament. The first petition, in

Originally published as 'The emerging political power of the elderly in Britain 1908–1948', *Ageing and Society*, 10, (1): 17–40 (abridged).

July 1939, asked for a doubling of the basic pension to £1, and collected an estimated five million signatures during six weeks of local canvassing. The Speaker remarked: 'This is a historic occasion. It is the first time in the history of this House that a petition has been presented accompanied by a demand.' This was a long way from the 'silent suffering' and 'passive protest' which the NCOAP had sought to articulate (Longstaff Dennison n.d. [c. 1919]:).[3]

Concessions gained during wartime followed a similarly piecemeal path to those granted after National Conference on Old Age Pensions (NCOAP) pressure during the 1914–19 period. What is particularly interesting about the Federation, however, is the way in which it attempted to raise public awareness at a time when pensions policy was about to undergo its most dramatic overhaul to date. Like the NCOAP the Federation was non-partisan, but, unlike its predecessor, its hands were not tied by affiliation to (and therefore responsibility for) the friendly society or trade union movement. This openness, together with the decentralised branch network, enabled initiatives to come 'from below', from older people themselves. Undoubtedly, there were echoes of an earlier campaigning style, but the rhetoric of the Federation – as reflected in the pages of *The Pensioner* – was altogether more direct and biting, more tangible. One issue cited a *Daily Herald* report on Nazi Germany which claimed that, 'About 40,000 [. . .] prisoners are between 65 and 85 years old. They live in barracks [. . .] and are allowed a shilling a day upkeep. *On this meagre subsistence allowance they die like flies.*' 'So what?' said the Federation, having shown by budgetary analysis that British pensioners also lived on just 7s a week. Their immediate reaction to the Beveridge Report's compromises was displayed graphically in a cartoon, the caption to which read 'Cheer up, Maggie, we shall get £2 a week when we are 97' – a bitter comment on the gradualist compromises of the new pensions scheme. A Pensioners' National Appeal had been taken up by the *Daily Dispatch* in 1938 and Ritchie Calder's articles in the *Daily Herald*, 'Life on 10/- a Week', provided a further boost for the 1939 agitation with their Orwellian revelations. The national press also used topical speeches from Annual Conference as front-page copy on occasion, but although Percy Cudlipp, the *Herald* editor, extended his patronage to informal negotiations with the BBC, Auntie declined to let Grandpa take the airwaves, despite repeated appeals.[4]

In keeping with the rank-and-file strength of the movement, pressure was applied most effectively at local level. By contrast with the 'insider' methods of the Old People's Welfare Committees it was also profoundly political, resembling 'the abrasive approach of 1960s pressure groups such as Shelter rather than the more staid "non-political" approach' of the voluntary organisations (Means and Smith, 1985: 69–70). Despite the qualified success of the 1939 escapade, *The Pensioner* remarked in April 1940 that 'To exert pressure on the

Government as a whole is to invite failure, as is demonstrated by the fate of many petitions.' As with the NCOAP, complaints raged against the 'same old twaddle' about costs of rearmament and fighting for a better world being trotted out in Parliament, but the style of attacking hypocrisy and injustice was wholly different. Birtles cited Roosevelt's dictum that, 'The function of a statesman is to yield to pressure', but since 'not the Government, only persons can have responsibility', the struggle was to be waged in the constituencies, against individual MPs. 'We must carry on our guerrilla warfare, sniping our members with postcards and letters' read the first *Pensioner* editorial.[5]

The problem as they perceived it lay with the centralisation of authority within the parties. This was clear, for example, with Labour's record over the past 20 years.

> One would think that, after all that time, a movement that really desired increased pensions and had failed, would have changed its tactics . . . the stronger a movement becomes 'institutionally' the weaker it becomes as an instrument for the benefit of the people.[6]

All hinged on accountability. Branches engaged in detailed correspondence with local MPs demanding explanation if Federation demands – £1 (later 30s) at 60 with no means test – were not being pursued. Several held public meetings where local MPs were put on their mettle and remorselessly pilloried if they failed to acquiesce. *The Pensioner* was, however, careful to note that 'It's the votes in Parliament that show up your MP, not what he says on the platform.' The division on the Determination of Needs Bill debate in February 1941 was reprinted from Hansard, citing all 173 who had voted for the continuance of means calculations together with the 'sincere few' (19) who had been carpeted for defying the Labour whip. This was a tactic borrowed from the NCOAP. However, the Federation used its local mass support to carry the campaign further. In 1943 Annual Conference carried a motion suggesting all local branches put forward their own candidates for municipal elections. Subsequently, Ernest Melling (the Federation's secretary) stood for Blackburn's staunchly Labour Trinity ward on a pensioners' independent ticket, while in the 1945 general election a mass meeting of 1200 pensioners endorsed Barbara Castle and John Edwards, 'not because they are Labour candidates, but because they will support YOU'.[7]

Between 1943 and 1948, several huge mass petitions were delivered to Westminster whilst the National Council of the Independent Labour Party decided 'to place the whole machinery of the Party at the disposal of the old folk'. In April 1944 an executive deputation to London met Liberals, Tories, the *Daily Herald* and the Assistance Board all within the space of two days (Carradice and Stanfield, 1943).[8]

In terms of consciousness-raising, their uncompromising approach surely paid dividends. However, the failure to influence policy decisions was most clearly evident in the outcome of discussions surrounding the Beveridge Report in 1942. On first intimation that an inquiry was to be conducted, the Federation responded cynically, commenting that, 'Whenever the Government gets itself into a fix [. . .] it appoints a committee. This is to enable breathing space.' Having engaged, none the less, in a protracted correspondence with the Committee to allow a memorandum to be submitted, an NFOAPA deputation finally gave oral evidence in May. They were especially critical of the voluntary organisations.

> They cannot touch even the fringe of what is required, are administering palliatives, mitigating the evil which needs totally eradicating. It is a National responsibility which should and must be primarily that of the Government.

As Means and Smith (1985: 70) point out, a concentration on pensions issues caused them to ignore inadequacies in medical and social provision whilst 'their campaigning style was unlikely to have been appreciated'.[9] Not surprisingly, when the Report was published, the Federation were far from satisfied.

> For all practical purposes, the Beveridge Report is useless [. . .] and we had better ignore it entirely, concentrating on action which will secure our just rights – AND NOW – not at some vague future time.

They went on to deride the 'screaming headlines', 'spate of glorification' and 'premature eulogies' which followed in its wake. They were perhaps justified in their anger at the relatively low priority accorded older people under the welfare state. Their complaint that they had been betrayed by a Committee 'set up as a result of the pressure by the NFOAPA upon individual MPs' was, however, some way wide of the mark.[10] In 1952 an NFOAPA pamphlet remarked that 'the essential strength of the Movement lies in its potential voting power'. Thirty-seven per cent of the electorate were then over age 50 (Melling, 1952). Today, as the postwar consensus crumbles and new conflicts impose on the agenda, a yet larger potential exists. But it is only a *potential* strength. [. . .]

Notes

1. See also *The Pensioner*, Feb. 1940; Mar. 1940; Apr. 1940; May 1940; Feb. 1941.
2. See also *The Pensioner*, Sep. 1940; Mar. 1941; June 1942; Aug. 1942; May 1944; Nov. 1942.
3. See also *The Pensioner*, Feb. 1940.
4. *The Pensioner*, Nov. 1942; Sep. 1941; Jan. 1942; Nov. 1940; Oct. 1942; Apr. 1940; Dec. 1947; Mar. 1940; Jan. 1943; Oct. 1943; Jan. 1947; Mar. 1947; May 1947; July 1940; Feb. 1940; May 1942; June 1942; Aug. 1943; May 1944. Birtles (n.d.) notes that, 'To get first-hand knowledge the *Daily Express* deputed one of their staff to go out and for a week

try to live on ten shillings. Each day he reported loss of weight . . . [he] acknowledged it was the most trying week of his life, and had borrowed three shillings and sixpence from the following week's allowance.

5. *The Pensioner*, Apr. 1940; Oct. 1942; Mar. 1942; Sep. 1942; Mar. 1940; Feb. 1940.

6. *The Pensioner*, Feb. 1941.

7. *The Pensioner*, June 1940; May 1941; Dec. 1941; Jan. 1941; May 1941; Mar. 1941; Apr. 1941; Sep. 1941; Aug. 1943. NFOAPA Headquarters, Blackburn: local press cuttings and campaign leaflets (1945).

8. See also *The Pensioner*, Sep. 1943; Sep. 1942; May 1944; Feb. 1945; Sep. 1946; Oct. 1948. House of Commons Debates 380, cols 1671-2 (31 May 1942); 393, cols 671-3 (3 Nov. 1943).

9. *The Pensioner*, Mar. 1942; June 1942.

10. *The Pensioner*, Jan. 1943; Feb. 1943; May 1942.

References

Birtles, J.C. (n.d.) *The Ties That Bind*. (Unpaginated.)

Carradice, D. and Stanfield, C. (1943) *Justice for the Old Folk*. London: Independent Labour Party.

Longstaff Dennison, J. (n.d.) [c.1919], *Plain Facts, Old Age Pensions As They Are and As They Ought to Be*.

Means, R. and Smith, R. (1985) *The Development of Welfare Services for Elderly People*. London: Croom Helm.

Melling, G. (1952) *The Federation Story*. (Undated.)

33

On being a woman in the pensioners' movement

Zelda Curtis

In 1982, as a community development worker with Camden Task Force,[1] an important part of my job was to provide information, resources and support for the Camden Pensioners' and Trades Union Association (CPTUAA), an affiliate of the Greater London Pensioners' and Trades Union Association (GLPTUAA).[2] Both organisations were renowned for their campaigning activities.

Their members had been leading trade unionists in their younger days, steeled in struggles for better pay and conditions for their members, and in their older age they were still in struggle for a better life for pensioners. Many of them, now well into their eighties, are still to be seen braving the elements to collect signatures on their petitions.

The Camden Pensioners, with whom I worked, mounted a campaign to get the standing charges abolished on gas and electricity bills. They demonstrated with their poster boards outside the showrooms, attracting much attention and gaining many hundreds of signatures for their petitions. The majority of those demonstrating were women, as were the majority of those signing. As women over 65 are amongst the poorest in this society, they were well aware, from their own experience, of the hardship created by the high charges.

Despite the preponderance of active, campaigning women in both the CPTUAA and the GLPTUAA, the men held the power in the organisations. It was not surprising - indeed, it could hardly have been otherwise. The men were mainly retired building workers and engineers and neither unions were renowned for their acceptance of equality issues. The men were of a generation that had not encouraged women into the union. Women's place, if not in the home, was certainly not to be in the positions of power. And their attitudes had not changed just because they had retired. Women's issues were not considered of importance and the slogan of the Women's Liberation Movement, 'the personal is political', was anathema.

Most disturbing was that the women colluded with the men. They deferred to what they seemed to consider men's greater aptitude for leadership. They accepted without question that their role was as minute-taker, tea-maker and organiser of jumble sales. Although, nationally, a few women did hold leading positions, particularly in the North West, many of the women members of the GLPTUAA were suspicious of feminist ideas. Their political affiliations had dissuaded them from thinking of their own specific needs as being of importance. They were used to campaigning alongside the men and they thought themselves equal to them. They had been active in the peace movement, which had always been considered a women's issue, and yet they allowed their own needs and demands to be subsumed within the men's national ones.

When I complained about the men's attitudes and the male-oriented language used in pensioners' meetings, they insisted that these were unimportant points beside the greater need to stand in unity with the men to win the demands of the British Pensioners' Charter:

1   A universal basic state retirement pension of not less than one-third of the average earnings for each pensioner.
2   Full health care provision including hospital and community care to be free and available at time of need and where needed.
3   Payment of an additional £5 a week heating allowance to all pensioners' households from 1 October to 3 March each year.
4   Christmas bonus of £50 to be paid to all pensioners free of income tax.
5   The death grant to be restored and renamed, more appropriately, the funeral grant and to be £400.
6   All payments to pensioners to be uprated at six-monthly intervals on the basis of the increase in earnings or the cost of living, whichever is the greater.
7   All pensioner households to be relieved of paying standing charges and for TV licences.
8   Free travel facilities to be available for all pensioners on bus, coach, underground and rail services, whether publicly or privately owned, nationwide.
9   All pensioners to be able to live in accommodation which is appropriate to personal needs and circumstances, including sheltered housing with lifeline facilities.
10 The full range of social and community services to be available to pensioners as and when needed. Pensioners to be entitled to invalid care allowance.

Note there is no specific mention of women. However, point 1 does acknowledge the right of each woman, regardless of her marital status, to have a state pension in her own right. This differs from the Declaration of Intent[3] of the National Pensioners' Convention, which still talks of 'couples'. It was Beveridge, of course, who originally institutionalised sexism in state pensions through his definition of women as dependants and as unwaged housewives. This is why many older women feel that the British Pensioners' Charter should, at the very least, include:

> recognition of the unpaid contributions of the women whose work is within the home, of assisting wives and of rural women, to the nation's economy by inclusion in contributory pensions.

This was one of the points in the Bill of Rights agreed in the older women's workshop at the EURAG (European Federation for the Welfare of the Elderly) Conference in 1988.

The gender-blindness of the pensioners' movement set the workers within Pensioners' Link thinking about a project specifically for and about older women and the issues that affect their lives. They sought to bring together older women to discuss and campaign around those issues and to raise their collective voice against ageism, sexism and racism.

By 1984 the Older Women's Project was in action and women members of the pensioners' movement were encouraged to attend its conferences, in which health, housing, transport and education were discussed. On health matters, the older women were concerned about the trivialising and dismissal of their treatable health problems and the dangers of over-prescription of drugs. They were worried, too, by the upper age limit set for screening of breast and cervical cancer. Most importantly, recognising the double disadvantage suffered by older black women and the huge gap in knowledge of their needs, they called for more research into the diseases which particularly affect them. They demanded that special attention be paid to cultural differences and the need for women medical staff, interpreters and special diets.

On housing matters, they were concerned about safety inside and outside the home. Because of the racism suffered by women of different ethnic groups on council estates, they demanded that anti-racist policies be put into practice. Accessibility and affordability were the major issues in the transport discussions, especially wheelchair access to the Underground. And self-defence and assertiveness training was thought to be essential to enable older women to deal with the violence and racial harassment directed against them.

The project then published their recommendations and promoted action on the issues raised. On one occasion, around 50 older women went to the House of Commons to meet with Jo Richardson, the shadow Minister for Women, to make her aware of their needs. Most of the women were active in their local community, often on Community Health Councils and on Carers' Committees, taking up the issues of concern to women.

During 1984/5 I served as a co-opted member of the Women's Committee of the Greater London Council (GLC), and one of the tasks undertaken by that Committee was to examine the position of women within the GLC 'Forum for the Elderly'[4] chaired by Councillor Harry Kay and having Jack Jones – a well-known ex-trade union leader – as one of its members. We were also to look at the Forum's attitudes to women's issues. The organisations represented on the Forum were: voluntary agencies working with older people; the Standing Conference of Ethnic Minority Senior Citizens; the Jewish Welfare Board; the Older Feminist Network; the various wings of the pensioners' movement; and the Transport and General Workers' Union (TGWU) Retired Members' Association. Unfortunately few of them attended regularly.

It seemed to the Women's Committee that the Forum lacked a women's perspective, and that it acted on the false premise that the interests of older women and men were identical. A paper was presented to the Forum from the Women's Committee on the special interests of older women, lesbians, and older women with disabilities. Older lesbians argued, for instance, that those responsible for old people's homes should recognise the need for single-sex homes and take into account the realities of lesbian family life. The Committee emphasised the need to enable women to influence the decisions that touch their lives. It called on the Forum to include a women's perspective in their future policy-making; to broaden the representation on the Forum to include organisations which work specifically with older women; and to ensure that the representation was not merely tokenistic.

The paper was not well received and Jack Jones was particularly incensed. He kept repeating that the women in the pensioners' movement would not agree with the demands of the Committee. Had we ever asked them their views, he demanded, not realising that the Women's Committee had heard those women's views through the conference they had organised, and in which I had facilitated an older women's workshop where they discussed the specific interests of women in the pensioners' movement.

After a heated discussion, it was decided to postpone any decisions until the representatives of the GLPTUAA and the TGWU retired members had had a chance to discuss the paper. Their comments were to be brought to a future meeting, but, with the abolition of the GLC and re-organisation of the Forum soon after, the matter rested there.

When finally I found it possible to join the movement myself, it was to the GLPA that I went, hoping that women's issues might be on the agenda. I was disappointed, though on attending the delegates' meeting I was encouraged by the forcefulness of some of the women in the face of the men's tub-thumping. Many of the men representatives there were left-wing demagogues able to sway the crowds. Yet, highly political as they are, the groups they represent are often social, i.e. groups of pensioners coming together mainly for tea and bingo, or lunch and a game of cards.

Having worked collectively most of my working life, I have never felt comfortable with the formality of their meetings, with their protocol and points of order. There is a whole trade union 'language' that women find difficult to penetrate. What usually happens at the delegates' meetings is that the men get up one after another to make lengthy speeches, often repeating what has already been said; and more often than not it is irrelevant to the matter under discussion. There is no real debate and women find it difficult to get into the discussion. But of late some of the women are challenging the apparently unseeing eye of the Chair when women raise their hands to speak.

The men are always keen to remind the world that it owes them a living because they fought in the Second World War. I have never understood the logic of that argument. They seem to think that they are entitled to benefits because they fought in a war, not because they have paid their insurance contributions and taxes throughout their working lives, as had their parents before them. They are supposed to be campaigning for universal benefits, so what about all the people who did not fight? Will they not have a state pension? When I challenged the 'World War' argument at one meeting, however, I was told it impresses the powers-that-be!

What worries me most, however, is the lack of real democracy in the pensioners' movement, as in so many other organisations. Officers are allowed to get away with creating and pushing through policies of their own and of manipulating the committees. It is not that the Chair or other 'leaders' do not work for the good of the organisation and the members it serves. The policies could be the best and be approved by members, but no one person can know best for all and power corrupts. It also stunts the development of other members and restricts the possibility of policy changes. It is not always the wish of the officer to wield the power or bear the burden of responsibility of putting forward ideas all the time. It is often the apathy of the membership that creates the situation. In the GLPA I believe it is the discipline learned in the trade union movement, the sense of 'loyalty above all' that precludes the members from challenging their leaders' lack of democracy. That sense of loyalty was also insisted upon in their political background. Whilst many would say that loyalty to leaders was necessary in order to win the struggle, my political experience makes me wary of such arguments. But class loyalty is very strong and whenever I point out an undemocratic decision I gain no support. I am made to feel like a traitor. Though some of the women in the local action groups complain bitterly that their chairperson is a dictator, I know that if ever he was attacked by an outsider they would close ranks to defend him. There is one member of the Executive who does challenge undemocratic acts, but he is a rare character – he also encourages debate on women's issues!

At the Birmingham 1992 National Pensioners' Convention many of the women delegates became extremely annoyed and frustrated. The report given to the Executive Committee of the GLPA showed that delegates had been pressured by the leaders to withdraw or remit certain resolutions without proper debate. One such was a motion on equal pension rights for men and women. After a clash of different motions, it was referred back to be clarified later by negotiation among the platform.

To the credit of the GLPA, one of its Executive Committee members pushed through a resolution on equalisation of state pension age at the TUC and got it carried unanimously, despite the leadership's opposition. The crux of the resolution was that the General Council should initiate a major broad-based campaign of opposition to the Social Security Advisory Committee recommendation that the pension should be equalised at age 65 for women and men. Recognising the threat this poses to women, the resolution was in favour of equality of state pension at age 60.

Whilst I was still rejoicing at that, I was astounded to hear a resolution moved at the GLPA Annual General Meeting later that year calling for the opening up of membership of the Association to those aged 60. I jumped to my feet to point out that there were already members aged 60 in the Association – they were called *women*. It seems that older women are invisible to many trade unionists and certainly to many retired ones. The whole movement seems to be gender-blind. The British Pensioners' and Trades Union Association, the national body, states in its constitution that it aims to 'involve the broad mass of pensioners, regardless of race, colour or creed'. No mention of gender. Yet women make up the vast majority of pensioner numbers.

Moreover, those women are worried that the government's 'care in the community' plans will actually mean older women having to care for even older relatives. Already they have learned of closures of council homes in the new round of cuts and of higher costs of meals-on-wheels. That's why 'care in the community' is a constant subject of discussion at delegates' meetings, and why it is one of the two major planks of its campaigning in 1993, the other being no means testing of benefits.

'Care in the community' was also one of the issues raised at a recent day's conference of 'black and ethnic elders' organised by the GLPA, whose representative on the Executive is a woman. The conference was organised to obtain the views of black and ethnic minorities on the 10 clauses of the British Pensioners' Charter. Hopefully the Charter will be changed soon to reflect issues of gender and ethnicity.

However, the Association has a hard battle to survive financially, even though the trade union movement has responded generously to its appeals. As always, the women members rally round. They organise jumble sales and Christmas draws and their fund-raising efforts help greatly to keep the GLPA afloat. I believe that it is high time the women's commitment was given greater recognition and that the issues that affect their lives be put on the agenda.

Notes

1. Task Force later became Pensioners' Link. In April 1993 the central office of Pensioners' Link lost its grant from the London Borough Grants Committee. At the time of writing some of the local centres have retained their funding and are continuing their work with pensioners. The older Women's Project (see below), with secure funding, is becoming a Membership Organisation and has changed its name to Association of Greater London Older Women (AGLOW).

2. The Greater London Pensioners' and Trades Union Association later became the Greater London Pensioners' Association (GLPA).

3. The Charter and the Declaration of Intent were discussed in the *GLPA Newsletter* in June 1992, thus: 'The decisions of the Birmingham Conference of the National Pensioners' Convention have brought the Declaration of Intent much closer to the British Pensioners' Charter. However, the role of the two documents is entirely different. The Declaration is a statement of agreed policy on matters affecting pensioners whereas the Charter translates that policy into simple terms for mass communication.'

4. The GLC Forum for the Elderly was initiated to give London's pensioners a way of getting their views heard by policy-makers. Seen as a partnership between the Council's elected members and representatives of elderly people's organisations, its aims were to provide a platform for elderly Londoners to raise their concerns and develop their ideas, to involve them in the development of policies, to look at issues from the perspective of pensioners and make representation to central government and other relevant bodies.

CONCEPTS AND VALUES

34

Ageism: concept and definition

Julia Johnson and Bill Bytheway

In an earlier paper we argued that the way in which ageism is defined affects not only the scope of gerontological inquiry but also wider political debate about policies relating to age (Bytheway and Johnson, 1990). Whereas the analytical relevance of the concepts of race and racism have been debated for years (Banton, 1977; Miles, 1989), little attention has been given to ageism. In this chapter, we briefly review how the concept of ageism has been used and then consider some of the problems in formulating a definition.

Butler's definition

Butler provided the first, and perhaps the most well-known, definition. In *The Encyclopedia of Aging*, published in 1987, he defines ageism as follows:

> Ageism is defined as a process of systematic stereotyping of, and discrimination against, people because they are old, just as racism and sexism accomplish this for skin colour and gender. (Butler, 1987: 22)

This formulation, reflecting a widely held view of ageism, incorporates a number of key words.

Old – The only reference to age is through the word 'old'. Butler relates his conceptualisation of ageism to a discernible group of people who can be referred to as 'old'. He, like many others, uses a number of other words to refer to this group – older, elders, elderly, aged – but not in a way which challenges the presumption of its existence. The pensioners' movement is well established in many countries, often with a multiplicity of organisations that draw upon memberships of people over a certain age. However, with the growth of the third age movement and radical changes in the regulation of retirement and

---

This chapter is based on a paper presented at the Second International Conference on 'The Future of Adult Life', Leeuwenhorst, The Netherlands, 1990.

pensions, the specification of the criteria determining who is old is becoming increasingly debatable.

Stereotyping – This is the attribution of a range of distinctive characteristics to all members of a group. Butler suggests that 'old' people are 'categorized as senile, rigid in thought and manner, and old fashioned in morality and skills'. There are two important aspects to stereotyping which need to be distinguished. One is the ascription of negative characteristics. Terms such as senile, rigid and old fashioned, are viewed negatively in popular opinion; most of us would feel offended if they were applied to ourselves. The second aspect is that stereotyping draws upon generalisation, and possibly upon valid scientific research. For example, 'old people are typically poor' is the kind of conclusion that might be drawn from research and indeed which might form the basis of anti-ageist action. Nevertheless, the statement, and the word 'typically' in particular, can foster the belief that 'all old people are poor': a classic stereotype which fosters a wide range of ageist responses, such as concessionary fares.

Discrimination – This is action taken in relation to all people of a certain group. An obvious example of ageist discrimination is the inclusion in a job advertisement of the statement: 'people over 35 need not apply'. Again discrimination is typically viewed negatively but it should be noted that there is always a 'positive' side: 'preferential consideration will be given to people aged 35 or under', for example. The important point about discrimination is that it is the exercise of power by an organisation over the individual.

Against – This directly implies conflict; in particular, conflict between old people, on the one hand, and those who stereotype and discriminate, on the other. Most writers on this subject identify older people as the victims of ageism. Some, however, see ageist conflict as involving not just 'the old' but all age groups, each stereotyping and discriminating against the others. Another tendency, not so clearly apparent, is to play down conflict, seeing ageism rather as a failure of societal attitudes. The conflict between age groups is echoed in the conflict between critics such as Butler and the ageism they seek to challenge. They are against ageism; ageism is something that has to be fought – military metaphors abound.

They – Who are 'we' and who are 'they'? Kuhn, in a discussion of being old in an ageist culture, asserts, 'we are a new breed of old people' (1977: 14). In contrast, 'we', for other writers, are service providers: 'Our society has a very negative attitude towards old age. This affects the way we treat elderly people, the expectations we have of them and the services we provide' (Dixon and Gregory, 1987: 20). The use of these pronouns creates a conceptual map around the authors' reasoning, causing groups of people to be variously included and excluded. In particular, Butler's mapping suggests that they, the old who are discriminated against, are indeed a category of people who are different from the implied 'us'.

Sexism and Racism – Butler's reference to sexism and racism is a near universal practice in writing about ageism. The two words 'just as' directly imply equivalence. Many use the parallel with sexism and racism as the basis of a definition of ageism, thereby ignoring what is distinctive and peculiar about age (something we come back to later). As Cole has commented about ageism: 'we do not yet have the careful, critical scholarship that might justify or illuminate its analogies to racism or sexism' (1986: 119). Others, fearing that age discrimination might be perceived to be no more than the latest fashion, are cautious about adding ageism to the anti-discriminatory agenda (Stevenson, 1989: 8).

Two broad tendencies

In reviewing different approaches to the conceptualisation of ageism, we have detected two broad tendencies. The first, well represented by Butler's definition, is to see ageism as something that relates solely to older people. This view is encompassed both by welfarists whose concern is with the needs of older people, and by political economists whose focus is on the relationship of older people to the process of production. What is common to both is the assumption that there are 'elderly people' who constitute a minority group that suffers a series of negative characterisations: for example, that they are 'a burden to society'.

The second tendency is to relate ageism, not just to older people, but to all people regardless of age. As Itzin puts it,

> Ageism is usually regarded as being something that affects the lives of older people. Like ageing, however, it affects every individual from birth onwards – at every stage putting limits and constraints on experience, expectations, relationships and opportunities. Its divisions are as arbitrary as those of race, gender, class and religion. Thus the chronology of ageing becomes the hierarchy of ageism. (1986: 114)

What this implies is that ageism affects us all throughout our lives: it is prejudice based on age not old age. As evidence of this, there is, first the growing importance that is given to individual age by social institutions such as the National Health Service or Social Security – being too old for an operation or too young for a welfare benefit, for example. Secondly, there is the lifelong fear of age, and the pressure to sustain a youthful outlook and appearance, fostered not least by an aggressive cosmetics industry. Within this perspective, it is not difficult to think of the tendency to separate off 'the elderly', and to express concern about the stereotypes and discrimination that 'they' have to suffer, as a clear example of ageist distancing.

Formulating a definition

The formulation of a definition which focuses upon ageism throughout the life course rather than upon 'old people', however, is problematic. Our individual relationship to socially constructed age categories is constantly changing as we age.

Biological variation is used to legitimate distinctions on grounds of gender and race, and in a similar way the biology of ageing is used to provide a scientific justification for particular social responses (Estes and Binney, 1989; Leonard, 1982). For example, a doctor may decide against a certain form of treatment on the grounds that the prognosis, based upon scientific evidence, is not good given the patient's age. Many such responses presume the inevitability of decline with age. Levin and Levin have argued that biological theories of ageing have prompted the association between ageing and decline:

> Both the theories and the research in physiological ageing have contributed to our expectation that the human organism will deteriorate with age. Psychologists of ageing seem to have taken the literature of physiological ageing as a model for their own work, assuming that the brain declines with age as the rest of the body does. Thus, like the literature in physiological ageing, the psychology of ageing has become a litany of decline in the mental adaptive capacities of humans. (1980: 10)

The idea that 'the human organism will deteriorate with age' unambiguously implies that 'inferiority' comes with age. Levin and Levin also argued that many social gerontologists as well as psychologists have adopted the biological model in documenting and explaining the decline of social life with age. Despite strenuous efforts to promote a more positive image of 'successful' ageing, the model of decline is still widely held, as is evident from the massive sales of ageist birthday cards. It is not difficult to see how belief in decline and in the inferiority of life in old age underlies many recent discussions about euthanasia. In this way, the model of biological decline is critical to ageism.

This model, however, does not adequately explain why 'the young' as well as 'the old' are marginalised, stereotyped and discriminated against, using exactly the same marker: chronological age. Kuhn (1978) seeks to forge an alliance between younger and older people, conceiving of both groups as adults who, through age, are on the margins of the labour force. Franklin and Franklin (1990) likewise examine the 'treatment of young and old people'. Their discussion of cultural, political and economic issues tends to focus upon the admission and discharge of individuals to 'ordinary adult life'. According to this approach, ageist discrimination originates in age-specific legislation regarding the labour market and, most directly, affects those on the margins of the labour force. It is not seen as directly affecting the very young or the very old or, indeed, those in mid-working life.

If we regard discrimination against young adults as an aspect of ageism, then we must take into account biological theories of development as well as those of decline. Both include presumptions about competence; in the case of the young competence is being acquired, and in the case of the old it is seen to be declining. Such theories are being used to legitimate institutional discrimination at both ends of the working life: the young are not yet old enough and the old have become too old. As we have seen in recent years, these forms of discrimination are not applied just to the hiring and firing of employees but also to the classification of those not in work: to reduce the embarrassment of the government, both the young and the old are increasingly being excluded from the official unemployment statistics.

Inclusion and exclusion

A definition of ageism that focuses solely on the points of entry and exit to the working population, however, neglects a critical feature of Itzin's perspective: how ageism places limits, constraints and expectations at *every* stage from birth onwards. Echoing theories of development and decline, but regardless of age, a person may simultaneously be told 'not to be so childish' and be accused of 'going senile', and another be told to 'grow up' and also be described as 'getting past it'. In all these instances, references to stereotyped ideas about age-appropriate behaviour are being used to exercise power, to put people down, to make them feel that they have 'failed' to develop properly and that they are declining in their capacities.

We consider the idea of middle-aged people being the agents of ageism, oppressing both the young and the old and only being threatened themselves 'in the future', to be inadequate. At the 'peak of maturity' as much as at the extremes of age, chronological age is used to mark out categories of people who are seen as similar or different to oneself. Since we all are constantly threatened by this form of interpersonal assessment, we seek to distance ourselves from the realities of ageing by having, as Matthews (1979) puts it, one definition for others and another for ourselves. In other words, 'we' seek to be included and to have 'them' excluded. To avoid exclusion, we hide our age by keeping it secret and by cosmetically treating its visible manifestations.

In attempting to remain included as we age, despite our experience of being excluded by younger people, we feel it is necessary to see other 'old people' as different from ourselves. Hence, far from being 'anti-ageist', we are inclined to draw upon our life-long training in ageism in relating to others. This is well illustrated by the common anecdote: 'Isn't it funny? She's 80 and she talks about visiting her "old people"!' Unlike the teller of the tale, the 80-year-old doesn't see herself as one of the old people.

Conclusion

This discussion suggests a short definition of ageism: the offensive exercise of power through reference to age. This accommodates both institutionalised ageism, including legislative discrimination against people over specific ages (like exclusion from jury service), and internalised ageism such as offensive interpersonal action (for example, calling someone an 'old bag'). It also covers benevolent patronage, perhaps the most pervasive form of ageism: 'keeping an eye on the old folk' and so on.

What is most difficult in developing appropriate responses to ageism is how to take 'proper' account of the reality of age. There is inevitably a certain truth behind the stereotypes. People born before 1940 do have personal memories of the Second World War; they do have a life expectation which is less than that of younger generations; they were socialised as children into a culture that is no longer dominant; they are statistically more vulnerable to a variety of threats to their well-being. The answer, perhaps, is to develop patterns of interaction that ignore the stereotypes and that collectively challenge the ageism of the institutions.

If people wish to take collective action as 'old people', they are obviously free to do so and, of course, they have every right to be impatient and indignant. It may be that their continued oppression will come to be known as 'oldageism'. But one senses that, for many older people, the inequalities that they would choose to challenge in the political arena are those based on other identities relating to gender, ethnicity, disability and class.

References

Banton, M. (1977) *The Idea of Race*. London: Tavistock.

Butler, R.N. (1987) 'Ageism', in *The Encyclopedia of Aging*. New York: Springer, pp. 22–3.

Bytheway, B. and Johnson, J. (1990) 'On defining ageism', *Critical Social Policy*, 29: 27–39.

Cole, T. (1986) 'The "enlightened" view of ageing: Victorian morality in a new key', in T. Cole and S.A. Gadow (eds), *What Does It Mean To Grow Old?* Durham, NC: Duke University Press, pp. 117–130.

Dixon, J. and Gregory, L. (1987) 'Ageism', *Action Baseline*, 34: 21–2.

Estes, C.L. and Binney, E.A. (1989) 'The biomedicalization of ageing: dangers and dilemmas', *The Gerontologist*, 29 (5): 587–96.

Franklin, A. and Franklin, B. (1990) 'Age and power', in T. Jeffs and M. Smith (eds), *Young People, Inequality and Youth Work*. Basingstoke: Macmillan, pp. 1–27.

Itzin, C. (1986) 'Ageism awareness training: a model for group work', in C. Phillipson, M. Bernard and P. Strang (eds), *Dependency and Interdependency in Old Age: Theoretical Perspectives and Policy Alternatives*. London: Croom Helm, pp. 114–26.

Kuhn, M. (1977) *Maggie Kuhn on Aging*. Philadelphia, PA: Westminster Press.

Kuhn, M. (1978) 'The gray panther rides again!', *New Age*, 5: 7–8.

Leonard, P. (1982) 'Editor's introduction', in C. Phillipson, *Capitalism and the Construction of Old Age*. London: Macmillan, pp. xi–xiv.

Levin, J. and Levin, W.C. (1980) *Ageism: Prejudice and Discrimination against the Elderly*. Belmont,CA: Wadsworth.

Matthews, S. (1979) *The Social World of Old Women*. London: Sage.

Miles, R. (1989) *Racism*. London: Routledge.

Stevenson, O. (1989) *Age and Vulnerability*. London: Edward Arnold.

35

'Us' and 'them'? Feminist research, community care and disability

Jenny Morris

Both disability and 'community care' are issues of fundamental interest to women yet the feminist concern with 'community care' has been partisan in that it is almost entirely from the point of view of non-disabled and younger women. The experience and interests of disabled and older women are missing from the terms of debate, from the research and from the development of theory. In order to understand how this has come about, it is necessary to go back to the origins of feminism's concern with 'community care'.

Feminist theory on the family

The feminist concern with 'community care' policies is integrally linked to feminism's central concern with women's position within the family. During the 1970s and 1980s, feminist academics developed theoretical analyses of the family and of the welfare state and the interrelationship between the two was particularly apparent in the boom in research and theorising on the issue of 'carers'. Feminists exposed the way that the state exploits women's unpaid labour within the home and the extent to which the policies of caring for elderly and disabled people within the community depend upon women's role within the family.

A key concern for feminists was to assess what social policies should be supported and campaigned for. Research and analysis was particularly directed at the question of whether, and under what conditions, 'care in the community' could be supported or whether alternative types of policy would further women's interests. [. . .]

Capitalism, according to McIntosh, depends on a family household system in which

This article is based on a chapter in the author's book, *Pride against Prejudice: Transforming Attitudes to Disability*, published by The Women's Press (1991).
From *Critical Social Policy*, 33, Winter 1991/2: 22–38 (abridged).

a number of people are expected to be dependent on the wages of a few adult members, primarily of the husband and father who is a 'breadwinner', and in which they are all dependent for cleaning, food preparation and so forth on unpaid work chiefly done by the wife and mother. (1979: 155)

This system also enables women – whose main role is unpaid caring work within the family, supported by the male wage – to be used as a reserve army of labour when required by socio-economic and technological developments.

The key issue for non-disabled feminists is that this family household system is based on women's economic dependence on men. Mary McIntosh, Elizabeth Wilson and other feminists also identified that the state has an important role to play in perpetuating and strengthening this family system and women's dependency within it (Wilson, 1977). It followed from this recognition of the role of the state that, if a feminist strategy was to be aimed at freeing women from their economic dependence, campaigns around equal pay and equal employment opportunities were not enough; it was also crucial to resist state policies which perpetuated women's role of providing unpaid labour within the home.

As McIntosh concluded, there were two aspects to the strategy which needed to be developed to address women's role within the family. 'What is called for', she said, 'is political struggle for state recognition of the needs of both sexes and all unwaged individuals, combined with a transformation of the dependent household so that women can participate in production on the same basis as men' (McIntosh, 1979: 170–1).

In respect of women's needs as 'unwaged individuals', the work of Hilary Land and others drew attention to the way in which the social security system perpetuated women's economic dependence on men. Various campaigns were waged around specific issues in an attempt to win financial support for women in their own right rather than as wives. This strategy was articulated by the adoption by the British Women's Liberation Movement in 1974 of the 'fifth demand' – that of legal and financial independence.

Feminists also attacked the family as the context in which women provide unpaid care. In the late 1960s and early 1970s the caring function which feminists primarily focused on was child care. From the late 1970s, however, feminists started to turn their attention to the caring tasks which are carried out within the family other than child care – the care of physically disabled people, of older people and of learning disabled people. This was partly prompted by the fact that during the early 1980s a radical Conservative government enthusiastically took up the issue of 'community care' in its task of bringing about a radical restructuring of the relationship between the state, the individual and the family.

Feminists and 'community care'

[. . .] Mary McIntosh's 1981 article in *Critical Social Policy* sets out the general terms of the debate which feminists developed during the 1980s. Although, in the context of the Tory ideological and financial onslaught on state benefits and services, much feminist energy of necessity has had to go into defending the welfare state, McIntosh argues the importance for feminists of getting our strategic priorities clarified. 'The problem', she says, 'is whether to press for equality with men, usually in terms of legal, political and citizenship rights, or to press for greater support and respect for women in their role as housewives and mothers' (1981: 37). [. . .]

Like many feminists McIntosh comes down firmly in support of the first strategy – that of placing women on the same footing as men – because this would undermine the dependency relationships within the family. As she writes, 'Women's liberation depends upon the radical transformation of [the] family' (1981: 38). The main tactic which McIntosh focuses on in this article is the demand for disaggregation in the social security and taxation system (i.e. the abolition of the treatment of the married couple as one unit for taxation and social security purposes), the motivation being that 'all women will have rights to full social security and that all men will lose the right to state back-up for keeping their wives in dependence' (1981: 39). It is no coincidence, however, that in a bracketed aside McIntosh states 'we should be mounting a much stronger criticism of present ideas of "community" and fighting for new forms of institutional care that avoid the problems earlier radicals have pointed to' (1981: 35). If women's dependence on men and their concomitant lack of economic independence as individuals is grounded in their caring role within the family, then it is but a short step to arguing that women should not do this caring and that such caring tasks should be performed outside the family.

The logic of a feminist strategy on community care policies seems inevitable. As Janet Finch says in an article published in 1984,

> We are clear what we want to reject: we reject so-called community care policies which depend on the substantial and consistent input of women's unpaid labour in the home, whilst at the same time effectively excluding them from the labour market and reinforcing their economic and personal dependence upon men.

Finch takes issue with socialists such as Alan Walker (1982), who holds the view that non-sexist modes of community care could possibly be developed through both the expansion of domiciliary services and a challenge to men's attitudes to caring. She argues that even if state provision expanded so that adequate care was provided by paid carers, the family will still remain the setting for community care, and since the family is the location of women's oppression, women's dependence would remain unchallenged.

This leads Finch to ask the question, 'Can we envisage *any* version of community care which is not sexist?' (1984: 7). Feminists researching on informal carers have generally agreed with her when she asserts that she cannot. The case is a strong one; all the evidence is that caring for adults within the home places a greater burden on women and that this caring role is a crucial part of women's dependence. Moreover, as Hilary Graham (1983) discusses, the association of 'caring for' with 'caring about' plays an important part in the social construction of what it is to be a woman in western society.

In the context of this analysis, feminists have difficulty supporting community care policies. This creates a dilemma. Either feminists have to support residential care or, as Finch says, conclude that alternative ways of 'looking after highly dependent people' cannot be developed without fundamental social, economic and cultural transformation (Finch, 1984: 16). [. . .]

'On balance', she says,

It seems to me that the residential route *is* the only one which ultimately will offer us a way out of the impasse of caring: collective solutions would, after all, be very much in the spirit of a socialist policy programme, and a recognition that caring *is* labour, and in a wage-economy should be paid as such, in principle should overcome some of the more offensive features of the various 'community' solutions. An additional bonus would be for the creation of additional 'real' jobs in the welfare sector. (1984: 16)

Finch goes on,

Working through precisely how such care could be provided in a way which does not violate the relational aspects of caring, nor individual autonomy and identity, and would actually be popular with those for whom it was provided, seems a difficult but a possible programme for both feminists and socialists concerned with this area of social policy. There is a particular urgency about this task, given the rising numbers of elderly people in the population between now and the end of the century. (1984: 16)

Gillian Dalley has taken up this challenge. In *Ideologies of Caring*, published in 1988, she argues strongly against community care policies and in favour of new forms of residential 'collective' care. She starts from the position that community care policies 'appear to be premised precisely on principles to which feminists are opposed – that is, upon the primacy of the family and the home-bound status of women within it. They are exact contradictions of the collectivist solutions to the problems of caring which feminists would propose' (Dalley, 1988: xii). Dalley not only criticises the failure to provide sufficient resources to enable a good quality of life within the community, but also argues that 'care in the community' is actually against the interests of both women and those people who they are supposed to benefit. [. . .]

Disabled and older people experience daily the inadequacies of 'community care' and would agree with everything that feminists such as Finch and Dalley say about the isolation, poverty and sheer hard work which too often characterise both their lives and that of their carers. However, disabled and older people as individuals and through their organisations have almost without exception put their energies into achieving a better quality of life *within* the community (taking this to mean outside residential care) and have thus maintained a (critical) support of community care policies – whilst recognising that the Conservative government may have some questionable motivations for promoting such policies. For those disabled people who have resisted residential care as the solution to their housing and personal care needs and insisted on their rights to live within the community, the approach of feminists such as McIntosh, Finch and Dalley to care in the community policies is very alarming. Are we right to be alarmed or should we be putting our efforts into demanding better forms of residential care, as they suggest?

'Us' and 'them'

We can go a long way towards answering this question when we recognise that for feminists writing and researching on carers, the category 'women' does not generally include those who need physical assistance. When Janet Finch asked the question 'Can we envisage any version of community care which is not sexist?' she went on to say, 'If we cannot, then we need to say something about how we imagine such people *can* be cared for in ways which we find acceptable' (1984: 7; italics in original). In order to understand how she, and other feminists, answer this question it is necessary to recognise who Janet Finch means when she says 'we' and whether 'we' are included in the term 'such people'.

The latter term refers to 'people (of whatever age, although this perhaps is an experience most common in old age) whose physical needs require fairly constant attendance or, at least, the constant presence of another person' (1984: 7). Throughout Finch's writing and that of other feminists on community care policies it is clear that the term 'we' quite definitely does not include 'such people'. When Finch and others are assessing what policies would be acceptable to 'us' she means what policies would be acceptable to non-disabled feminists.

Much of the research that feminists have engaged in on caring explicitly separates out non-disabled women from disabled women. Gillian Dalley (1988), for example, refers to 'women and dependent people' as if they are two completely separate groups, whose interests, what is more, are in conflict. She introduces her book by saying, 'This book is about dependent people and the women who usually care for them' (1988: 1). This separation of 'women' from disabled and older people (who are treated as genderless unless their gender, as in Clare Ungerson's research [Ungerson, 1987], is of significance to the carer) is evident in most of the feminist research on caring and has major implications for the questions and issues which feminists consider important. Finch and Groves (1983), for example, identified that the equal opportunity issues around community care were those concerning the sexual division of labour between men and women as carers. In none of the pieces of research is there any analysis of equal opportunity issues for disabled and older women.

This separating out of disabled and older women from the category of 'women' comes about because of a failure of the feminist researchers concerned to identify with the subjective experience of 'such people'. The principle of 'the personal is political' is applied to carers but not to the 'cared for'. This general tendency is articulated by Clare Ungerson's account of why the issue of caring is of personal significance to her. She writes

> my interest in carers and the work that they do arises out of my own biography. The fact that my mother was a carer and looked after my grandmother in our home until my grandmother's death when I was 14 combines with the knowledge that, as an only daughter, my future contains the distinct possibility that I will sooner or later become a carer myself. (Ungerson, 1987: 2)

Lois Keith, a disabled feminist, commented on Ungerson's inability to see *herself* (and not just her mother) as potentially a person who needs physical care:

> Most of us can imagine being responsible for someone weaker than ourselves, even if we hope this won't happen. It is certainly easier to see ourselves as being needed, than to imagine ourselves as dependent on our partner, parents or children for some of our most basic needs. (Keith, 1990)

[. . .] Like most feminists who have written on this subject, Ungerson fails to incorporate into her analysis the fact that, not only are most carers women (although, as I shall discuss later, not such a large proportion as feminists have assumed), but so are most of those who receive 'care'. Her analysis of social processes involved in the issue of caring must remain incomplete while she considers only one part of the caring relationship and, far from being exciting, research such as hers is profoundly depressing from the point of view of disabled and older women who are yet again marginalised – but this time by those who proclaim their commitment to 'women-centred issues'. Even Suzy Croft (1986), who started to challenge the concepts of independence and dependence, acknowledging the important role of radical disability organisations, still failed to break out of the analytical straitjacket which divides 'women' from disabled and older people.

The failure of feminist researchers and academics to identify with the subjective experience of those who receive care has meant that they have studied caring situations where there are seemingly very clear distinctions between the person who cares for and the person who receives care. Their assumptions have led them to seek out carers and the most common source of identifying potential interviewees is organisations (statutory authorities and voluntary organisations) to whom people have identified themselves as carers. However, a situation in which one party to a relationship has a clear identity as a carer while the other is clearly cared for can only represent one type of caring relationship – and may, in fact, not be the most common. If we focused not just on the subjective experience of those identified as carers but also on the other party to the caring relationship we may find that in some situations the roles are blurred, or shifting. We may also want to expand our definition of caring for to encompass not just physical tasks but also the emotional part of caring for relationships. Research carried out by disabled feminists would, therefore, focus not so much on carers as on caring.

Feminist research on carers is a valuable application of the principle 'the personal is political' and I do not underestimate the importance of the higher public profile of the needs of carers which this research has helped to bring about. However, the failure to include the subjective experience of disabled and older people has meant that the feminist analyses and strategies stemming from the research have a number of limitations. Most importantly it has resulted in a dilemma being posed between 'care in the community' or residential care, which is in many ways a false dichotomy. It is also evident that, not only are the attempts to encompass the interests of disabled and older people merely token gestures, but the interests of carers have not been fully addressed either. [. . .]

References

Croft, S. (1986) 'Women, caring and the recasting of need', *Critical Social Policy*, 16: 23–39.

Dalley, G. (1988) *Ideologies of Caring: Rethinking Community and Collectivism*. London: Macmillan.

Finch, J. (1984) 'Community care: developing non-sexist alternatives', *Critical Social Policy*, 9: 6–18.

Finch, J. and Groves, D. (1983) *A Labour of Love: Women, Work and Caring*. London: Routledge & Kegan Paul.

Keith, L. (1990) 'Caring partnership', *Community Care*, 22 February. INSIDE supplement, pp. v–vi.

McIntosh, M. (1979) 'The welfare state and the needs of the dependent family', in S. Burman (ed.), *Fit Work for Women*. London: Croom Helm, pp. 153–72.
McIntosh, M. (1981) 'Feminism and Social Policy', *Critical Social Policy*, 1: 32–42.
Ungerson, C. (1987) *Policy is Personal*. London: Tavistock.
Walker, A. (ed.) (1982) *Community Care: the Family, the State and Social Policy*. Oxford: Blackwell/Martin Robertson.
Wilson, E. (1977) *Women and the Welfare State*. London: Tavistock.

36

Philosophical perspectives on quality of life

Andrew Sixsmith

Introduction: some ideas about the 'good life'

Some of the earliest ideas about well-being and quality of life are provided by the Greek philosophers and, indeed, many of their principles are firmly lodged in the popular consciousness of what constitutes the 'good life'. For example, hedonism holds that the sole good in human life is pleasure. The modern view of hedonism is one of living a life of wantonness and abandon, seeking pure pleasure regardless of any consequences. A more accurate account is one of living pleasurably, but moderately, recognising the fact that too much of a good thing can have very negative outcomes, such as the rotten hangover that usually follows on from too much drink.

The Greeks also gave us some very different perspectives on the nature of well-being. Stoicism can be seen as a way of overcoming adversity, of facing the many problems that one will encounter in life. The key principle is to be indifferent to the external world. By cultivating this indifference and learning to accept the inevitable then an individual will be no longer in the power of others or of external influences. Cynicism is a similar philosophy of consolation, where the world is seen as basically bad and the things that are conventionally held to be valuable – honour, property, pleasure – are all worthless. If the individual relies on these external things, then he or she may be betrayed by them. Personal salvation and virtue can be found only within the individual and thus a virtuous and happy life will be one that is frugal and simple. The rejection of worldly pleasures can also be found in asceticism and Christian ethics:

> We are God's heirs and Christ's fellow-heirs, if we share his sufferings now in order to share his splendour hereafter. (Romans 8. 17)

This brief discussion illustrates the very diverse views about well-being and perhaps should warn us that we are unlikely to come up with a straightforward definition of the 'good life'. However, there are three philosophical approaches, which are of particular significance to the discussion of quality of life: utilitarianism, Aristotelian philosophy, and existentialism.

Utilitarianism

The central question within utilitarian thought is how can we determine whether any action is right or wrong? This issue was resolved by the principle of 'utility', developed by philosophers such as John Stuart Mill and Jeremy Bentham. Utilitarianism holds that an action is right if it produces the greatest good or 'happiness' for the greatest number of people:

> Utility, or the Greatest Happiness Principle, holds that actions are right in proportion as they tend to promote happiness, wrong as they tend to produce the reverse of happiness. By happiness is intended pleasure, and the absence of pain; by unhappiness, pain and the privation of pleasure. (Mill, 1972: 6)

This 'greatest good' principle has had enormous influence on welfare thinking and social and economic policy within the western, liberal tradition. The ideal of utility has also been central to the conceptualisation of individual well-being, motivation and quality of life. From a utilitarian perspective, people are seen as rational beings, whose actions are aimed at maximising their well-being, or utility. Individuals undertake a kind of cost-benefit exercise that involves adding together all the 'goods' that accrue in their life and subtracting from that all the 'bads'. Well-being occurs when the 'goods' outweigh the 'bads'. This model is implicit in the way many social scientists have examined quality of life, particularly within economics and psychology. Indeed, Bentham gave us what is perhaps the first ever life-satisfaction scale in what he called the 'Hedonic Calculus', which evaluated the amount of pleasure of an action according to certain components, such as intensity of pleasure and its duration. By quantifying well-being in this way, it is possible to measure it empirically, allowing comparisons to be made between individuals or relating well-being to factors such as poverty, health and so on.

However, it is important to consider the limitations of the idea of well-being as utility. Can people really put a value on the different aspects of their life? Can they simultaneously consider all aspects of life and put them into a 'happiness equation'? Is happiness, or utility, the only motivating factor behind human behaviour? Are all people alike in the way they perceive happiness, and evaluate their lives? Are people's preferences and desires stable or do they change over time? Cannot people be mistaken about what is in their best interests?

Aristotle and happiness

Utilitarianism is concerned with the effects or outcomes of an action. Everything we do, and everything that happens to us, has benefits or disadvantages. An action is 'good' if the beneficial effects exceed the negative ones, with 'happiness' as the key to the 'good life'. Happiness is also seen as the supreme good by Aristotle in his *Nichomachean Ethics*, but his interpretation of human well-being departs from the utilitarian version in a number of important ways (Megone, 1990).

Aristotle's concern is with the means by which happiness is achieved. He argues that if we understand the essential nature of our being then we will also understand the nature of our well-being. Aristotle talks about man's 'function'. If a thing or person has a function or purpose then its best state will be when it is fulfilling that purpose. One can identify purposes in all manner of things: eyes, feet and so on, all have some purpose. But the notion of 'essence' implies some characteristic that is exclusive to the phenomenon in question. So what is man's characteristic purpose or function that distinguishes him from all other things? Aristotle identifies this as 'rational activity', or the operation of reason and intellect in one's life. The actions of animals are not guided by 'reasons' in the same way as is human action and thus intentional action is the unique quality of being human. Following on from this, the best state of being for a human would be to lead a fully rational life. While the 'perfect' life would be one of pure contemplation, the exercise of rationality in all our everyday actions would be the key to happiness and fulfilment in a practical sense.

This account of happiness may not ring entirely true to our modern ears – for example, with regard to the precedence of the intellect over other aspects of life. However, Aristotle raises certain issues which are crucial to a discussion of quality of life. First, from an Aristotelian perspective, well-being is not a state or an 'object', but an 'activity', where happiness is a kind of 'by-product' of the way we act in the world. If happiness were a state, then it 'might belong even to a man who slept all through his life, passing a vegetable existence' (Aristotle, 1955: 326). In this sense, well-being cannot be considered as something independent of our actions; what we do will determine whether we are happy or not.

Secondly, Aristotle's account of well-being derives from an examination of essential human nature. True happiness can only be achieved if our actions are guided by the fundamental principles implied by our nature. In effect, this provides us with a code of behaviour by which our actions are judged as 'good' or 'bad'. Our personal well-being will therefore depend on the extent to which we live our lives by this moral code. In the *Nichomachean Ethics* Aristotle goes to considerable lengths to outline key 'virtues', such as courage, patience and truthfulness, by which we ought to live our lives and thereby achieve our potential for happiness.

An existentialist perspective

'Existentialism' is a very diffuse body of work that should be seen as a 'movement' rather than a 'philosophy' in a conventional sense, encompassing philosophers and writers such as Martin Heidegger (1962) and Jean-Paul Sartre (1957). However, there are certain themes which recur within existentialist writing that set it very much apart from the philosophies of Mill and Aristotle.

From an existentialist point of view, the utilitarian assertion that well-being can be reduced to a straightforward comparison of pleasure and pain would be rejected as a facile interpretation of the richness and complexity of human existence. Existentialism also departs from the Aristotelian tradition by examining, not our intrinsic nature as 'beings', but the nature of what Heidegger calls our 'being-in-the world'. We are 'trapped in existence' – we cannot escape from having to deal with our own being and everyday life. Fundamentally, we are 'coping' rather than 'knowing' beings and in this respect human activity is not something that is as inherently rational as we may think. Our general state is one of habituation, ignorance, confusion, doubt and uncertainty, while many of the circumstances in which we find ourselves are largely outside our control. We might look for rational explanations, but life is very much about conflict, contradiction, dilemma and ambiguity, where the competing strands in our lives are often irreconcilable. Life is rarely easy and personal well-being is not so much about being happy, but about how we face up to and deal with the situations we encounter.

The idea of 'facing up to life', of struggling to transcend the contingencies of life, is at the core of the existentialist view of human being. While much of life might be structured by external factors, we do not have to live our lives according to a predetermined blueprint, but are free to make choices within available options. So how do we make our choices in life? Arguably, the common way of being is governed by conformism; doing what others want you to do, a kind of socially-defined, 'unauthentic' self. This amounts to self-deception, where we evade personal responsibility by acting in the ways that are expected of us or following the well-trodden paths of life. By taking this perspective, existentialism rejects the essentialism of Aristotle. For thinkers such as Sartre, there are no codes of conduct to which we can turn for guidance. Any action which does not derive from the exercise of one's absolute freedom of choice is an act of 'bad faith'.

As an alternative, Sartre offers us 'sincerity' or 'authentic being'. This is not a matter of being true to one's own 'nature', for even this places limits on our capacity to choose and transcend what we already are. Rather it is a matter of looking at and understanding and facing the challenge of the possibilities of our being, a task in which we are completely alone. Of course we cannot hope to attend to every minute detail of our life and authenticity should be perhaps seen as a 'way of being' rather than a 'state of being'. In other words, it is not so much what we do but the way that we do it. We may fail in what we do, we may indeed feel unhappy, but at least we can say we tried, whereas acting in 'bad faith' tends to come back at us in feelings of guilt, remorse and regret.

Conclusion: the search for meaning

In quality of life we have a powerful but highly problematic concept that defies any attempt at systematic definition. Various philosophies appear relevant to our discussion, but provide very different perspectives on the nature of human well-being. All have their strengths and weaknesses and I would not like to suggest that any one is 'better' than another. Nevertheless, there is considerable intuitive truth about the existentialist emphasis on the complexity and ambiguity of human being. Is our well-being really something that can be easily translated into straightforward formulas of happiness and virtue?

This point is made by Victor Frankl (1964) when he considers the lives of people who might not be seen as 'happy' in a conventional sense. He argues that even in the face of great adversity people do find a reason for their existence and illustrates this in an account of his own experiences in a Nazi concentration camp. Despite great suffering he retained the will to survive:

> There is nothing in the world, I venture to say, that would so effectively help one to survive even the worst conditions, as the knowledge that there is a meaning in one's life. There is much wisdom in the words of Nietzsche: 'He who has a why to live for can bear almost any how'. (Frankl, 1964: 105–6)

The situation that Frankl endured is perhaps the worst that most of us are able to conceive of: suffering, uncertainty about whether you will live or die, the loss of loved ones. Yet amidst these horrors many people did find meaning in their life, whatever its specific source. For Frankl, it was the reconstruction of a confiscated manuscript on scraps of paper; for one of his comrades it was the meaning found in personal sacrifice. Perhaps there is a general lesson to be learned here: that our well-being lies in our capacity to find meaning and to conduct life accordingly.

References

Aristotle (1955) *Ethics* (trans. J.A.K. Thompson). Harmondsworth: Penguin.
Frankl, V. (1964) *Man's Search for Meaning*. London: Hodder & Stoughton.

Heidegger, M. (1962) *Being and Time*. (trans. John Macquarrie and Edward Robinson). London: SCM Press.

Megone, C.B. (1990) 'The quality of life: starting from Aristotle', in S. Baldwin et al. (eds), *Quality of Life: Perspectives and Policies*. London: Routledge, pp. 28–41.

Mill, J.S. (1972) *Utilitarianism*. London: Dent. (Originally published in 1861.)

Sartre, J.-P. (1957) *Being and Nothingness*. (trans. Hazel E. Barnes). London: Methuen.

37

Religion and aging

David O. Moberg

Age differences in religious indicators

Public opinion polls provide national information on religious behavior and attitudes. The Gallup poll (Princeton Religion Research Center, 1982) has included questions about religion for half a century, so some comparisons can be made over time as well as between subsamples of the population. One question it has asked since 1939 is 'Did you, yourself, happen to attend church or synagogue in the last seven days?' In February 1939, 41 per cent of all adults answered affirmatively. The lowest recorded point of 37 per cent was reached in 1940. It then rose to the highest levels on record – 49 per cent in 1955 and 1958 – and remained in the upper forties until 1964 (45 per cent). The subsequent gradual decline to the 1971 figure of 40 per cent can be attributed largely to reduced attendance by Catholics following the Second Vatican Council. The national figure has fluctuated between 39 per cent and 42 per cent ever since.

Of greater significance here are the large differences by age. In the typical year of 1986, for instance, only 33 per cent of the adults polled under the age of 30 attended church or synagogue in a typical week, compared to 49 per cent of those aged 65 and older. Most early Gallup polls used '50 and older' for the oldest age grouping, but the same pattern of highest weekly attendance by the highest age group consistently emerges.

The most complete Gallup survey with comparisons by age had a stratified sample of 1485 adults in 1981. It showed that old people are also more likely than others to be church members and to participate in groups for Bible study or prayer and meditation, although the charismatic renewal movement attracts more middle-aged people. Older adults are also more likely to consider religion to be very important in their lives (67 per cent), to seek God's will through prayer (84 per cent), to believe that God loves them even though they may not always please him (94 per cent), to try hard to put their religious

From K.F. Ferraro (ed.), *Gerontology: Perspectives and Issues.* New York: Springer, 1990, Chapter 10, pp. 179–205 (abridged).

beliefs into practice in relationships with all people (89 per cent) to receive a great deal of comfort and support from their religious beliefs (87 per cent), to believe in the divinity of Jesus Christ (93 per cent), to wish their religious faith were stronger (84 per cent), and to welcome social changes that make religious beliefs play a greater role in people's lives (88 per cent).

Two-fifths of the elders say they have been 'born again' or have had a turning point in life when they committed themselves to Christ. They are more likely to watch religious television programs than others, and over a third (36 per cent) are involved in charitable or social service activities, but less than a fifth (compared to more than a third of those under 30) have received any religious education or training within the past two years. They are more apt to rate themselves high for living a very Christian life (41 per cent in the two highest of 11 categories) and to have high levels of spiritual commitment (66 per cent).

Various research projects also have revealed the importance of religion among older people. Although limited by problems of sampling, cross-sectional rather than longitudinal design, and other qualifications, most have found that private religious devotions like prayer and Bible reading, use of mass media religious programs, strength of faith, religious beliefs, and other indicators of commitment are higher for older than for younger age groups. [. . .] Stronger religious commitment helps to explain the large number of old people in many churches. In 315 United Methodist churches in Kansas, for example, 30.4 per cent were aged 65 or older (Oliver and Carey, 1988).

There are wide variations by ethnicity, social class, denomination and other characteristics. Thus national data on elderly blacks shows no decline in church attendance with increasing age despite increased health disability. Their subjective religiosity is significantly higher than that of younger respondents. The church is very important in their lives, but no evidence supports the deprivation compensation model that claims religious participation is a form of alternate gratification for people of low socio-economic status (Taylor, 1986). Gitelman (1976) found that most aged urban poor blacks emphasize the importance of religion in their daily lives. Over three-fourths said they belonged to a church, and almost as many said religion was extremely important, with another one-fifth saying it was important. Nearly three-fourths said they pray a lot. In contrast, over three-fourths of the urban poor Jews were not synagogue members; most noted that religion was not very important in daily life and had difficulty naming specific activities to serve, worship or express their faith. Yet 85 per cent of the blacks and 76 per cent of the Jews said that they either were more religious now than in their youth or that they had always been religious [. . .]. Gitelman attributed the low level of Jewish religious practice to the removal of resources like kosher butcher shops, spiritual leaders and synagogues from their neighborhoods. A Midwestern study of Jews found that older men were much more likely than others to belong to five or more Jewish organizations and that elderly women had stronger religious commitment than younger women (Kart et al., 1987).

Age-period-cohort explanations

Any attempt to explain why senior citizens are more religious than middle-aged and young adults must face the age-period-cohort issue. One possibility is that the elderly generation experienced more religious training during their early socialization, but evidence on this subject is not clear. In the Duke Longitudinal Studies of Aging, church activities increased in late middle age, then leveled off in the seventies, with decline beginning at the fourth round at an average age of about 80 (Palmore, 1981). Despite the decrease among the old-old that is associated with increased physical limitations and transportation problems, polls have persistently found the highest levels of church attendance among those past 60 for at least half a century. If higher levels of religiousness were strictly a cohort phenomenon, one would expect the pattern to change over time, each successive (younger) generation being less religious in old age.

The generational differences could be a consequence of the period effects of having different kinds of experiences during the life cycle. World War I, the deadly flu epidemic of 1919/1920, the Great Depression of the 1930s and World War II produced numerous disruptions that strongly affected older Americans. Events on the religious scene also influenced their beliefs, attitudes, affiliation and activities. Not least among these were the revivalism of Dwight L. Moody, Billy Sunday and thousands of less well known evangelists; the Pentecostal movement; the fundamentalist-modernist controversies; the Scopes trial, and the immigration of millions of European Catholics (see Moberg, 1984a). Yet younger generations have had analogous experiences, such as the changes associated with World War II, the wars in Korea and Vietnam, the assassinations of John and Robert Kennedy and Martin Luther King, Jr., the Billy Graham crusades, the Charismatic Renewal Movement and the tensions related to such controversial public policy issues as the legalizing of abortion and the place of religion in public schools. The web of period effects is so tangled that it is impossible to identify any specific pattern of events that could have made the oldest generation 'more religious' than the others.

The explanation that stands up best, hence, is that the aging process itself contributes to a deepening of religious concern in the later years, especially on the private, nonorganizational level. Yet to acknowledge that is not to have a firm grasp on the causal processes that are involved. Is disengagement from other responsibilities responsible?

(Perhaps people have more time to devote to religion during retirement.) Are the elderly so obviously near the end of earthly life that they devote increased time to 'preparing for their finals'? (Is there an existential fear of death and, as that inevitable event approaches, an enhanced desire to prepare to face one's ultimate destiny and Creator?) Have we been socialized or 'programmed' by our culture to be busy activists until deteriorating bodies force us to slow down? (Does society teach us that religion is chiefly a compensation for those who are deprived and a comfort for those who cannot be 'useful' – the deprivation hypothesis?) Is there within each person a longing for reconciliation with Deity and a desire for unity with God that is squelched by the pressures of life during youth and middle age but released by freedom from social constraints in late life? (Many Christians believe that this is a universal desire that is suppressed only when people allow 'the world' to squeeze them into its mold.) Obviously there is a need for careful research to test these and other plausible hypotheses, as well as for personal reflection, conversations with mature adults and interdisciplinary sharing of perspectives from various theological and philosophical world views. [. . .]

Religion and life satisfaction

Numerous studies have found a positive relationship between various measures of religiosity and high levels of morale, life satisfaction, psychological health, successful aging and other indicators of well-being. One of the first behavioral scientists to call attention to this was psychologist George Lawton (1943). On the basis of extensive counseling with older people, he listed trust in God or 'health of the spirit' as second only to good health as a source of contentment in late life, placing it ahead of a cheerful state of mind, money, friends, a gainful occupation, pleasant relationships with family members, the satisfaction of doing things for others, and ordinary kindness and consideration from other people.

Many studies from the late 1940s through the 1960s (summarized in Gray and Moberg, 1977: 66–120) found positive correlations between religion and personal adjustment in old age. Detailed analyses in one concluded that the correlation between church membership and good adjustment should not be attributed to membership per se but was a consequence of the intervening variables of religious beliefs and activities (Moberg, 1951). Similarly, among older Mexican-Americans, the main effect of church attendance on positive life satisfaction is eliminated among men by removing the effect of health indicators, while for women attendance remains a strong predictor even after taking the effects of health into account (Levin and Markides, 1988). Dropouts from a longitudinal study of mostly Mexican-Americans also reduced the significance of attendance for life satisfaction (Markides et al., 1987).

Recent research has verified that elderly people with high levels of religious activities and beliefs are psychologically healthier than those with low levels (Morse and Wisocki, 1987), that belief in life after death is a stronger predictor of well-being and world view than frequency of church attendance (Steinitz, 1980), that among those past age 75 only health accounts for more of the explained variance in morale than religious behaviors and attitudes (Koenig et al., 1988), that the positive relationship between religion and subjective well-being is even stronger among older than among younger samples in 28 studies on the subject (Witter et al., 1985), that the normal elderly who were widowed during the Duke Longitudinal Study on Aging adapted with emotional stability supported by deep religious faith, that a lack of fear of death was associated in the same study with frequent Bible reading, belief in a future life, and religious conceptions of death, and the 'religious activity and attitudes are correlated with happiness, feeling useful, and personal adjustment' (Palmore et al., 1985: 457).

Spiritual well-being

Any attempt to develop a holistic understanding of aging must include attention to the human spirit. Sturzo (1947), an Italian social scientist, emphasized that humanity is engulfed by the supernatural, the 'true life' that surrounds the natural outward life much as the atmosphere surrounds the earth. Hence, even those who deny the reality of the supernatural live within it and are spiritual beings. There are many evidences that human nature either is basically spiritual or has a very important spiritual component (Moberg, 1967). Because few are clearly empirical by positivistic definitions, skeptics rightly argue that one cannot prove this by the 'scientific method', but neither can they disprove it by that method.

The National Interfaith Coalition on Aging (NICA) concluded that spiritual well-being is central to all concerns of 'the religious sector', but its survey to discover what the religious bodies were doing revealed a wide variety of implicit definitions. NICA developed a working definition: 'Spiritual well-being is the affirmation of life in a relationship with God, self, community and environment that nurtures and celebrates wholeness' (Thorson and Cook, 1980: xiii–xiv). That definition and related research support the hypothesis that health of the human spirit is central to the well-being of the whole person. All valid indicators of spiritual wellness correlate positively with measures of mental, physical and social wellness.

The most widely used research instrument dealing empirically with spirituality is the Spiritual Well-Being Scale developed by Paloutzian and Ellison (1982). Ten of its Likert-type items constitute a Religious

Well-Being Scale and 10 an Existential Well-Being Scale. Its results correlate highly with other measures of spiritual wellness, strongly indicating its benefits (Ellison, 1988; Moberg, 1984b, 1986).

The nursing profession has done significant work on spiritual wellness. It has added 'spiritual distress' to its diagnostic classifications (Kim et al., 1984) and initiated studies of that subject. For example, the grounded theory research of Hungelmann et al., (1985) concluded that spiritual well-being involves harmonious interconnectedness between self, others, nature and Ultimate Other (God or Life Principle). It exists throughout and beyond past, present and future time and space and 'is achieved through a dynamic and integrative growth process which leads to a realization of the ultimate purpose and meaning of life' (1985: 152). Nursing research also has found that religious and spiritual resources help patients to cope with cancer (Sodestrom and Martinson, 1987), chronic illness (Miller, 1983: 27), hemodialysis (Baldree et al., 1982), and other diseases and treatments. The contributions of nurses to the spiritual health of patients are being increasingly recognized within the profession (see Fish and Shelly, 1988). [. . .]

References

Baldree, K.S., Murphy, S.P. and Powers, M.J. (1982) 'Stress identification and coping patterns in patients on hemodialysis', *Nursing Research*, 31: 109–11.

Ellison, C.W. (1988) 'Spirituality: theory, research and application'. Unpublished manuscript, Alliance Theological Seminary, Nyack, NY.

Fish, S. and Shelly, J.A. (1988) *Spiritual Care: The Nurse's Role* (3rd edn). Downers Grove, IL: InterVarsity Press.

Gitelman, P.J. (1976) 'Morale, self-concept and social integration: a comparative study of black and Jewish aged, urban poor'. Unpublished doctoral dissertation, Rutgers University, New Brunswick, NJ.

Gray, R.M. and Moberg, D.O. (1977) *The Church and the Older Person* (rev. edn). Grand Rapids, MI: Eerdmans.

Hungelmann, J., Kenkel-Rossi, E., Klassen, L. and Stollenwerk, R.M. (1985) 'Spiritual well-being in older adults: harmonious interconnectedness', *Journal of Religion and Health*, 24: 147–53.

Kart, C.S., Palmer, N.M. and Flaschner, A.B. (1987) 'Aging and religious commitment in a midwestern Jewish community', *Journal of Religion and Aging*. 3 (3/4): 49–60.

Kim, M.J., McFarland, G.K. and McLane, A.M. (1984) *Classification of Nursing Diagnoses*. St Louis, MO: C.V. Mosby.

Koenig, H.G., Kvale, J.N. and Ferrel, C. (1988) 'Religion and well-being in later life', *The Gerontologist*, 28: 18–28.

Lawton, G. (1943) 'Happiness in old age', *Mental Hygiene*, 27: 231–7.

Levin, J.S. and Markides, K.S. (1988) 'Religious attendance and psychological well-being in middle-aged and older Mexican-Americans', *Sociological Analysis*, 49: 66–72.

Markides, K.S., Levin, J.S. and Ray, L.A. (1987) 'Religion, aging, and life satisfaction: An eight-year, three-wave longitudinal study', *The Gerontologist*, 27: 660–5.

Miller, J.F. (1983) *Coping with Chronic Illness: Overcoming Powerlessness*. Philadelphia, PA: F.A. Davis.

Moberg, D.O. (1951) 'Religion and personal adjustment in old age'. Unpublished doctoral dissertation, University of Minnesota, Minneapolis, MN.

Moberg, D.O. (1967) 'The encounter of scientific and religious values pertinent to man's spiritual nature', *Sociological Analysis*, 28: 22–33.

Moberg, D.O. (1984a) *The Church as a Social Institution* (2nd edn). Grand Rapids, MI: Baker Book House.

Moberg, D.O. (1984b) 'Subjective measures of spiritual well-being', *Review of Religious Research*, 25: 351–64.

Moberg, D.O. (1986) 'Spirituality and science: the progress, problems, and promise of scientific research on spiritual well-being', *Journal of the American Scientific Affiliation*, 38: 186–94.

Morse C.K. and Wisocki, P.A. (1987) 'Importance of religiosity to elderly adjustment', *Journal of Religion and Aging*, 4 (1): 15–26.

Oliver, D.B. and Carey, L. (1988) 'A survey of aging and aging-related programs in Kansas area United Methodist churches', *Quarterly Papers on Religion and Aging*, 4 (4): 1–8.

Palmore, E.B. (1981) *Social Patterns in Normal Aging*. Durham, NC: Duke University Press.

Palmore, E.B., Busse, E.W., Maddox, G.L., Nowlin, J.B. and Siegler, I.C. (eds) (1985) *Normal Aging III: Reports from the Duke Longitudinal Studies, 1975–1984*. Durham, NC: Duke University Press.

Paloutzian, R.F. and Ellison, C.W. (1982) 'Loneliness, spiritual well-being, and the quality of life', in A. Peplau and D. Perlman (eds), *Loneliness: A Sourcebook of Current Theory, Research and Therapy*. New York: Wiley InterScience, pp. 224–37.

Princeton Religion Research Center (1982) *Religion in America*. Princeton, NJ: Gallup Poll.

Sodestrom, K.E. and Martinson, I.M. (1987) 'Patients' spiritual coping strategies: a study of nurse and patient perspectives', *Oncology Nursing Forum*, 14: 41–6.

Steinitz, L.Y. (1980) 'Religiosity, well-being, and Weltanschauung among the elderly', *Journal for the Scientific Study of Religion*, 19: 60–7.

Sturzo, L. (1947) *The True Life: Sociology of the Supernatural* (trans. B.B. Carter). London: Geoffrey Bles.

Taylor, R.J. (1986) 'Religious participation among elderly blacks', *The Gerontologist*, 26: 630–6.

Thorson, J.A. and Cook, T.C. (eds) (1980) *Spiritual Well-Being of the Elderly*. Springfield, IL: Charles C. Thomas.

Witter, R.A., Stock, W.A., Okun, M.A. and Haring, M.J. (1985) 'Religion and subjective well-being in adulthood: a quantitative synthesis', *Review of Religious Research*, 26: 332–42.

38

Gerontological approaches to quality of life

Beverley Hughes

The concept of quality of life has played a central role in the evolution of social gerontology. It can be argued that concern about the quality of life of older people generated the questions within research, policy and practice which have led to the emergence of social gerontology as a discipline. And yet, perhaps because the concept was part of the birth process, its definition has become more complex and confused as the infant has grown and developed. [. . .]

In summary, although there has been, over the past 25 years or so, a growing concern within research and policy arenas with the quality of life of old people, neither within the research community nor amongst policy-makers has there been a systematic attempt to clarify and define the concept or how it might be measured. Whilst the concept has been fundamental to the development of social gerontology, different studies have used different definitions and different instruments. This is at least in part because quality of life presents important conceptual, definitional and methodological problems for social gerontologists. [. . .]

The concept of quality of life

The concept of quality of life is multi-dimensional and has no fixed boundary. As with similar concepts of 'need', 'well-being' or even poverty (for example, Mack and Lansley, 1985; Wilkin and Hughes, 1987), there is much room for debate not only about the *constituent elements* of the concept, but also about the *standard* for each constituent element below which the quality of life would be said to be unacceptably low.

Constituent elements

Various studies have brought together different combinations of elements to investigate the quality of life of old people in different

Originally published as 'Quality of life', in S.M. Peace (ed.), *Researching Social Gerontology: Concepts, Methods and Issues*. London: Sage, 1990, Chapter 4, pp. 46–58 (abridged).

environmental settings. Over a wide range of research, much of which has focused on the impact on old people of institutional environments, particularly residential homes (in Britain) or nursing homes (in the United States), the broad categories of elements included can be summarised as follows:

- *individual characteristics of old people*: for example, functional abilities, physical and mental health, dependency, personal characteristics such as gender, race and class (Wilkin, 1987).
- *physical environmental factors*: for example, facilities and amenities, standard of housing, control over environment, comfort, security, regime in care settings (Willcocks et al., 1987).
- *social environmental factors*: levels of social and recreational activity, family and social networks, contact with organisations (Booth, 1985).
- *socio-economic factors*: for example income, nutrition, standard of living, socio-economic status (Townsend, 1981).
- *personal autonomy factors*: ability to make choices, exercise control, negotiate environment (Evans et al., 1981).
- *subjective satisfaction*: the quality of life as assessed by the individual old person (Wilkin and Hughes, 1987).
- *personality factors*: psychological well-being, morale, life satisfaction, affect, happiness (Wilkin and Hughes, 1987).

Standards

For any particular element, there also has to be a decision about the standard at which quality of life will be assessed as poor, acceptable or good. Although it is not difficult, per se, to define in an a priori way that, say, below a certain level of income an acceptably good quality of life cannot be achieved, the difficulty lies in the ability for researchers, and people in society generally, to reach a consensus on what that particular level should be. And yet without a degree of consensus, the ability of research to make progress through time, for studies to build upon each other, for findings from different studies to be compared and contrasted, is severely restricted.

The concept of quality of life, however, is more than that of, say, 'standard of living', although standard of living would be one element of the quality of a person's life. 'Quality' cannot be reduced to a series of objectively defined standards, nor can it be encompassed entirely by subjective satisfaction expressed by the individual. On the one hand, it must be grounded in theoretical constructions of ageing, but it also relies upon normative judgements of either the researcher or the researched. It is a multi-dimensional concept which has to be conceptualised as a matrix, or network, of interrelated elements whose integration determines the overall quality of life for a particular individual. The task facing social gerontologists is to define and operationalise that concept in ways which make it a simpler task to assess an individual's quality of life and make comparisons with the lives of others in similar or different settings. There can be no single way of defining and measuring quality of life which is applicable to all types of research. However, the concept offers social gerontology a rich vein for progress not only in knowledge about old people but also in the development of theoretical constructs and research methodology, provided the definitions and methodological problems can be addressed in a systematic way. [. . .]

Objective and subjective dimensions

'Life quality includes both the *conditions* of life and the *experience* of life' (George and Bearon, 1980: 2; my emphasis). The integration of objective and subjective elements within the boundary of a single – albeit multi-dimensional – concept has been recognised as a fundamental problem in the definition and measurement of quality of life (George and Bearon, 1980). Whilst most researchers have acknowledged these two dimensions, there has been disagreement on their relative importance. In relation to the experiences of people with a mental handicap, for instance, Beswick and Zadik (1986) argue that quality of life 'is an individual subjective concept'. Thus, its measurement 'should identify individual – even idiosyncratic – needs, the relative subjective importance of those needs and the extent to which a person feels they are being met. . . . It follows that it may be illogical to try and develop meaningful group measures of quality of life' (1986: 1). The work of Havighurst and his colleagues within social gerontology has, to some extent, endorsed this stance with the implicit assumption that quality of life can be wholly or largely defined and measured by life satisfaction indices (Neugarten et al., 1961).

However, to abandon the application of the concept to group populations entirely on the grounds of the difficulty of integrating its objective and subjective elements would be to deny gerontological research vital evidence of how the elderly population fares in relation to other sections of society and, indeed, how quality of life varies between different groups of old people, across time or across cultural and ethnic factors. [. . .]

Cultural dimensions

The impact of cultural experience upon quality of life is considerable and researchers must take this dimension into account both in designing research instruments and in interpreting data. Personal characteristics such as class, race and gender are powerful intervening variables which will have a determining effect not only on the conditions of life people experience but also on their expectations and values and thence upon their subjective views of what constitutes 'good' or 'bad' quality of life. Indeed, one can argue that age itself will also be an intervening variable in that people of different ages in the same culture, with different historical experiences of life conditions and social attitudes, will define quality of life differently. Faragher (1978) has emphasised the importance of this issue for the current generations of old people, whose experience of deprivation and hardship during war years, of the development of welfare provision within the punitive ideology of the Poor Law is likely to result in expectations which are much lower than those of people, yet to become old, who have experienced a society with richer and more comfortable conditions of life.

The negative social construct of old age, outlined by Phillipson (1982), has not only obscured the positive aspects of old age, but has also, in its uniform greyness and pessimism, presented a false image of homogeneity amongst the elderly as a social group. Thus, the idea that old age itself is the great leveller, the most powerful determinant of quality of life, has become deeply entrenched in western ideology and has served to obscure the connection between poor quality of life in old age and the economic and social conditions which affect people throughout their lives. The political and economic factors which cause poverty in old age for some social classes are denied, whilst the condition of old age itself is defined as the problem. Thus, not only does this view fail to acknowledge the evidence of a wide range of quality of life amongst old people (see for example, Townsend, 1981), it has also prevented examination of the impact of class, race and gender on quality of life in old age. [. . .]

References

Beswick, J. and Zadik, T. (1986) 'Evaluating quality of care: an editorial in introduction', in J.Beswick, T. Zadik and D. Felce (eds), *Evaluating Quality of Care: Proceedings of a Conference held on Friday 4 July 1986*. Conference Series: Midlands Division of the British Institute of Mental Handicap.

Booth, T. (1985) *Home Truths: Old People's Homes and the Outcome of Care*. Aldershot: Gower.

Evans, G., Hughes, B. and Wilkin, D. with Jolley, D. (1981) *The Management of Mental and Physical Impairment in Non-specialist Residential Homes for the Elderly*. Research Report No. 4. Manchester: University Hospital of South Manchester, Psychogeriatric Unit Research Section.

Faragher, T. (1978) *Notes on the Evaluation of Residential Settings*. University of Birmingham: Clearing House LASS Research, No. 2: 59-85.

George, L.K. and Bearon, L.B. (1980) *Quality of Life in Older Persons: Meaning and Measurement*. New York: Human Sciences Press.

Mack, J.H. and Lansley, S. (1985) *Poor Britain*. London: Allen and Unwin.

Neugarten, B.L., Havighurst, R.J. and Mobin, S.S. (1961) 'The Measurement of life satisfaction', *Journal of Gerontology*, 16: 134-43.

Phillipson, C. (1982) *Capitalism and the Construction of Old Age*. London: Macmillan.

Townsend, P. (1981) 'The structured dependency of old people', *Ageing and Society*, 1 (1): 5-28.

Wilkin, D. (1987) 'Conceptual problems in dependency research', *Social Science and Medicine*, 24 (10): 867-73.

Wilkin, D. and Hughes, B. (1987) 'Residential care of elderly people: the consumers' views', *Ageing and Society*, 7 (2): 175-201.

Willcocks, D.M., Peace, S.M. and Kellaher, L.A. (1987) *Private Lives in Public Places: a Research-based Critique of Residential Life in Local Authority Old People's Homes*. London: Tavistock.

39

Measuring quality of life

Michael Bury and Anthea Holme

In the lives of the very old, as in the lives of people at all stages of the life course, material circumstances and health are central to the quality of life. Without an adequate level of both (defined within the context of prevailing values), the pleasure of living, it is held, is likely to diminish. [. . .]

In order to arrive at a fuller picture of the lives of the very old, [however], we need to know what *meanings* are attached to both material circumstances and health, and how they fit in with other valued areas of life. [. . .] In order to serve this purpose we offer an initial definition of quality of life in the context of old age and then discuss some of [its implications]. [. . .]

Defining the concept

Of all the discussions of quality of life and the elderly currently available, George and Bearon's (1980) influential résumé is perhaps the most useful for our purposes. In their discussion, they recognise the difficulties of definition but attempt to bring together the two main sets of factors: objective conditions and subjective evaluations.

'Objective conditions' refers to the assets (we might say, resources) which people can call on to deal with life's challenges, particularly their health and their financial security. Despite all their present complexity in the context of the very old, they are clearly central to the quality of life assessment. 'Subjective evaluations' refers to a range of life experiences, and includes: 'perceptions of well-being, a basic level of satisfaction or contentment, and a general sense of self-worth'.

This dual concept, which includes 'the conditions of life and the experience of life', may be put more schematically, thus:

Originally published as 'The quality of life', in M. Bury and A. Holme, *Life after Ninety*. London: Routledge, 1991, Chapter 5, pp. 82–96 (abridged).

Dimensions of Quality of Life

Objective conditions

General health and functional status
Socio-economic status

Subjective evaluations

Life satisfaction and related measures
Self-esteem and related measures [. . .]

Subjective measures of quality of life

As far as the subjective dimensions of quality of life are concerned, these combine several measures concerning life satisfaction which can be summarised in two basic ways. [First,] life satisfaction may be used as a general or 'global' measure of past, present or (anticipated) future states, and may be expressed in terms of happiness or a sense of well-being with life as a whole. Second, particularly with respect to residential arrangements and day-to-day experiences, including inter-personal relationships, it may be possible to link life satisfaction to specific aspects of experience, for example family interaction. Horley (1984: 124) maintains that this latter domain of quality-of-life measures, including 'day-to-day specific action . . . has been virtually ignored to date'.

Measures of self-esteem, by contrast, direct our attention to social psychological components of experience. For George and Bearon (1980: 6) the essential evaluation here is of the self as an object and of judgements about the degree of success in 'personal interaction and negotiation with the environment'. At the social level, 'status attainment' through the life course may produce a sense of success or failure (Riley et al., 1988), whereas satisfaction or dissatisfaction with relationships may have a particular influence on psychological status. In this way measures of well-being may be contrasted with psychological measures of self-worth.

The ability to negotiate change and to make effective choices, however, directs attention to the relative power held by individuals and their carers, as well as other significant individuals in the person's life. The increased reliance with age on formal services may run the risk of increasing feelings of being in need or dependent, or reinforce a sense of loss of role thus reducing self-esteem. George and Bearon (1980) make the point that there is frequently a set of delicate 'trade offs' to be made here, in opting for different kinds of living arrangements. [. . .]

Following our earlier delineation of quality-of-life measures, we may usefully distinguish two broad subjective dimensions here. The first concerns overall or specific kinds of 'life satisfaction' and the second concerns factors related to 'self-esteem'. Attention to the quality of life in these senses fits in well with an emphasis on biography or life course. It unlocks an investigation into the relationships between memories and perceptions people hold of the past as well as of the present and future.

A survey of the circumstances of a *current* group of very old people tells us little in itself about the 'historical' influences that have shaped the present. However, the often repeated call for longitudinal studies (e.g. Kalache et al., 1988) may underestimate the possibilities of studying components of the quality of life across the life course, in cross-sectional data. As Medley (1980) argues, we cannot wait 50 years to address matters of substance in the ageing field.

Relying on recall [. . .] has, of course, many problems, but research has been able to demonstrate some important connections between judgements of quality of life in the present, the past and the future outlook. Staats and Stasson (1987), for example, show that future expectations of the quality of life are closely linked to current outlook in that present happiness or unhappiness colours perceptions of the future. Stones and Kozma (1986) put this in the context of 'propensities' built up over time. By this they mean that the outlook of elderly people, as it has developed through significant phases of the life course, creates a 'cognitive style' which informs decision-making in day-to-day settings. This, in turn, creates a 'propensity' for the situation to become self-fulfilling in the future, though of course this is not an ineluctable causal sequence. Over time people seek out those circumstances where their underlying philosophy of life is reinforced. This philosophy of life, and its formation in historically specific circumstances, provides a sense of continuity between personal and public events.

At the personal level, the term 'events' refers here to two sets of experiences. The first are the anticipated events that structure the life course of most individuals [. . .]; leaving the parental home, setting up a home of one's own, marriage and children, the breaking away of children, exiting from the labour market and possible bereavement in later life. The full range of these events is, of course, particularly relevant to the very long lived.

The second are those events that cut across hopes and expectations; the loss of a child, or of a job, the onset of poor health or the unexpected experience of bereavement (in our study, for example, an instance of the loss of a son in a plane crash). Much of the research on 'life events' concentrates, in adult life, on this latter group of events and their impact on mental health, especially through their lowering of self-esteem (see, e.g., Andrews and Brown, 1988; Brown and Harris,

1978). Here, we wish to comment briefly on the role of both sorts of events in terms of life satisfaction as well as self-esteem.

Research on the experience of events across a long life course reveals how important their timing is. It seems clear that most of us operate with a definite 'social clock' which guides our expectations of events within the biographical context (for a broader discussion of time and the life course, see Young, 1988). Such expectations influence whether events are anticipated or unanticipated, the latter having more negative implications for the quality of life than the former. For example, to suffer the onset of a serious disabling illness at an early age, particularly in a historical setting where such an occurrence is relatively rare, can create a sense of being 'cheated' out of expected life stages (Bury, 1982).

Such biographical disruption is likely to have profound effects on the response of the individual to subsequent experiences. As argued earlier, the onset of disabling illness in later life may be accompanied by a greater sense of acceptance or even stoicism. It may be that biographical timing rather than passivity helps explain such acceptance, a factor that needs to be borne in mind in proposals for more active medical treatment for the very old.

Fallo-Mitchell and Ryff (1982) draw attention to two key variations in the nature of 'social clocks' which are important for our discussion. First, they argue that different birth cohorts may have quite different expectations of events. Thus, expectations of the age at which one should marry or leave the parental home may be significantly influenced by cultural patterns as well as individual variations. The entry to and exit from age-related 'role structures' is governed by structural features and people's active response to them (Riley et al., 1988: 251). Perhaps many of the clashes between generations are to do with the 'clash of clocks' implied here.

Second, there are potentially significant differences in expectations between the sexes. Fallo-Mitchell and Ryff (1982: 265) review the expectations of women across the life cycle and conclude that their findings 'suggest the existence of social clocks that serve to sanction the appropriate times for events in the female life cycle'. Serious departures from such expected timings may have important influences on the quality of life, especially for women who may be particularly affected by such events. Overall life satisfaction continues to rise for men across the life course, even into later years, whereas it tends to 'plateau' for women (Medley 1980: 198). [This proved to be] of particular relevance to our own study of very old people.

At a social psychological level, it has also proved useful to investigate the impact of past experiences and events on the quality of life. Murphy (1982) has provided evidence to link both personality factors and life events in the past with current mental-health status. In a study of elderly people suffering from depression, she was able to show that poor relationships prior to the onset of old age were significantly associated with the current onset of illness. Low self-esteem and unhappiness brought over from the past into old age increased vulnerability to depression in the face of life events such as bereavement or physical illness.

Those who had experienced good relationships in the past were more likely to be able to withstand the impact of changes and negative events in old age. As Murphy reminds us, "Tis better to have loved and lost than never to have loved at all.' Thus, good experiences in the past can have a considerable bearing on the present. They may reduce vulnerability to the negative effects of threatening life events. Needless to say, the causal pathways between events and quality of life are difficult to establish, and it is not the purpose of the present study to try to do so. What is clear, however, is that negative or unanticipated events do not produce serious effects on self-worth or self-esteem in any simple way. Coping mechanisms may intervene to offset the impact of events or bolster a vulnerable personality.

In this connection, research on the impact of social and leisure activities and of social support on the quality of life is of importance. The distinction between objective and subjective dimensions is difficult to sustain here, as these factors might more properly be seen as objective indicators of quality of life in their own right. Be that as it may, there is considerable evidence that patterns of social life, including leisure activities, influence the quality of life.

Remaining active and having adequate social support are likely to contribute to the quality of life in a residential setting. As Bulmer (1987: 60), however, has argued, patterns of social ties and activities vary considerably in adult life, and these may have lasting effects on expectations. He points out that in adult life, middle-class or professional groups have extensive social networks often based on work during adult life, compared with working-class groups who do not (for a more general discussion of these class differences, see Allan, 1979). This kind of variation warns against making too many assumptions about the role of social activities and support across the life course.

Mutran and Reitzes (1981) provide a useful approach to the linking of activities with both broader social indicators and objective measures on the one hand, and with well-being on the other.

In this way it is possible to address more 'mediated' links that might help predict well-being. Among very old people, as we shall see, many activities may be noticeable by being either severely reduced or absent, though this is not always the case. By the age of 90, well-being may be predicated on a more 'passive' life-style in the present, though, of course, valued memories of social life in the past may remain intact. Moreover in very old age it may be that satisfaction with leisure is more important than activity itself (Ragheb and Griffiths, 1982).

In summary, subjective measures of the quality of life, such as those of life satisfaction, well-being or self-esteem, direct our attention to important events and their effects on individuals throughout the life course. They also relate to important changes in the position of the very old in a changing social environment. Our own emphasis on the subjective dimensions of very old age means that we should give considerable weight to the interaction between these components. [. . .]

References

Allan, G. (1979) *A Sociology of Friendship and Kinship*. London: Allen & Unwin.

Andrews, B. and Brown, G.W. (1988) 'Social support, onset of depression and personality: an exploratory analysis', *Social Psychiatry and Psychiatric Epidemiology*, 23: 99–108.

Brown, G.W. and Harris, T. (1978) *The Social Origins of Depression*. London: Tavistock.

Bulmer, M. (1987) *The Social Basis of Community Care*. London: Allen & Unwin.

Bury, M.R. (1982) 'Chronic illness as biographical disruption', *Sociology of Health and Illness*, 4 (2): 167–82.

Fallo-Mitchell, L. and Ryff, C.D. (1982) 'Preferred timing of female life events; cohort differences', *Research on Aging*, 4 (2): 249–67.

George, L.K. and Bearon, L.B. (1980) *Quality of Life in Older Persons: Meaning and Measurement*. New York: Human Science Press.

Horley, J. (1984) 'Life satisfaction, happiness and morale: two problems with the use of the subjective well-being indicators', *The Gerontologist*, 24 (2): 124–7.

Kalache, A., Warnes, T. and Hunter, D.J. (1988) *Promoting Health among Elderly People*. London: King Edward's Hospital Fund for London.

Medley, M.L. (1980) 'Life satisfactions across four stages of adult life', *International Journal of Aging and Human Development*, 11 (3): 193–209.

Murphy, E. (1982) 'The social origins of depression in old age', *British Journal of Psychiatry*, 141: 135–42.

Mutran, E. and Reitzes, D.C. (1981) 'Retirement, identity and well-being: realignment of role relationships', *Journal of Gerontology*, 36 (6): 733–40.

Ragheb, M.G. and Griffiths, C.A. (1982) 'The contribution of leisure participation and leisure satisfaction of older persons', *Journal of Leisure Research*, 14 (4): 295–306.

Riley, M.W., Foner, A. and Waring, J. (1988) 'The sociology of age', in N.J. Smelser (ed.), *Handbook of Sociology*. London: Sage.

Staats, S.R. and Stasson, M.A. (1987) 'Age and present and future perceived quality of life', *International Journal of Aging and Human Development*, 25 (3): 167–76.

Stones, M.J. and Kozma, A. (1986) 'Happiness and activities as propensities', *Journal of Gerontology*, 41 (1): 85–90.

Young, M. (1988) *The Metronomic Society*. London: Thames & Hudson.

POLICY AND POLITICS

40

Ideology and the private sector of welfare

Roy Parker

The private sector of care is not different simply because of the commercial considerations that underlie its provision. It arouses strong ideological sentiments because it is assumed to be based upon and guided by a different social philosophy from either the public or voluntary forms of provision. Each sector attracts support or opposition in *principle* as well as in relation to what it actually achieves or fails to achieve. This is partly because performances are evaluated differently according to what people see as desirable or undesirable. There are widespread beliefs that the private sector of welfare is either inherently superior or inherently inferior to publicly organised services. That being so, it [seems sensible to note] the main lines of argument that are employed to support these two positions and to see how far they are compatible with the evidence.

Those who favour a market system of welfare appear to see its advantages as essentially fivefold:

- that it offers consumer choice;
- that it is flexible;
- that it dispenses with the heavy hand of bureaucratic control;
- that it encourages competition which leads to efficiency; and
- that it weans people from a reliance upon collective forms of provision in favour of self-reliance, thereby reducing public expenditure.

The problems of securing *consumer choice* in dependent old age are considerable whatever the system whereby services are provided. Once a person is dependent and, in particular, once their mental capacities are impaired, their ability to make choices declines, not because they do not have preferences but because they are often not able to convert these preferences into reality. What sick or dependent

From I. Sinclair, R. Parker, D. Leat and J. Williams, *The Kaleidoscope of Care*. London: HMSO, 1990, Chapter 20, 349–61 (abridged).

people mostly want is not to be sick and not to be dependent. Informed choice also depends upon the possession of information. Our skill in picking and choosing in the marketplace tends to be related to our familiarity with the range of goods or services and with their prices. If we are inexperienced we look to others for advice and guidance. Many of those whose help we enlist will have experience of buying and using the commodities themselves. However, almost by definition, those who advise the elderly will have had no such experience; nor will they have experienced the states of dependency in which the elderly find themselves. The dependent elderly face many problems but their very dependence also presents a problem to which other people have to seek solutions on their behalf. The elderly person may well regard the solutions that are contrived for them as distasteful and unwelcome.

For reasons like these 'choice' is inherently difficult to ensure and there is little evidence to suggest that one system provides for it better than another. This is particularly so in relation to entry into residential care and to the selection of particular establishments (Sinclair, 1988). The 'democratisation' created by the availability of board and lodging allowances may have increased relatives' or social workers' choice but seems to have done little to enhance or expand the choice of the individual old person. However, the picture may be somewhat more optimistic when we turn from residential care to private help in the home. What little we know about it suggests that the private informal market for paid assistance does enable elderly people to have more choice and also to exercise more control; but that depends, of course, upon their ability to pay.

In general 'the *earlier* elderly people obtain services' the greater the likelihood that they will be able to make their own choices. In the public sector the allocation of scarce resources is usually made on the basis of the existence of needs that are sufficiently pronounced to warrant priority; where services are rationed by the severity of need they are likely to be provided at a late stage in the development of dependency when crises are most common and when choice is made that much more difficult. By contrast, because the private market generally eschews this criterion in favour of ability to pay, it is more likely to offer some elderly people a better choice. The popularity of buying into schemes of sheltered housing with a home or nursing home on the same site may owe much to the opportunity they offer elderly people to make contingency plans before a stage of advanced dependency is reached.

The second claim made for the private sector is that it is *flexible*, or at least that it is more flexible than public services. There seems to be evidence both for and against this view. Certainly many of the private domiciliary services appear to be flexible in relation to what they are prepared to supply and when. In the residential sphere the picture is more complicated. Some private residential homes are obviously flexible about who they admit (or retain) but others are not. This seems to turn in part upon their resources and equipment: under-staffed and under-capitalised homes are unlikely to be able to be flexible.

Of course, much depends upon precisely *what* flexibility one has in mind. For example, as well as flexibility about admissions to residential homes and nursing homes there is also the question of flexibility in regimes and this appears to be influenced by the style of leadership and by the amount of individual attention and privacy that it is possible to provide with different staffing ratios, different amounts of space and different financial constraints.

In principle, there seems to be nothing inherent in the private system that promotes greater flexibility than the public sector except that decisions about who is to receive a service are based upon demand rather than need; because of this there may be a greater willingness to respond to a wider variety of tastes, requirements and expectations. On the other hand, the application of tight financial criteria may well lead to considerable inflexibility. There is undoubtedly a great deal of variation in the private sector in this matter, whereas in the public sphere it is more likely that local policies will exist that impose a degree of uniformity; but these may or may not encourage flexible practices.

If one important aspect of flexibility is the ability or willingness to redeploy resources if better ways of meeting the needs of the elderly are indicated, then there seems to be no evidence (in terms of location or, say, a shift from residential to community care) that the private sector is more flexible than the public domain. Indeed, quite the opposite; except, of course, that private enterprise (at least in the residential field) has responded swiftly to changes in the financial incentives that governments offer.

The idea of sectors being more or less flexible is grounded in comparisons. However, in reality it is hazardous to generalise, not least because one sector may perform well on one dimension of flexibility but not on another. It is also hard to reach firm conclusions because of the diversity that exists within each sector; because of the lack of information about what goes on in detail from day to day and because we are unsure how that is experienced by different elderly people.

The claim that the private sector is more flexible than public services also reflects the conviction that it avoids the worst features of cumbersome *bureaucratic control*. Yet [. . .] the development of the private sector of welfare for the elderly is closely associated with the expansion of regulation. Where public monies are involved, and where there are major concerns about the protection of the consumer, the private sector is likely to generate bureaucratic involvement. How this is evaluated depends, of course, on what kind of bureaucracy we are talking about; it also depends upon the level of control that is exercised over the other sectors. For example, as the Wagner report on residential care pointed out, the evidence of 'chronic mismanagement, staff shortages and poor standards of care' revealed by independent reviews of local authority homes in the London boroughs of Brent and Camden, followed by 'the truly horrific abuses' described by the inquiry into Nye Bevan Lodge in Southwark, emphasised that simply because a service is publicly provided it does not follow that it is well regulated (Wagner Committee, 1988).

The fact that private residential homes and nursing homes are widely advertised suggests that *competition* exists; but this may be very uneven around the country depending upon the overall level of provision and the alternatives that are available. However, the idea of competition depends to a large extent upon the information that consumers have in the first place and then upon the possibility that they can switch from the service they dislike to one that appears to offer an improvement or a lower price. This may be true at the point of entry, but once in residential care the elderly cannot easily change their minds in the way that a purchaser in the shops can, and those who might act on their behalf may well be reluctant to subject an infirm elderly person to the upheaval of a move unless there are compelling grounds for doing so. Furthermore, for those in receipt of financial support from public sources the question of competitive prices is hardly relevant. However, competition for those residents who pay their own fees and are literally more mobile may be more lively at the upper end of the market.

What active competition there is at present may be for the goodwill of the major referral agents. In those circumstances the competition may be centred on official recommendation or approval. However, there are undoubtedly areas where demand is so buoyant that, beyond this, little competition exists. It will be interesting to see what effect the introduction of local authority contracting for service has upon competition within the private sector of care. One suspects that different areas will experience different developments depending upon the state of the local market, the terms and conditions of the contracts that are drawn up and the degree of selectivity that local authorities impose upon the agencies with which they are prepared to negotiate. There is, of course, also the question of inter-sector competition; but because of the lack of information we do not really know, for example, whether the private and voluntary homes are in competition and, if they are, how that competition is manifested and conducted.

When we turn from private residential care to other private services there is scant evidence of active competition mainly, it seems, because a large part of the provision is informal and because in areas where it is organised there is usually only one company. It is conceivable that private domiciliary services might compete with private residential services but in the present state of uneven development that seems to be most unlikely.

In short, therefore, it is hard to discover how much private welfare competition exists in particular areas, what form it takes and thus what its results are. Where competition does occur it may lead, for example, to standards being set at the lowest acceptable level in order to achieve commercial viability: much depends upon the elasticity of demand in different sub-markets. To conclude that competition leads to greater or lesser efficiency goes well beyond the available evidence. What may be important is that the existence of private, voluntary and public services provides an opportunity for cross-evaluation.

Finally, the notion that the availability of private care encourages *self-reliance* and *reduces public expenditure* is clearly seriously challenged by the developments in private residential care that have sprung from public subsidisation. It is possible that the present cost to the Exchequer of board and lodging allowances greatly exceeds what would have been required in order to provide comparable services in the public sector or alternative community-based services.

Few elderly people can plan to be financially self-reliant without having more income during earlier phases of their lives; later, when their needs emerge, few insurance companies are interested in the high-risk business that they represent. Without the means (both financial and institutional) of preparing to be self-reliant in old age it becomes necessary for those who would use private-for-profit services to be protected in some way at public expense from the prices that prevail.

Other forms of 'self-reliance' in aged dependency will also be limited. The issue of to whom elderly people turn for help and on what terms may be more important. The use of a publicly supported private sector, for instance, does not necessarily safeguard self-reliance; it is simply a particular way of responding to dependency. However, we should not dismiss too quickly the importance to the elderly person of the terms upon which services are offered. For instance, the opportunity to pay directly for service may be a significant component of feeling self-reliant even when the money is a transfer payment from the state that happens to be routed via the old person. In our society it is as much the appearance of having money that confers status and power as the actuality.

If one looks at the arguments that are usually deployed by those who view private systems of welfare with disfavour and suspicion then it is possible to identify five principal criticisms:

- that private provision is not necessarily determined by need;
- that it is not susceptible to integrated planning;
- that private services may expose vulnerable and dependent people to exploitation;

- that private welfare leads, inevitably, to greater inequality; and
- that because the market relies upon the realisation of profit from essentially individual transaction it cannot embrace the idea of collective responsibility and hence the notion of social unity through interdependence.

Looking back at the evidence of the extent to which different sections of residential care cater for people with a variety of levels of dependency, there is little doubt that private homes and nursing homes accommodate many who are in considerable *need*. Whether their needs could be better met in other ways is another matter and a question that can be legitimately asked of all three sectors. On the other hand, private domiciliary care appears more often to be provided in inverse proportion to need. Yet matters are not as straightforward as that, for such a proposition tends to assume that wants and needs are exclusive conditions. What the operation of the price mechanism does is to remove the necessity to define need. The consequence is, of course, that the possibility of giving precedence to those in greatest need in a systematic fashion is forgone.

Since the private sector operates to make a profit and to satisfy demand rather than need, it follows that it is difficult to incorporate it in any *integrated plan* that is concerned with the distribution of total welfare resources, whether nationally or locally. It can be done more easily where private services are directly substitutable for public services or where they depend heavily upon public monies. Governments can use financial incentives and disincentives (as shown by the history of the location of industry) to affect what welfare businesses do. However, there are comparatively few examples of the positive and deliberate use of these mechanisms (rather than their use in reactive and remedial ways) in the welfare field, and even when they are employed the initiatives seem to be dogged by unforeseen and perverse consequences.

One of the most important things that elderly dependent people need is other people to care for them. Those who challenge the propriety of developing private-for-profit caring services often base their criticism upon the view that *profit and care are incompatible*, or at least that sooner or later they will be in conflict and that profit will then always emerge the victor. It is certainly the case that private care businesses will not continue for long if they are uneconomic and, in that sense, the proposition has some truth in it; but that does not mean to say that considerations of profitability will always prevail or that profitable enterprises are uncaring. Indeed, those in favour of a market economy argue strongly that profit *enables* society to be more caring. For those who take the opposite view, however, there is an inherent likelihood that the pursuit of the one will prejudice the other. Conversely, of course, it has to be said that the absence of a profit motive is no guarantee that good standards of provision will be preserved. Budgetary and other limitations (not least the standard of management and the availability of good staff) may be as severe an obstacle to providing high-quality service as the need to make a profit.

Whether or not the enlargement of the private sector of welfare leads to more *inequality* depends upon two things. First, it depends upon the prevailing distribution of income and wealth and, secondly, upon the level and character of public intervention. [It has been] argued that inequality in old age is growing and that it may become greater still. If that is so, then systems of private welfare are likely to feed upon and reflect those inequalities. Certainly they will do nothing to reduce them. We may speak of a mixed economy of welfare but, in these circumstances, it is more likely to be a segregated economy of welfare based upon ability to pay. To the extent that intervention by the state in the private welfare market encourages access independently of ability to pay, then those consequences can be mitigated. However, even with heavily subsidised private services there appear to be pronounced tendencies towards inequality of access, whether by social category or by geographical area.

Finally, there remains the central philosophical issue about the social *distribution of responsibility*. It is undeniable that the principles of private enterprise reflect, in one way or another, an individualistic view of how responsibility for personal well-being should be allocated. By contrast, public provision financed from general taxation signifies the acceptance of a collective responsibility. It is obvious that both systems and both sets of principles can become contaminated and distorted; but that does not deny the fundamental difference between them nor the fact that their enlargement or diminution has an important symbolic significance, although, in practice, little difference may be observed in what they provide on a day-to-day basis.

Hence the debate about the contribution, place and future of the different sectors of welfare for the elderly cannot be conducted wholly in empirical terms; there are matters of moral and political philosophy at stake as well. That that is so is no reason to disregard the enormous gaps in our knowledge, particularly of the sphere of private welfare. Indeed, quite the contrary, for only when the empirical questions are better answered will the questions of value be more clearly exposed.

References

Sinclair, I. (1988) 'Residential care for elderly people', in I. Sinclair (ed.), *Residential Care: the Research Reviewed* (Vol. 2 of the Wagner Report). London: HMSO, pp. 243–91.

Wagner Committee (1988) *Residential Care: a Positive Choice, Report of the Independent Review of Residential Care, Chaired by Gillian Wagner*. London: HMSO.

41

Housing and community care

Robin Means

This article is based upon the assertion that housing is a crucial, even if often-neglected, dimension of community care. Research evidence has repeatedly indicated that many elderly people do not enjoy living in institutions yet have illness and dependency problems which could have been coped with in their own homes (Booth, 1985; Townsend, 1962). There is evidence that many people enter residential homes or fail to leave hospital care primarily because of housing problems (Sinclair, 1988). Housing disrepair and housing costs can be a major source of worry to elderly people, irrespective of whether they are owner occupiers or rentiers (Coleman and Watson, 1987). Frail, sick or disabled elderly people are likely to spend large periods of time at home and therefore the quality of that environment is likely to be crucial to their mental health and general well-being (Harrison and Means, 1990). Elderly owner occupiers have equity stored up in their homes and this raises the question of whether such equity can be used to maintain their homes or even to meet some of their health and welfare needs (Mackintosh et al., 1990). Finally, the house-building industry has come to see the accommodation and care needs of older people as an important niche market through the development of sheltered house for sale schemes (Williams, 1990). All these points support the view that housing is the foundation of community care (NFHA and Mind, 1987).

Despite this, debates about housing in later life and community care have, until recent years, been very narrow. In the 1950s, 1960s and 1970s this debate focused almost entirely on sheltered accommodation. The majority of early sheltered housing schemes were built by local authorities (100,000 units in England and Wales by mid-1983) but housing associations have increasingly become involved. [. . .]

Several points need to be made about this tendency to treat sheltered accommodation as the apparently sole housing component of community care for older people. First, it remained a form of provision for a minority and the vast majority of elderly people

Originally published as 'Community care, housing and older people: continuity or change?', *Housing Studies*, 6 (4), 1991: 273–84 (abridged).

remained in non-sheltered housing in owner occupation, private renting and social renting. [. . .] Second, the growth of sheltered accommodation began to undermine the clear distinction between 'ordinary' housing and institutional care. Indeed, the emphasis on sheltered accommodation as a form of social care has intensified in recent years with the development of 'Category 2½', or very sheltered housing schemes, by some housing associations and local authorities. These schemes offer increased support services and a higher level of staffing in an attempt to help very dependent people avoid institutional care (Tinker, 1989).

The third point concerns the fact that sheltered housing may be a component of community care policy but it is often not part of a 'staying put' policy since by definition such schemes tend to be age-specific, purpose-built property into which people move from their previous homes. Therefore, if the previous home does represent a store of memories and cherished experiences, then this store will have to be abandoned in order to obtain the high-quality housing and warden support services offered by many sheltered housing schemes. Indeed, a cynical interpretation of their development by local authorities would be that they reflected the need to offer a 'carrot' to persuade elderly people to transfer from larger family council houses. [. . .]

The final point concerns the reasons why the tenants of sheltered housing schemes decide to move. Research by Butler et al. (1983) found that better housing had mattered more to most residents than the existence of an alarm system or a warden. This led them to argue:

> What is not altogether clear is why somebody living in poor housing conditions should be seen as a candidate for a form of specialised housing, when apparently their requirements could have been met in other ways – either by home improvements or a move to better quality housing. (Butler et al., 1983: 39)

More recently Oldman (1986) and Wheeler (1986) have asked why the special needs of some older people should lead to the development of segregated housing. Both authors argue that a focus on age-related physical needs is used to disguise the social and economic disadvantage of the majority of elderly people.

Elderly people did appear in more general debates about housing but usually in terms of them providing an explanation for certain housing problems (Means 1987). As council tenants they have often been seen as living in inappropriately large homes needed by families on the waiting list, while as reluctant private landlords they have been used as one explanation for the decline in the private rented sector. Perhaps most importantly, as owner occupiers they were often seen in the 1970s as an obstacle to urban renewal through their reluctance to take out home improvement grants.

Progress appeared to be made in 1978 when the government published a discussion document called *A Happier Old Age* (DHSS/ Welsh Office, 1978) [. . .] which claimed that what was needed was the development of a wide range of housing options for elderly people, backed up by a high level of co-operation between housing, health and social services in planning and providing facilities. The days of a narrow focus upon standard sheltered housing schemes appeared to be over.

To a limited extent, these hopes were realised and a wider range of housing options did emerge in the 1980s (Mackintosh et al., 1990). Very sheltered housing schemes have already been mentioned, but further variations have included the emergence of both sheltered housing for sale and part-ownership sheltered housing schemes. Many local authorities have explored the use of mobile wardens and dispersed alarm systems to support individual elderly people in their own homes. Insurance companies have developed home equity release schemes to enable elderly owner occupiers to 'unlock' some of the capital in their homes. The early 1980s saw the emergence of 'Care and Repair' and Anchor 'Staying Put' schemes to advise elderly owner occupiers on how best to repair their properties, while a new improvement grant system has just been introduced which is far more flexible in terms of being able to fund small repairs, although it is a system in which larger grants are now based on means testing (Leather and Mackintosh, 1989).

However, these assorted initiatives do not add up to a coherent set of housing policies and housing developments which are broadly supportive of community care objectives. Instead, the 1980s have seen growing housing inequalities both between tenures and within tenures. First, there has been the attempt by central government to turn council housing into a form of welfare housing for marginal groups (Forrest and Murie, 1988). [. . .] Second, there have been growing inequalities between owner occupiers in terms of house values and housing disrepair. One dimension of this has been the north–south divide in house prices, but another has been the continued housing disrepair problems faced by elderly owner occupiers. [. . .]

The long-term impact of the 1988 Housing Act and the 1989 Housing and Local Government Act is not yet known, but many fear a reduction of rented accommodation affordable for those on low incomes (Clapham, 1989; Willmott and Murie, 1988). The housing benefit system is meant to cushion the blow of rising rents in local authority and housing association property, but this is becoming more and more problematic for elderly people because of restrictions on capital savings and steepening [benefit] tapers (Bull and Poole, 1989). The 'lucky' ones entitled to benefit face dependence upon a complex means-tested benefit and possibly the prospect of a sense of stigma because of their reliance upon a residualised welfare state. The 'lucky' who are too 'well off' to qualify for state subsidy may in reality be part of what Bull and Poole (1989) call 'the not rich, not poor'. These are elderly people who are too poor to take full advantage of what the private market can offer but who are considered too rich in terms of income or savings to qualify for state benefits and/or for socially rented housing.

Housing and community care in the 1980s therefore represent something of a paradox. Housing options and innovations have increased but most of these have been small-scale and targeted at only some types of elderly people. As Clapham and Smith (1990) argue, this has represented substantial material gains for a limited number of elderly people but at the cost of the danger of increased stigma for some users and, also, at the cost of being a device by which the failure to implement a more fundamental shift of housing policy to help all those on low incomes and in housing need can be justified and rationalised.

So where do housing and housing policy fit into the proposed changes of the Griffiths Report (1988) and the White Paper, Department of Health (1989)? Both reports are concerned to enable people to remain in their own homes wherever possible. However, the Griffiths Report is far more dismissive of housing policy and housing agencies than the White Paper. Under 'Responsibilities', the Griffiths Report states:

> The responsibility of public housing authorities (local authority housing authorities, Housing Corporation, etc.) should be limited to arranging and sometimes financing and managing the 'bricks and mortar' of housing needed for community care purposes. [. . .] (1988: 16)

To say the least, this represents a minimum recognition of the pioneering role of housing associations and local authorities in 'special needs' housing for people with mental health problems and learning difficulties. [. . .] There have been difficulties, one of which is funding new developments since financial viability often depends upon them being registrable as residential homes. The Griffiths Report needed to say much more on how to open up the finance of 'bricks and mortar' for housing schemes targeted towards particular community care groups in a way that created financial incentives to minimise the dependency-inducing features of design and staffing. [. . .]

The White Paper on community care (Department of Health, 1989) has taken a much broader and a more positive view of housing [. . .]. It stresses that suitable good quality housing is essential to an overall community care strategy. The new means-tested improvement grant system, Care and Repair schemes and Staying Put schemes are all mentioned in section 3.5 of the chapter on the roles and responsibilities of social services authorities. [. . .]

Future prospects

[. . .] The positive statements within the White Paper should not be overlooked or undervalued. In order to produce community care plans, social services departments are being encouraged to work collaboratively with health authorities, housing departments and housing associations. These plans will be vetted by the Social Services Inspectorate of the Department of Health and the Inspectorate will expect social services departments to address housing issues in some depth. Hopefully, this will be backed up by social services staff becoming not only more aware of housing issues and problems, but also more astute about how these can be tackled.

Their ability to tackle such problems will partly depend on whether certain other initiatives flourish. Perhaps the most important of these is the new home improvement grant system with its ability to help people with disabilities and elderly people who need small repairs carried out. However, a major question mark hangs over the extent to which local authorities will be in a financial position to fund discretionary small repair grants and the extent to which elderly people will apply for larger grants given the introduction of means testing (Leather and Mackintosh, 1989). The second initiative concerns 'Care and Repair' and 'Staying Put' type projects and whether the government will decide to support their development as a national system of advice for elderly owner occupiers. Existing research underlines the ability of these agencies to improve housing conditions and to support elderly people in their own homes (Harrison and Means, 1990; Leather and Mackintosh, 1990). [. . .]

If 'Care and Repair' and 'Staying Put' type projects were to develop into a national network of home improvement advice agencies for elderly owner occupiers and if the new improvement grant system is well resourced, then something like a national strategy for elderly owner occupiers might be seen to emerge, and one backed up by a growing awareness from social services about the importance of housing problems in undermining the ability of elderly owner occupiers to remain in their own homes. However, this scenario is based upon some very large assumptions. Overall pressures upon social services departments may undermine their ability or willingness to fully address housing issues. [. . .]

Even more worrying are the bleak prospects for socially rented housing. In previous research, the author has illustrated the enormous demand for good-quality council housing from those who feel trapped in poor-quality owner-occupied property or in private renting (Means, 1988). This escape route seems likely to be increasingly cut off as the overall council stock continues to decline and the remaining properties show rising rents.

The ability or willingness of housing associations to further develop their role in the provision of socially rented housing for elderly people is equally unclear. This sector is, also, facing the introduction of higher rents for new developments under the 1988 Housing Act. [. . .]

It should be remembered that this is an issue not just for sheltered housing schemes but also for more general small unit developments since the majority of existing housing association tenants are not in sheltered housing (NFHA, 1985).

Having said this, it is clear that certain housing associations intend to become major providers of social care services, including residential care. [. . .] It is also likely that some associations will 'offer' to use their existing sheltered housing schemes as a resource unit from which to provide such services as day care, meals on wheels and home care to the local neighbourhood. In general the contract economy seems likely to draw certain housing agencies further into the provision of social care rather than housing services. It is too early to predict how extensive this development will be, or whether it will benefit the elderly consumer.

Conclusion

The references in the White Paper on community care (Department of Health, 1989) about the importance of housing to older people are welcome. However, similar statements were made in *A Happier Old Age* (DHSS/Welsh Office, 1978) yet only limited progress was made in the decade after its publication in terms of collaboration between different agencies and innovative projects. Indeed, the overall housing situation deteriorated in terms of prospects for many low-income elderly people in both owner occupation and renting. A similar pattern seems likely to emerge with the White Paper.

The final comment concerns 'well off' elderly people. Increasing talk is heard of the grey economy and the growing importance of 'well off' elderly people as a ripe market niche awaiting appropriate responses from the private sector (Booz, Allen and Hamilton, 1988). There is no doubt that growing numbers of elderly people will have the financial resources to 'buy in' at least some of their home care needs in later life from the private sector, without any need to subject themselves for case management assessment. [There is some] scope for releasing equity tied up in property. However, it does need to be remembered that state and occupational pensions remain poorly developed in this country relative to the rest of Europe (Bosanquet et al., 1990) and that the bulk of elderly people within the foreseeable future will not be able to 'self-provision' all their needs in the last years of their lives. Their quality of life will continue to depend at least partially upon the housing and social care policies of central and local government.

References

Booth, T. (1985) *Home Truths: Old People's Homes and the Outcome of Care.* Aldershot: Gower.

Booz, Allen and Hamilton (1988) 'The elderly market - a strategy on innovation', *Financial Viewpoint,* April.

Bosanquet, N., Propper, C. and Laing, W. (1990) *Elderly Consumers in Britain: Europe's Poor Relation?* London: Laing and Buisson.

Bull, J. and Poole, L. (1989) *Not Rich: Not Poor - a Study of Housing Options for Elderly People on Middle Incomes.* London: SHAC/Anchor Housing Trust.

Butler, A., Oldman, C. and Greve, J. (1983) *Sheltered Housing for the Elderly.* London: Allen & Unwin.

Clapham, D. (1989) 'The new housing legislation: what impact will it have?', *Local Government Policy-Making,* 15 (4): 3-10.

Clapham, D. and Smith, S. (1990) 'Housing policy and "special needs"', *Policy and Politics,* 18 (3): 193-206.

Coleman, L. and Watson, S. (1987) *Women over Sixty: a Study of the Housing, Economic and Social Circumstances of Older Women.* Australian Institute of Urban Studies, Publication Number 130.

Department of Health (1989) *Caring for People: Community Care in the Next Decade and Beyond.* CM 849. London: HMSO.

Department of Health and Social Security/Welsh Office (1978) *A Happier Old Age.* London: HMSO.

Forrest, R. and Murie, A. (1988) *Selling the Welfare State: the Privatisation of Public Housing.* London: Routledge.

Griffiths Report (1988) *Community Care: Agenda for Action.* London: HMSO.

Harrison, L. and Means, R. (1990) *Housing: the Essential Element in Community Care - the Role of 'Care and Repair' and 'Staying Put' Projects.* London: SHAC and Anchor Housing Trust.

Leather, P. and Mackintosh, S. (1989) 'Means testing improvement grants', *Housing Review,* 38 (3): 79-80.

Leather, P. and Mackintosh, S. (1990) *Monitoring Assisted Agency Services: Part I, Home Improvement Agencies - an Evaluation of Performance.* London: HMSO.

Mackintosh, S., Means, R. and Leather, P. (1990) *Housing and Later Life: the Housing Finance Implications of an Ageing Society.* SAUS Study No. 4. Bristol: School for Advanced Urban Studies, University of Bristol.

Means, R. (1987) 'Older people in British housing studies: rediscovery and emerging issues for research', *Housing Studies.* 2 (2): 82-98.

Means, R. (1988) 'Council housing, tenure polarisation and older people in two contrasting localities', *Ageing and Society.* 8 (4): 395-421.

NFHA (1985) *Developments in Housing for Older People.* London: National Federation of Housing Associations.

NFHA and Mind (1987) *Housing: the Foundations of Community Care.* London: National Federation of Housing Associations.

Oldman, C. (1986) 'Housing policies for older people', in P. Malpass (ed.), *The Housing Crisis.* London: Croom Helm.

Sinclair, I. (1988) 'Residential care for elderly people', in I. Sinclair (ed.), *Residential Care: the Research Reviewed* (Vol. 2 of the Wagner Report). London: HMSO, pp. 243-91.

Tinker, A. (1989) *An Evaluation of Very Sheltered Housing.* London: HMSO.

Townsend, P. (1962) *The Last Refuge.* London: Routledge & Kegan Paul.

Wheeler, R. (1986) 'Housing policy and elderly people', in C. Phillipson and A. Walker (eds), *Ageing and Social Policy: a Critical Assessment*. Aldershot: Gower, pp. 217-33.

Williams, G. (1990) *The Experience of Housing in Retirement: Elderly Lifestyles and Private Initiative*. Aldershot: Avebury.

Willmott, P. and Murie, A. (1988) *Polarisation and Social Housing*. London: Policy Studies Institute.

42

Workers versus pensioners

Paul Johnson, Christoph Conrad and David Thomson

The rapid ageing of the populations of all industrial countries over the next 40 years will be an economic and social transformation of vastly greater magnitude than the 1970s oil price shock or the 1980s recession. Unlike the economic difficulties of the last two decades which arose suddenly and with little warning, the timing and extent of population ageing are fairly predictable, because we know now within narrow boundaries how many people of working age and how many elderly will be alive in 20 or 30 years' time. This process of population ageing is likely to have a profound impact on many established social customs and institutions such as the pattern of work and retirement, the functioning of welfare systems, and the nature of family relationships. The anticipation of this demographic shift and its attendant social and economic problems must lead us to question whether the principles of our social institutions related to work and leisure, income and transfers are well adapted to these future challenges. A growing number of observers think the answer is no. [. . .]

The demographic background

The essence of the demographic problem is quite simple – the proportion of old people in the population of industrial societies is increasing and the proportion of people of normal working age is falling. However, [. . .] the dynamics of this demographic change are quite complex and vary to a surprising degree between countries. All developed countries have seen an increase in average life expectancy over the course of the twentieth century as nutrition and hygiene have improved and medical advances have increased the survival chances of the young. [. . .] Yet despite impressive increases in longevity, the

From P. Johnson, C. Conrad and D. Thomson, *Workers versus Pensioners*. Manchester: Manchester University Press/CEPR, 1989, Introduction, pp. 1–16 (abridged). This book derived from a conference on 'Work, Retirement, and Intergenerational Equity, 1850–2050: The Social Economy of the Second Half of Life', organised by the Centre for Economic Policy Research and held at the St John's College, Cambridge, in July 1988.

root cause of 'population ageing' lies not in our success in extending the life course, but in our failure to produce more children.

In 1950 the total fertility rate, which measures the expected number of births per woman aged 15–44, was well over 2.1 (the population replacement rate) in all the countries of Western Europe and North America. Today only Ireland continues to experience above-replacement fertility, while in West Germany and Denmark total fertility has fallen to the unprecedented level of 1.4. [. . .]

The ratio of persons aged 65+ per 100 persons aged 15–64 in Europe stood at 15.1 in 1960 and is expected to be 29.1 by 2025; in West Germany the ratio in 1960 was 16.0, but the very low fertility rates of today mean that the expected ratio in 2025 will be 36.5. [. . .]

Why does this matter? An increase in the average age of the population need not engender any inevitable economic problems. [. . .] However, increased longevity has not been matched by an extension of the working phase of life; the trend has been for the normal age of retirement to fall rather than rise. Furthermore, the typical age for commencement of work in the labour market has risen over the last century as a larger proportion of children have been educated for a greater number of years. These long-term changes in the nature of the employment contract, with work starting later and finishing earlier, have led to a progressive shortening of the productive phase of life despite the overall improvement in health and higher chance of survival which together have worked to increase the productive potential of the individual.

An inevitable corollary of this reduction in the number of years spent in employment is an increase in the length of life spent dependent on the effort and output of that section of the population currently engaged in productive work. ('Productive' is being used here in the conventional but limited sense of remunerated activity, and no comment is being made about the possible wider meanings of the term.) Whether the retired population is supported from its own savings or from state pension and welfare payments does not affect the general proposition that the present consumption of the aged (and children) is provided for by the current output of productive workers. However, the specific pension arrangements that have evolved in each country do determine the nature and degree of exchange or transfer between particular age groups or generations, and in most developed countries it is the state pension and welfare systems that have emerged as the prime agents for transferring resources from productive to non-productive sections of the population. [. . .]

The welfare contract

There is considerable variation in the financial and administrative detail of the different national systems for the transfer of resources from productive workers to non-productive pensioners, but they have tended to follow similar trends since the Second World War. [. . .] The case of the United States [. . .] serves as an illuminating example. In the immediate post-war period the proportion of the workforce covered by the US contributory state pension scheme – Old Age and Survivors Insurance (OASI) – grew rapidly, and the real value of the pension payment rose sharply. [. . .] Revenue rose more rapidly than expenditure, and it therefore seemed appropriate to increase pension payments for retirees to a level far above that which could be justified on an actuarial basis by reference to the contributions those retirees had themselves made. [. . .]

In the 1970s, however, as the OASI system matured, the ready sources of additional revenue dried up. By that time the coverage of the scheme had expanded to include nearly all adult workers, so that the scope for finding additional revenue by incorporating new groups of hitherto uninsured workers disappeared. Moreover, larger numbers of workers were beginning to enter retirement and carried with them the expectations of high and rising pension levels such as they had seen their older colleagues enjoy. However, contributions from the current workforce were no longer high enough to sustain these expanded pensions. The social security system faced bankruptcy, and the financial crisis was exacerbated by the reduction in the rate of economic growth and rise in the level of unemployment that accompanied the oil price increases of 1974 and 1979. [. . .]

The way welfare and pension systems reacted to the similar range of problems they faced in the 1970s has led David Thomson (1989) to argue that welfare states may be one-generation phenomena. [. . .] He suggests [. . .] that there has been an unconscious but nevertheless consistent and successful attempt by one broad birth cohort, which reached adulthood during and just after the Second World War, to secure for themselves the main benefits of the post-war welfare state. This 'welfare generation', as Thomson calls them, have gained heavily throughout their lives from welfare and tax systems which provided them with highly subsidised property purchase, large child benefits and an expanding educational system when they were at the stage of family formation and now with greatly increased pension rights as they enter retirement. [. . .] People of the 'welfare generation', he argues, have always been net beneficiaries of the welfare state, and wish to remain so into their very comfortable retirement [. . .]. Crucial to the argument is the reluctance of the 'welfare generation' to curtail their claim on the welfare state at a time when welfare budgets are overburdened, and when many people of working age are themselves dependent on the state because of high rates of unemployment. Despite a clear rise since the mid-1970s in the number of young adults with dependent children living at or below the poverty line, the real value of welfare benefits and tax concessions to this age group has fallen, whereas the increasingly asset-rich elderly have maintained or improved the value of their state pension entitlements. In this economic environment, suggests Thomson, there is a strong incentive for younger voters to break with this implicit welfare contract which seems always to work to their disadvantage, and to support the dismantling of the national welfare system and a return to private provision. Intergenerational competition, therefore, may affect not just the relative welfare of the old and the young, but can also threaten the very existence of state welfare systems. [. . .]

This idea of an intergenerational conflict for resources between the young and the old has been rejected by a number of commentators who argue that generation or birth cohort is not an appropriate unit of analysis (Binney and Estes, 1988; Easterlin, 1987). To talk of a 'welfare generation' or of competition for resources between the young and the old implies a degree of homogeneity among the elderly population that may not exist. Class divisions or (because so many of the very old and very poor elderly are women) gender divisions within the aged population may be as significant as any divergence in the age profile of poverty between those over retirement age and those with dependent children. [. . .]

Perhaps not surprisingly, given the newness of the generational approach to social analysis, there exists disagreement amongst those who believe that the intergenerational framework is an appropriate way to think about the dynamic impact of modern welfare states. In particular, there is debate about how an optimal degree of intergenerational exchange might be decided upon. [. . .] Norman Daniels (1989) is concerned to point up the confusions that abound in talking about justice between age groups and generations. The two are distinct, and yet individuals are members of both at once. As a result two separate questions are being merged and misconstrued in most discussions of 'generational equity' [. . .]. On the one hand there is the age group issue – what is due in terms of justice to those who are young or old today. On the other, modern societies face the generation question – what is due to those who may be elderly now, but who perhaps have a peculiar history of contribution to or benefit from society's taxation and benefit programmes. Daniels argues that little is to be gained by searching first for justice between generations: that way lies acrimony, divisiveness and constant tinkering with policies. The long-term interests of all will best be served if primacy is given to determining what a just society wants for the elderly and others, since all now enjoy the near-certain prospect of passing through all ages themselves. [. . .]

The labour contract

[. . .] The discussion by Anne-Marie Guillemard (1989) of the trend towards early withdrawal from the labour force shows that the average retirement age has fallen in all developed countries over the last 20 years, and that this has occurred independently of any alteration in the age limits for the receipt of state old-age pensions or other welfare benefits. If this trend towards earlier retirement could be reversed the effect on intergenerational transfers between productive and non-productive sections of the population would be immediate and significant, because the additions to the labour force would also be subtractions from the dependent population.

To see what scope exists for reversing the trend towards early retirement, we need to consider why people leave the labour force, and how these decisions are influenced by social security and pension rules [. . .]. Individual choices and circumstances play a part; people may opt for early retirement because they no longer need or want to work, or they may be forced into retirement because they lose the mental or physical capacity for employment. Improvements in the fitness and nutrition of the population over the course of the twentieth century indicate that the reduction in the average age of retirement has not occurred because of an absolute decline in the health of older people, although changing popular and medical perceptions of fitness and disability may have worked to counter any objective improvements in health. It seems more likely that the labour force supply of older people has fallen over time because their increasing wealth and pension entitlements have reduced their need for an employment income. However, it can be said with confidence that not all retired people have left employment from choice [. . .].

A much discussed model developed by Lazear (1979) explains why employers have curtailed their demand for older workers in terms of economics. In large, modern corporations the fixed costs associated with hiring and training a worker are substantial and in order to minimise these costs employers attempt to restrict staff turnover. One effective way to do this is to pay seniority increments to staff with a certain number of years' service. These bonuses are not related to the specific job done by the worker or to his or her productivity – their purpose is to establish an earnings gradient which will provide an incentive for workers to stay with their employer. However, the very nature of seniority payments means that at some point an older worker is likely to be paid a wage or salary greater than his marginal product – in other words, he will be a net cost to the employer. At this point the employer needs to shed this worker, but a straightforward policy of dismissal of older workers would serve to undermine the employee loyalty which it is the purpose of the earnings gradient to promote. The socially acceptable way to shed older workers is, therefore, to offer them early retirement with an advantageous pension arrangement. As long as the cost to the employer of the early retirement settlement is less than the cost of the continued employment of the unproductive worker up to normal retirement age, early retirement is the employer's preferred choice. As Stephen Sass (1989) demonstrates in his investigation of US private and union pension schemes, it is also the preferred choice of labour organisations. [. . .]

Early retirement seems, therefore, to be in the interest of everyone directly involved in it, if not for the bulk of the working population who have to support the cost of generous pension arrangements either through increased taxes, increased private pension contributions, or increased prices for the products of the companies that promote these expensive early retirement policies. A higher level of labour force participation among older people, which would appear to be in the interest of all western societies now facing the problems of population ageing, seems not to be in the interest of any of the parties involved in the decision – a clear case perhaps of the public good and individual self-interest in conflict. Until recently national governments themselves favoured early exit from the labour force as a means of alleviating the pressure on the labour market. Serious doubts about the cost and the effectiveness of such policies have emerged (Holzmann, 1988) but the aim of shifting jobs from the old to the young is still quite popular. The situation therefore looks like a conflict between two public goods – the short-term labour market concern and the long-term pension cost concern. Although one cannot expect to reverse the trend to earlier retirement by political decisions alone, governments will have to make up their mind which way to go on this issue [. . .].

Policy options

[. . .] The working of both the welfare contract and the employment contract in modern industrial societies serves to exacerbate the economic and social problems that are a concomitant of population ageing. The problems are manifest and obvious, the solutions less straightforward. If no action is taken to deal with the incipient crisis of population ageing, then it seems certain that western societies will experience major social and economic dislocation, and they may experience this relatively soon. [. . .]

There is a further reason for action to be taken now [. . .]. Few people have the opportunity and resources to change their pension plans and pattern of asset accumulation after their mid-forties, so that their social and economic expectations of retirement tend to be set at least 20 years before normal retirement age. If new attitudes to retirement will be needed by the third decade of the next century to cope with the cost of an ageing population, then it is the expectations and actions of today's 20- and 30-year-olds that should be the focus of attention.

Many governments have already enacted certain measures to dampen the expectations of retirees in the twenty-first century, for example by increasing payroll taxes, reducing early retirement incentives and revising the automatic increase of benefits (Holzmann, 1988; ILO, 1987; Schmähl, 1989). These reforms, however, do not touch the principles of existing systems and seem to allow only for cosmetic reactions to the inbuilt inequities. They may even worsen the inequity felt by younger workers.

The most obvious and accessible area for immediate government action is the welfare contract. [. . .] There can be no justification for a pension scheme that takes from poor parents and children and gives to rich pensioners. Of course, many of today's pensioners are poor, and no doubt there will be poor pensioners in 50 years' time, but current trends indicate that pensioners as a whole are getting wealthier. A move from a universal to a needs-related pension system would seem to be both fair and efficient, but politically hardly 'saleable' as yet, before the effects of ageing are more widely considered and discussed. Whether any western government has either the political will or the electoral strength for such a move remains to be seen; recent retrenchment in welfare spending has impinged very little on the retired population, despite the fact that pension expenditure is the most costly element in all western welfare states.

Any action to alter the nature of the employment contract will be more difficult because [. . .] all parties concerned with the decision seem to prefer early retirement. The legislation enacted in the United States by President Reagan to raise in steps the normal age of receipt of the OASI pension from 65 to 67 between the years 2003 and 2027 is not likely to have any effect on the downward trend in the actual age of retirement from paid work unless the demand for labour increases considerably at the same time. It may be possible to encourage the employment of older workers through various tax concessions, but these would have to be large to overcome the effect of the earnings gradient. Perhaps the shortage of young workers over the next decade will begin to undermine ageist employment policies. [. . .]

The economic and social problems associated with population ageing in industrial societies are not short-term phenomena like balance of payments crises or periods of inflation which can be corrected through monetary or fiscal policy. Even if fertility rates could be brought back towards replacement levels in all countries within a decade, the problems of population ageing would still be apparent in our demographic structure for the next 50 years. It is this long-term aspect which makes population ageing such an unpalatable issue for governments and administrations which are interested in solutions rather than problems, and which like to parade the effectiveness of their solutions at appropriate points in the electoral cycle. Yet it is the long-term nature of the problem that makes it imperative that action is taken now to cope with the costs of population ageing that will become most apparent in 30 years' time. If no action is taken, the competition for resources between workers and pensioners will break the fiscal basis of modern welfare systems, and quite possibly this will undermine the democratic consensus upon which the western economies are based.

References

Binney, E.A. and Estes, C.L. (1988) 'The retreat of the state and its transfer of responsibility: the intergenerational war', *International Journal of Health Services*, 18: 83–96.

Daniels, N. (1989) 'Justice and Transfers Between Generations' in P. Johnson, C. Conrad and D. Thomson (eds), *Workers versus Pensioners*. Manchester: Manchester University Press/CEPR, pp. 57–79.

Easterlin, R.A. (1987) 'The new age structure of poverty in America: permanent or transient?', *Population and Development Review*, 13: 195–208.

Guillemard, A. (1989) 'The Trend Towards Early Labour Force Withdrawal and the Reorganisation of the Life Course: a Cross-national Analysis' in P. Johnson, C. Conrad and D. Thomson (eds), *Workers versus Pensioners*. Manchester: Manchester University Press/CEPR, pp. 164–180.

Holzmann, R. (1988) *Reforming Public Pensions: Background, Pressures and Options*. Paris: OECD.

ILO (International Labour Office) (1987) *Demographic Development and Social Security (Report II)*. Geneva: ILO.

Lazear, E.P. (1979) 'Why is there mandatory retirement?', *Journal of Political Economy*, 87: 1261–84.

Sass, S. (1989) 'Pension Bargains: The Heyday of US Collectively Bargained Pension Arrangements' in P. Johnson, C. Conrad and D. Thomson (eds), *Workers versus Pensioners*. Manchester: Manchester University Press/CEPR, pp. 92–136.

Schmähl, W. (ed.) (1989) *Redefining the Process of Retirement in an International Perspective*. Heidelberg: Springer.

Thomson, D. (1989), 'The Welfare State and Generation Conflict: Winners and Losers' in P. Johnson, C. Conrad and D. Thomson (eds), *Workers versus Pensioners*. Manchester: Manchester University Press/CEPR, pp. 33–56.

43

The new prospects for retirement

Michael Young and Tom Schuller

Seventy is younger now than it was yesterday.

(Mrs Barker, Plumstead)

The social history of Britain which pioneered the new industry has in one variation or another been followed almost everywhere, from the United States to Germany, from France to Japan, with the new order being wrenched out, time and time again, from the bosom of the family. Pre-industrial society rested on this single ancient institution which, for millennia, had an all-embracing sweep, performing all functions and straddling all ages. The family produced its own food and clothing, educated its children, sustained its old and controlled its members so that they served these ends. The family was the great generalist, as with a much reduced role it still is.

The new age-locked society has been made possible by the gains in productivity which industry has brought about. When the family was both economy and society it had one great disadvantage: domestic production did not yield much more than a basic living. Before the coming of industry men, women and children had to work from almost the cradle to almost the grave because they were at the margin of subsistence. There was little or no room for people of any age who could not grow and rear the food they ate and make the goods they consumed. Almost every consumer (outside the landowning classes) had to be a producer as well. Who would not toil, should not eat. [. . .]

Separating off the ages

It was the factory that put an end to the all-age family as the unit of production and brought into existence age-classes where there had been none before. The gains in productivity brought about by the factories and the associated agricultural and other improvements allowed masses of people, for the first time in human history, to live above the subsistence level. But the fact of there being gains did not in

---

From *Life After Work*. London: Harper Collins, 1991, Chapter 1, pp. 1–26 (abridged).

itself dictate the manner in which they should be distributed. The surplus above subsistence was not used as it would have been if the family had remained the altogether dominant institution. For then the extra productivity might well have been used, not, as it was in practice, to relieve the old and the young from the obligation to contribute to their own upkeep, but to spread the benefits of extra leisure and income across all age groups, without any of them being required to give up work entirely. The world would have had a different notion of full employment from the one that has been adopted. Full employment would have been in existence wherever children started work early, as they had done before, and older people continued to work late, as they had done before, so that people of all ages would have been doing paid work but with ever decreasing hours for all of them. Leisure would have been spread around evenly instead of being so heavily concentrated at each end of the age spectrum. Everyone of any age could have had time for education just as everyone would have had to spend time on work. Consumers and producers would have remained the same people, and no new age-classes created of consumers who were not allowed to be producers. This is all now a might-have-been but not necessarily a will-never-be; the might-have-been could be revived in a new form in the future. [. . .]

The option was never weighed up and then, after proper reflection, rejected. If it had been, the subsequent history of the industrial world, without schools confined to children and without children and old people being excluded from work, would have been so different as hardly to be imaginable. As it is, the family as the generalist has given way to industry as the specialist. Specialisation has been demanded by the growth of an ever more complex economy and, as it turns out, of an evermore fragmented society. The globe has been pulled together into one network by specialised communications but pulled apart by new and equally specialised institutions for industry and education, health and amusement, which have taken over what the family, as an all-age affair, once did largely on its own.

The reduction of the family's productive role has had a marked effect on incentives. Industry has always needed workers who want more goods and services and want them insatiably. If workers had ever been satisfied with what they had, industrial discipline would have disappeared. [. . .]

The situation would have been still more worrying if children and older people had remained bread-winners as well as bread-eaters. As it was, their gradual removal from the labour force meant that workers had more dependants, more people to work for, more needs that had to be satisfied. Their altruism made workers into work-horses.

The removal of the young and the old from the labour force also strengthened incentives in another way. If they had not been removed, increasing leisure would have been spread around all ages instead of being concentrated on young and old. [. . .] Part of the fear of those whose business is business was that, if their employees had too much free time, work would cease to be salient in their lives. [. . .]

The rise of the state

The role of the new nation-state in the whole transformation was crucial. The family did not give up its functions willingly: it fought strongly against the take-over. The tenant farmers held out against enclosure of their lands; the families dependent upon the domestic handicrafts all over Britain put up trenchant opposition to the new machines even when they did not go so far as to join the Luddites; after education was made compulsory in 1870 some poor parents rioted against the new schools which were going to take their children and their children's labour away from them. In all phases of the long struggle the state was engaged on the other side, harnessing its sovereign force and its money to put down the traditional comprehensive family and subtract from it some of its more crucial functions, or (as in education) force itself on the family as a partner. Though always in the name of reform and always to demonstrate a perfectly genuine benevolence for the interests of the young and the old, the state appropriated some of the main roles of the family. It weakened the family's own basic framework for distributing its resources between all its members according to their needs and challenged its mini-collectivist sentiments with an individualism more in tune with the exigencies of industry. The fulcrum of modern society has been the alliance between the state and industry. [. . .]

Meanwhile the old had to be prevailed upon to withdraw from the labour market. They had to recognise that to 'retire', once their duty to avoid, had now become their duty to honour. Eventually common parlance had to give retirement its new meaning and its new respectability. None of this would have been done without the state. Characteristically, it was the civil service that invented retirement in its modern form and tied it down to specific ages. [. . .] Compulsion was brought in to enforce retirement just as it was put behind education in its modern form. Since then policy (always backed by the rigours of the law) has lurched from one shaky rationalisation to another, with 70 being fixed as the qualifying age for a non-contributory pension in 1909, and 65 for a contributory pension in 1925. The practice became still more ridiculous in 1940 when the retirement age for women was settled at 60, five years younger than for the husbands whom they usually outlived, and still outlive, by a handsome margin. [. . .]

Thus it has been laid down that people's life-cycles should be cut into the standard segments we know today. The state has used its compulsory powers to decree that when they pass one birthday they have to enter school and at another leave the workforce, and, historically, employers have aped the state. [. . .]

The two extreme age-classes have been swollen out by a series of steps, each of them peculiar to the one or the other. The elongation of retirement has followed on the improvements in health. Better health is one of the results of a higher standard of life when this has taken the form of more and better food and this has benefited those who used to eat too little, even if it has harmed those who eat too much; alongside this have come better sanitation and better housing; better medicine and better health care. Being more healthy, people live longer. But the retirement age has not been raised in line with the gain in life expectancy. If the gain had since 1940 been wholly used for extending working life, the standard retirement age would already be 70 and on the way up to 75 in 2025. But as it is, with no such adjustment, the number of people in Britain entitled to draw a retirement pension has been rising steadily. [. . .] It has become less and less true that work-enders are also life-enders.

Superimposed on this major trend, common to all industrial societies, has been another of more recent origin which has been common to most – the practice of leaving work earlier. Men though not women have been ending their paid jobs a good deal earlier than they used to. [. . .] The labour market has changed its shape, perhaps permanently, which means that to the growing numbers of people who are over the normal retirement age now have to be added the many who have retired below it. [. . .]

Class comparisons

The new age-classes [. . .] are not unlike the ordinary social classes. Both kinds of class in their modern forms had their origins in the industrial revolution. [. . .] But the age-classes are not formed out of the occupational structure: their members do not have ordinary occupations – the result being that the young have not yet been caught up in the ordinary class structure and the old have to some extent left it behind. In many ways, rather than describing behaviour only in terms of the general inclusive system of social classes, it says more about people, and is also descriptive of their way of life, to consider them as starting in one age-class, then entering an occupational class, and ending in another age-class.

In another respect the age-classes and the main occupational classes – that is, the working class, the middle class and so forth – are alike: the boundaries of each have become more fuzzy. [. . .] More difficult to place in the ordinary class system are people like businessmen who have much money but little education or actors and parsons who are the opposite. This is especially so for people who have started life in one social class and then as a result of social mobility moved into another.

The boundaries of the age-classes have also become more blurred. The pensionable ages laid down by the state have retained their immense influence. A majority of people still retire at these official ages. But the trend we have just mentioned towards earlier work-ending has been increasing the variability of the leaving ages and will presumably do so still more in the future, and people can now draw a state pension without having to give up work. At the other end of the spectrum many youngsters involved in government training schemes have been paid and have had work experience without being in ordinary employment. [. . .] Moreover, it is not just the age-boundaries themselves that have become blurred. Older people can in their own way be as trendy and almost as responsive to fashion as the younger, and romance is as much something for them as for their grandchildren.

But for all that, the age-classes, if definable at the margin with less precision, remain intact in so far as they comprise vast sections of the population. Their members are mostly still characterised by not being able to work [. . .] and, as a consequence, young and old are dependent in whole or part on the state for their support [. . .]. The state which played such a crucial part in bringing the age-classes into existence is still the prop, indeed the legislator, without which the two age-classes on which we are concentrating could not exist. The new age-class structure is therefore particularly open to challenge. What the state can do, the state can undo. [. . .]

The fault-lines in society

The expansion of the two age-classes at the extremes has been obscured by their failure to attest their own difference from others and their own common interests with each other. Their class-consciousness has not been raised to the point where in any numbers they call their lot into question. For the old the class struggle has been gentle; grey power is rarely manifest. So far it is only the young with their youth culture who have begun to stake out a claim to an independent identity. But the importance of the new class of the young, and still more of the old, has been partially hidden from view for the reason we have already given. They have not become distinctive classes because in so far as they have had an ideology it has not been that of a leisure-based class but has remained a work-based one. [. . .] The old – our main interest here – will not become a fully fledged age-class until they have created a way of life which is distinctive from that of the still-working classes.

[. . .] We believe that the situation is changing rapidly. The age-classes could be subordinated to the other classes much more easily when they were relatively small than they can now that nearly half the population is in one or other of them, with numbers increasing every day. The social controls which maintain the dominance of the work ethic are still in force, and stem in part from the state; but they are no longer so effective. Social change always becomes predictable when fault-lines appear in society. The fault-lines arise from deep-lying inconsistencies. Our argument is that there is a growing inconsistency between the size of the age-classes and their subordination. [. . .] [Institutional] control has become anachronistic. It treats some people who are adults in most meanings of the word as though they are still children, and others who are still as fit and energetic as ever as though they have passed over a date-line from which there can be no return. [. . .]

The need for new terms

[. . .] As we said earlier, the word retirement came into use in this context in the last century. We think it should in due course be retired to the obscurity from which it emerged. It was once appropriate enough. Retirement was a kind of postscript to work which only had to be defined negatively, because the period used to be short. [. . .]

All that has changed. The message that comes with the farewell present (if there is one) can wish the recipient a long and happy retirement but, if it is to be a long one, retirement is no longer the right word for what is no longer the same experience. [. . .] Once it can be detached from work this whole stage of life cries out to be regarded in a different light, as something more positive, not derived from work in the way a pension is derived from the work that preceded it, but distinctively worthwhile in its own right.

The term we have used instead of retirement is 'third age'. It refers to the phase which can now last for 20, 30, even 40 years of active life after leaving work and which would in Britain alone account for some 10 million people. [. . .]

The term we prefer is of French origin, as used in *Les Universités du Troisième Age*, and the clubs with the same name which proliferated in France in the 1970s and 1980s. It has infiltrated into English and gained some currency through the University of the Third Age which was started in the early 1980s. At the time of writing the British U3A has over a hundred branches. The new attitude which is called for by demography, if by nothing else, could be helped along by the new term as it takes its place in the progression described by Laslett: 'First comes an era of dependence,

socialization, immaturity and education; second an era of independence, maturity and responsibility, of earning and of saving; third
an era of personal fulfilment' (1989: 4). [. . .]

The potential for fulfilment

'An era of personal fulfilment' sounds very hopeful, and it would be
wholly unrealistic to suggest that this is what necessarily happens in
the third age. [. . .] When we refer to the third age in this way, what
we are emphasising is its potentiality rather than its actuality. We are
thinking of older people as having a certain kind of freedom – a
negative freedom from coercion – which they may or may not convert
into another kind of freedom, the positive kind. 'Freedom from' is
contrasted with 'freedom for' and the particular 'freedom from' which
is possessed by the age-class is freedom from work. Instead of catching
the same train every morning and strap-hanging to the same little
desk, people can go fishing, read, dig the garden or do anything else
that they could not do while bound into the daily round of work.

But what if they don't? Many of the people we interviewed were
aware of being deprived of the freedom *to* work. Some of them wanted
to go on earning as much as they could for as long as they could, and
if that is what they wanted they should be able to do so. Others liked
their jobs, however contrary it may seem, precisely because their jobs
did limit their freedom. They were now uncomfortable because they
could do what they wanted to do instead of what they were told to do
by an employer who paid them to do what they were told, supported
not just by a command of money but by a work ethic [. . .]. Such
people had so successfully internalised the imperatives of a society
devoted to work that they could not happily choose something
different. [. . .] So we are not by any means resting our argument on
the claim that all people at this stage of life like being free, merely that
they can be. Our particular interest [. . .] is in seeing who, when they
have the chance, ventures out and who pulls back. [. . .]

Reference

Laslett, P. (1989) *A Fresh Map of Life*. London: Weidenfeld and Nicolson.

44

Older people in Europe:
social and economic policies

Alan Walker and Jens Alber

Employment policy issues

While the member states of the [European] Community may view with pride the emergence of more balanced age structures among their populations, this change, and the pace at which it is taking place, raises a number of important policy issues. For example, population ageing is posing a challenge to policy-makers in member states because retirement or old-age pensions are already the largest item in their social security budgets. This is particularly the case for those countries that have previously instituted major reforms to public pensions and are now facing the twin financial implications of population ageing and pension system maturation. Moreover, at a time of economic recession, concerns about the financial stability of pensions and wider social security systems inevitably become more urgent.

The health services of member states can claim considerable credit for the decline in mortality over the last 30 years. In some countries life expectancy has increased significantly as a result – by 10 years for women in France, Italy and Spain. However, this success, particularly the fall in mortality rates among older people themselves, has increased the demand for health and social care. The rapid increase in the numbers of very elderly people (mainly women) also has important implications for the provision of care both informally, by families, and formally, by the public, private and voluntary sectors. The issue of

From *Older People in Europe: Social and Economic Policies: The 1993 Report of the European Observatory*, by Alan Walker, Jens Alber, Anne-Marie Guillemard and, in collaboration with Juan Antonio Fernandez Cordon, Aurelia Florea, Kees Knipscheer, Olgierd Kuty, Éamon O'Shea, Heloisa Perista, Merete Platz, Gaston Schàber and Dimitris Ziomas (Commission of the European Communities, Directorate General V, Employment, Social Affairs, Industrial Relations). The three main chapters of the report contain detailed syntheses of material provided in national reports from the 12 EC countries. Of the extracts reproduced here, the first two main sections, 'Employment policy issues' and 'Recent developments in pension policy' are by Alan Walker, while the final section, 'Recent policy developments (in health and social services)', is by Jens Alber.

how to provide care for increasing numbers of frail older people (albeit a minority of all older persons) is one that is currently confronting all governments and millions of ordinary families throughout the Community.

Over the last 20 years there has been an accelerating trend towards early labour force exit among older workers. In several member countries this has been encouraged by public policy in response to rising unemployment. Now some states are facing the problem of how to reverse this trend in order to compensate for a fall in the supply of young labour market entrants or to reduce the cost of early retirement.

Population ageing also presents important challenges to the social cohesion of member states and the Community as a whole. The main issue here is the extent to which the rapid changes in the age structure of populations can be managed in ways that maintain the relatively high levels of intergenerational solidarity in EC countries and which also ensure the continuance of social integration among older people and their families. [. . .]

Recent developments in pension policy

The national reports highlight three important issues with regard to current and future pension policy: adjustments in the scope and coverage of pension systems; the growth of private supplementary and additional pensions; and the equal treatment of men and women and the introduction of greater flexibility in retirement.

Adjustments in the scope and coverage of pensions

[. . .] The combination of economic recession, pension system maturation and population ageing has put pressures on public spending and, in some countries, even threatens another fiscal crisis. As a result most EC countries have either taken action to limit pension spending or, at least, are considering such action. But although cost containment seems to be the main engine driving discussions about pension reform, it is not the only one, nor is it the only factor explaining recent developments. Thus it is possible to distinguish two contrasting motivations behind current or planned adjustments in the scope and coverage of pensions, and a third which combines both of them. [. . .]

First of all, there are those countries that have limited the rise of pension costs by altering the public pensions contract in some way. This usually entails either adjusting the contributions or inflation-proofing conditions or raising the retirement age. [. . .] Those that have taken action so far are the UK and Germany, while those in the process of taking action or about to do so are France, Italy and Greece. [. . .]

Secondly, despite an overarching concern with the cost implications of population ageing [. . .], some countries have been extending their pension coverage recently. In fact the balance sheet shows that actually, up to the start of 1993, more countries have been extending provision than cutting back. For example, Belgium, Denmark and Luxembourg have recently increased the flexibility of their pension system. In 1990 Spain decided to upgrade pensions at least in line with the consumer price index and link increases in the married person's pension to the minimum interprofessional wage. [. . .]

Turning, thirdly, to those countries that appear on both dimensions of pension policy – expansion and contraction – Germany represents the leading example. Thus the 1989 reform law, being implemented from 1992, extended the recognition of informal care by awarding three contribution years' credits for each child. In addition the 1989 law gave credits for periods of care for frail persons – a major innovation in EC pension provision. Persons regularly providing care on an unpaid basis for at least 10 hours per week are treated as if they had pension contributions and earned 75 per cent of the average wage. [. . .]

Overall, then, it appears that the last four to five years have seen a continued improvement in the scope and coverage of national pension systems in the majority of member states, despite the fact that the most talked about issue seems to be cost containment.

The expanding private sector

The dominant EC pension model consists of an earnings-related basic pension scheme supplemented by a voluntary occupational one. In most countries the occupational pension sector has played an increasing role over the last two decades. The private sector includes occupational schemes, applying to groups of employees which are usually administered by employers, and personal pensions consisting of individual contracts with insurance companies. In recent years the common 'defined benefit' occupational scheme has been partly replaced, in some countries, by the 'defined contribution' or 'money purchase' scheme whereby the actual pension received depends on the outcome of capital investments rather than being based on a pre-defined formula linking pensions to earnings. Such schemes obviously introduce an element of uncertainty into future retirement income. [. . .] The governments of some countries have been trying to increase the role of private pension schemes partly in response to concerns about the mounting costs of public pensions.

Examples of countries with large occupational pension sectors include the Netherlands and Germany. [. . .] Both countries illustrate the problems associated with such pension schemes. For example they usually exclude part-time and low-paid workers – exclusions which affect women more than men. [. . .] In addition to this fundamental deficiency there are the well-known problems of lack of full inflation-proofing and loss of pension rights when employees change employment. [. . .]

There is also the potential danger that insolvencies may result in the loss of pension funds. Under German law entitlements do not end with insolvency. [. . .]

As noted above, the growth of private pension schemes has sometimes been the result of conscious government policy. In 1988 both the Belgian and British governments introduced tax incentives to encourage employees themselves to make personal pension savings as a means of reducing reliance on the public pension scheme. [. . .] Both countries are lowering the value of these incentives in 1993. [. . .]

It is likely that private occupational and personal pensions will increase in importance in the future, as governments see them as, at least partial, alternatives to the public sector. This also applies to the one northern EC country that has traditionally had a very small occupational pension sector – Denmark – which, in 1991, saw the introduction of such pension schemes for the majority of those in employment.

Equal treatment and flexible retirement

The majority of EC pension systems are characterised by inequalities between men and women. Until recently five member states also had lower state pension ages for women than for men. As a result of a series of judgements by the European Court over recent years the discriminatory nature of dual pension ages has been called into question. Belgium took action from the start of 1991 to equalise pension ages but Greece, Italy, Portugal and the UK still have a different age for men and women. The Italian government is in the process of introducing pension reforms that will gradually raise the pension ages for both sexes to 65, and the British government has published a consultation document putting forward a number of options of pension age equalisation.

Belgium is the only EC country to have introduced, in 1991, a flexible pension age: from 60 for both men and women, with a loss of one-fortieth and one-forty-fifth of the pension per year up to the age of 65. But six member states – Denmark, France, Germany, Italy, Luxembourg and Spain – have partial pension schemes in place. The earliest of them was established in Denmark where partial pensions have been payable to those aged 60 to 66 since the start of 1987. The partial pension is paid according to the reduction in the number of hours worked and at most it may contribute 90 per cent of the shortfall in income. The option of combining a half pension and a half salary was introduced in Luxembourg in April 1991. [. . .]

Recent policy developments [in health and social services]

[. . .] Recent policy developments centre on five major issues:

- to contain the heavy growth of health expenditure;
- to define policy priorities for the rapidly growing group of elderly persons;
- to provide adequate coverage for the growing need of long-term care;
- to reorganise residential care;
- to introduce new incentives for the development of community care and informal care.

Ever since the beginning of the 1960s the health sector has been one of the most rapidly growing expenditure fields in social policy. When the recession following the two oil price shocks of the 1970s led to growing public deficits, most European countries sought to curb the rate of health expenditure growth. Reforms were initiated which led to a reduction of the number of hospital beds, to capped budgets for various medical services, and to increased private cost-sharing. In most countries, however, the increases in health expenditure kept outpacing the rate of economic growth throughout the 1980s. While the health expenditure ratio of the 12 EC-member countries averaged 6.8 per cent in 1980, it rose slightly further to an average of 7.1 per cent in 1990. To combat further growth several countries such as France, Germany and the UK introduced not only new austerity measures, but also structural reforms which aimed at subjecting the providers of health services to more effective cost controls. [. . .]

The new emphasis on cost-efficient health care services entails a series of very difficult decisions: is it acceptable to have dual health care systems with basic services for all and more expensive services only for a privileged few? Can health care services be rationed? If so, who shall have priority in access to costly services? And, by implication, the most difficult of all decisions: who shall live? In this situation, several national governments are seeking to define priorities in health care, and to develop new care mixes which shift the long-standing priority for the sector of acute care to better-balanced provisions in favour of the long-neglected sector of long-term care.

As part of this ongoing process, several countries are drafting plans, or are at least establishing commissions, for the development of future policy programmes for the elderly. Belgium introduced a Round Table of Health Experts in 1988. Denmark passed a series of national framework acts for old age policies in the late 1980s. In France [each department since 1982] has been obliged to develop a gerontological plan, and, (in 1991) the government introduced a multi-year programme for the future development of care. [. . .]

In most of the new policy statements there is consensus that long-term care for elderly people is a new standard risk of social security which needs to be covered by some sort of public provision. The issue of a public 'dependence insurance' or 'long-term care insurance' looms particularly large in countries which do not have a national health service, or whose sickness insurance schemes cover nursing care and home care services for older people only partly. Ongoing debates over a long-term care insurance are reported for Belgium, France, Germany and Luxembourg, i.e. all four countries which adhere to traditional sickness insurance schemes. In these countries, the social welfare schemes designed for the support of low-income families are increasingly burdened by growing expenditures for care purposes. Therefore the local authorities exert pressure to introduce new types of social security schemes which cover the growing risk.

In Germany the national government has just introduced a bill for an almost universal compulsory insurance scheme for long-term care. The new scheme is to be financed on a pay-as-you-go basis with a contribution rate of 1.7 per cent of gross earnings shared equally by employees and employers. [. . .]

As practically all recent policy statements of the various national governments agree that community care should have priority over residential care, the residential care sector is undergoing a rapid transformation. Access to residential care is being increasingly made contingent upon the decisions of screening committees which assess clients in order to establish which type of care is most suited and most cost-efficient. [. . .] As [such professional assessment] procedures are explicitly designed to substitute more expensive kinds of provision by less expensive ones, there is a risk that the margin of individual choice of the client will be limited. Therefore, adequate participation rights of the clients, or of organisations representing their interests, should be introduced as safeguards in the case of a disagreement with professional judgements.

Several countries recently witnessed marked increases in commercial nursing homes (though such homes do not exist at all in Denmark). Belgium, Portugal and the UK are the most notable examples of this new trend. The expansion of for-profit residential care calls for new regulatory measures which overcome traditional differences in the regulation of public and private sector homes. [. . .]

In the sector of domiciliary care there have been some interesting policy changes which aim at overcoming the distinction between nursing care and home care, and at providing new incentives for informal care. Denmark made home help services a public service free of charge in 1989. As from July 1992, further payment of the service will be income tested for old age pensioners, but for more than 90 per cent of the clients the service will continue to be free of charge. The Netherlands extended the scope of its exceptional medical expenses scheme to cover a certain amount of home help services. [. . .] Belgium, France, Portugal and Spain have introduced various programmes for foster families which host people in need of care. [. . .] France (1989) and Portugal (1991) have recently adopted national laws regulating the relationship between foster families and their guests. In addition, French private households employing care-takers are exempted from social insurance contributions, whereas people giving care in private households receive certain tax credits. [. . .]

PASTS

45

Born 1898; a brief group biography

Mark Abrams

In mid-1977 there were 2,840,000 people in Great Britain aged 75 or more – 896,000 men and 1,944,000 women. A little over half of them were aged 75 to 79: the age of the median man in the 75 or over population was 78, and that of the median woman was 79. The purpose of the following notes is to remind the reader of some of the main events in the social and personal environment in the early life of this median person and thus help to indicate the values and experiences that shape his, or rather her, attitudes and judgements today. Since two-thirds of those aged 75 or more are women the 'biography' is more appropriately developed in terms of a girl born in 1898.

If born in London (or indeed any other large city) the circumstances of her parents and home have been described in considerable detail in the 17 monumental volumes of Charles Booth's *Life and Labour of the People in London*; the first volume of this appeared in 1889 and the final one in 1897 – a few months before her birth in 1898. Booth's survey showed that one-third of all London families were living at or below the subsistence level, i.e. lacked sufficient income to afford a diet that would keep them above the starvation level. And over 30 per cent of London's population were living under conditions of gross overcrowding – i.e. at a density of two or more persons per room. From his findings Booth concluded that the principal causes of this widespread absolute poverty were not to be found in 'crime, vice, drinks or laziness, [but in the] lack of work, death of husband, sickness, trade misfortune, old age and accident'.

Shortly afterwards Seebohm Rowntree's study in York showed that at the end of the nineteenth century such poverty was not limited to Britain's largest cities. His report, *Poverty: a Study of Town Life* (1901)

From *Beyond Three-Score and Ten: a First Report on a Survey of the Elderly*. Mitcham: Age Concern England, 1978, pp. 6–7.

using an extremely austere measure of poverty (e.g. 21s 8d. per week to cover all the needs of a family of five – broadly at 1977 prices equivalent to £16) showed that in York 28 per cent of people, because of either primary causes or secondary causes (i.e. 'wasting' part of the household income on the purchase of furniture or newspapers), fell below even this miserable poverty line.

If our median child of 1898 was born in the countryside then the chances are that her material background was even worse. In 1903, P.H. Mann, stimulated by the work of Booth and Rowntree, applied the latter's techniques to an agricultural village in Bedfordshire where the Duke of Bedford was 'the greatest landowner, houseowner, and employer of labour in the district'. Mann, however, made one adjustment to Rowntree's measure of poverty. Since, in his words, 'wood, brush, thorn etc. could be picked up free' (report in Galton et al., 1905), he decided that a family of five could survive on 18s 4d. a week (i.e. approximately £14 at present prices). Even with this reduced dividing line he found that 41 per cent of working-class people in the village were in primary poverty and another 9 per cent (through 'bad management' and 'drink') were in secondary poverty. (And at the time of Mann's survey 25 per cent of Britain's population lived in rural districts.)

As a young child the visits she made to her grandparents might be clouded by their poverty; in the 1890s of all those in England and Wales aged 65 or more nearly 30 per cent were described in the official statistics as 'paupers' (i.e. they drew Poor Relief) and well over a quarter of these 'paupers' lived in the workhouse. Those elderly paupers who were not admitted to the workhouse might, if they qualified as 'the deserving poor', receive from various sources, including parish pay, 7s 6d. a week, or 12s. for a married couple.

A year or two before the outbreak of World War I our median respondent left school at the age of 14 (or 13 if she was bright enough to pass a special examination) in time to see her older brothers and, a little later, her father, join the Armed Forces; in many cases her mother also was mobilised for the war effort (as a munition factory worker, or as a land worker) and possibly finished the war either as a widow or as the wife of a wounded war casualty. (During World War I 744,000 men serving with the British Forces were killed and 1,693,000 were wounded.)

Then, by the time the 1921 Census was taken and our median girl was 23 years of age she was either already married (not very likely) or, more probably, out at work; and 'out' should be taken literally; in 1921 of all women in employment in Britain over 20 per cent were in private domestic service. An almost equal number worked in the textile mills of the North and the garment workshops of London.

Marriage came late in those days and by the time the 1931 Census was taken nearly one-third of the contemporaries of our median woman were still single although they were now in their early thirties. In part this lack of husbands would be due to the fact that after the end of World War I hundreds of thousands of young people, mainly men, decided to seek a better life outside Britain. Between 1919 and 1931 the loss of emigrants from this country ·to the United States, Canada, Australia, New Zealand, etc. was an average of over a quarter of a million people a year.

For the next three of four years she, and most other people, considered themselves lucky if they had a job at all. In 1934, when the worst of the Great Depression had passed, in the average month 17 per cent of the 13 million manual workers covered by the unemployment insurance scheme were out of work. From then on conditions continued to improve but even so at mid-1939 the proportion of workers unemployed was only slightly under 12 per cent; and for those unfortunate enough to live in the industrial cities of Lancashire and the Tyneside the ratio was closer to 20 per cent.

Even those with jobs were hardly steeped in affluence. At the last pre-war official earnings survey in October 1938, the weekly pay of the average adult male manual worker was 69 shillings and that of the average woman worker aged 18 or more was less than half that at 32 shillings (their rough equivalents at today's prices would be £35 and £16).

When World War II broke out our median 1898 infant had entered her forties and by the time food rationing finished in 1954 she was well past middle age. However, she had witnessed the post-war expansion of the welfare state and was able, provided she had paid the necessary contributions and had retired from paid employment, to draw a weekly retirement pension of £2 on reaching the age of 60 in 1958 (roughly equivalent to £8.50 today).

[. . .] Since then the real value of her pension has increased, the health and social services have expanded, housing conditions have improved, concessionary fares on public transport have been offered her, but these have all come late in life. For many women who are now approaching 80 the first three-quarters of their lives were lived against a background of abject poverty, hard work, danger and wretched housing. It would not be surprising if their present criteria of what the need, of what they are entitled to, and of what gives them satisfaction are modest.

It should also be remembered that in one important respect the men and women aged 75 or more who were interviewed in 1977 are exceptional – they have survived. And that by itself makes them remarkable; of all the babies born in Britain at the beginning of this century almost one-third had died by 1946 and another 40 per cent by

1977. Our respondents were drawn from the 30 per cent who have survived.

Reference

F. Galton, Durkheim E. et al., (1905) *Sociological Papers*. London: Macmillan & Co.

46

Oral history as a social movement: reminiscence and older people

Joanna Bornat

What I want to talk about is a movement with very recent origins. Fifteen years ago or so there was little to show in history books, in social work textbooks or in publishing, of any idea that ordinary older people's life experience might be of interest or of any value. [. . .]

About 10 years ago there were three rather isolated areas of work which quite separately were beginning to make an impact, but which had yet to influence each other. In history, psychology and in community publishing during the 1960s and early 1970s some new and challenging ideas were beginning to take shape. They generated ideas which, when they came together in the early 1980s, were to change care work practice with elderly people, widen learning opportunities across the age range and produce a rich yield of historical evidence from all corners of the British Isles. I want to begin with a brief account of the development of those three areas of work.

Oral history origins

Oral history, treating recollection of experience as valid evidence, has its own long history, as Paul Thompson (1978) has shown. Traditionally, and until the mid-nineteenth century, historians regarded spoken testimony with as much reverence as they treated documents recording events, laws and customs. Indeed the recollections of the famous, rich and influential in society have always had a place in accounts of wars, political change and custom. The place of the diary and of memoirs of politicians and opinion leaders has rarely been challenged by historians whose skills include deciphering documents and piecing together the past from written records. This practice left us with a history that was narrow in content and often uncritical in method. The personal accounts which remained to us represented only a narrow range of social and economic

From *Oral History*, 17 (2) Autumn 1989, pp. 16-24 (abridged).

viewpoints tending to concentrate on what was public and political at the highest levels of society. Daily life, insofar as it was chronicled through parish and census records, and the detailed surveys of Booth and Rowntree, was passed through the filter of bureaucratic form-filling or of record-keeping of observers external to the daily lives under scrutiny. There were few accounts from women, from minorities, from deviant groups, and in content the bias neglected accounts of family life, social customs, working life, old age, neighbourhood, community and undocumented events hidden from history.

Oral history turns the historian into an interviewer and changes the practice of the historian into a personal interaction with the past within living memory. Listening to someone describe their first day at work, school days, participation in unofficial strikes, childbirth, courtship, housework, historians have learned to broaden ideas of what history is about. It was in the late 1960s that oral history began to establish itself in Britain. At that time, two large surveys, at the Universities of Essex and Kent, used interviews with a large sample of older people as respondents. These led to many other research projects (see, e.g., Davidoff and Westover, 1986) and to writing which made use of the memories of elderly people to explain areas of the past previously unrecorded. It was significant for the development of oral history that the more successful and long lasting of those two university-based initiatives was in a department of sociology. This theoretical context gave oral history in Britain a distinctively humanistic bias which contributed to its later broadening out into less formally academic areas of work and research (see Plummer, 1983). [. . .]

Community publishing origins

At about the same time as oral history methods were beginning to have an impact on the world of historical research, there were other developments going on. Community publishing evolved in the early 1970s with a form and content which opened up new possibilities for access to audiences and to new writers. In many respects community publishing represents the 1970s' expression of the University Settlement movement of over a hundred years earlier. In the 1970s teachers, graduates, community activists living and working in the more deprived areas of inner cities encouraged working-class people to write and produce their own art and literature. The Centerprise Publishing Project is one such enduring example. In an account of their first five years' work, Centerprise showed how people in the London Borough of Hackney devoured the pamphlets of autobiography and reminiscence which, amongst others, a dressmaker, a shoemaker and a cab driver had written (Centerprise, 1977). Dot Starn's *When I Was a Child*, published in 1973, sold 1000 copies in the first three months. Arthur Newton's *Years of Change* sold 400 copies in four years. Other community groups in Bristol, Manchester and Brighton were at the same time publishing local people's writing and finding a mass readership amongst people who could identify with childhood experiences of family life, growing up, migration to England, finding work and struggling through, when it was written by their contemporaries and described streets, experiences and even individual people they could remember. Ordinary people became their own historians and biographers and many took an active part in editing, designing and promoting their books.

These community publishing projects and countless others since have been funded by a variety of sources, by local government, charitable trusts, commercial sponsors, and, latterly and most ironically, as a response to widespread unemployment, by central government, thanks to the Manpower Services Commission's short lived Community Programme. They developed and refined a medium for reminiscence, the cheaply produced illustrated booklet. From towns and cities the length and breadth of the British Isles, there is now an enormous literature of people's history published in this format. Almost exclusively this has been written by older people or edited from accounts recorded with their help. [. . .]

Psychology of old age origins

The third area in which new ideas were taking shape during the 1960s and 1970s was in the psychology of old age. This change has been discussed in detail elsewhere by people more qualified than me (e.g. Coleman, 1986). Starting in the United States, psychologists interested in the ageing process began to question the idea that reminiscing was an abnormal or pathological activity, something to be discouraged. Robert Butler published a paper in 1963 which was to excite and interest those working with more frail elderly people. He used the idea of 'life review' and argued for a perspective which accepts looking back over a past life as a normal and universal experience in old age. [. . .]

Partly in response to the very great enthusiasm which Robert Butler's work gave rise to, Peter Coleman's later influential study, *Ageing and Reminiscence Processes*, argues for a more qualified perspective on reminiscence as therapy (1986: chapter 10). His research found older people who were unwilling or unhappy reminiscers.

The emergence of *Recall*

During the 1970s three areas of work were emerging. Each of these involved older people and each emphasised the importance of recalling the past. These three areas might have developed independently, they might have had little impact beyond the boundaries of influence of their various practitioners. In order for the qualitative and quantitative leap forward to have taken place, something else needed to happen. [. . .]

Without wanting to sound too dramatic, or monocausal, I want to argue that the one event which was to draw attention to oral history with older people was the publication in November 1981 of Help the Aged's tape/slide programme *Recall*. The simplicity and apparent comprehensiveness of sequences of images and sounds covering the first 80 years of the twentieth century made *Recall* an instant success. Hundreds of sets of the package sold in the first few years and it continues to sell well today, even in the face of several competing formats and versions. [. . .]

Recall's origins lie in the arts. As an architect, Mick Kemp was interested in the meaning of the environment for mentally frail older people. His project workers were art students with an interest in images and self-expression. For them history was something which older people generated or could be encouraged to create, given the right cues and stimuli. The philosophy behind *Recall* was very much one which gave equal validity to the memories of all older people. As an historian who came in at a later stage in the development of the packages I well remember conflicts between those whose main concern was to evoke responses, and those people, like me, who wanted both to evoke and *inform*. Thus an early version of the First World War sequence focused almost exclusively on life in the trenches since this was what the elderly men they met talked about. After discussion amongst members of the production team and further testing with groups of older men, and women, the sequence finally included images of women's work and life on the home front. *Recall* in its final form invites recognition of past events and experience, but it also stirs up what may have been forgotten and it introduces the idea of differing experience and perspective on the past.

The second point I want to draw from the *Recall* experience concerns opening up opportunities to more people to become oral historians. Care staff and community workers with a background in historical research can reasonably be expected to be few in number. And even those who have an interest in local history find that they have no opportunity to follow their interest within working hours. History is not a subject area for social or health services training. What *Recall* provided and still provides is a technologically simple means to exploring the past. This opens up possibilities to residential, community and hospital care staff and to anyone else who can find a slide projector, cassette player and a screen or white wall. Slide/tape production has, in my opinion, many advantages over video. It allows for larger images, it can easily be interrupted with a clear still picture and it requires fairly low level technology.

Equipped with *Recall*'s slide/tape packages, staff-led reminiscence sessions took off in homes and centres all over the British Isles. The idea caught on not just because the packaging was simple and the images and sounds highly evocative. The impact of *Recall* lay in the responses of the audiences and groups of older people. Very quickly the issue became not just one of how to show *Recall*, but how to manage and develop work with groups convened to watch and take part. The evidence that reminiscing is stimulating and enjoyable was immediately available.

Reminiscence: a movement

Recall is not the whole story of course. Oral history, community publishing and life review were having their own impact with groups of workers and older people at this time. *Recall* had captured a market of interested people who it seems were awaiting an opportunity to explore the memories of the older people they knew. What followed over the next eight years in Britain at least was something like an explosion of interest in reminiscence work with older people. There have been several local editions of *Recall*, there have been television programmes, radio programmes, videos, training packs, large-scale exhibitions like *Exploring Living Memory*, workshops, journal articles, conferences, courses, booklets, plays, films, almost every possible medium has been explored. Inevitably reminiscence work developed a systematisation and 'reminiscence therapy' became the talking point amongst workers caring for older people. Courses emerged with freelancing practitioners offering training in this new area of work.

The impact on oral history, community publishing and in psychology has been selective. Perhaps because some of the most enthusiastic proponents of reminiscence work with older people were also oral historians, it's possible to say that in Britain, with some exceptions, oral historians have taken a rather different approach to colleagues in other continental European countries. We'd like to think we've sustained an awareness of the meaning of reminiscence in the lives of older people. For some of us the separation between oral history and reminiscence risks the distancing of older people in the process and weakens their control over what is produced. The pursuit of oral history is a goal which we all share, whether we work as individual researchers of any age or in groups with older people. Reminiscence work implies a more active role for those whose memories are sought and it introduces goals and objectives which can be personal, social and, of course, historical. [. . .]

Reminiscence: the debate about therapy

Within psychology and in work with more frail elderly people debates continue. Surprisingly, given the extent to which reminiscence work has been taken up in homes and hospitals around Britain, there has been very little research and evaluation into its outcomes for older people. But perhaps it is because of the general level of enthusiasm and the sense of being part of something akin to a social movement that there tend to be strong claims for the positive benefits of the work, and very few pauses for comparison or reflection.

A recent paper brought together in a critical review much of the evidence from the work of psychologists working in the field of reminiscence with older people. Susan Thornton and Janet Brotchie (1987) looked at clinical and experimental evidence for therapeutic outcomes for reminiscence activities with elderly people. Their conclusions confirm what some of us had suspected. Based on available evidence there is no safe case to be made for reminiscence on its own bringing about change in the mental abilities of elderly people who may be experiencing depression or low self-esteem as a result of organic illness.

Early in the days of the Reminiscence Aids Project there had been a hope that, somehow, by encouraging the use of memories, mentally frail people would improve their grip on reality. More recently, experimental research has shown small improvements in some measures of functioning amongst non-confused elderly people (Hobbs, 1983) but it isn't clear that the results can always be shown to be directly the result of reminiscing. The strong case for a therapy status for reminiscence has yet to be found or proved.

Does the lack of status as a therapy matter? As Andrew Norris (1989) points out, simply awarding reminiscence work the title of therapy would only mean that it joined a number of other similarly dubiously labelled activities. Within the context of hospitals, gardening has become 'horticultural therapy', reading is 'bibliotherapy' and listening to or playing music is 'music therapy'.

There may be good reasons for avoiding the label therapy. Again Andrew Norris (1989) argues that 'the main function of labelling . . . seems to be to validate [these activities] as legitimate activities in which professional people are entitled to engage'. Taken further, Mike Bender (1989) argues it could mean that *only* professionally qualified people are entitled to take up activities labelled as therapies. This would certainly have unhappy outcomes for the practice of reminiscence work.

One of the strengths of reminiscence work with older people is its openness in terms of process and skill base. Following Andrew Norris it is possible to see reminiscence work as being utilised in a range of therapeutic approaches. He argues for a role for a reminiscence approach in bereavement counselling, insight-based psychotherapy, in cognitive therapy, in reality orientation with people suffering from dementia, in providing stimulation for confused elderly people and in goal planning in more behavioural models of psychotherapy (Norris, 1989). By avoiding the label of therapy we can continue to enjoy the advantages of working flexibly and in a variety of settings. [. . .]

Reminiscence work in residential homes and hospitals

Psychologists, nurses and occupational therapists working in hospitals and residential care workers and social workers in community-based settings, have all found reminiscence work useful and appropriate with groups and with individual elderly people. Approaches vary. John Adams (1988) talks eloquently about the way his continuing care ward was transformed by the introduction of posters from the First World War as talking points. The elderly women on the ward talked about their experiences of the Blitz, visitors stayed on, maintenance men lingered to hear stories. Many of these women had only a fragmentary account to give of their past lives because of their present confused states. It was through the stimulus of reminiscence and by staff and relatives picking up on comments about their pasts that a more detailed, and more sensitive picture of their earlier lives began to unfold.

At Claybury Hospital in North-East London, people with depressive illnesses have been encouraged to write scrapbooks and include photographs of themselves as a means to self-discovery and restoring confidence and renewed insights into themselves and family members (Nance, 1988). Mel Wright and Martin Truelove, social workers in South London and Bradford, have used reminiscence projects with housebound elderly people. In South London a newsletter focused on life on an inter-war housing estate and encouraged a small group of housebound people who otherwise had little contact to share memories of the early years of the estate (Wright, 1986). In Bradford, volunteers were recruited to take down the memories of housebound elderly people. In one case this resulted in 10,000 words of testimony from a post-war refugee (see, *Oral History* 16, no. 2 1988, p. 4). [. . .]

Early on in *Recall*'s development it was suggested that the programme could have some use in training staff. It is probably true to say that the implications for caring relationships were not fully realised at first. [Today] things look very different. Most people who have responsibility and involvement in training care staff and others agree that insights gained from reminiscence sessions have had a profound effect on the relationships of staff and the elderly people they work with. [. . .]

Amongst the best and most committed carers, interests lie in de-routinising reminiscence activities. In group sessions these workers are their best enthusers and resourcers. Some have become part-time researchers into memorabilia and local history, others give accounts of sessions which have brought out the most reticent group member. In some homes and hospitals, knowledge of individual past lives has led to outings and visits, closer staff and relatives involvement and shared experiences from personal histories (Gibson, 1989).

Successful reminiscence work depends less on the accurate remembering of the past and more on the process of exchange and listening. It is this understanding which has captured the interest and commitment of people working with more frail and dependent elderly people. [. . .]

References

Adams, J. (1988) 'Ghosts of Christmas past', *Nursing Times*, 84 (50), 14 December: 62–4.

Bender, M. (1989) 'Reminiscence: applications and limitations', *PSIGE Newsletter*, 29: 22–7.

Butler, R. (1963) 'The Life Review: an interpretation of reminiscence in the aged', *Psychiatry*, 26: 65–76.

Centerprise (1977) *Local Publishing and Local Culture: an Account of the Work of the Centerprise Publishing Project, 1972–1977*. London: Centerprise Publishing Trust (136 Kingsland High Street, London E8).

Coleman, P.G. (1986) *Ageing and Reminiscence Processes: Social and Clinical Implications*. Chichester: Wiley.

Davidoff, L. and Westover B. (eds) (1986) *Our Work, Our Lives, Our Words: Women's History and Women's Work*. London: Macmillan.

Gibson, F. (1989) *Using Reminiscence: a Training Pack*. London: Help the Aged.

Hobbs, A.N. (1983) 'A study to determine some effects of the Help the Aged's *Recall* audio-visual programme'. Unpublished Dip. Psych. dissertation, the British Psychological Society, Leicester.

Nance, A. (1988) 'Reminiscence with the elderly in hospitals', in *Living Memories: Recalling and Recording the Past*. London: London History Workshop and Thames Television.

Norris, A. (1989) 'Reminiscence-based psychotherapeutic work with elderly people'. Paper presented at the Winter Meeting of the Belgian Society of Gerontology and Geriatrics, Ostend, February.

Plummer, K. (1983) *Documents of Life: an Introduction to the Problems and Literature of a Humanistic Method*. London: Allen & Unwin.

Thompson, P. (1978) *The Voice of the Past*. Oxford: Oxford University Press.

Thornton, S. and Brotchie, J. (1987) 'Reminiscence: a critical view of the empirical literature', *British Journal of Clinical Psychology*, 26: 93–111.

Wright, M. (1986) 'Priming the past', *Oral History*, 14 (1): 60–5.

47

History of migration to the United Kingdom

John Young and James George

Seeking out a 'cause' or a 'reason' for a particular migration is problematic. One helpful approach which, at least to some extent, can be applied as an explanatory model is the notion of 'pull/push' factors. The pushed group would be characteristic of the refugee. Some refugees are political and others economic, but both groups effectively seek to escape from intolerable personal circumstances within their own country. [. . .] The pull factors operate where an individual or group have been attracted to Britain for self-betterment and (usually) a potentially more prosperous way of life. The best contemporary example here is the migration of the South Asians from the Indian subcontinent. In the main these represent people who had a reasonably satisfactory way of life but saw greater prospects for training and earnings in Britain. [. . .]

Elderly people of Afro-Caribbean origin

The great majority of elderly people from the West Indies came to the United Kingdom in the boom period after the Second World War. However, Britain and the Caribbean Islands have had a close association for nearly three centuries. Initially, this was through trade with the financially successful seventeenth-century triangular trading route between Britain, the African Coast and the Caribbean Islands, with the infamous middle passage of slave carriage to the islands. Later, the sugar plantations of Jamaica, Barbados, Trinidad and other islands of the British West Indies were under direct rule as part of the British Empire. The islanders were therefore imbued with British values and surrounded by Empire trappings. There was a strong feeling of identity with the 'mother country' which was reinforced by an educational system which strongly emphasised a sanitised version of British society. For the better educated and ambitious, however, there were few opportunities for advancement as middle and top civil

From A. Squires (ed.), *Multicultural Health Care and Rehabilitation of Older People.* London: Edward Arnold with Age Concern, 1991, Chapter 2, pp. 17–27 (abridged).

service posts were occupied by graduate career diplomats from Britain. A restlessness developed based in part on self-betterment, and in part on a desire to visit the 'mother country'.

The Second World War provided an important opportunity for many to realise their ambitions. The hunger for labour to drive the war machine in Britain stimulated a Caribbean labour recruitment campaign. Several thousand joined the RAF and were trained as engineers and mechanics. These people found themselves reluctantly repatriated after demobilisation: many would have preferred to stay. They returned to a deteriorating Caribbean economy which was dependent on sugar exports and suffered greatly during a commodity price collapse. There was escalating unemployment and general despair. Prospects of self-betterment in Britain seemed obvious. There was also a sense of adventure – almost a pilgrimage to the centre of the Empire which was fuelled by encouraging stories from the repatriated ex-servicemen.

The start of the post-war Caribbean population migration is usually attributed to the docking at Tilbury on 22 June 1948 of an old troop carrier called the *Empire Windrush* [. . .]. It was much publicised at the time. Some 500 Jamaicans suffered the uncomfortable journey; many were returning ex-RAF servicemen but there was a rude shock for others with their first sighting of dirty streets, slums and ruins and early experience of the British uncharitable weather.

In the 10 years following the arrival of the *Empire Windrush*, 125,000 West Indians came to Britain. Up to a quarter were highly trained with professional and managerial skills. These people had the greatest difficulty in obtaining work in a Britain that was poorly prepared to receive an influx of black workers. Their arrival rapidly exposed latent racism within British society. There was much political confusion engendered on the one hand by a fear of 'open access' for all Commonwealth citizens, and on the other the need for extra labour to satisfy a rampant expanding economy with production increases of 8 per cent per annum at this time. In the event, so acute was the labour shortage that policy was dictated by the pressing practical needs of the day and active immigration from the West Indies was encouraged by a recruitment drive and assisted passage [. . .]. Most of the new arrivals worked in public transport or the health service, with a smaller number in manufacturing. Many intended originally to return home with proof of their success. Return without it would be a sign of failure which some could not consider. [. . .]

It is important to remember that there are very distinct differences in culture and previous experience between people from different islands in the Caribbean. Over half the West Indians who came to Britain came from Jamaica: others came from Guyana, Barbados, Trinidad and Tobago. Those from the island of Dominica had a colonial heritage which was French. Many West Indians are Christians; the largest group are Pentecostalists, some are Anglicans or Baptists and a few are Methodists or Roman Catholics. It has been from this background that the ethnic Caribbean elders have emerged. [. . .]

East African Asians

These settlers came to Britain from Uganda, Kenya and Tanzania in the late 1970s and early 1980s. They constitute a distinctive group of Asian settlers in that they are 'twice removed' having originally left India during the early part of the twentieth century as indentured labour to build the Kenya/Uganda railways. This first intercontinental journey had been stimulated by the prospect of financial self-improvement. Many of these Asians remained in the East African countries forming the administrative and operative personnel of the railways they had helped build. They had predominantly occupied East African townships where they formed isolated pocket communities. But it was this isolation which led to their displacement following independence for the East African colonies. The Asian labour force had provided highly skilled personnel, both middle-level administrators and professionals. Independence of the African countries was followed by a policy of Africanisation which most affected the public services and was felt especially strongly by the South Asians. [. . .] These circumstances led to the migration of South Asians to countries abroad. For the Ugandan Asians, the displacement was far more acute when, in short order, they were ousted by the policies of General Amin in 1972.

Although the East African Asians are distinguished by their common background of 'twice migrated', this common background should not obscure the several different cultures contained within this apparently homogeneous group. There are Hindus, Muslims, Gujaratis and Sikhs. Within this caveat, however, many East African Asians do share certain common features which distinguish and set them aside from Asians migrating to Britain directly from the Indian subcontinent. First, they had a long-established urban background and were familiar with town life in contrast to the mainly rural Asians from the Indian subcontinent. They brought with them a range of managerial and professional skills. They were also relatively prosperous and had a certain amount of capital which freed them from the poor-quality housing occupied by many immigrants in the United Kingdom and provided them with a more secure foothold in a foreign land. This meant that they were more able to establish themselves in successful small businesses. [. . .] They also had the benefit of migrating as whole family units. Clearly this produced a potential for much increased personal strength and mutual support and is in sharp contrast to the Indian subcontinent Asian experience. Here it was largely individuals who migrated, rather like expeditionaries attempting to find a foothold and, perhaps at a later stage, being joined by their families.

Elderly people of Vietnamese origin

[. . .] Since the Communist victory in Vietnam, and the subsequent unification of that country in 1975, several thousand Vietnamese refugees have been resettled in Britain. The majority come from North Vietnam and most are ethnic Chinese who speak both Cantonese and Vietnamese. [. . .]

For many, the exodus was desperate and harrowing in small overcrowded boats with little food and few personal possessions. They spent varying times in cramped reception centres in Hong Kong before dispersing mostly to Britain or America.

On arrival in Britain the refugees spent between three months and one year in reception centres. Here they learnt about the British way of life, were taught English and were prepared for resettlement. [But learning] a new language and culture represented an ambitious task and many left the reception centres only poorly equipped to cope with their new environment and with a less than adequate grasp of the English language. A further factor was that of 'displacement shock' [and] the additional tension of coming to terms with an uncertain future in a hugely different culture [. . .].

Unfortunately, there was not sufficient vacant housing in any one local authority in Britain to accommodate significantly large groups of Vietnamese families. Rather, they were dispersed throughout small towns in the United Kingdom in small groups of four to ten families. [. . .] Unfortunately also, they arrived on the employment scene just as unemployment reached its highest. [. . .] Not surprisingly, those who found work mainly found unskilled jobs [. . .].

Elderly Chinese

Large-scale migration of Chinese to Britain is quite recent compared with the number of Chinese who left for the Americas, Australia and South East Asia as 'coolies' and contract labourers in the nineteenth century. The vast majority have come from Hong Kong and therefore differ from earlier migrants who predominantly originated from the Chinese provinces of Gwandong and Fujina. The late nineteenth-century Chinese were forced out by the oppressive regime of the last Manchu emperors.

The earliest Chinese arrivals at the end of the last century contained a significant proportion who were fleeing American persecution as they were driven from their homes in California. Other Chinese entered Britain after jumping ship seeking better paid work. Some continued to work in the dockland areas but increasingly the Chinese became associated with the laundry trade. These Chinese immigrants were principally seeking rapid accumulation of wealth before returning home to Southern China. Setting up a laundry required little capital but involved great physical toil. They established the early Chinatowns in London, Manchester and Liverpool.

The much larger-scale Chinese immigration took place in the 1950s and 1960s. It was stimulated by a great enthusiasm and fashion for Chinese food and a rapid expansion in the Chinese restaurant trade. Many of the Hong Kong Chinese who came to Britain at this time relied on contacts already established here to find employment. These contacts were often brothers, uncles, cousins, fellow villagers or friends. Family emigration took place in stages over several years. Many of the Chinese elders, therefore, may be fairly recent emigrants who came to join their sons and daughters. They may encounter considerable difficulties adapting to a new culture compounded by language and literacy problems and ill health due to a lifetime of work in kitchens or on the land. The Hong Kong Chinese community in Britain is widely scattered, working mainly in Chinese restaurants in almost every town in Britain. The larger communities are in London, Cardiff, Manchester, Burnley and Liverpool.

Elderly people of Cypriot origin

The first major group of Cypriots, who are mainly Greek-speaking, came during the 1930s and worked predominantly in the clothing industries.

In the late 1950s and early 1960s further Greek and Turkish Cypriots came to Britain for work or to escape the political situation in Cyprus. After the crisis in 1974, Cypriot residents were joined by thousands of homeless relatives. The majority of Cypriots have settled in London. Many are now elderly and, although literate in Greek or Turkish, may be unable to cope with spoken English and have become socially isolated.

Elderly people of Central and Eastern European origin

Jewish refugees from Russia and Romania came to Britain to escape persecution at the end of the nineteenth and the beginning of the twentieth century. The influx was numerically very large and was particularly noticeable because of the rather small numbers of Jewish people living in Britain before this time. These new immigrants were a culturally distinct section of the Jewish people who spoke Yiddish and were concentrated in a limited range of workshop trades rather than the familiar shopkeeper and merchant role. Many had had the original intent of reaching the expanding North Americas and had intended to use Britain as a staging point but settled here instead. They settled predominantly in the East End of London, and in Leeds and Manchester. Further Jewish refugees came to settle in Britain to escape Nazi persecution.

After the Second World War, large numbers of people from Central and Eastern Europe were actively recruited by the government to work in British industry. Apart from the Poles, these included Ukrainian, Czechs, Romanians, Germans, Yugoslavs, Estonians and Latvians. Subsequently, almost 20,000 newcomers arrived from Hungary after the 1956 unrest. [. . .] The Eastern European elderly are by no means a homogeneous group, having several different cultures and religions. They may be Jewish or alternatively belong to many Christian denominations including Orthodox, Roman Catholic, or Lutheran.

South Asians from the Indian subcontinent

There is a long established tradition of migration from the Indian subcontinent to a wide scatter of countries. For example, between 1834 and 1937 the total migration from India has been estimated at approximately 30 million, but, of these, 24 million returned leaving only 6 million as permanent migrants. This pattern of essentially short-term migration has persisted. Much of this early migration was for indentured or contract labour and only within the British Empire, as it then was. East and South Africa, the West Indies, and South East Asia, particularly Malaya and parts of Borneo, have considerable settlements of Indians. Subsequently, political and social changes closed many of these old migration inlets. Demographic, economic and, in some cases, political developments in the Indian subcontinent continued, however, and increased in intensity as factors pushing towards emigration. After 1955, migrants from India and Pakistan began to enter Britain in increasing numbers. They came from the Punjab, particularly districts of Jullundar and Hoshiarpur, and from the central and southern parts of Gujarat, from the West Punjab in Pakistan, the northwest frontier area and Mirpur district of Kashmir, and the Sylhet district of Bangladesh. This wide scatter of small geographical pockets of migration sources can be seen in Figure 47.1. These migrants comprise widely different cultural, religious and language backgrounds as indicated in Table 47.1.

The factors underlying the stimulus for emigration of these various groups are very mixed. Undoubtedly, however, the established tradition of migration for people living in these areas has acted as an

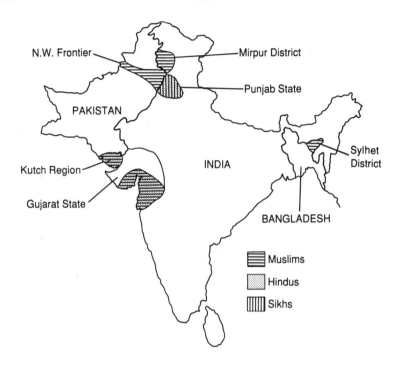

Figure 47.1 *Diagram showing the major areas of the Indian subcontinent from which people have migrated to the United Kingdom*

Table 47.1 *Asians in the United Kingdom*

Country of origin	Province of origin	Language	Main religion
India	Punjab	Punjabi/Hindi/Urdu	Sikhism
	Gujarat	Gujarati	Hinduism
Pakistan	Punjab	Punjabi/Hindi/Urdu	
	Mirpur	Mirpuri/Punjabi	Islam
	North West Frontier	Pashto/Punjabi/Urdu	
Bangladesh	Sylhet	Bengali (Sylheti dialect)	Islam
Africa			
Kenya			
Tanzania	Majority	Gujarati/Punjabi/	Hinduism
Uganda	from	English/Swahili	Sikhism
Malawi	Gujarat		and Islam

influential backdrop. The Sikhs of Punjab, in particular, have proven themselves to be the most adventurous of Indian migrants and are now widely dispersed in many parts of the world. [. . .] The people of Bangladesh [. . .] are a seafaring nation and many were driven by poverty and drawn by ambition to leave their homes at an early age and to work in the merchant ships of the Raj. Some settled in the cities of Britain where their presence has been the stimulus for further migration, from the Sylhet district in particular. Many well-educated people from Pakistan and Bangladesh followed a tradition of obtaining higher British qualifications to gain top-level jobs at home. Most returned but some stayed behind or returned after brief visits to their homeland where they were not fully satisfied with their way of life. The break up of East Pakistan in 1971, resulting in the birth of Bangladesh, was a major factor in a much larger wave of migration. At this time 'push' factors due to political uncertainties, unstable economy and poor job opportunities took precedence over the previous 'pull' factors. The settlers entering Britain at this time (and also large numbers to other European countries, the USA and Canada) were essentially economic refugees escaping from an uncertain rural life and farming and seeking a more prosperous standard of living in industrial work in Britain. Most of these settlers have retained strong links with their homeland and indeed many have returned upon retirement.

Elderly people of Irish origin

There was a major influx of Irish migrants, particularly in the 1920s and 1930s, many from rural areas. The men took up labouring and navvying jobs and the women tended to be employed in domestic service. Many of the men were employed 'on the lump' with wages being paid in cash and they were encouraged to avoid tax and insurance. Many of their employers took no interest in the welfare of their workforce and working conditions were hard with illness and industrial accidents common. Lack of proper employment, insurance and tax records often prevented these people from claiming welfare benefits. Many lived in poor housing conditions in inner cities on inadequate diets. These difficulties have often followed elderly Irish people into old age resulting in poor mental and physical health.

Conclusion

The post-war industrial prosperity in Britain has provided the general backdrop attracting a diverse range of migrant settlers. Several of the larger groups have been discussed above but there are many numerically smaller but equally important settlers who have not been included. Many of these people are now entering old age when ill-health becomes an increasing threat. Neglect of previous background and culture, and of the circumstances stimulating the migration, are particularly detrimental during illness when trust, empathy and openness may become jeopardised by unintended misunderstandings. A little extra time and patience may be all that is required to avoid this outcome.

48

Glimpses of a lost history

Paul Thompson

What was it like to grow old in the past in Britain? For the moment we can only piece together fragments of evidence. The history of ageing in this country has still to be written. Much of it is now irrecoverably lost; for the lack of interest in the experience of ordinary old people shown by historians is mirrored in the scanty documentation which survives from the past. Like ordinary people in general, old people usually show up vividly in the record only when they become a problem. At death, in the moment of passing, all secure an entry, and some a lasting monument; but of most people's later life little is ever known, or now knowable. Such a silence is itself significant. It reflects powerlessness. It also reflects ambivalence.

A rounded picture of later life over the past two or three centuries is thus impossible. But we do know enough to be able to pick out some clear changes, and continuities too, by tracing particular themes. Let us begin with social attitudes to ageing. How different were they in the seventeenth century from today? 'In early modern England', Keith Thomas has written, 'the prevailing ideal was gerontocratic: the young were to serve and the old were to rule.' It was assumed that wisdom, as the sum of experience and self-control, grew with age. The image of God as an old man was echoed throughout society. The church itself was headed by elderly archbishops and the law by aged judges. In the printer's workshop the oldest workman would be 'father' of the chapel. Children were taught to show their parents obedience, duty and respect, taking their hat off to their father as a matter of manners, and at solemn moments kneeling to receive his formal blessing. Communities were typically run by the 'anciently of the parish'. Often this was reflected in the village church, where the old sat in the best seats and the young at the back (Thomas, 1976: 5-7).

Yet alongside this ideal - perhaps in part provoked by it - ran strong counter-currents. In reality the key positions of power in both

From P. Thompson, C. Itzin and M. Abendstern, *I Don't Feel Old: Understanding the Experience of Later Life*. Oxford: Oxford University Press, 1990, Chapter 2, pp. 19-43 (abridged). This source contains extensive illustrative material, full references and footnotes.

politics and the law were normally held by men in their forties and fifties. The elderly could not sustain the more strenuous manual work in agriculture or the crafts. Respect did not prevent children from rebelling against their parents. And the grave, sober image of old age was a constraint on social behaviour. The elderly who expressed continuing sexual interests would be mercilessly ridiculed by the youth groups of their village. There was a widespread mocking of 'old fools'. 'Old people commonly are despised', observed Richard Steele, 'especially when they are not supported with good estates', while another commented in 1621 how, in contrast to the common 'pleasure in infants' shown by women, 'old people are burdensome to all; neither their talk nor their company is acceptable' (Thomas, 1976: 43–5).

This ambivalence towards the old is clearly shown in the traditional seven stages of life. [. . .] There were two concurrent stereotypes of the old. One was as strikingly negative as the other was positive. Either could be drawn on, to support respect or scorn. And the balance of early modern attitudes to the old looks a good deal less favourable when we realise that the terms of chronological age used then were quite different from those in use today. Their Old Age, from 50 to 62, we now see as part of Middle Age. Our Young Old Age they saw as Senility; our Old Old Age was beyond the focus of their conventional wisdom.

This pushing onwards of the chronological stages over the centuries partly reflects a second, more fundamental transformation: the cumulative impact of changes in health and demography. The direct impact of improving health in later life has been relatively recent. But the position of older people is also shaped by general birth and death rates. Thus in a rapidly growing population there will be relatively few older people, as in many contemporary Third World countries; while in a stagnant population they will be relatively more numerous, and more of them will lack the support of children. Hence in late nineteenth-century France the aged were already a more prominent group, almost twice the proportion in England at the same time: indeed, there were proportionally somewhat fewer old in booming Victorian England than in 1700. But these changes through the birth rate remained relatively modest in this country until the present century. Right through from the seventeenth until the early twentieth century those who reached the age of 60 years remained a small but quite steady 5–7 per cent of the English population (Laslett, 1977: 181–96; Wrigley and Schofield, 1981: 216). By 1900, however, the birth rate was plunging as couples chose to have fewer children, just as improved health had also begun to have a marked impact; and it is the *combination* in the twentieth century of a now almost stagnant population of small families with a new fall in death rates which explains the striking rise of over 60-year-olds to form over 20 per cent of our population today and why, more than in any previous generation, such a high proportion of them are without children.

It is partly that old people themselves are living longer. A late Victorian at 60 could look forward to scarcely a dozen more years of life; a contemporary 60 year-old man can expect almost twenty more years and a woman even more. But the impact of the fall in death rates among younger age groups (which began earlier, in the mid-nineteenth century) has been still more dramatic. In the past, death struck through the life cycle. Children were especially vulnerable, but many also died in young or middle adulthood. By 50 a married man or woman was as likely as not to have suffered widowhood, and would have already lost half his or her contemporaries: in contrast to a mere twentieth today. Hence far more people *enter* old age. But they pay an unexpected price, which is itself one of the underlying differences between old age in the past and in the present.

The withdrawal of earlier death has been so marked that today most English people will have no direct experience of the grief of bereavement until they lose their own parents, when they are themselves well into middle age. For the young, death is so unreal that it has become a pleasure to play with, part of the fantasy of violence. Then suddenly, unprepared by experience, as they become old they are struck by the unfamiliar, relentless impact of death combing out their social world, remorselessly striking down their family and friends. [. . .]

It is above all women who are living longer. In 1800 there were roughly equal numbers of older men and older women, but today there are three women to every two men. Since women in general have less social prestige than men, this in itself tends to reinforce negative attitudes to the elderly. But the imbalance affects women more directly. The majority of men who survive can expect to have the support of a wife up to the age of 85, but any woman over 72 is more likely to be a widow left on her own. While men today enjoy later life as one of a couple, for women the experience is most often solitary. There was no such sharp contrast in the earlier past (Wall, 1984).

Less dramatically, the health of the surviving has improved. Doctors in early modern England had developed no special skills for dealing with the health of older people. Probably most of those surviving were reasonably active, as they would die rather quickly when they succumbed to their first serious illness at this stage of life. However, they would have been commonly toothless, since false teeth were a luxury until the nineteenth century. And enough elderly people did survive as chronically sick, physically maimed or mentally impaired to sustain the most negative seventeenth-century images of old age as 'a perpetual sickness', 'a disease', a time of impotence in the widest sense, 'the dregs . . . of a man's life' (Thomas, 1976: 42). [. . .]

England's very unusual system of inheritance is of particular interest because of its continuing influence in later centuries, both on the fate of older people and also more generally on the English class system. The English aristocracy pursued the principle of independent homes for the older generation to its ultimate conclusion. Despite the vast size of their houses and the numerous servants surrounding each aristocratic family, on the death of a Victorian head of household 'his or her resident family was expected to leave to make way for the incoming heir and his or her family. The widowed mother and any unmarried siblings living at home usually had to move out' (Gerard, 1982: 33). [. . .] It was especially through this single-minded concentration of resources through inheritance on a principal heir that the English aristocracy were able to tighten their grip on the land. Farm families by contrast increasingly sold off their holdings, in order to secure their own last years and at the same time allow equal treatment of their children. [. . .]

Those with significant property to leave were of course a minority. But it seems to have been equally rare for young couples in the poorer classes to help their ageing parents by providing them with houseroom. Thanks to the recent statistical work of demographic historians we now have quite detailed information on with whom the old lived in England from early modern times onwards. These statistics can easily seem impenetrable and tedious, but they have important light to throw if we can tease out their implications.

Studies of household listings reveal comparatively few three-generational homes in England from the sixteenth century onwards: a mere 5 per cent on average. This is half the typical findings for France, and far less than the third or more often reported from Eastern Europe or from Japan in the same centuries. The English figure climbed briefly to 9 per cent in the mid-nineteenth century and then fell back to a mere 1 per cent today. But although these figures do tell us how few families had a grandparent in their own home, they can be misleading. The grandparent could have been living a few houses away. Indeed, an international survey of old people in Britain, Denmark and the United States in the 1960s found over 40 per cent of them living within ten minutes' journey of their children in all three countries. This could well have been true in the past too: we do not know. Also, the figures depend on how many grandparents were alive in the population. Typically, because people elsewhere married much younger than in north-west Europe, they became grandparents younger – so there were simply more grandparents around. A large part of the contrast results from this. All the same, if we turn the figures about and look at them from the point of view of the older generation themselves, we still find that in early modern England only 10 per cent of 60-year-olds were living with their married children or grandchildren. This is startlingly lower than the figures of over half reported from Eastern Europe and the Far East; and it also looks as if co-residence was much more common in southern France, and also in post-colonial America. This contrast has continued. In Britain today only 9 per cent of those over 60 live with another relative apart from their own spouse, in contrast to 12 per cent in the United States, 14 per cent in France and 29 per cent in Japan and China (Thompson et al., 1990: 257–8).

The consequence of these household arrangements today are that a very high proportion of older people live alone. The longer they live, the higher the figure climbs. In early modern England the proportion of solitary 65-year-olds was only 10 per cent, while in the mid-nineteenth century it came as low as 7.5. In the East there were almost none. Today it has risen to over 40 per cent in Britain, Scandinavia and North America, and 30 per cent in France, in contrast to less than 7 per cent in China and Japan. To put it another way, the English have always been prepared to let some of their old live alone. But one of the great changes from the past is that this possibility of living alone is swiftly becoming a probability (Anderson, 1988: 436; Laslett, 1976; 110).

Yet a closer look behind these stark figures suggests that the English have not been so peculiarly heartless. Their housing was very early on more ample. They were also early in being especially mobile, no longer tied to land which could easily be sold. So with each generation there was a 'scattering of children at marriage', which left scarcely one couple in 10 with married children in the same parish. On the other hand, there were much more likely to be single children still living at home. Women bore children late; widowed men commonly remarried quickly to a younger woman so that there was another batch of younger children in the family; and most children married late. There must have been many daughters like Margaret White, who described in the 1590s how she stayed on living with her widowed father, 'guided him and his household, and was continually with him in his sickness until his death' (Macfarlane, 1986: 92–3).

In practice the widowed of any age were much more likely to stay in their own homes than to move to find support. The early modern English household listings show that over half (55 per cent) of all over 60-year-olds lived with relatives apart from their spouse, and by far the most common of these were unmarried children still living in the parental home. But the pattern varied distinctly between the married and widowed. Nearly all the married couples kept their own homes, half still with children, a quarter with other kin or lodgers, and a quarter on their own. Of the widowed and single, by contrast, only two-thirds now lived on in their own homes, usually with their children or lodgers, or very rarely grandchildren, but 12 per cent on their own. Over a third had moved, roughly half into their children's or grandchildren's homes, and half to live as 'lodgers' – sometimes with other kin – or go into institutions. Thus overall only one in eight 60-year-olds were solitaries or institutionalised. In England, as elsewhere 'even though their help could not be counted upon', children and kin were providing the greatest share of support for the older generation of their families (Laslett, 1977: 201).

Nevertheless, what remains especially striking and distinctive is the English reluctance to take back the elderly within the home as *dependants*. When, during the nineteenth century, there was briefly a sharply rising proportion of widowed older people living with relatives, this was above all in the cotton and pottery towns, where married women factory workers were exceptionally common. Grandmothers could therefore join their children's households to fulfil a direct need as child-minders. Thus of the widowed, over 85 per cent were living with relatives in Preston in 1851, and 72 per cent in the Potteries; while in the market town of Ampthill, only 61 per cent [were] (Anderson, 1971: 55; Thompson et al., 1990: 258). Elsewhere the great majority of the older generation continued to run their own homes. And when they could no longer do so, they were more likely to become independent lodgers than to move in under their own children's roof. The other side to English hesitation in offering houseroom was a belief in the independence of the old.

(* * *)

Independence of course demands economic means: and this brings us to a last and equally basic issue. What resources were open to older men and women in the past? [. . .]

The great majority [. . .] carried on working as long as they possibly could. At any age, most men were still at work. There are instances of 90-year-olds still at work in seventeenth-century England. Even in the 1900s the national census returns show over 60 per cent of men over 65 employed, in England, the United States, and France. [. . .] The proportion in work had begun to fall, however, and from the 1930s dropped rapidly: according to official figures, today in England a mere 7 per cent of men over 65 remain employed. The earlier situation lingered longest in the countryside. In England older men could get contract work for hedging and ditching, maintaining public spaces, or minor building repairs, which allowed them to work at their own pace (Thomas, 1976: 38). [. . .]

The lighter work to which men tended to shift as they got older was generally worse paid. Work for older women was as badly paid, but for many it was more of a gain because they had not earned at all while their children were young. [. . .]

A third possibility, at first unusual but slowly growing with time, was retirement in the modern sense, on a pension. Retirement for men of property was, as we have seen, an accepted practice in early modern England. The merits of pensions, extending this practice to those on salaries, were debated from the late seventeenth century onwards, with leading advocates including Daniel Defoe, and later the radical Thomas Paine of the French Revolution years. The first small groups to be provided with pensions were the lower-paid naval warrant officers in 1672, and soon afterwards customs officers; while an Act of 1749 set up a scheme for master merchant mariners. The pioneering general pension scheme was, however, for the civil service: first established in 1810, by 1859 a full pension scheme allowed retirement at 60. The first commercial companies to follow suit were public utilities such as some railway and gas companies, which started pension schemes for their clerical staff from the 1840s onwards. These early pension schemes were all rewards for loyalty to a narrow group of white-collar staff, whose salaries were insufficient to allow them to retire like more prosperous middle-class professionals.

It was only in the late nineteenth century that a sustained campaign for pensions for manual workers began. Among the pioneers, the Great Western Railway scheme of 1865 was notably early. It was followed by some other railway and gas companies, and from the 1900s a range of well-known paternalistic companies: Cadbury, Colmans, Coats, Cunard, Wills, Marconi, and many others. Their paternalism was sometimes explicitly mixed with the desire 'to take the fire out of the socialist cause'. Strikers could find their pension rights withdrawn. In this period, however, by far the largest occupational scheme was the independently organised Durham Miners' Permanent Relief Society, originating in the 1860s, which by the 1890s had 140,000 contributing members and 4000 pensions being paid out.

All these advances were dwarfed by the step forward made with the introduction of a national state Old-Age Pensions scheme in 1909 for *all* those over 70 on incomes of less than 10 shillings weekly – roughly a charwoman's wage. It could not be taken along with poor relief, and those with criminal records were excluded; it was only available at 70, not 60; and it was set at a very mean level, a mere 5 shillings, below the bare minimum which Seebohm Rowntree calculated was then needed for subsistence. It was a supplement for the 'deserving poor', rather than a true pension. Yet its impact in allowing ordinary retired workers some self-respect was enormous.

Paradoxically the introduction of the state pension seems to have ended independent activity by workers' organisations, with even the Durham miners' scheme fading out between the wars. From the 1930s, on the other hand, the big insurance companies moved in strongly to fill the gap between the state pension and the standard of living for which most workers hoped, setting up occupational pension schemes for firms on a contract basis. The 1930s also saw a vigorous campaign for better pensions for women, which led to the introduction of a state pension for women at the age of 60 in 1940. Men remained eligible only at 65. Public and private sector schemes together covered one in eight workers in 1936, and one in three by 1956 (Hannah, 1986: 6–40; Thomas, 1976: 38–40).

By this time retirement schemes were not merely rewards for work and service. They also reflected a growing belief that it was in the general interest for the old to stop working: a fundamental change in attitude. [. . .]

What of those who could not work, and were ineligible for pensions; or, as more often recently, whose pensions were insufficient? We have already seen through looking at where the widowed lived that in England, as throughout the world, the family was the biggest single resource for older people in trouble. [. . .]

Inevitably there were always ways in which these 'family obligations' could be evaded. Alan Macfarlane has recently argued that the social pressure to enforce them was less strong in England than elsewhere. Certainly the fear of abandonment in old age has never been more powerfully put than in *King Lear*. On the other hand – and the two aspects of English attitudes could indeed be different sides of the same coin – there was an especially clear and early assumption of community obligation to support the aged poor. In the Middle Ages the lord of the manor was regarded as legally responsible for the relief of the poor and one-quarter of the church tithes were also customarily set aside for this purpose. After the Reformation these traditions were regularised in a unique Poor Law which made each parish responsible for its own poor, and obliged it to finance its aid by levying a poor rate on its inhabitants (Macfarlane, 1986: 105–8).

This communal support for older people in early modern England could be on a remarkably generous scale. For the elderly, the history of welfare provision seems to have been less a story of steady progress over the centuries than an oscillation between phases of relative generosity and meanness. From the seventeenth until the early nineteenth century, parish records suggest that over one-half of widows would normally have been provided with regular pensions on the rates; and still more remarkable, when compared with working-class incomes, these pensions were *twice* as good as those offered by state pensions today (see Figure 48.1). The mid- and late-nineteenth century saw a savage counter-attack on this system, with a reduction of pensions to a mere third of the value of the average working man's wage, and a concerted attempt to shift more of the burden back onto the family (Thomson, 1984).

Some Poor Law Guardians made attempts to enforce the new legal obligations which the 1834 Poor Law imposed on children to support their parents with money. In one case, for example, Reepham magistrates in Norfolk sent two brothers to prison for two months as a penalty for not supporting their mother, although both men were close on 60 and had wives and children themselves. But the new law failed to change normal practice, and such cases remained rare. It seems that

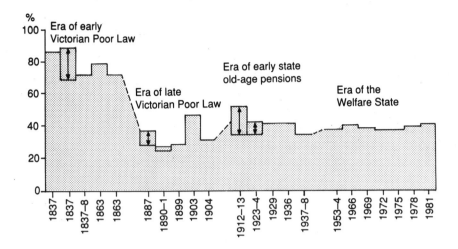

Figure 48.1 *Pensions and working-class incomes, 1837–1981, showing standard old-age pension as a percentage of gross income of a working-class adult. Boxed shaded areas represent extreme limits, where assumptions had to be made about family size (Thomson, 1984: 453)*

these obligations were found more likely to stir up serious friction within families than to rally family help. Charles Booth noted in the 1890s that many sons would prefer to move rather than accept legal compulsion, and that their own old parents would often see relief as a right: 'the aged prefer a pittance from the parish (regarded as their due) to compulsary maintenance by children; compulsion makes such aid very bitter' (Booth, 1894: 226). The simple truth was that, in any case, few such poor families would have had cash that they could have regularly given away. On the other hand, among more prosperous working-class families customs were changing as real wages continued to rise. One Suffolk farm servant paid 5 shillings every week in the 1900s to help a sister keep their 80-year-old mother. A skilled Nottingham engineer's daughter of the 1920s remembers her father 'would never go to see his parents unless he could take them some money. . . . Three pound notes were usually left discreetly on the table after tea. It was never mentioned.' And a study in the 1940s reported that one person in every five over 60 was receiving some form of financial support from a son or a daughter (Thompson et al., 1990: 258–9).

More immediately, however, the new policy was imposed through suspending pensions to the elderly themselves, and insisting that those on relief should move into the prison-like workhouses built in each Poor Law district after 1834. As a result, in the 60 years from 1851 the proportion of old people living in institutions almost doubled, rising to over 7 per cent of men over 65 and nearly 10 per cent of those over 75, and slightly over half this figure for women. Since the 1900s, despite the increasing numbers of the elderly, the proportion has again fallen back by more than a third. The regime of the workhouse was deliberately deterrent, and at least up to the 1890s married couples would be forced to live apart within it. Little beyond food was provided: not even false teeth to eat with. Middle-class visitors entering a workhouse for the first time could be deeply shaken by the harsh indignity of the prison-like routine, the grotesque, despairing toothless faces, 'the forlorn, half-dazed aspect of these battered human hulks who once were young'. There was no need 'to write up the words "Abandon hope all ye who enter here"', George Lansbury wrote of the Poplar workhouse. 'The place was clean: brass knobs and floors were polished, but of goodwill, kindliness there was none' (Lansbury, 1928: 135–6).

Not surprisingly, only families in real difficulty were prepared to see their own older generation end their lives in such a place. One survey of aged inmates of the Newington workhouse in south London showed that a mere 16 out of 725 had any relatives with even the space to take them in. Even in 1930, when the most draconian workhouse rules had been eased, another London survey of aged applicants for relief found that half had no family at all. [. . .]

It took the rise of the socialist movement to turn the tide. George Lansbury himself became one of the first reforming Poor Law Guardians in East London in the 1890s, and the social legislation of the Liberals, including the state Old-Age Pension introduced in 1908, was a direct response to the rising political influence of the labour movement. Nevertheless, the move back towards a more generous welfare policy for older people was hesitatingly slow. The pension was fixed well below subsistence level. Walter Greenwood (1935: 180) portrayed an old-age pensioner in the 1930s who had to live on sixpence a day after he had paid his rent. He could afford nothing for tobacco:

> I don't eat breakfast, just a cup of tea and a bit of toast if I can spare it. The butcher lets me have a pound of dripping now and then and I can make it last. Dinner I boil myself just a few potatoes, and I eat them with a piece of bread. . . .
>
> There's a pal of mine who works at the wood yard and he brings me a bag of bits of wood that's been left over. He comes once a week with it and I've got to be careful to make them last. That's my biggest worry, keeping warm. Sometimes I can't sleep I get that cold.
>
> They give me the newspaper from next door when they've finished with it. And I go to bed as soon as it gets dark. It saves burning light and fire, and I can listen to next door's wireless if they've got it turned on loud. You can hear it plain through the wall.

Poverty surveys support Greenwood's account. In London, for

example, Llewellyn Smith (1932: 208) reported that 'lack of warmth seems to be a greater hardship than lack of food'. Rowntree's three surveys of York show that as working-class living standards gradually rose because of wage gains, smaller families and, from the 1940s, full employment, poverty became increasingly concentrated among older people. In 1900 they were no more often in poverty than the working class of any age, but by 1935 they had become significantly more vulnerable, and in 1950 the elderly comprised over two-thirds of all the poor (Rowntree, 1910: 38–51; 1941: 156; Rowntree and Lavers, 1951: 34).

The surveys also show that older people continued to be found in some of the very worst housing. In Rowntree's examples of typical streets in 1900, in the poorest streets up to a third of the householders were widows, in contrast to less than 5 per cent in the best working-class districts. Roberts has recalled the houses in his own slum district of Salford where two or more 'old maids', or 'old faggots' as the teenagers mockingly called them, lived together (Roberts, 1976: 87). Just the same refuges of the elderly also appear in the *Social Survey of Merseyside* of 1934, where they made up a third of the tenants of the largest multiple households. In one, for example, a casual labourer and his wife in their sixties lived with a woman of 79, her son of 57 who was a street matchseller, and six younger tenants; in another a woman of 68 was subletting to another woman of 65, a crippled woman of 60, and two others; while in a third household a 71-year-old sandwich-man lived with an unrelated widow and widower of the same age and two younger tenants (Caradog Jones, 1934: 122–7). Deprived, and often also dirty, these ageing social outcasts, rather than ask help of the community, chose to huddle together.

The poverty surveys are also remarkable in another way. They are the first published documents from which we can glean personal details about ordinary older people in significant numbers. Rowntree's investigators sketched in details of each household. These show that half the older men were still at work. Still more of the widows went out as chars or washerwomen, and a few minded children. The atmosphere of the homes varied. At one extreme, an invalid widow was described as a 'disreputable' hawker who 'ought to be in workhouse. Hawks when able . . . House very dirty, probably used as a house of ill-fame.' At the other, in a respectable working-class street, were the old couple living 'on his means . . . "Resting after a life's hard work."' (Rowntree, 1910: 38–51).

Llewellyn Smith's London survey of the 1930s similarly provided nutshell portraits of many old people, combining what the interviewers noticed with comments from the older people themselves (1932: 57–67). Again, the contrasts are striking. Thus one couple living in a basement were 'respectable', 'very superior and very particular about cleanliness'; the wife spent most of her day on housework and mending clothes, while the husband 'does such things as chopping the wood and mends anything that is broken. In the evening they both listen-in [to the radio] and enjoy it very much, especially the Sunday evening sermons.' By contrast, a single old woman who lived in 'some very nasty flats in a very poor street' seemed to be 'rather a grubby woman. Her clothes were very very untidy, not very clean and not too well cared for. . . . I rather wondered whether she drinks, as when I went in in the morning there was a large bottle of beer on the table. She seemed to be quite a cheerful old woman.' However, 'she said that she now has really no friends or relations in the world and there are times when she feels very lonely. She is very frightened of falling ill in that flat as she has no one to look after her.' Another widow of 84 'had outlived all her old friends' and did not get much support from her children. She seemed 'rather frightened of her daughters and they seem to treat her very badly . . . One cuts her dead in the street if she ever sees her.' Several others, on the other hand, were 'on the best of terms' with their children, including two in shared households and another couple who said 'their children are very good to them; one daughter does their washing for them and their daughter-in-law goes up nearly every day to do their shopping for them'.

Of particular interest here are the minority of notably active older people, like the man whose 'great hobby is making toys for his grandchildren and great-grandchildren'; or the amateur painter always at his easel 'if the light is good enough'; or the old sailor, disabled for 50 years, yet 'a very contented old man', who spent his time cooking, cleaning, and reading 'either novels or the newspaper'. He had sublet part of his house to a married daughter, and would also play with his grandchildren, 'amusing them when they come back from school'. He was also clearly fond of his daughter and 'likes her company'. Significantly, he said he was 'on the best of terms with her as they are quite independent of each other. He says that he would not get on so well with her if he had his meals with her, but as he lives quite separately they are very friendly and he likes to know that they are near if he wants company.' [. . .]

These rare but vivid glimpses of the extraordinary variety of life experiences among the older generation in the early twentieth century are not only precious in themselves, but suggest the dangers of generalising about the earlier past to make up for the lost history of ageing. Certainly the historical evidence as a whole gives little support for the quite widespread belief that older people in the past enjoyed a much more secure and respected position than they do in the present. The one undoubted gain has been improved health, and with it longer life itself. But the continuities are equally striking. There have always been a minority of wealthy older people and a majority struggling to survive in poverty. The rise of the welfare state has brought much earlier retirement from work, but has had little impact on the low incomes typical of later life both past and present. Nor has there been much change in the pattern of support from the family. Throughout this period older men and women in this country have preferred to live in their own homes and have maintained a strong belief in independence.

Within these continuities, the individual variety is also significant. There have always been some old people who were influential and highly regarded, in contrast to the many others who were treated with ridicule, antagonism, or at best patronised as dependants. And as we have seen, the life-styles of older men and women have been equally varied.

References

Anderson, M. (1971) *Family Structure in Nineteenth Century Lancashire*. London: Cambridge University Press.

Anderson, M. (1988) 'Households, families and individuals in 1851', *Continuity and Change*, 3: 421–38.

Booth, C. (1894) *The Aged Poor in England and Wales*. London: Macmillan.

Caradog Jones, D. (1934) *A Social Survey of Merseyside*. Liverpool: University of Liverpool.

Gerard, J. (1982) 'Family and servants in the country-house community in England and Wales, 1815–1914'. PhD dissertation, University of London.

Greenwood, W. (c. 1935) *How the Other Man Lives*. London: Labour Book Service.

Hannah, L. (1986) *Inventing Retirement: the Development of Occupational Pensions in Britain*. Cambridge: Cambridge University Press.

Lansbury, G. (1928) *My Life*. London: Constable & Co.

Laslett, P. (1976) 'Societal development and aging', in R. Binstock and E. Shanas (eds), *Handbook of Aging and the Social Sciences*. New York: Van Nostrand Reinhold. pp. 87–116.

Laslett, P. (1977) *Family Life and Illicit Love in Earlier Generations*. Cambridge: Cambridge University Press.

Macfarlane, A. (1986), *Marriage and Love in England: Modes of Reproduction 1300–1840*. Oxford: Basil Blackwell.

Roberts, R. (1976) *A Ragged Schooling: Growing Up in the Classic Slum*. Manchester: Manchester University Press.

Rowntree, B.S. (1910) *Poverty: a Study of Town Life*. (Originally published 1901.) London: Macmillan.

Rowntree, B.S. (1941) *Poverty and Progress*. London: Longmans.

Rowntree, B.S. and Lavers, G.R. (1951) *Poverty and the Welfare State*. London: Longmans Green.

Smith, H.L. (1932) *The New Survey of London Life and Labour. Vol 3*. London: King.

Thomas, K. (1976) 'Age and Authority in Early Modern England', *Proceedings of the British Academy*, 62: 205–48.

Thompson, P., Itzin, C. and Abendstern, M. (1990) *I Don't Feel Old: Understanding the Experience of Later Life*. Oxford: Oxford University Press.

Thomson, D. (1984) 'The decline of social security: falling state support for the elderly since early Victorian times', *Ageing and Society*, 4 (4): 451–82.

Wall, R. (1984), 'Residential isolation of the elderly: a comparison over time', *Ageing and Society*, 4 (4): 483–503.

Wrigley, E.A. and Schofield, R.S. (1981) *The Population History of England 1541–1871: A Reconstruction*. London: Edward Arnold.

49

Social services for elderly people: from Beveridge to Thatcher

Robin Means

Residential care and the National Assistance Act 1948

Section 21 of the National Assistance Act 1948 states: 'it shall be the duty of every local authority . . . to provide residential accommodation for persons who by reason of age, infirmity or any other circumstances are in need of care and attention which is not otherwise available to them'. Other sections deal with how such residential accommodation was to be managed (Exchequer contributions, charges, etc.), contributions to voluntary organisations, the registration of private old people's homes and the compulsory removal of old people from the community. Local authorities were not given any general power to promote the welfare of old people. Instead section 29 stated this power should only cover those who 'are blind, deaf, or dumb and other persons who are substantially and permanently handicapped by illness, injury, or congenital deformity'. Equally, local authorities were not given further power to provide directly domiciliary services for elderly people. The National Health Service Act 1946 had given local [health] authorities the power to develop home help services for a range of groups including 'the aged'. As a result, local authorities would not be allowed to develop their own meals-on-wheels services, chiropody facilities, laundry services, visiting schemes or counselling services. [. . .]

Why did this heavy emphasis upon residential care exist within the Act? What effect did it have upon the subsequent development of welfare services for elderly people?

There seems to have been little if any discussion amongst senior civil servants and politicians about any alternative strategy of state support for elderly people in the 1940s (Means and Smith, 1985). The 'able-bodied' elderly should live in their own homes on their pension

Originally published as 'The development of social services for elderly people: historical perspectives', in C. Phillipson and A. Walker (eds), *Ageing and Social Policy*. Aldershot: Gower, 1986, Chapter 5, pp. 87–106 (abridged).

and with support from their family (i.e. daughters or daughters-in-law). The long-term 'sick' should be in hospital. The long-term 'frail' should live with their families or enter a local authority residential home. This lack of imagination about services seems to have reflected the dominant belief that 'frail' elderly people could not manage in their own homes unless living with other members of their family; domiciliary services provided by the state and voluntary organisations could not offer sufficient support for this group. For example, the Nuffield Provincial Hospital Trust founded a meals-on-wheels scheme in Essex in 1947, and the Assistance Board were informed of which groups this was to cover. One of these was 'feeble old people, living alone' but the Trust stressed that 'the ideal solution in such cases will be admission to a residential home, but in view of the lack of such accommodation a mobile meals service would be of value as a preventative measure'. Domiciliary services were seen very much as a second-best alternative. [. . .]

Another reason for the emphasis upon residential care in this period was that existing institutional provision was extensive and a cause of public controversy. [. . .] One example of [. . .] criticism was a letter [. . .] which appeared in the *Manchester Guardian* in March 1943. This letter recalled a visit to 'a frail, sensitive, refined old woman' of 84 who was forced to live in the following regime:

> Down each side of the ward were ten beds, facing one another. Between each bed and its neighbour was a small locker and a straight-backed, wooden, uncushioned chair. On each chair sat an old woman in workhouse dress, upright, unoccupied. No library books or wireless. Central heating, but no open fire. No easy chairs. No pictures on the walls. . . . There were three exceptions to the upright old women. None was allowed to lie on her bed at any time throughout the day, although breakfast is at 7 a.m., but these three, unable any longer to endure their physical and mental weariness, had crashed forward, face downwards, on to their immaculate bedspreads and were asleep. (Quoted in Samson, 1944: 47)

The response to the letter was sufficiently intense and voluminous to encourage an official from the Public Assistance Division of the Ministry of Health to provide an interview on the criticisms to a *Manchester Guardian* reporter. [. . .] Overall he emphasised that the war had interrupted the early stages of substantial improvements in the care of old people but that experiments in evacuation hostels had underlined the need to develop small homes with relaxed rules (Means and Smith, 1983). Public assistance institutions were an embarrassment to the Ministry of Health because they were out of step with the ideological consensus being built around the Beveridge Report (1942). They needed to be defused as a potential political issue and this was a central task of the 1948 Act. [. . .]

The implementing circular for the 1948 Act instructed local

authorities to concentrate on building Homes for 30–35 residents, and that all Homes should be run 'with a simple code of rules designed for the guidance, comfort and freedom of the residents'.

The 'reform' of residential care in the 1948 Act was greeted with enthusiasm by the bulk of the press, most politicians and many local authority staff (Means and Smith, 1985). One public assistance officer from Middlesex County Council, for example, claimed that:

> The old institutions or workhouses are to go altogether. In their place will be attractive hostels or hotels, each accommodating 25 to 30 old people, who will live there as guests not inmates. Each guest will pay for his accommodation – those with private incomes out of that, those without private incomes out of the payments they get from the National Assistance Board – and nobody need know whether they have private means or not. Thus, the stigma of 'relief' – very real too, and acutely felt by many old people – will vanish at last. (Garland, 1948: 36)

Residential homes in the 1950s and 1960s

[. . .] The years immediately after the Second World War have been characterised as an age of austerity in which there were restrictions on many aspects of public expenditure. Britain – and many other parts of the world – was undergoing the strains of moving from a war to a peacetime economy. With respect to capital projects, there was a shortage of labour and building materials and this drastically affected plans to build new residential homes for elderly people. [Table 49.1 underlines the extent of restrictions, especially upon new homes.] Highest priority was given to what was seen as productive investment (e.g. industrial estates, new towns, housing for families) – the economically active of the present or the future, or to national security. [. . .] It was not until the early 1960s that the construction of purpose-built residential homes was accelerated. [. . .]

Peter Townsend (1964), in *The Last Refuge*, [. . .] showed that in 1960 former public assistance institutions were still the mainstay of local authority residential provision for handicapped and elderly people. Such accommodation 'accounted for just over half the accommodation used by county and county borough councils, for just under half the residents and for probably over three-fifths of the old people actually admitted in the course of a year' (Townsend, 1964: 29). As a result, *The Last Refuge* is often remembered as an attack upon what was often called 'the workhouse legacy' (Ryan, 1966). The research, however, represented an indictment of all forms of local authority residential care including converted properties and new purpose-built homes. Residents from all three types of homes suffered from a loss of occupation; they felt isolated from family, friends and community; they failed to make new relationships; they experienced a loss of privacy and identity; and there was a collapse of powers of self-

Table 49.1 *Council homes opened for old and handicapped persons in England and Wales, 1948–60*

Year	No. of homes opened	Of which newly built
1948	97	0
1949	103	0
1950	138	1
1951	112	5
1952	130	5
1953	119	17
1954	99	15
1955	57	13
1956	73	22
1957	72	29
1958	53	26
1959	55	27
1960	76	47
Total	1184	207

Source: Townsend, 1964: 22

determination. Townsend concluded that the long-stay institution failed to give residents 'the advantages of living in a "normal" community' (1964: 190) and should be abandoned as an instrument of social policy. The alternative was to improve financial benefits, expand sheltered accommodation and develop preventive medical and domiciliary services. [. . .]

The Last Refuge and other associated work on institutions (Barton, 1959; Meacher, 1972) represented a challenge to dominant conceptions of social and medical need in old age. The primacy of residential homes in local authority welfare provision was [under severe attack]. And yet the theme taken up by state officials in relation to *The Last Refuge* was not the failure of most residential homes to meet the social needs of most elderly residents but rather the necessity of replacing a limited number of inadequate buildings. In the same year as the publication of *The Last Refuge*, local authorities were asked by the Ministry of Health to submit ten-year plans for the development of their health and welfare services, for 1963–73. In terms of the proposed capital programme, just over half the money was to be devoted to residential homes for elderly people [. . .]. The stated policy of the Ministry of Health was that local authorities should build new purpose-built residential homes to replace all unsatisfactory premises whether former public assistance institutions or converted dwellings, and to bring the provision of places in homes for elderly people by all 146 local authorities up to the national average in 10 years' time. Residential provision for elderly people continued to expand – it dominated the capital expenditure of local authorities (Bosanquet,

1978), and provided accommodation for an increasing percentage of the elderly population (Thomson, 1983). [. . .]

By the 1970s many commentators were beginning to agree with the early critics of residential homes that they 'have come to loom larger and larger as things that are good in themselves rather than as practical solutions to a pressing difficulty' (Bosanquet, 1978: 109). [. . .]

Domiciliary services and 'family' care

[. . .] The optimistic tone of the debate about residential 'hotels' did not survive the pressures discussed in the previous section. By the early 1950s, a consensus [appeared to have] developed amongst [civil servants], politicians and the professions that elderly people should remain in their own homes for as long as possible for their own happiness and also to reduce financial pressure on the state. [. . .]

Yet this consensus is illusory – there has always been conflict over how to define 'for as long as possible'. This conflict is at the core of the debate about the respective roles of the state, the voluntary sector and the 'family' in the care of dependent elderly people. More specifically, it opens up the question of why the state has proved so reluctant to develop domiciliary services that might delay the point at which institutional care is the only feasible option for many elderly people.

Older people and the family

[. . .] Numerous commentators during the 1950s claimed that the creation of the so-called 'welfare state' had undermined 'family' responsibility towards a number of groups including elderly people. The medical profession, geriatric social workers, the local authority associations and leading members of the voluntary pressure groups were all willing to express this view at various times. This attitude seemed especially acute within the medical profession because of a belief that hospital beds were being blocked by the refusal of relatives to offer a home to elderly patients. Thompson, for example was associated with surveys of hospital provision for the elderly sick in the Birmingham area during the late 1940s and he warned:

> It is . . . possible that slackening of the moral fibre of the family and a demand for material comfort and amenity outweighs the charms of mutual affection. . . . The power of the group-maintaining instincts will suffer if the provision of a home, the training of children, and the care of its disabled members are no longer the ambition of a family but the duty of a local or central authority. (Thompson, 1949: 230)

[. . .] It is clear that two questions were frequently posed during this period: did the 'family' still accept its 'responsibilities' towards elderly parents? And did domiciliary services and provision from voluntary organisations support or undermine the 'family' in this respect? [. . .]

Empirical evidence during this period gave an unequivocal answer to these two question. Families did 'care' and the bulk of this tending was carried out by wives, daughters and daughters-in-law. The overall message of such research was that the 'belief in the decline in filial care of the elderly is unfounded and an as yet unproven myth' (Lowther and Williamson, 1966). The most influential demolition of this myth is again associated with the work of Peter Townsend (1957; Townsend and Wedderburn, 1965; Shanas et al., 1968). [. . .]

The research results proved that disability in elderly people was more widespread amongst those living in their own homes than those in institutions. However, those in their own homes tended to have more extensive family resources than those in institutional care. Such relatives, and especially female relatives, provided an enormous amount of domestic and nursing care which far outstripped anything provided by the state or voluntary organisations. The minority of elderly people who did receive such services tended to be similar to those in institutional care – they lacked 'family' resources. [. . .] Rather than being restricted from a fear of undermining the family, domiciliary services needed to be rapidly expanded to support families and help the isolated. Other academics (Meacher, 1970) were able to develop these ideas through their own research and to argue for the development of an overall preventative health and social service strategy that would offer support and guidance to all elderly people rather than the narrow band already seeking institutional care. [. . .]

[The golden age of domiciliary services?]

[. . .] Research has made a strong case for a major shift of emphasis from residential care to domiciliary services in local authority provision for elderly people. Why did this not occur? At first glance, politicians and [civil servants] do seem to have agreed about the need for an expansion of domiciliary services. Voluntary organisations were encouraged to develop such services as visiting schemes and luncheon clubs (Ministry of Health, 1962). The legal obligation of local health authorities to provide chiropody services under the 1946 Health Service Act was confirmed in 1959 (Ministry of Health, 1959). The 1962 amendment to the National Assistance Act 1948 gave local authorities the power to develop their own meals-on-wheels services. The Health Services and Public Health Act 1968 and the Chronically Sick and Disabled Persons Act 1970 both considerably increased the power of local authorities to provide domiciliary support services. Such lists of legislative developments and exhortation by circular can give the impression of unimpeded incremental progress towards a more 'liberal' policy of social welfare provision for elderly people. However, there is a major difference between legislative intent and service development. Local authority provision remained dominated by residential care throughout the 1960s and early 1970s.

One explanation for this situation is that many welfare 'professionals' refused to accept that domiciliary services could be cost-effective in helping frail and sick elderly people to remain outside institutions. [. . .] This continued belief in the utility of residential care may have retarded the development of domiciliary services. Nevertheless, other commentators made exactly the opposite argument. Residential homes were expensive; an expansion of domiciliary services would be a cost-effective response to this situation by encouraging relatives to carry on caring for their elderly relatives rather than requesting their admission to a residential home (Sheldon, 1960).

The interesting question becomes why the first rather than the second argument continued to hold sway despite the large volume of research evidence that pointed in the opposite direction.

Townsend (1981) has pointed to the self-interest of those who work in the residential sector. [Other] research has underlined that self-interest was equally strong in those voluntary organisations involved in domiciliary service provision. These organisations often used pressure-group tactics in a prolonged campaign to restrict the development of local authority powers in relation to meals-on-wheels and related services. Such campaigns took place in an environment whose medical and social work 'professionals' were primarily engaged in a debate about the macro restructuring of the NHS and the personal social services rather than the details of service delivery for elderly people (Means and Smith, 1985).

However, one other influence upon the continued predominance of residential care will be explored in more detail; welfare services for elderly people only achieve any status on the political agenda during periods of demographic 'panic' and/or fiscal crisis. Arguments over the hospital/residential care divide in the 1950s were conducted against a background of concern about the rising elderly population. The demographic projections of the Royal Commission on the Population (1949) had created concern about the future 'burden of dependency' that would have to be carried by the working population; those over 65 would rise by 2 to 3 million over the next 30 years which was defined as problematic because 'the old consume without producing which differentiates them from the active population and makes them a factor reducing the average standard of living of the community' (Royal Commission on Population, 1949: 113). This created a climate in which the relative merits of hospital and residential care would be high on the agenda of [civil servants] and politicians. Adjournment debates about services for elderly people were a frequent feature of the House of Commons during the 1950s. The population projections, however, proved inaccurate, which led some critics to deride 'the noisy barrage of faulty statistics' (Titmuss, 1955: 47). The Guillebaud

Report (1956) ensured that the cost of the NHS was no longer defined as a political issue during the late 1950s and 1960s. [. . .]

Services for elderly people only re-emerged as a major political issue [in the mid-1970s] when [concern about overall public expenditure levels] coincided with renewed fears about population trends. The 'burden of dependency' debate was about to be reopened (see Walker, 1980). At first, this situation persuaded central government to agree that domiciliary services needed to be expanded to reduce pressure on residential care. The priorities document of the DHSS (1976) argued that the more domiciliary services can be expanded, the more the pressure on residential accommodation and hospitals can be eased. The government had, therefore, decided to allow for a 2 per cent increase in meals-on-wheels and home help provision although this would be balanced by a cut in the capital programme for residential accommodation and day care.

All of us are now only too aware that a new 'golden age' for domiciliary services was not about to be ushered in. Sophistication in the packaging of such services may have improved through various social work experiments and research projects (DHSS, 1983) but this [. . .] occurred against a background of concern from [civil servants] and politicians about the need to restrict the expectations of elderly people and their relatives about the overall availability of domiciliary services. This [was] a central message of various government documents [of the late 1970s and early 1980s], perhaps best summed up in the often quoted statement [from the first Thatcher government's White Paper, *Growing Older*], that 'care in the community must increasingly mean care by the community' (DHSS, 1981). [. . .]

References

Barton, R. (1959) *Institutional Neurosis*. London: John Wright and Sons.

Beveridge, W. (1942) *Social Insurance and Allied Services*. Cmnd. 6404. London: HMSO.

Bosanquet, N. (1978) *A Future for Old Age*. London: Temple Smith.

Department of Health and Social Security (1976) *Priorities in the Health and Personal Social Services*. Consultative document. London: HMSO.

Department of Health and Social Security (1981) *Growing Older*. Cmnd. 8173. London: HMSO.

Department of Health and Social Security (1983) *Elderly People in the Community: Their Service Needs*. London: HMSO.

Garland, R. (1948) 'End of the Poor Law – and a new era dawns in British social welfare', *Social Welfare*, 11 (2): 36–7.

Guillebaud Report (1956) *Report of the Committee of Enquiry into the Cost of the National Health Service*. Cmnd. 9663. London: HMSO.

Lowther, C. and Williamson, J. (1966) 'Old people and their relatives', *The Lancet*, 21 March: 1460.

Meacher, M. (1970) 'The old: the future of community care', in P. Townsend (ed.), *The Fifth Social Service: a Critical Analysis of the Seebohm Proposals*. London: Fabian Society. pp. 80–109.

Meacher, M. (1972) *Taken for a Ride*. London: Longman.

Means, R. and Smith, R. (1983) 'From public assistance institutions to "sunshine hotels": changing state perceptions about residential care for elderly people', *Ageing and Society*, 3 (2): 157–81.

Means, R. and Smith, R. (1985) *The Development of Welfare Services for Elderly People*. London: Croom Helm.

Ministry of Health (1959) *National Health Service Act, 1946, Section 98: Chiropody Services, Circular 11/59, 21 April*. London: HMSO.

Ministry of Health, (1962) *Development of Health and Welfare Services: Co-operation with Voluntary Organisations, Circular 7/62, 12 April*. London: HMSO.

Royal Commission on Population (1949) *Report of the Royal Commission*. Chaired by Viscount Simon and Sir Hubert Douglas Henderson. London: HMSO.

Ryan, T. (1966) 'The workhouse legacy', *The Medical Officer*, 11 November: 270–1.

Samson, E. (1944) *Old Age in the Modern World*. London: Pilot Press.

Shanas, E., Townsend, P., Wedderburn, D., Friis, H., Milhoj, P. and Stehouwer, J. (1968) *Old People in Three Industrial Societies*. London: Routledge & Kegan Paul.

Sheldon, J. (1960) 'Problems of an ageing population', *British Medical Journal*, 23 April: 1225.

Thompson, A. (1949) 'Problems of ageing and chronic sickness', *British Medical Journal*, 30 July: 250–1.

Thomson, D. (1983) 'Workhouse to nursing home: residential care of elderly people in England since 1840', *Ageing and Society*, 3 (1): 43–70.

Titmuss, R.M. (1955) 'Age and society: some fundamental assumptions', in *Old Age in the Modern World: Report of the Third Congress of the International Association of Gerontology*. Edinburgh: Livingstone, pp. 46–9.

Townsend, P. (1957) *The Family Life of Old People*. Harmondsworth: Penguin.

Townsend, P. (1964) *The Last Refuge*. London: Routledge & Kegan Paul. (abridged)

Townsend, P. (1981) 'The structured dependency of the elderly: the creation of social policy in the twentieth century', *Ageing and Society*, 1 (1): 5–28.

Townsend, P. and Wedderburn, D. (1965) *The Aged in the Welfare State*. London: Bell.

Walker, A. (1980) 'The social creation of poverty and dependency in old age', *Journal of Social Policy*, 9 (1): 45–75.

50

The historical development of geriatric medicine as a speciality

Helen Evers

The ways in which a society copes with the major events of birth, illness and death are central to the beliefs and practices of that society and also bear a close relationship to its other major social, economic and cultural institutions. [. . .] treatment of those who are [. . .] dependent on others is a revealing indicator of the social values lying behind the allocation of [. . .] resources. [. . .] understanding the beliefs and practices associated with health and healing and the social processes involved contributes to a deeper understanding of [. . .] society. (Stacey, 1988: 1)

Means and Smith (1985) observe that examining the past history of services for old people can throw light on today's policy and practice issues. The history of geriatric medicine in Britain reflects societal responses to old age. It is a fascinating story of inspired and dedicated individuals, of professional interests and conflicts and of trends in social and health policy on older people. This chapter sketches some landmarks in the development of geriatric medicine, and illustrates the associated conflicts and dilemmas, some of which are still evident today. It also discusses some of the benefits resulting from developments in geriatric medicine. Fuller accounts are given by Carboni (1982) and Jefferys (forthcoming).

Emergence of 'old age' as a category has been influenced by medical analyses of the problems of old age. Kirk's observation (1992) that over 100 works on ageing and medical problems were published during the nineteenth century is evidence of the increasing medicalisation of old age at that time. He describes Canstatt's textbook on the clinical medicine of old age of 1839 as particularly important because, although old age was itself considered as a disease in the book,

it seeks to define the relationship between 'involution' and disease, [. . .] general and specific manifestations of disease in old age; and it emphasises the need to deal seriously with elderly patients. (Kirk, 1992: 487)

In Britain, the development of geriatric medicine as a specialty dates from the 1930s as will be outlined below.

Warren's contribution to the early development of geriatric medicine

Marjory Warren (1897–1960) was a key figure in the development of geriatric medicine. She was appointed Assistant Medical Officer at the West Middlesex County Hospital in 1926, and promoted to Deputy Medical Superintendent in 1931. In 1935, the hospital took over responsibility for the former Poor Law infirmary. The idea was to improve medical care for the 'chronic sick', many of whom were old, and looked after in 'human warehouses', being kept in bed in overcrowded and environmentally depressing wards.

Warren was faced with some 700 patients, with whom she set to work on classification, treatment and rehabilitation. About 200 'relatively able-bodied' patients were transferred to a nearby residential home, and a further 150 transferred to the care of psychiatric staff, leaving some 350 'really chronic sick patients to be cared for and treated' (Warren, 1948: 45). Warren published numerous papers documenting her work and reflecting on the need for a specialty of geriatric medicine.

She admonished the medical profession and society:

> It is surprising that the medical profession has been so long in awakening to its responsibilities towards the chronic sick and the aged, and that the country at large should have been content to do so little for this section of the community. Today, owing to the ageing of the population, the general shortage of nurses and domestic help [. . .] and the fact that more women are employed [. . .] the problem has reached enormous dimensions. [. . .] To all who have studied the subject it is obvious that the specialised care and treatment of these folk is of great economic importance and calls for immediate attention. (Warren 1946a: 841)

In Warren's view, doctors were uninterested in the old because they were poor, and because greater time and patience were needed to investigate many of their conditions. 'Cure' is harder to achieve and amelioration takes longer:

> The majority of these patients have ceased to be engaged in active work of an essential nature and hence their return to health is less advertised than in the case of a worker returning to his job, and is therefore less spectacular. (Warren 1946b: 384–5)

Higher death rates and the multiple pathology typical of old age were also cited by Warren (1946b) as inclining the medical profession to lack of interest in old people.

She was struck by the plight of 'the untreated case':

> Only those who have had charge of such patients can know anything of their misery and degradation. Having lost all hope of recovery, with the knowledge that independence has gone, and with a feeling of helplessness and frustration, the patient rapidly loses morale and self-respect and develops an apathetic or peevish, irritable, sullen, morose, and aggressive

temperament. [. . .] Lack of interest in the surroundings, confinement to bed, and a tendency to incontinence soon produce pressure sores, with the necessity for more nursing, of a kind ill appreciated by the patient. An increase in weight [. . .] and an inevitable loss of muscle tone make for a completely bedridden state. Soon the well-known disuse atrophy of the lower limbs, with postural deformities, stiffness of joints, and contractures, completes the unhappy picture of human forms who are not only heavy nursing cases in the ward and a drag on society but also are no pleasure to themselves and a source of acute distress to their friends. Still, alas, in this miserable state, dull, apathetic, helpless, and hopeless, life lingers on sometimes for years, while those round them whisper arguments in favour of euthanasia. (Warren 1946a: 841–2)

Warren was also concerned about the costs to society of failure to respond to health care needs of the ageing population. Establishing geriatric medicine as a specialty, with new initiatives in training doctors and carrying out research, would facilitate 'The proper care of the aged chronic sick [which] requires knowledge of the elderly and sympathy with their particular requirement' (Warren 1943). Over 50 years later, Warren's pronouncements still have a familiar ring about them.

Matthews (1984) summarises the innovations Warren introduced:

1 classifying patients into five groups (ambulatory, continent bed-ridden, incontinent women, senile but untroublesome and finally those with senile dementia), which were then separated into discrete wards for planned care and treatment;
2 improving the environment to facilitate rehabilitation – this included repainting and improving the lighting, improving the conditions generally, as well as introducing equipment for rehabilitation;
3 establishing a multidisciplinary team to assist in medical and social rehabilitation of patients.

Warren's work came to the attention of Dr Sturdee at the Ministry of Health, and in 1947 a small number of pioneering practitioners established the Medical Society for the Care of the Elderly, which became the British Geriatrics Society in 1959.

Factors contributing to the development of geriatric medicine as a specialty

A variety of issues significantly influenced the growing specialisation of geriatric medicine. The Local Government Act of 1929 enabled county council public assistance committees to hand over former Poor Law infirmaries to health committees in order to improve care of the aged and chronic sick. This created an imperative for action, as exemplified in Marjory Warren's early work.

At the beginning of the Second World War, the Emergency Medical Service was established and there was a massive decanting of patients, including many old and chronic sick people, from London hospitals. Later, old and chronic sick people were moved from air-raid shelters and the temporary rest homes for those made homeless by the bombing and accumulated in public assistance institutions and hospitals outside the cities. The 'problem' of old and chronic sick people became an issue: patients from these groups were seen as blocking scarce hospital beds.

After the war, the Ministry of Health continued to be concerned about this problem, as well as the plight of the old people themselves. There was interest in the innovative work of the early pioneers, and, besides, there were pressures to find jobs for doctors returning from war duties.

At the inception of the NHS, the medical profession were concerned that the new health service might be swamped by the old, who, formerly, did not have automatic right of access to all the hospitals (Thomson et al., 1951). Marjory Warren and others had demonstrated the potential for rehabilitation, and the need to prevent clogging of NHS hospitals put this issue in the spotlight.

Key features of practice in the developing specialty of geriatric medicine included recognition that 'bed is bad', a phrase coined by Cosin, a surgeon who pioneered early mobilisation of older patients after treatment for fractures of the femur. The importance of home and family context to successful treatment and rehabilitation was recognised. The principle of 'floating beds' and rotating admissions – 'six weeks in, six weeks out' – was established, to serve the twin purposes of rehabilitation and of providing relief to carers. Eric Brooke, of Carshalton, faced with huge waiting lists in the 1950s, made a virtue out of a necessity and introduced the practice of domiciliary assessments, which often led to interventions other than hospital admission.

The 'community orientation' of the embryonic specialty was a feature from the outset: Warren wrote of the desirability of maintaining old people in their own homes whenever possible.

Development and change in post-war geriatric medicine

The development of public health medicine and epidemiology had an important influence on the new specialty. Sheldon's seminal work *The Social Medicine of Old Age* (1948), a survey of a random sample of old people at home, made a major methodological contribution to knowledge about health, illness and life-styles in old age. Research and documentation of practice in clinical geriatrics began to form a distinctive knowledge base for the developing specialty (e.g. Howell, 1944).

The policy climate from the 1950s on was ripe to support the development of a power base for geriatricians. Concern about the 'rising tide' of old people, and growing emphasis on the need for community care to save money as well as to meet needs, lent support to central pillars of geriatric practice: e.g. multidisciplinary teamwork, community orientation, holistic health and social care. Development and innovation in age-related comprehensive geriatric services flourished despite constant difficulties with resources, during the post-war period (see e.g. Horrocks, 1982).

The first Chair of Geriatric Medicine in Britain was established in Glasgow in the late 1960s, and by 1992 there were 23 such posts. The concerns of the early days were predominantly about service development and organisation. While this continues to be an issue, consolidation of scientific respectability, through academic medical research, is also to the fore.

The medical profession at large had a strong interest in supporting the development of geriatrics as a solution to the management of long-stay care. But geriatricians had no wish to serve as 'clinical undertakers' (Kemp, 1963) for the rest of the medical profession. They aimed to develop distinctive expertise and practice both for the benefit of patients and to move away from being custodians of 'no-hopers' towards improving rehabilitation, turnover and 'cure'.

Prestige within hospital medicine relates partly to high technology and perceived success in terms of rapid turnover. Geriatric medicine's early responsibility for long-stay patients, and an inheritance of poor facilities and resources, meant that it was not a popular choice for specialism. Only a minority of doctors saw this scenario as a challenge with which they personally wished to engage. Trends in geriatric medicine have been towards increasing turnover rates, which, arguably, has served the interests of geriatricians as well as patients. The specialty now has less difficulty in recruiting high-calibre staff.

Past issues, current issues?

The relationship of geriatric medicine to other specialties has been the subject of debate since the early days. As we have seen, much of the specialty's distinctiveness has derived from its particular approach to practice and service organisation, with the emphasis on holistic care, through multidisciplinary teamwork, and its community orientation, including the commitment to relief care and rehabilitation.

Partly with recruitment and resourcing difficulties in mind, various forms of integration with other specialties, particularly general medicine, have, from the 1970s, become widespread. Integration has the advantage of fostering 'better inter-specialty understanding, more efficient operation, better educational opportunities and better deployment of staff' (Harrison, 1992: 29).

Patients should benefit from the broader-based understanding of geriatric practice characteristic of a service which integrates general and geriatric medicine. While the separate specialty of geriatric medicine has raised the profile of the distinctive health care needs of older people, and stimulated innovative service responses, integration may serve to counter the widespread negative social pressures to marginalise older people.

As Harrison points out, there may be some disadvantages for patients looked after by 'integrated' services. Continuity may be disrupted when they are transferred between acute, slow-stream rehabilitation and long-stay beds. Further, in the acute context, Harrison is concerned whether the pressures on nursing staff may jeopardise the holistic approach fostered in the best of specialist geriatric departments.

Rapid growth in the specialty of psychogeriatric medicine has been important. Improved services for those with functional and organic mental illness in later life have had a major impact on geriatric services. As with geriatric medicine, the trend is away from direct long-stay care provision. This may have benefits for patients, but there may be disadvantages for carers.

Debates about long-stay care stimulated the birth of geriatric medicine as a specialty and continue to be a major issue today. Professional interests, concern about the quality of life of older people and about costs to society are consistent themes throughout the period since the 1930s. Now, as then, questions about who should be responsible for long-term care – lay carers, social or health services – and who should pay remain central to social and health policy.

There has been a rapid growth of private sector nursing and residential care which was fuelled by the availability of social security funding. With the implementation of the NHS and Community Care Act (1990), public financial support of residential care will only be available contingent upon assessed need for such care. Warren (1943) argued that all long-stay care provision should be under medical control. Today, many consultants in geriatric medicine envisage an increased responsibility in relation to residential and nursing home care, which, they suggest, could benefit service-users (Harrison, 1992). As in the early days, they would focus on improving diagnosis, care and rehabilitation, and fulfil a 'gate-keeping' function vis a vis a hospital. However there is a danger here of the daily lives of older people in homes becoming dominated by the medical paradigm.

Conclusions: benefits to patients?

The emergence of geriatric medicine as a specialty has given a high profile to the particular considerations for medical care of older people, and stimulated innovative approaches and positive developments in service delivery.

While the record of higher and more rapid turnover may benefit patients, there is a possibility that patients may be discharged 'quicker and sicker' (Schorr, 1992). Continuing conflicts over long-stay care and under-resourcing remain a problem. Grimley Evans (1992) argues that physiological need and not age should determine service provision. He warns that age is not a sound medical basis on which to draw service boundaries. In the new market economy of health, the specialist geriatric service may legitimise unjustifiable rationing in relation to people who happen to be old.

It is difficult to reach unequivocal conclusions as to the extent of geriatric medicine's positive benefits in health care of older people. We should compare the British situation to that of other countries where the specialism has not become established. Is geriatric medicine an ageist practice for containing the potentially limitless demands for health care among older people, under the control of geriatricians acting as 'clinical undertakers' in the service of the more glamorous factions of the medical profession (Kemp, 1963)? Evaluating the outcomes for patients of the development of geriatric medicine is complex. But it would be a misinterpretation as well as a grave disservice to the inspired individuals, past and present, who have shaped and continue to shape the specialty to dismiss it as merely an ageist response to a series of demographic, political and professional pressures.

References

Carboni, D. (1982) *Geriatric Medicine in the United States and Great Britain*. London: Greenwood Press.

Evans, Grimley J. (1991) 'Aging and rationing' *British Medical Journal*, 303, 12 October: 869-70.

Harrison, J. (1992) *Geriatric Medicine in South Birmingham: 1992-1997 and Beyond*. A report to the Chief Executive. South Birmingham Health Authority, Birmingham.

Horrocks, P. (1982) 'The case for geriatric medicine as an age-related specialty', in B. Isaacs (ed.), *Recent Advances in Geriatric Medicine*. Vol. 2. Edinburgh: Churchill Livingstone.

Howell, T. (1944) *Old Age: Some Practical Points in Geriatrics*. London: H.K. Lewis.

Howell, T. (1962), 'Some differences between geriatrics and general medicine', *Concord*, May: 47-8.

Jefferys, M. (forthcoming) *History of Geriatric Medicine*.

Kemp, R. (1963) 'Old age a regret', *The Lancet*, 2 November: 897-900.

Kirk, H. (1992) 'Geriatric medicine and the categorisation of old age - the historical linkage', *Ageing and Society*, 1 (4): 483-97.

Matthews, D. (1984) 'Dr Marjory Warren and the origin of British geriatrics', *Journal of the American Geriatrics Society*, 32: 253-8.

Means, R. and Smith, R. (1985) *The Development of Welfare Services for Elderly People*. London: Croom Helm.

Schorr, A. (1992) *The Personal Social Services: An Outside View.* York: Joseph Rowntree Foundation.

Sheldon, J. (1948) *The Social Medicine of Old Age.* London: Oxford University Press.

Stacey, M. (1988) *The Sociology of Health and Healing.* London: Unwin Hyman.

Thomson, A., Lowe D. and McKeown, T. (1951) *The Care of the Ageing and Chronic Sick.* Edinburgh: E. and S. Livingstone.

Warren, M. (1943) 'Care of the chronic sick: a case for treating chronic sick in blocks in a general hospital', *British Medical Journal*, 2: 822, 25 December.

Warren, M. (1946a) 'Care of the chronic aged sick', *The Lancet*, 8 June: 841–3.

Warren, M. (1946b) 'Geriatrics: a medical, social and economic problem', *Practitioner*, 157: 384–90.

Warren, M. (1948) 'The evolution of a geriatric unit', *Geriatrics*, 3: 42–50.

51

History of old age in western culture and society

Georges Minois

It is the tendency of every society to live and to go on living: it
extols the strength and the fecundity that are so closely linked with
youth and it dreads the worn-out sterility, the decrepitude of age

(de Beauvoir, 1977: 46).

Simone de Beauvoir's statement is particularly well confirmed by [this
study of the great ancient civilisations]. Over and above their minor
variations, the general impression is one of pessimism and hostility
towards all-conquering age. In spite of [. . .] various pleas in defence
[. . .], it is clear that youth has always and everywhere been preferred
to old age. Since the dawn of history, old people have regretted their
youth and young people have feared the onset of old age. According to
western thought, old age is an evil, an infirmity and a dreary time of
preparation for death. Even the latter is often envisaged with more
sympathy than is decrepitude, because death means deliverance.
Christian thought has always tried to reconcile and familiarise its
adherents with death, the door to eternal life. Pagan and neo-Platonic
thought preferred suicide to decrepitude. This is an incontrovertible
fact, which cannot be concealed behind a few rare instances of
peaceful and happy old age. Such people may appear happy, but their
lives were bitter indeed. The fountain of youth has always constituted
western man's most irrational hope.

The situation of old people expresses the ambiguity of the human
condition more fully than do the other ages of life. Living in this
world, they are already felt no longer to belong to it. The activities,
attitudes and distractions of the young are forbidden them. The only
role allowed them is an inhuman one: unfailing wisdom, without
error or frailty. To be accepted, an old man must be a saint.
Condemned to veneration or detestation, he no longer has the right
to commit the slightest mistake, he who enjoys so much experience,
he who can no longer surrender to the slightest urge of the flesh, he

From *History of Old Age: from Antiquity to the Renaissance*. Cambridge: Polity Press, 1989,
pp. 303–7.

who is so worn and shrivelled, he must be perfect, or he will become revolting and doting.

> If old people show the same desires, the same feelings and the same requirements as the young, the world looks upon them with disgust: in them love and jealousy seem revolting or absurd, sexuality repulsive and violence ludicrous. They are required to be a standing example of all the virtues. Above all, they are called on to display serenity; the world asserts that they possess it, and this assertion allows the world to ignore their unhappiness. The purified image of themselves that society offers the aged is that of the white-haired and venerable sage, rich in experience, planing high above the common state of mankind; if they vary from this then they fall below it; the counterpart of the first image is that of the old fool in his dotage, a laughing-stock for his children. In any case, either by their virtue or by their degradation, they stand outside humanity. (de Beauvoir, 1977: 10)

This is undoubtedly the main conclusion. From antiquity to the Renaissance, however societies evolved, they remained fundamentally based on physical strength and bodily vigour; the conditions were unfavourable to old age from the start. However, variations of detail appear within this framework, which contribute towards the local and temporary amelioration or deterioration of the situation of old people. Any search for a regular evolution from ancient Egypt to the Renaissance would indeed be vain, given the great difference between the countries and civilisations involved. [. . .] The course of history traces neither a hyperbola nor a parabola, but a capricious arabesque which eludes every attempt at equation by the human brain. The condition of the old was determined by several components which did not necessarily evolve in the same way, and an improvement in one sector might well be accompanied by a deterioration in another. At no time did all the favourable conditions combine.

What were these different factors which came into play to define the social status of the old? The first was undoubtedly their physical frailty. Consequently, the condition of the old was worst in those societies which were most anarchical and least policed, relying on the law of the strongest, as in the Merovingian world and in the Middle Ages as a whole. Conversely, in more structured societies, where the state and the law had more authority and could enforce order, the weaker elements were more protected against physical aggression by the strong. This was the case in Rome and under the absolute monarchies of the sixteenth century.

The second factor making up old age was the knowledge and experience due to long life. Thus civilisations which relied on oral tradition and custom were kinder towards the old. In such societies, they acted as links between the generations and as the collective memory. They were called on during the long evenings and at legal proceedings, as was the case in Greece and especially in the Middle Ages. On the other hand, the advance of the written word, of archives and laws recorded in writing, were unfavourable to them. Their knowledge of custom was rendered useless. The printed book was for a while the old man's enemy. In this sense, Rome and the Renaissance boded ill for him. These legalist civilisations had less need of their old people's customary experience. Added to which the relative acceleration of history during the Renaissance contributed to relegating them to the category of antiquated and useless things.

Harvey C. Lehman assessed the positive and negative qualities of old age as regards cultural evolution as follows:

> Whatever the causes of growth and decline, it remains clear that the genius does not function equally well throughout the years of adulthood. Superior creativity rises relatively rapidly to a maximum which occurs usually in the thirties and then falls off slowly. Almost as soon as he becomes fully mature, man is confronted with a gerontic paradox that may be expressed in terms of positive and negative transfer. Old people probably have more transfer, both positive and negative, then do young ones. As a result of positive transfer the old usually possess greater wisdom and erudition. These are invaluable assets. But when a situation requires a new way of looking at things, the acquisition of new techniques or even new vocabularies, the old seem stereotyped and rigid. To learn the new they often have to unlearn the old and that is twice as hard as learning without unlearning. But when a situation requires a store of past knowledge then the old find their advantage over the young. (1953: 330)

The third factor is their altered features. Societies which indulged in a cult of physical beauty tended to depreciate old age. This was particularly obvious in Greece and during the Renaissance. Societies which entertained a more abstract and symbolic aesthetic ideal were, conversely, less revolted by wrinkled faces because they were aiming at a spiritual beauty above and beyond the visible; this was the case in the Middle Ages especially.

Age also serves to increase the number of one's relations, as new generations appear and matrimonial alliances are contracted. Civilisations which experienced the extended and patriarchal family, which supported those members who were incapable of work, did help the old more. This was generally the case in the remotest ages, at the beginning of a new civilisation, for instance, or during periods of crisis; in archaic Greece, at the beginning of the Roman republic, or during the early Middle Ages. Periods of relative equilibrium, on the other hand, generally witnessed the disintegration of the group in favour of the conjugal family – as in classical Greece, imperial Rome, the 'classical' Middle Ages and the Renaissance, which all tended to neglect their old.

Old age can also be a time when worldly goods accumulate, ensuring the material security and prestige of old persons in the ruling classes. Societies where movable wealth, which is essentially personal, played a great role allowed many old people to achieve a superior status, as in the merchant and banking circles in Rome, at the end of the Middle Ages and the Renaissance. However, the corollary to this concentration of wealth within the hands of old people was that the young were impatient and sometimes murderously jealous of them. Where landed property predominated, belonging to the family group, the inverse situation arose and was less favourable towards the elder members.

Generally speaking, the periods known as transitional were less unfavourable towards the old than the stable periods known as classical. The times of upheaval, when the prejudices and rigid structures characteristic of settled times were lost, were more open to a variety of talents, more friendly towards difference and less encumbered by aesthetic, moral or social taboos. While these periods were undoubtedly difficult for everyone, old people were less rejected; every age suffered the common lot of a precarious existence. The Hellenistic world, the time of the Germanic invasions and the early Middle Ages were less hard on the old than were classical Greece and Rome, or the Renaissance.

Added to which, the general attitude towards the old of every society tends to assume a particular colour within each social category. It has always been better to be old and rich than old and poor. Charity is all that can be hoped for in the latter event, where the elderly are totally dependent on others. In short, there has never been a golden age for the old, but a chaotic evolution at the whim of the desynchronised values of civilisations.

The concept of retirement did not exist in any of these ancient periods, with the exception of a few privileged cases. Such distinctions as existed were between two categories of old people: the active old, who, in spite of their age, continued to exercise a profession and who merged into the mass of adult people so far as their contemporaries were concerned; and the inactive old, who were forced by their decrepitude to rest, and were classed [. . .] among the infirm and the sick. There was thus no limit and old age disappeared. This constituted their main difficulty, resulting in the weakness and misery of the old in the past. In societies which were still very closed, where a person's status and membership of a group were the sole guarantors of his social acceptance, where an isolated individual could not survive, an old person was not recognised as such. So he had no rights and was entirely at the mercy of those around him. This was the social circle which, in the final analysis, created the image of old people, starting from the norms and human ideals of their age.

Each civilisation has its model old person, and judges all its old accordingly. The more this model is idealised, the more demanding and cruel the society is, and so long as this trend is not reversed, old people will not be truly integrated within the group. Every description encountered above has in fact been a judgement; there have always been good or bad old people, who conform to a greater or lesser degree to the established ideal. When these societies begin with reality and experience as they know them instead of starting off with an abstract model, they take a great step forward. For this, we must wait for the advent of the social sciences, of psychology and geriatric medicine. The old should be studied and society adapted to meet their needs, rather than the reverse. It should be recognised that old people have their needs, including physical ones, and that they should be allowed to satisfy these needs, instead of decreeing that the old man is wise and trying to force him so to become.

References

de Beauvoir, S. (1977) *Old Age* trans. P. O'Brian. Harmondsworth: Penguin.
Lehman, H.C. (1953) *Age and Achievement*. Princeton, NJ: Princeton University Press.

FUTURES

52

The politics of age

Russell A. Ward

It is support *by the aged* of old-age politics which will determine the future vitality of the senior movement. Their widespread participation depends upon emerging feelings of *aging group consciousness*, defined as

> elderly persons who become aware, not merely that they are old, but that they are subject to certain deprivations because they are old, and they react to these deprivations with resentment and with some positive effort to overcome the deprivation. Further, they are aware that most, or all, older persons are subject to these deprivations, and they feel a positive sense of identification with other elderly persons for this reason. For them, the elderly are a group, and not merely a category. (Rose 1965b: 19)

This consciousness contributes to feelings of belonging to a *subculture of the aging*. There is evidence that older people who identify themselves as 'old' are more liberal, particularly on issues affecting the aged, such as government intervention in inflation and medical care (Bengtson and Cutler, 1976).

Does this kind of age consciousness exist? Arnold Rose (1965a, 1965b) has argued that a subculture is already developing among older people in American society, which he attributes to such recent trends as the growing number and proportion of older persons in the population, better health and education among the aged, the emergence of 'retirement communities' and the emergence of unifying grievances such as the cost of health care. Others have argued, however, that the aged do not constitute a true 'minority group' partly because they lack widespread feelings of group identity and readiness to organize on their own behalf (Rosow, 1974; Streib, 1965). Such feelings depend on more than just age.

There are understandable barriers to the feelings of group solidarity represented by aging group consciousness, not the least of which is resistance to the perception of personal aging because of the stigma

From *The Aging Experience: an Introduction to Social Gerontology*. New York: J.B. Lippincott Co, 1979, pp. 371–7.

attached to old age. 'But old people are also mirrors for one another, mirrors in which they do not care to see themselves – the marks of old age they behold vex them' (de Beauvoir, 1972: 472). The aged are also not accustomed to thinking in terms of age identification. Other bases of differentiation have been salient throughout their lives – race, sex, ethnicity, religion, social class. The older college-educated, middle-class white may feel he has little in common with the older lower-class black. Feelings of age solidarity are further minimized by contacts with other segments of society through the family or the mass media and the use of them as reference groups. These 'bonds of pluralism' limit feelings of alienation from the larger society (Seeman, 1975). Poor health and transportation problems accompanying old age may also prevent older people from associating with one another.

There are conditions which might foster aging group consciousness, however. What is required is a perception of similarity with age peers based on past experiences and current common fate. Proximity, in the form of some type of age-segregated situation, would allow older people to develop a sense of the situation of age peers and of their similarities in interests, needs and attitudes. Hochschild's (1973) study of Merrill Court shows the development of this sense of community in an age-segregated setting. Membership in such age-segregated residential settings is still not widespread, however, and the development of solidarity typically requires homogeneity on factors other than age. This type of age concentration can result in aging group consciousness, but not as a widespread phenomenon throughout the older population.

Membership in old-age associations may also foster aging group consciousness. One study found that participation in age-graded groups fostered greater activist self-interest based on age – greater desire for political change, more receptivity to appeals for organized political activity, and an increased willingness to engage in activist political behavior (Trela, 1972). Groups like the NCSC (National Council of Senior Citizens) and AARP (American Association of Retired Persons) can provide an opportunity for older people to more clearly define their interests and the political problems which confront them *collectively*, but membership in such groups still accounts for only a small minority of the older population.

As with class consciousness (Laumann and Senter, 1976), aging group consciousness implies certain perceptions by the individual. There must be a recognition by the older person that his life chances depend on the *group*, rather than just personal resources. This implies an awareness of the age stratification system and the extent to which one's own relative position is determined by it. Thus, the aging group conscious would attribute problems to the age-based system rather than to personal failure. There is little evidence of such feelings among the aged, and stigma combined with cross-generational associations will probably limit its emergence. There is also little evidence that the aged view the age stratification structure as undesirable or changeable, perceptions which Laumann and Senter suggest are related to group consciousness. Indeed, there is evidence that older people attribute greater legitimacy to norms of age-appropriateness than younger people.

Rosow (1974) has argued that the stigma attached to old age will continue to be a barrier to group identification and that, while there seems to be growing concern about the problems of the aged, the age stratification of modern societies will still dictate low status and restricted roles for them. He further argues that the aged will still be substantially disadvantaged, giving them little effective social leverage or political power. Binstock (1974) is also skeptical about the possibility of 'senior power', arguing that the aged will continue to be too heterogeneous to form an effective political bloc.

The picture is not all one-sided, however. The aged are not quiet when it comes to voting, political interest and the like, and they can be quite 'liberal' about programs which would directly benefit them. (Aren't we all?) The growing size of the older population, rising interest in gerontology, the visibility of old-age associations and the ability of some older groups to coalesce despite their internal cleavages all indicate the possibility of continued or growing political activism by the aged. More important, the sources and facilitators of political activism still exist and may increase in the future.

Social movements arise from feelings of alienation, relative deprivation and status inconsistency. Status inconsistency is the feeling that one's status in one area is out of line with one's status in another area, providing conflicting expectations, instability of the self and a perception that rewards do not correspond with one's aspirations (Trela, 1976). Combined with feelings of deprivation compared to other groups or to one's expectations, this can create a preference for change in the political order, in the form of either political liberalism or extremism. Feelings of status inconsistency and relative deprivation may occur in older people, particularly those who move from higher middle-aged status to a lower status in old age (loss of authority, financial problems). The Townsend Movement was a response to status loss caused by the Depression and consisted largely of professionals, businessmen and skilled workers who had been driven into the ranks of the deprived aged (Trela, 1976). We have also seen that the aged often experience heightened alienation, particularly political powerlessness, which can lead to political activism. Members of one old-age movement, the McLain Movement, tended to feel dissatisfied and distrustful (Pinner et al., 1959).

Paradoxically, these feelings of status inconsistency and alienation may rise as we alleviate some of the most dire economic and medical problems of older people. Betterment of individual status may heighten feelings that the position of older people *as a group* is unjust. Thus, institutional ageism may be more pronounced for older people who are better off individually, but still treated as 'just another old person'. The 'young-old' in particular can be expected to push for more meaningful involvement in community life (Neugarten, 1974).

It must be recognized, however, that status inconsistency and alienation present only a *potential* for political mobilization which may not be realized. Most older people do not see the political system as unresponsive or illegitimate, despite increases in alienation with age. Their relative satisfaction with political affairs, combined with well-established norms of self-reliance and a reluctance to burden other generations, limits the development of political activism. Additionally, downward mobility experienced by the aged does not necessarily result in generalized alienation or distrust. Tissue (1970) found that older recipients of public assistance from middle-class backgrounds were dissatisfied with their own situations, but had not lost faith in the fairness of the larger social order. Thus, rather than political activism, status inconsistency and relative deprivation may result in stress-related psychological problems or social withdrawal (disengagement) (Trela, 1976).

Studies of student activism suggest that alienation in itself is also not enough to create political activism but that high perceived powerlessness in relation to the *system* must be combined with a low sense of *personal* powerlessness (Seeman, 1975). Older people tend to be more fatalistic than young people, however, and if aging results in lower self-esteem, this may also lessen feelings of personal efficacy (Ragan and Dowd, 1974). Other potential psychological accompaniments of aging, such as disengagement, conservatism and interiority, would also limit activism, and the lack of political efficacy is compounded by low income and poor health. In addition, minority-group elderly, such as Mexican-Americans (Torres-Gil and Becerra, 1977), have encountered a long history of intimidating barriers to political participation.

But, since many of these psychological traits represent cohort differences rather than the effects of aging, feelings of political efficacy should be higher among older people in the future. Future older people will be better equipped for effective political involvement, because of higher levels of education, and more accepting of protest politics (Table 52.1). If such attitudes reflect a political 'generation', they will be carried throughout the life cycle, and there is some indication that this may occur. A followup of former civil rights activists found that they had neither 'matured out' of their activism nor 'dropped out' because of disillusionment (Fendrich, 1974). They were concentrated in knowledge and human service industries and in change-oriented voluntary associations, and they were still committed to radical political and economic change.

Table 52.1　*Per cent approving 'non-conventional' political participation, by age*

Per cent approving of	Age	
	18–35	60+
Protest politics	26.4	10.2
Civil disobedience	22.0	9.3
Sit-ins	10.8	3.2

Data are from the University of Michigan Center for Political Studies 1972 national presidential election survey.

Source: Cutler and Schmidhauser, 1975: 402. Reprinted by permission.

Ragan and Dowd (1974) point to other developments which might enhance future political activism by the aged. Increased involvement in age-graded voluntary associations and lobbying groups such as AARP may increase feelings of political efficacy to combine with subjective dissatisfaction and political distrust. Area Agencies on Aging are supposed to encourage political participation by older people in the development of services. Increased attention by the media to the problems of older people also contributes to an ideological basis for political movements.

So there is a *potential* for aging group consciousness and political activism. The very fact that societies are age-stratified is an objective basis for age consciousness, since the relative position and status of the aged are structurally determined. Since older people already constitute about 15 per cent of eligible voters and tend to vote regularly, they are a potential 'swing' vote in close elections. It is true that 'there is no evidence to indicate that aging-based interest appeals can swing a bloc of older persons' votes from one party or candidate to another' (Binstock, 1974: 202–3). But objective reality may be less important than the perceptions of political leaders. One indication of the perceived importance of older voters is the appearance of the National Council of Senior Citizens on the 'enemies list' of the Nixon administration.

There is no reason to believe that 'senior power' can ever occupy a position of overriding political importance, that older voters will polarize around a few issues, or even that the aged can achieve the status of organized labor or organized business. The interests and needs of older people will continue to be seen as one set of problems among many others. But there is also no reason to expect that old-age activism will fragment and die out in the foreseeable future. National old-age associations are now well-established on the political scene, and are both visible and accessible. Support from older masses may well increase among future cohorts, and people will continue to participate in old-age social movements for a variety of reasons: their friends belong, they agree with the group's purposes, they see the movement as a way to achieve their own goals, they can utilize their political expertise, or they simply have time on their hands (Ragan and Dowd, 1974). The aged will represent an important force in pressing for political and social change. Whether they will be effective in pursuing their goals and interests depends on many things, including receptivity from the larger society and competition with other groups making claims, and predictions are fraught with uncertainty.

References

Bengtson, V. and Cutler, N. (1976) 'Generations and intergenerational relations: perspectives on age groups and social change', in E. Shanas and R. Binstock (eds), *Handbook of Aging and the Social Sciences*. New York: Van Nostrand Reinhold.

Binstock, R. (1974) 'Aging and the future of American politics', in F.Eisele (ed.), *Political Consequences of Aging. Annals of the American Academy of Political and Social Science*, 415: 199–212.

Cutler, N. and Schmidhauser, J. (1975) 'Age and political behavior', in D. Woodruff and J. Birren (eds), *Aging: Scientific Perspectives and Social Issues*. New York: D.Van Nostrand.

de Beauvoir, S. (1972) *The Coming of Age*. New York: Putnam's Sons.

Fendrich, J. (1974) 'Activists ten years later: a test of generational unit continuity', *Journal of Social Issues*, 30: 95–118.

Hochschild, A. (1973) *The Unexpected Community*. Englewood Cliffs, NJ: Prentice-Hall.

Laumann, E. and Senter, R. (1976) 'Subjective social distance, occupational stratification, and forms of status and class consciousness: a cross-national replication and extension', *American Journal of Sociology*, 81: 1304–38.

Neugarten B. (1974) 'Age groups in American society and the rise of the young-old', in F. Eisele (ed.), *Political Consequences of Aging. Annals of the American Academy of Political and Social Science*, 415: 187–98.

Pinner, F., Jacobs, P. and Selznick, P. (1959) *Old Age and Political Behavior*. Berkeley: University of California Press.

Ragan, P. and Dowd, J. (1974) 'The emerging political consciousness of the aged: a generational interpretation', *Journal of Social Issues*, 30: 137–58.

Rose, A. (1965a) 'The subculture of aging: a framework for research in social gerontology', in A. Rose and W. Peterson (eds), *Older People and Their Social World*. Philadelphia, PA: F.A. Davis.

Rose, A. (1965b) 'Group consciousness among the aging', in A. Rose and W. Peterson (eds), *Older People and Their Social World*. Philadelphia, PA: F.A. Davis.

Rosow, I. (1974) *Socialization to Old Age*. Berkeley: University of California Press.

Seeman, M. (1972) 'Alienation and engagement', in A. Campbell and P. Converse (eds), *The Human Meaning of Social Change*. New York: Russell Sage.

Seeman, M. (1975) 'Alienation studies', *Annual Review of Sociology. Vol 1*. Palo Alto, CA: Annual Reviews.

Streib, G. (1965) 'Are the aged a minority group?', in A. Gouldner and S.M. Miller (eds), *Applied Sociology*. Glencoe, IL: Free Press.

Tissue, T. (1970) 'Downward mobility in old age', *Social Problems*, 18: 67–77.

Torres-Gil, F. and Becerra, R. (1977) 'The political behavior of the Mexican-American elderly', *The Gerontologist*, 17: 392–9.

Trela, J. (1972) 'Age structure of voluntary associations and political self-interest among the aged', *Sociological Quarterly*, 13: 244–52.

Trela, J. (1976) 'Status inconsistency and political action in old age', in J. Gubrium (ed.), *Time, Roles, and Self in Old Age*. New York: Human Sciences Press.

53

Ageing in developing countries: has it got anything to do with us?

Alex Kalache

I well remember my first impressions on my arrival in Britain in 1975. From my personal professional perspective in Brazil, this country seemed at first *the* place in which to grow old. As it happened, I was living opposite a private home for the elderly in a leafy street in North London. In those days private meant well looked after – care first, profits to follow. I introduced myself to the staff and visited the home; clean, aired, a well-maintained internal garden, residents able to bring their belongings and furniture to private, spacious, single rooms, and they all seemed happy! The whole place exuded dignity.

A few weeks later the first shock. A handful of statistics lost in a footnote in an obscure medical journal: over three-quarters of the doctors (all grades) working in geriatric medicine in England and Wales were foreigners, the great majority originated from the Asian subcontinent. Three-quarters?! Why was it that the British qualified doctors did not seem to be attracted to what surely ought to be one of the most important medical specialities in a country with so many old people around? What followed was a survey trying to elicit the factors that influenced geriatricians to choose the speciality and a study on medical students' attitudes towards the problems of older people. I then learnt that all was not rosy in this greying society. Although the country was, relatively speaking, affluent and prosperous, there was no political will to provide older people with the services and the resources required. How strange that in one of the first ageing societies, clearly a triumph of humankind, ageing should be regarded as an insurmountable problem which is not accorded priority. A telling statistic is that in 1992 elderly-related charities attracted £28 million from public donations in the UK; animal-related ones attracted £43 million.

My interest in ageing then started. The next question was why populations age. The equation says declines in mortality rates are followed by declines in fertility rates. All very simple. All very familiar. Was it not what was already happening in Brazil and other developing countries? It surely was. But why? Were these declines the result of socio-economic development? That was the trigger for the demographic transition in western developed countries. A gradual improvement in living standards over many decades; better housing, nutrition, working conditions, sanitation – the result: lower mortality. Better education, opportunities, higher expectations (particularly for women) – the result: lower fertility. The transition was well on course, if not completed, long before major developments in medical technology largely available only after the Second World War.

Was the same happening in the developing world? Most certainly not. People could still live in absolute poverty, with no water supply let alone sewerage, unemployed, malnourished, in the periphery of the big cities or abandoned in the countryside. However, their chances of premature death had diminished. Either through effective treatment or through primary prevention, most of the previously fatal infectious diseases were being controlled by medical technology, irrespective of the conditions these people lived in. Vaccines, antibiotics, combined with a few other measures, were doing the trick. No matter if they would return to the same appalling environments – technology was there for a quick fix. As for fertility, this was being regulated by new technology: oral contraceptives, intra-uterine devices, injectable contraceptives, surgical sterilisation. A higher education level was no longer required for women to control the size of their families.

My perception of the situation was rather blurred at first. The theories of 'development' had been firmly entrenched in western thinking, to the point that most of us believed in them. Things were 'getting better' and that is why life expectancy was on the increase. My perception was blurred too because of major environmental and social changes; I was beguiled by the glossy image of 'modernisation'.

Take Brazil as an example. In less than 40 years the proportion of urban dwellers has increased from one-third to three-quarters of the population. This is more striking yet when we think of the absolute numbers involved: from about 20 to over 100 million urban dwellers by 1990. This major shift creates powerful images. No longer a backward, rural country with poor peasants living in remote areas with their many scarcely dressed children, Brazil was 'miraculously' transformed in the 1960s, and 1970s by industrialisation (facilitated by the huge reservoir of cheap labour controlled by the draconian fist of a centralised state) and the advent of big agro-business. Within the last 30 years entire populations have left the countryside (where the prospects of ever owning any land had become even more remote) and started the painful process of squatting in the ill-served, poorly maintained, illness-ridden peripheries of the cities.

'Modernisation' (as a synonym for 'improved', 'better', 'more just') found an unexpected ally in one of its sub-products – the media, in particular, television. Huge investments were made on telecommunications – admittedly as a means of social and political control – resulting in a spread of information unprecedented in human history. Suddenly, with the pressing of a magic button, the whole world compressed in your living-room. No matter if the household is miserable, in a slum area, surrounded by open sewers, the adults unemployed, the children not receiving any kind of formal education, a television set is still affordable. If not, they can watch the round-the-clock programming on their neighbour's set. At the neighbours, they can watch *Neighbours*, or any of the other countless soap operas, home-made or imported, mostly portraying the lives and dramas of middle-class characters, heroes and heroines whose dreams and dilemmas have very, very little to do with their own harsh realities. It is one of the perverse ironies of the 'global village' that a poor woman in a slum area in São Paulo or in a remote hut lost in the Amazon region (yes, because television reaches even there) can suffer for Joan Collins in *Dynasty* – or for a well-off divorcee from Copacabana in the struggle for independence from her ex-husband.

This daily bombardment of model roles of values and attitudes, may take a while to influence people. But after 10, 20 years, after a whole generation is exposed to it day after day, year after year, the effects are only too visible, in terms of dress codes, life-styles, expectations, smoking, drinking, independence and . . . fewer children. Couples should produce one or two children, no more – this is the almost universally preferred family size as expressed in various studies by women in Brazil, irrespective of whether they hold a university degree or are illiterate, if they live in luxury or in squalor (IBGE, 1982; SNPES, 1987). Modern reproductive technology makes their wishes feasible. A recent nationwide survey has shown that 75 per cent of sexually active women aged between 15 and 45 are 'protected' by some form of contraception. Of these, 44 per cent have already been sterilised, 40 per cent are using the pill and close to 10 per cent use either an intra-uterine device an injectable hormone or another modern form of contraception (Arruda et al., 1986). The fact that close to 50 per cent of the women actively pursuing control of their family size have already been sterilised – compared to less than 1 per cent of men – is an indictment of a society. This is 'modernisation' at work, driven by vested interests. Female sterilisation is happening not only on request from women themselves: doctors can charge much higher fees for a Caesarean section than for a normal delivery, higher still if accompanied by a tubal ligation – resulting in the highest rates of Caesarean sections in the world. 'Voluntary' organisations funded mostly by the West are all there eager 'to help'. Moreover, in some parts of the country a woman will only get a job contract after exhibiting her medical certificate of sterilization.

Demographic transition is no longer what it used to be. However it takes time for people – researchers included – to realise it. Demographic revolution it should be called now. The consequences are far-reaching. In a country like Brazil no longer are infectious diseases the leading causes of death. The first four are cancer, cerebrovascular diseases, myocardial infarction and other forms of cardiovascular diseases. However, the next three are gastroenteritis, problems originated from the perinatal period, and respiratory infections in childhood. And to compound the epidemiological nightmare, the following three are accidents (road and other forms, mostly at work) and homicide – the hallmark of social violence in a country where the extremes of social injustice have been accentuated in the name of 'structural adjustment'.

Let me return to my first memories of Britain and how soon I realised that ageing was not perceived as a priority in this rich, industrialised country. Despite the resources which are available, despite the longer period of time for the demographic transition to take place (and, consequently, time to adjust to it), ageing is still a neglected subject area in western countries. It attracts little research funding (compared to other, more glamorous topics) and 'natives' do not seem to be interested in pursuing a career related to it. The privilege (and I do mean privilege) is left for foreigners who might find it more difficult to compete for jobs in other sought after areas.

In developing countries too there are problems. It is a fallacy to say that there the extended families will take care, that they will absorb the potential problems. They will not. Research findings are showing unequivocally that family resources are already stretched to the limit and that older people are the first to suffer (Ramos, 1988). Besides, how could traditional models of care survive intact when there are so many older people to be looked after by increasingly fewer potential carers? Everywhere women now have other interests and expectations and it would be naive to expect them to get back home to care for their increasing number of older relatives.

In Brazil the lack of resources is compounded by the lack of clear policies. Instead, ad hoc 'solutions' are implemented. Already now half of the social benefits paid by the Brazilian government are directed towards those aged 50 and over, who represent only 10 per cent of the population. By the year 2010 the proportion will be increased to 20 per cent. If the current status quo goes on unchecked there will be virtually no resources to invest in children – either for their education or for health care. The future of the country will be in jeopardy.

Furthermore Brazil is in debt. The economy is strangled by interest rates to be paid to the international banking systems. Politicians are scared by the signals of social convulsion. The social fabric is stretched to its limit, with an inflation rate running at close to 1000 per cent a year. Something has to be done to keep the country rolling, hence the mania for exporting. Anything will do: cash crops – such as soya beans, coffee, cacao and so on (at the expense of food production for internal consumption) – minerals, manufactured goods, produced cheaply by keeping the workers under strict control, and, yes – oh yes! – the Amazon. Why not? There, within reach, all those resources! Cut it down, pack it up and export it to the eager consumers of the rich world.

The challenge facing developing countries is tremendous. Ageing is at the core of it and the gerontological community elsewhere in the world will do well in assisting the pursuit of appropriate solutions. Not only will they find immensely interesting research possibilities, but it will be in their interest too. Failing to meet the challenge will contribute more pressure on governments which are becoming desperate. The consequences will affect all of us: a threat to the environment and an explosive social context. However, the benefits will also be shared by all of us: a fairer society, a rich country to become a partner for mutual development; and for gerontologists, the multiple opportunities for interchange and for stimulating research programmes. The time to start doing something positive is now and this involves not only gerontologists but funding agencies, bilateral organisations and the voluntary sector. In the West, it took far too long to realise that ageing was a fundamental issue to be addressed by society. In less developed countries we do not have that time to spare now.

References

Arruda, J.M., Rutenberg, J., Morris, L. and Ferraz, E.A. (1986) *Pesquisa Nacional Sobre Saude Materno-Infantil & Planejamento Familiar, Brasil, 1986*. Rio de Janeiro: Benfam.

IBGE (1982) *Perfil Estatistico de Crianças e Mães no Brasil*. Rio de Janeiro.

Ramos, L.R. (1988) 'A multidimensional survey on the elderly living in the community in São Paulo, Brazil'. PhD thesis, University of London.

SNPES (1987) *Assistencia Integral a Saude da Mulher – Material Instrucional*. Ministerio de Saude.

54

Paths for future population aging

Jill S. Grigsby

The age structure of a population is the result of the three basic population processes: fertility, mortality and migration. When these processes are constant for many years, a stable age structure emerges (Coale, 1964). Changes in fertility, mortality or migration will produce immediate changes in the age structure, as well as long-term effects. For example, the post-war baby boom of the United States initially made the population age structure younger. As the members of the baby boom cohort age, the US population also ages, even if there are no future changes in fertility, mortality or migration, due to the momentum inherent in the existing age structure and vital rates. Age structures, therefore, reflect current patterns of fertility, mortality, and migration, as well as the effects of these processes in the past (Coale, 1964). [. . .]

Four stages of demographic transition

In all parts of the world, the demographic transition is under way, although the pace and stage of the transition varies. First, in most of Africa and some parts of Asia and Latin America, mortality is still moderately high (life expectancy at birth of around 50 years) and fertility has not yet begun to fall. For these countries, the age structure is growing younger because mortality declines tend to occur first at the younger ages, as more babies survive into childhood. This initial 'younging' of the population provides momentum for large population growth when these children themselves reach childbearing ages. Reducing fertility rates, along with continued efforts to sustain the mortality declines under way – particularly infant and child mortality – should be the primary aims of societies beginning the demographic transition.

The second stage of the demographic transition is occurring in Asian and Latin American countries, where fertility declines are beginning to take place, setting a foundation for significant population aging in the

From *The Gerontologist*, 31 (2), 1991: 195–203 (abridged).

twenty-first century. Each woman, on average, is having fewer children, thus increasing the proportional size of the older population. Population policies for these societies also need to focus on fertility reduction in order to stave off large population growth. Although population aging is not yet a major issue for these countries, policy-makers should begin to incorporate plans for dealing with population aging into their overall policy agenda (Martin, 1990).

The third stage of population aging is under way in several developing countries, particularly in East Asia, that have recently experienced fertility and mortality declines. Their demographic transition has occurred much more rapidly than that of the western world, and, consequently, population aging will take place more quickly (Martin, 1988; US Bureau of the Census, 1987). A notable example of extreme population aging expected to transpire during the early part of the twenty-first century is China (Grigsby and Olshansky, 1989). Most of these countries recognize the need to continue strong fertility-reducing policies and already are aware that population aging is just around the corner.

Finally, in the developed world where most societies have completed the demographic transition to low rates of mortality and fertility, population aging is well in process and will continue into the next century, because even after fertility and mortality have stopped declining, the age structure needs some time to adjust to the new levels (US Bureau of the Census, 1987). Post-transition societies have also experienced fluctuations in fertility, producing baby booms and baby busts, which have both immediate and longer-term impacts on the age structure and the social institutions that address age-specific issues – for example, the need for schools, hospitals, prisons and long-term care facilities. [. . .]

Examples of population aging

The continuum of population aging can be illustrated by using the examples of Nigeria, Brazil, the Republic of Korea (South Korea) and the Federal Republic of Germany (West Germany prior to 1990). [. . .]

One way to display the age structures of populations is with population pyramids. Figure 54.1 shows the 1985 age structures of these four countries that exemplify the continuum of aging. In Nigeria, mortality has begun to fall, but fertility is still high; thus, the population is quite young. The broadened base of Nigeria's population pyramid reflects its recent declines in mortality at the younger ages. Brazil is further along in the demographic transition, as fertility and mortality are both lower than in Nigeria, yet Brazil's age structure also looks fairly young, although the base of the pyramid is beginning to narrow as fertility declines. South Korea has experienced dramatic

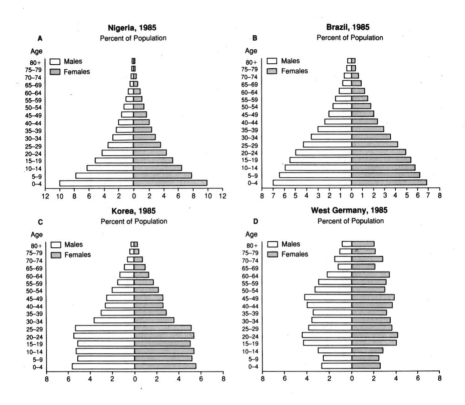

Figure 54.1 *Population age structures for Nigeria (A), Brazil (B), South Korea (C) and West Germany (D), 1985, as estimated by United Nations (1982)*

declines in fertility and mortality in the last two decades. Hence, its age structure is more rectangular than Brazil's, particularly at the younger ages. West Germany's population represents a post-transition society, where fertility and mortality are both low, although fluctuations in fertility can produce bumps in the age structure, so that the population 'pyramid' can resemble an hourglass rather than a rectangle.

These four populations were projected forward to the year 2025 (Figure 54.2), using a cohort-component methodology (The Futures Group, 1986) with medium-level fertility and mortality rates from the United Nations (1982). Even with fertility projected to decline, Nigeria's population pyramid demonstrates that the age structure will remain relatively young. Brazil's population age structure in 2025 also will continue to resemble a pyramid, although it shows swelling in the upper ages. By 2025 South Korea's age structure will become a rectangular one, except for the relatively smaller birth cohorts at the

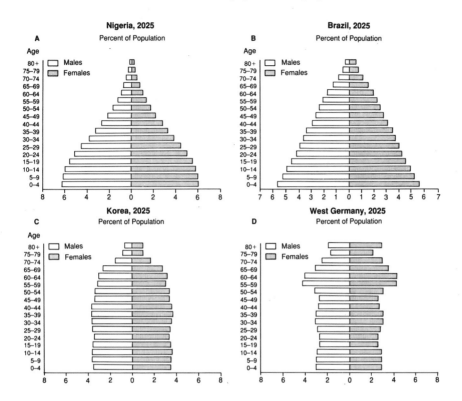

Figure 54.2 *Population age structures for Nigeria (A), Brazil (B), South Korea (C) and West Germany (D), 2025, as projected (see text)*

oldest ages. West Germany's age structure, which in 1985 began to resemble an inverted pyramid due to extremely low fertility, should revert to rectangular shape as fertility rises to replacement level [by 2025][1], although some demographers doubt that fertility in developed societies will increase this much (Westoff, 1983).

Population aging can be measured in ways other than constructing age-sex pyramids (Shyrock et al., 1976). The most common measure of population aging is the proportion or percentage of the population that is 'aged', although countries vary in their definition of which age marks old age. In some countries, retirement (particularly for women) can be as early as age 55, although ages 60 or 65 are more typical. Even in the United States, programs and services use different chronological markers of old age (Binstock et al., 1983). For international comparisons, the US Bureau of the Census (1987) refers to persons age 55 and over as 'older', persons 65 and over as 'elderly', and persons age 80 and over as the 'oldest old'. [. . .]

As the proportion of the population that is older increases, the older population itself also ages. In Nigeria approximately one-fourth of the elderly population was age 75 and over in 1985. Brazil's and South Korea's 1985 elderly populations were somewhat older than Nigeria's. By 1985, close to one-half of West Germany's elderly population was age 75 and over. The proportion of the elderly population in the oldest old category ranges from 9 per cent in Nigeria to 21.9 per cent in West Germany. Because their older populations are already fairly old, Brazil's and West Germany's older populations will become somewhat younger between 1985 and 2025. The elderly populations in Nigeria and South Korea, however, will age, with substantial increases in the age group 80 and older.

Measures of population aging that take into account age groups other than older ones also show a consistent pattern. [. . .] The aged/ youth ratio, with the older population as the numerator and the younger population as the denominator, arguably provides the best indicator of population aging. It is very small in young populations and very large in old populations. The aged/youth ratio (population 65 +/ population 0–14) shows how much further along West Germany is in the aging process than the other three countries. There were 116 persons age 65 and older for every 100 persons under age 15 in West Germany by 1985, whereas the comparable values for the other three countries are all less than 20. Like other measures, this one shows that South Korea will experience the greatest amount of aging between 1985 and 2025, as its aged/youth ratio will quadruple.

In contrast, the dependency ratio — (population 0–14) + (population 65 +)/(population 15–64) — with the young and old populations as the numerator and the working-age populations as the denominator, is much less sensitive to changes in the age structure. In 1985 Nigeria, the youngest population, had the largest dependency ratio, and West Germany, the oldest population, had the smallest. By 2025, however, the dependency ratios of these four countries show no clear pattern and do not differ greatly from one another. South Korea has the smallest dependency ratio in 2025, whereas West Germany's is the largest, but only slightly larger than Nigeria's and Brazil's. Population aging, therefore, tends to decrease the dependency ratio; however, the final stage of the demographic transition, when fluctuations occur in fertility, along with mortality improvements in the oldest ranges, can bring about increases in the dependency ratio. [. . .]

Population aging generally refers to proportional increases in the older population. Another important outcome is the growth in numbers of the older population, because demand for programs and services reflects the numbers of individuals and their appropriate characteristics. In 1985, West Germany had the largest number of persons age 65 and older of the four countries, although the growth of its older population will level off in the next century. Around 2010, however, Brazil's elderly population will surpass West Germany's in size and continue to grow in an exponential fashion. Nigeria and South Korea will also experience exponential growth among the elderly population. In fact, in all four countries, the elderly population is projected to increase faster than either the younger age group or the working-age population (Grigsby, 1988).

The oldest old populations (age 80+) are projected to increase at even faster rates than the 65 and older populations over the next 40 years. Between 1985 and 2025 the size of the oldest-old population in West Germany will fluctuate, reflecting the fluctuating fertility rates in the middle of the twentieth century. By 2025 the oldest-old population in Brazil is expected to grow almost two and a half times its size in 1985. In South Korea and Nigeria, the 80 and older age group will quadruple by 2025. [. . .]

Discussion

[By 2025], population aging is projected to take place in all parts of the world, not just in the more developed countries. Demographic transition theory predicts that, once under way, fertility and mortality declines eventually produce rectangular age structures, not unlike those of Western Europe today. Population policies that attempt to increase fertility in order to keep a society from aging only postpone and may even exacerbate future population aging. The question, therefore, is not how to stop population aging, but how to plan for it and turn it into an advantage. [. . .]

Of the four countries, South Korea is projected to have the greatest amount of population aging. By 2025, South Korea's age structure will be rectangular, as it will have joined the ranks of developed countries that have completed the demographic transition. This population-aging process will continue in South Korea even after fertility and mortality have reached their low levels, because it takes time for the age structure to adjust to changes in vital rates. Yet by 2025 South Korea is projected to have the lowest overall dependency ratio of these four countries because of the proportionately large working-age population. South Korea, therefore, needs to take advantage of this period when the traditional labor force is large to continue economic growth. At the same time, South Korea needs to incorporate the contributions of its relatively young older population and begin to address the health care in income needs of the growing oldest old population. [. . .]

In all four countries, projected mortality declines at the older ages mean that the older population will itself grow older. The oldest old population (ages 80 and older) will experience greater growth than any other age group in all four countries. All four countries need to address not only general issues of population aging, but also more specifically the even greater needs of the oldest old population.

Although population aging often connotes negative images, it also generally results in an overall lower dependency ratio, due to the large decline in the population under age 15, an age group that needs a large investment of societal resources for economic development to continue (Coale and Hoover, 1958; Preston, 1984). Furthermore, in the early stages of population aging, the working-age population increases proportionally, as we see for both Nigeria and Brazil, thus facilitating the transition of the dependent population from the younger to the older ages, which can require a shift in the public and private sectors. For example, as the school-age population declines in size, educational institutions may increasingly serve the needs of working-age and older populations, in retraining workers or providing intellectual stimulation. Fluctuating fertility, however, can produce baby booms that contribute to higher dependency burdens during the childhood years and later on as they reach the oldest ages, as will happen in the United States.

Population aging around the world is inevitable for the twenty-first century, given current projections of declining fertility and mortality, although the United Nations' (1982) projections do not include any possible effects of the AIDS epidemic on mortality or fertility levels. Demographic changes that have already occurred have created a momentum for aging in the developed world and in several developing countries, such that any changes in fertility and mortality will have a relatively small effect on the age structure. Reversing population aging would require an increase in mortality or fertility. There is no question that raising mortality is undesirable, but raising fertility may be just as problematic. First of all, once fertility has reached low levels, it is very difficult to encourage individuals to have larger families (Westoff, 1983). Moreover, raising fertility means creating a baby boom birth cohort, which US experience has shown can be difficult for a society to absorb. When the size of birth cohorts fluctuates, social institutions like hospitals, schools, prisons and the economy must continually adjust. Raising fertility will also cause a short-term rise in the overall dependency ratio by increasing the proportion of younger persons. Finally, as the projections for West Germany show, a rise in fertility will not reverse population aging, just moderate it. Population aging, therefore, should not be something that countries should try to avoid, but rather should be viewed as an outcome of desirable demographic progress that nevertheless requires adjustment from social institutions.

Note

1. Editors' Note – the population projections in this article concerning West Germany do not take into account the changes brought about by the re-unification of Germany in 1990.

References

Binstock, R.H., Grigsby, J.S. and Leavitt, T. (1983) 'Targeting strategies under Title III of the Older Americans Act'. Working paper no. 16. Waltham, MA: National Aging Policy Center on Income Maintenance, Brandeis University.

Coale, A.J. (1964) 'How a population ages or grows younger', in R. Freedman (ed.), *Population: the Vital Revolution*. New York: Doubleday.

Coale, A.J. and Hoover, E.M. (1958) *Population Growth and Economic Development in Low-Income Countries: a Case Study of India's Prospects*. Princeton, NJ: Princeton University Press.

The Futures Group (1986) 'Demproj, Version 2.62'. Glastonbury, CT: Author.

Grigsby, J.S. (1988) 'The demographic components of population aging'. Working paper. Ann Arbor, MI: Population Studies Center, University of Michigan.

Grigsby, J.S. and Olshansky, S.J. (1989) 'The demographic components of population aging in China', *Journal of Cross-Cultural Gerontology*, 4: 307–34.

Martin, L.G. (1988) 'The aging of Asia', *Journal of Gerontology*, 43: 599–613.

Martin, L.G. (1990) 'The status of South Asia's growing elderly population', *Journal of Cross-Cultural Gerontology*, 5: 93–117.

Preston, S. (1984) 'Children and the elderly: divergent paths for America's dependants', *Demography*, 21: 435–57.

Shyrock, H.S., Siegel, J.S. and Associates (1976) *The Methods and Materials of Demography*. New York: Academic Press.

United Nations (1982) *Demographic Indicators of Countries: Estimates and Projections as Assessed in 1980*. New York: Author.

US Bureau of the Census, K. Kinsella (1987) *Aging in the Third World*. International Population Reports, Series P. 95, No 79. Washington, DC: US Government Printing Office.

Westoff, C.F. (1983) 'Fertility decline in the West: causes and prospects', *Population and Development Review*, 9: 99–104.

55

Can we survive the world revolution?

Alexander King and Bertrand Schneider

The world view

The Club of Rome is an organisation of 100 people from 53 countries: none have any political ambitions, and few have anything culturally or ideologically in common, except their concern for the future of humanity. The Club was set up in 1968, that year of demonstrative world-wide unrest: the founders were concerned that governments could not - and would not - foresee the consequences of the sustained material growth of the twentieth century, or consider what quality of life the new general affluence should make possible. Its first commissioned report, *The Limits of Growth*, came out in 1972. [. . .]

Now the Club, seeing that the apparently rigid world situation of 20 years ago has dissolved into a perhaps terrifying - or perhaps hopeful - fluidity, has produced a sequel called *The First Global Revolution*. This starts with an immense yet simple presumption - that we are in the early stages of forming a new world society - as different from today's society as was post-industrial-revolution life from societies in the preceding agrarian millennia. 'This new revolution has no ideological basis: it is being shaped by . . . social, economic, techno-logical, cultural and ethical factors.' The new world, as yet demographically very young, is dense with information technology, confused about morals and ethics, and in social and educational chaos.

Humanity, says the report, is having to grope towards understanding this new world, and, at the same time, learning how to manage the new world - and not to be managed by it. It must invent its future: 'Humanity has to visualise the sort of world it would like to live in, make the vision realistic and sustainable, and mobilise the human energy and political will to make it happen.' And *now*. 'History is unlikely to provide another opportunity as promising as today's - and it is essential for humanity to find the wisdom to exploit it.' The report identifies three immediate areas of needed change:

Edited from a *Guardian* newspaper article, 'Can we survive the world revolution?', 12 September 1991, based upon A. King and B. Schneider, *The First Global Revolution*. Hemel Hempstead: Simon & Schuster, 1991.

- the conversion of the world from a military to a civil economy;
- the containment of global warming, reduction of emissions of carbon dioxide, tropical reforestation, conservation of traditional energy forms and development of alternative ones;
- the recognition of the disastrous effects of the First World's exploitation of Third World poverty – which accelerates exhaustion of natural resources, leads to corruption and short-term agricultural and social development.

And beyond that (see 'Problems' and 'Resolutions', below) the report describes a vacuum in public affairs constricting long-term thinking, and a human malaise inhibiting behaviour for the common good. It believes that it is possible for humanity to live through the revolution – mostly by what it calls 'learning the way into a new era'. The guiding principles of the new approach are:

- participation from *everyone* in seeking the way through the intertwining complex of problems;
- recognition that motivations determining human behaviour contain possibilities of positive change;
- acceptance that dramatic solutions are unlikely to come from leaders of governments – but real solutions may come from thousands of small, wise decisions made daily by ordinary people;
- acceptance that all privilege must be complemented by responsibility.

The only hope, it concludes, is in worldwide action derived from common understanding of the perils: that upsurge of wisdom can probably only come through the inner development of each individual – something religions have attempted to make possible through history, with few outward signs of success. We can't expect miracles. But we have to construct a holding position. It's our only possible future.

Problems

Order in a society is determined by the cohesion of its members. But general religious faith has evaporated in many countries, and respect for the political process has also faded; minorities are less willing to respect the decisions of the majority. A vacuum has been created. [. . .]

We can but hope that the semi-chaos which is now taking over will eventually provide the material for a self-organised system with new possibilities: but human wisdom must be marshalled quickly if we are to survive. The collapse of communism in the Eastern European countries and the Soviet Union is a major and unsettling factor in this coming turn of the century: the new hands that are to be dealt in the card game of politics are unlikely to be assessed at their true value or their political consequences evaluated until at least two or three decades have gone by. [. . .]

This period of absence of thought and lack of common vision – not of what the world of tomorrow will be, but of what we *want* it to be so that we can shape it – is a source of discouragement and even despair. It would seem that men and women need a common motivation – a common adversary – in order to organise and act together. In the vacuum such motivations seem to have ceased to exit – or have yet to be found. [. . .]

Children watch television and learn about all aspects of human life. They learn to be persons with individual choices, inclinations and freedoms. Not having been given the means to discern what is fundamental in traditions and values, and what is merely their formal expression, the younger generation is rejecting traditions and values as a whole. Parents now have to seek their consent and negotiate their own formerly unquestioned authority. How do they react to this reversal, where the exercise of authority is disrupted? [. . .]

Many of their elders are inclined to return to traditional roots of culture and religion, convinced that this will provide the only way out of a reality of misery and despair. But in many cases this need is perverted into fundamentalism and fanaticism, an expression of the immense disappointment with the western model of modernisation and consumption which has never kept its promise in most developing countries and has dehumanised industrial regions.

The traditional concept of nation is partly disappearing in the wave of internationalisation. The rebirth and reinforcement of xenophobia and racism can be explained by the millions of migrants in Asia, Africa, America and Europe who are felt to be a menace to the equilibrium of countries and a serious threat to national cultural identities just when these identities are being questioned by their own adepts. And individuals feel insecure facing the building of interregional organisations such as the European Community, where people fear they will lose their soul. Yet the revival of specific cultural identities and the definition of vast regional units *are* compatible. The apparent conflict arises from the difficulty of reconciling them within the existing political systems rigidly set within nation-states.

The current human malaise appears to be a normal stage of this great transition. Rebirth cannot take place immediately or without pain: it cannot disregard the diversity of societies and cultures, discount tradition. But the malaise is also a reflection of the present dangerous march towards a schizophrenic world, with these unresolved deep dichotomies:

- the disparity between the rich and the poor, with an increasing number of people living in absolute poverty;

- the disparity between those who do, and those who do not, have access to knowledge and information;
- the discrimination against religious and ethnic minorities, and against the old;
- the absence of equal dispensation of social justice;
- the lack of equivalence of rights and duties, of privilege and, responsibility;
- the balance between discipline and licence;
- the ambiguity between economic growth and the quality of life;
- the caring community versus the impersonal welfare state;
- the lack of balance between spiritual and material needs.

Resolutions

Any change implies learning and self-examination: and since changes are succeeding one another with unprecedented speed, the challenge is not to adapt once and for all to a new situation, but to live in a permanent state of adaptation facing uncertainty and the new dimensions of complexity affecting our world. This mutant situation does not mean that human beings should passively allow themselves to be modelled by the changes and suffer them without reaction, or live under permanent stress.

Education – in the sense of learning how to learn, indeed, learning how to change – is the key to the quality of human resources: enabling people to participate intelligently in society, accept responsibility and achieve human dignity. [. . .]

Education should have these objectives: acquiring knowledge; structuring intelligence and developing the critical faculties; developing self-knowledge and awareness of one's gifts and limitations; learning to overcome undesirable impulses and destructive behaviour; permanently awakening creative and imaginative faculties; learning to play a responsible role in society; learning to communicate; helping people to prepare for change; enabling them to acquire a global view. [. . .]

People who have been brought up to stand on certitudes will increasingly have to live in a world of complexity and uncertainty: they need new powers, which they can actually find within themselves: 'the human being is a thinking reed', wrote Pascal. But that which is cerebral and intellectual in human beings cannot approach so mysterious a truth as reality unless there is equally a resort to the apparently irrational, the intuitive and the emotional, the foundation of human relationships.

The role of science is to uncover knowledge, providing new data, the raw material of information. Today we have enormously greater amounts of information than our forefathers had, but there are few signs that human wisdom has increased significantly over the last 5000 years: the pursuit of wisdom is the essential challenge that faces humanity. [. . .]

Despite the unwanted side-effects of technology, generalised expectations of ever-increasing affluence flowing from it and of more material possessions persist within an economic system that is driven by consumer spending and credit availability. The materialistic technology-based approach to development has penetrated societies and cultures of all types, and even the most rigid, fundamentalist cultures find it impossible to resist the promise of power and affluence which it appears to offer. The goal of material affluence seems to generate greed and selfishness. The imperative need now is to attempt to master technology within a human framework, so as to contribute to the general and sustainable well-being of people in this and succeeding generations: technology must come within a holistic, global and even cosmic comprehension, and material advances must be balanced by cultivating social, moral and spiritual ambitions. The components of the corpus of society and of the individual's being are out of balance; the emotional, spiritual and even the intellectual elements have been overwhelmed by the weight of our physical triumphs. [. . .]

The global society we are heading towards cannot emerge unless it drinks from the source of moral and spiritual values which provide its dynamics. Beyond cultures, religions and philosophies, there is in human beings a thirst for freedom, aspirations to overcome our limits, and quest for a beyond. [. . .]

Humans have a need for a sense of a self if they are to lead a life of decent human dignity. In western societies with their shallow consumerism. 'I am what I own' or 'I am what I do', the more fundamental aspects of life have shrunk, including those of religion, ethnic identity, inherited values and beliefs. Such a situation leads to hyper-individuality, selfishness, over-consumption, as well as an excessive search for distraction, for instance in television viewing and drug addiction. There is a clear need for a new approach in which values are deliberately invoked to provide goals and a sense of meaning for the individual. Change, however, is too often seen as a threat to the self. There is a need for a value system which would provide a basis of stability to the life of individuals and of society; and also for a vision of a systematic world capable of leading to a systematic future.

In fact, there is a need for a new ethical vision, which has to encompass:

- the ethics of nature, imposed by global environmental issues;
- the ethics of development resulting from the increasingly unbearable gap between the rich and the poor;

- the ethics of money, because it is divorced from economic realities and dominates the ambitions of too many individuals;
- the ethics of images, which should rule over the media and modulate the influence of television in excessive dramatisation of the image;
- the ethics of solidarity – since the dimension of the problems posed to humankind today requires co-operation between human beings as a condition of their survival.

Author Index

Subject Index